Anyone Can...Arts
DRAWING MAGIC
Guidebook 1

By Peter Kraus

Anyone Can...Arts Publishing
www.anyonecanarts.com

Dedicated to my dad, whose delightful sketch of a pony opened the doors to the magical world of drawing for me.

ACKNOWLEDGEMENTS

My many, many thanks to the following people
for their valued support and encouragement.

Karen Higgins
Kristin Alonso
Angie Harris
Patti Riseling

GREETINGS
from Professor Pencil

Did you know...
from the moment you began forming the alphabet, you were
DRAWING?

Take the picture above, for instance. Observe that the capital "A" also works for the cabin's gable. Next study "B" and its contribution to the siding. Then, glance at "C," symbolizing a waning moon.

Get the connection? There's more to duplicating even a single letter than you might think. *DRAWING* ABILITY is needed and frankly, you've already proven YOU HAVE IT.

So, what's next? To broaden your horizons. You see, from my experience as a teacher, I've discovered there isn't just one way to draw; there are many. That's why this combination guide book/work book, complete with diagrams and instructions, not only acquaints you with a variety of methods, but also shows you how to apply them effectively; from start to finish.

Since approaches and preferences vary from person to person, please keep in mind, the exercises I've assembled and devised are not intended to represent completed works of art, ready to hang. The things to draw are intentionally simple to make concepts and procedures easy to understand and use. Once learned, they can be adapted to anything, no matter how elaborate.

Whether you are a beginner or advanced student, there's something for everyone. But be forewarned. The chapters are linked. As principles are introduced, they interact with others. Follow the course in sequence and you will benefit from the full array.

Get ready to have some fun, and prove to yourself that ANYONE CAN DRAW!

HELPFUL HINTS

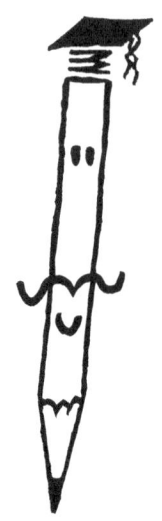

The following suggestions are very important. Please pay close attention.

1. Read directions carefully and stick to the program.
   Principles mesh. It's unwise to skim or skip around.

2. Be sure you don't miss the FOLLOW UP after each chapter.
   These summarize and shed further light.

3. Finish only one exercise in any one period and let the lessons sink in.
   Should you feel rushed, confused or fatigued, stop and regroup. Then resume when refreshed.

4. For review, by all means refer to previous chapters. Repeat all, or parts, as often as you like.
   Consult the glossary (at the back of the book) whenever you need word clarification.

5. Your attitude is important. If bored, angry or frustrated, it's not a good idea to press on, or
   tackle something new. Wait until you're relaxed and your positive outlook returns.

6. Avoid talking on the phone, watching TV, or some other distraction.
   Budget an hour or two, just for you, and focus on drawing without interruption.

7. Whenever you begin a new segment, or continue where you left off, always put your favorite
   music on and your cares aside.

8. Don't hurry. Move at a comfortable pace. FORGET ABOUT TIME.
   Your thoughts should be on your drawing, NOT on how long it takes.

9. ELIMINATE preconceived notions and pressures like how good you think your results should be.
   To expect your work to absolutely match the printed illustrations is impractical.
   Strive for knowledge.

10. Remember, you're learning. Those of you who set your sights mainly on the final outcome, rather
    than on the steps that get you there, are apt to miss the mark.

11. While doing the exercises, you may find certain procedures will seem more to your liking than
    others. Please keep an open mind. The quick convenient way is not necessarily the
    best. Stay receptive to all possibilities. In the event you feel the urge to judge, at least be fair.
    Rate your success AFTER you've completed the entire course.

12. If you haven't already done so, please see *"Greetings from Professor Pencil,"* on the previous
    page, and take his words of wisdom seriously. Most of all, enjoy yourself.

Draw for pleasure.
The fun is in the doing.

MATERIALS

Standard Size (8 ½"x 11") White Unlined Paper

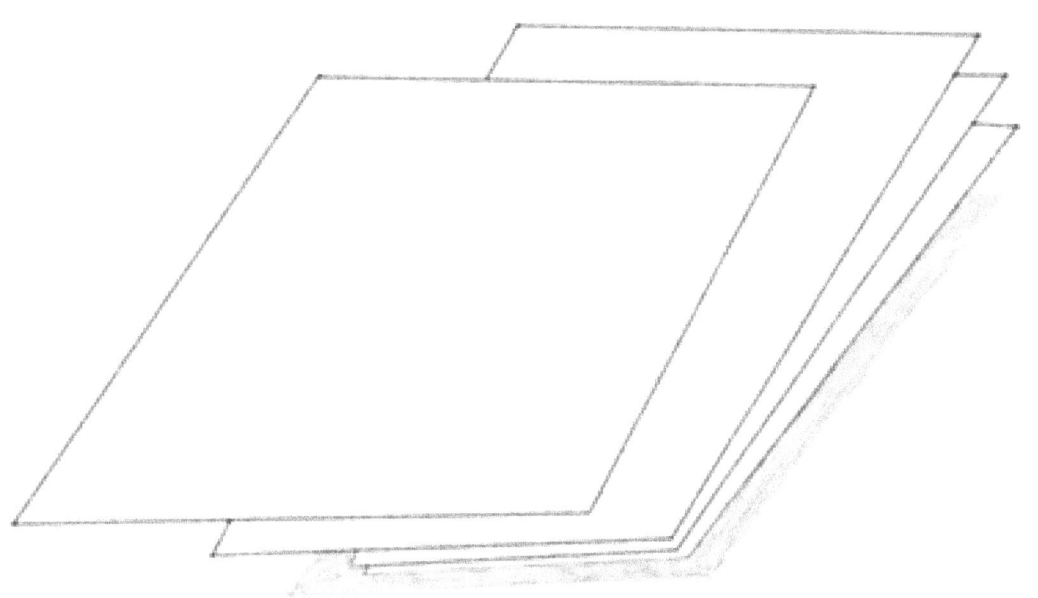

A couple of standard #2 pencils

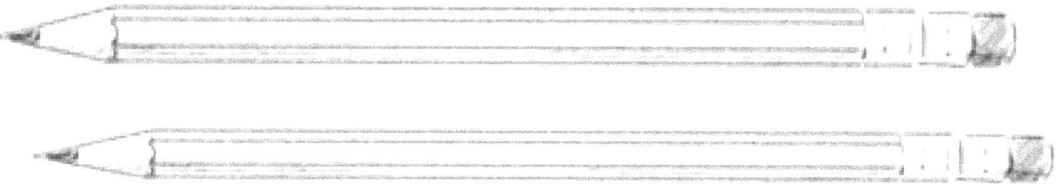

Eraser

Pencil Sharpener

ANYONE CAN...ARTS
DRAWING MAGIC
Guidebook 1

A copy of this book is filed with the United States Library of Congress.

ISBN 978-1466459496

Published by Anyone Can...Arts
www.anyonecanarts.com

Printed in the U.S.A.

CONTENTS

CHAPTER 1   The Overall Method.............................1

CHAPTER 2   The Attach Method......................25

CHAPTER 3   The Sideways Approach......................47

CHAPTER 4   The Inverse Method..........................71

CHAPTER 5   The Streamline Approach...................83

CHAPTER 6   The Crisscross Method......................91

CHAPTER 7   The Ad-Lib Method..........................115

CHAPTER 8   The Actual Subject Approach.............127

CHAPTER 9   The Random Mode..........................153

CHAPTER 10   The Squiggle Method.......................173

CHAPTER 11   The Freestyle Approach....................183

CHAPTER 12   The Chiaroscuro Method..................213

STUDENT GALLERY...234

GLOSSARY..236

INDEX..246

*EACH JOURNEY BEGINS
WITH THE FIRST STEP.*

Enjoy your odyssey.

*Take delight in your voyage
as well as your destination.*

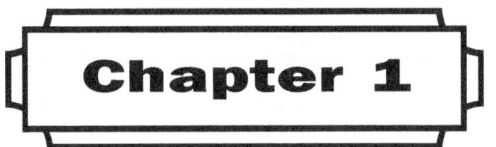

THE OVERALL METHOD

For a warm up, we are going to draw the following 6-sided shape.

(Without a Ruler)

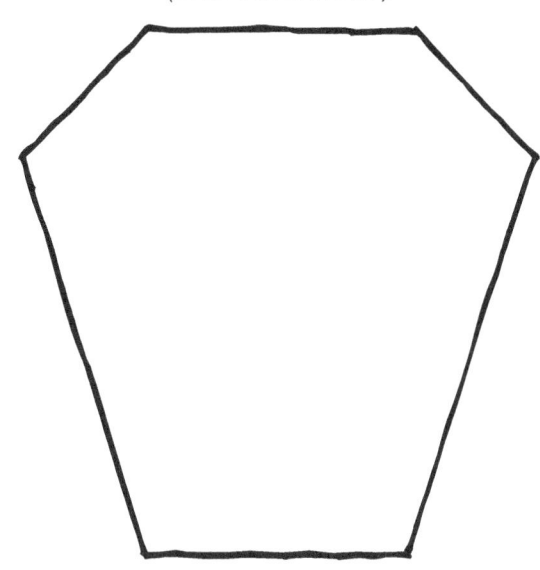

A cinch, right? So much so, you just might get
the urge to grab a pencil, and dive right in.

If you do, a word of caution: you could be in for a surprise.

Here are some typical results.

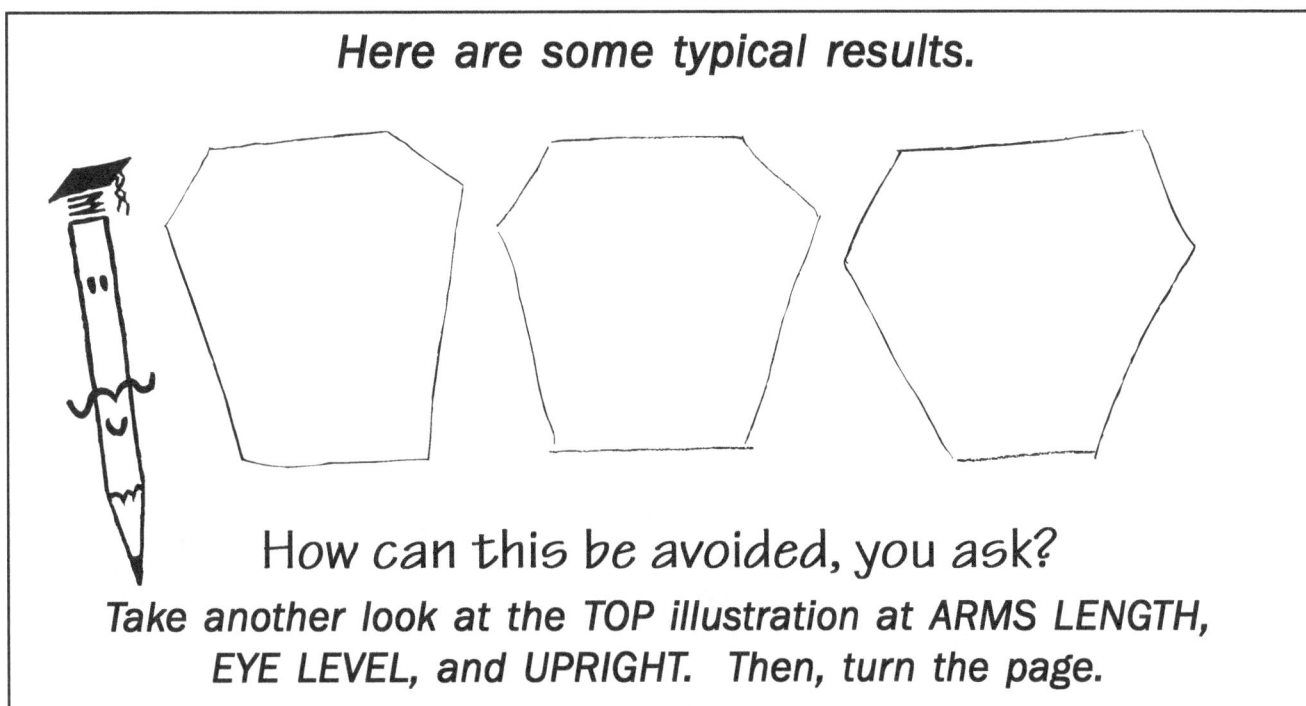

How can this be avoided, you ask?

*Take another look at the TOP illustration at ARMS LENGTH,
EYE LEVEL, and UPRIGHT. Then, turn the page.*

Having had a second glimpse, would you say the figure is taller than its span across?

If you said "yes," and I agreed with you, we'd both be wrong.
The overall size (length and width) **is the SAME.**

See for yourself! Place YOUR pencil *directly* on the illustrated version marked "A" below, as shown. Make certain your eraser tip touches the far LEFT corner. Then, line up your THUMBNAIL with the RIGHT, opposite corner. If you are left-handed, go from right to left. Either way, the procedure will confirm the figure's maximum span, *sideways.* Next, while holding the distance, rotate your arm to an *upright* position, so that your eraser tip is even with the top left corner of the figure, and over the pencil drawing marked "B." OK, now look where your thumbnail is. It lines up with the bottom left corner, doesn't it? What does this mean? It means you've just verified that the full extent in both directions is identical.

Illustration 1-1 Pencil reading comparison reveals *maximum* length and width are IDENTICAL.

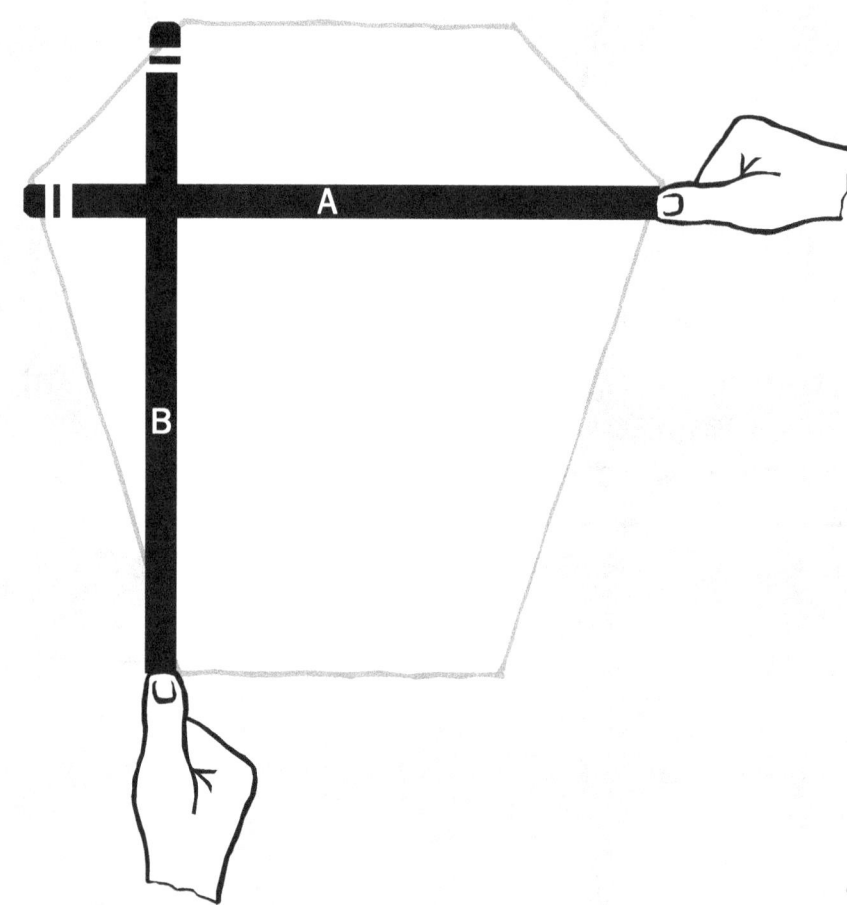

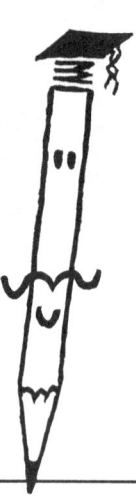

Amazed? Now, you know one of the main reasons
why artists use their thumb.
It helps them avoid false impressions.

Curious to learn more secrets?
Terrific! Keep going!

WHY DRAW WHEN THERE ARE CAMERAS AND COPY MACHINES?

I'll tell you why.

The drawing experience is a **marvelous adventure**, filled with many choices and usually a single, very special purpose; a desire to create the likeness of something with your **unique, personal touch**. In order to achieve this, generally there are three requirements which, thank goodness, you **ALREADY HAVE!**

I'm referring to your **eyes, head and hands,** of course. Picture them as though they were a scanner, computer and printer, all turned on and working. Next, imagine the scenario. From the instant your human scanner (vision) takes in the sights, the computer portion (your brain) kicks in to register the information. Soon thereafter, the printer (your hand, holding the pencil) carries out the message. The snag is, what you see and what turns out may be two different things.

Now, before you jump to any conclusions, please don't misunderstand. I'm not suggesting there is anything wrong with your ability. Your peepers, your thinking cap and fingers work just fine, but there is more to drawing than that. You need to know *WHAT to look for,* and *HOW to transfer* your observations accurately onto paper with confidence and ease. That's where this book comes in. It's your own private guide, so let's get underway.

In this chapter we will begin exploring several **basic drawing components**. First, I'll introduce a duo which generally operate well together. They are called REFERENCE POINTS and ALIGNMENTS.

WHAT ARE REFERENCE POINTS & ALIGNMENTS?

Essentially, **ALIGNMENT** is a word used to describe when two (or more) positions LINE UP. WHERE they start and stop are the REFERENCE POINTS. Put another way, think of **ALIGNMENTS** as **IMAGINARY BRIDGES,** and the *places they link* as **REFERENCE POINTS.**

Interestingly enough, you may be pleased to learn you've already put REFERENCE POINTS and ALIGNMENTS to use. The moment you took *pencil readings* (previous page), the process was activated. For example, you found a HORIZONTAL ALIGNMENT when you positioned your pencil *sideways* from mid-corner to mid-corner. In turn, those *positions* became REFERENCE POINTS. If this didn't tickle your funny bone, you also located another set, or VERTICAL ALIGNMENT, when you placed your pencil even with the *top* left corner, then lined up the *bottom* left corner with your thumb. Above and beyond that, when your compared the two OVERALL horizontal and vertical spans you discovered they were the same length.

So you see, with just a few basic checks for reference points and alignments you gain a better understanding for how shapes are STRUCTURED (put together). That is, assuming you give yourself the opportunity to look. And, now that you have an idea of how alignments and reference points work, next let's explore the way by which your observations are generally transferred to paper. What I'm referring to is the actual *connection* between reference points: namely, that all important, yet often taken for granted, and misunderstood LINE.

THE *STRAIGHT* LINE
ANOTHER VALUABLE COMPONENT

1. _____

2. _____

3. _____

Artistically speaking, all three lines can be considered STRAIGHT.

LINE 1 was done **WITHOUT a** straight edge and is classified as **a CONTINUOUS straight line.** Why? Because it was created by **CONSTANT** pencil contact with the paper, from beginning to end.

LINE 2 was also achieved **"FREEHAND"** (without a ruler or straight edge). However, the pencil point was occasionally **LIFTED and REPLACED**. This formed short, overlapping strokes, which enabled adjustment to take place along the way and remain on track from start to finish. As a result, the procedure is generally known as a **SKETCH** line.

LINE 3 was clearly fashioned using the side of a RULER or other device. Compare it to the other two lines. Notice THEY show PERSONALITY and CHARACTER, much like your individual signature. In contrast, the *ruled* line seems visibly STIFF and ORDINARY. No matter how many are made, or who makes them, they would appear about the same. The moral of the story is, **DRAW FREEHAND!** That's the route to your personal touch.

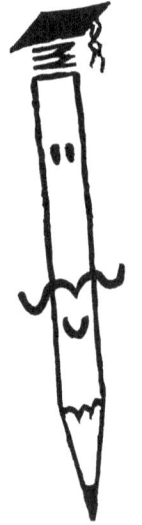

The next page is your chance to become better acquainted with STRAIGHT lines.

Worksheet A   Practice Straight "CONTINUOUS" Lines

Remember when you were a kid and learned to connect the dots?
Guess what? You get to put that knowledge to good use!

DIRECTIONS: *LIGHTLY* connect PAIRS of CONSECUTIVE numbers, *without lifting your pencil until a line is done* (per example #1 to #2). For longer spans, it may be wise to place small reference points, in between, starting with the midway point.   This can help you stay on course, while linking PAIRS of numbers such as #4 to #5.

IMPORTANT: Please note, there is a NUMERICAL GAP between each intended pair of numbers. After you bridge your first line from #7 to #8, ***DON'T link #8 to #10***. Number 9 is omitted, so the next set becomes #10 to #11. Then, you jump to #13, and connect it with #14. The procedure provides the opportunity to direct your hand from right to left, left to right, up to down, down to up, and diagonally. If you've got notions about erasing, or rotating your paper and using the side of your pencil as a straight edge, please forget it. The objective here is to practice drawing **FREEHAND** (without devices and/or shortcuts).

1   2   4   5

7   8   10   11

14   13

16   17

23   19

25   22   20

    29   37   38

         31   35

                                   40

        41

            43   44

                                   46

            47

  28   32   34

26

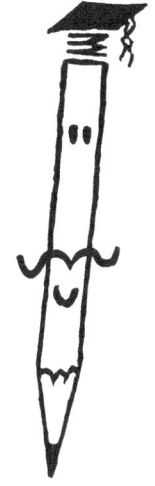

Had enough practice with CONTINUOUS straight
lines? OK. Sample the other type (following page.)

Worksheet B   Practice Straight "SKETCH" Lines

DIRECTIONS: Similar to line example #50 to #51 and #53 to #54, *LIGHTLY* connect *SETS* of *CONSECUTIVE* numbers with short, straight, "FREEHAND" *OVERLAPPING strokes.* That means, you can advance along your line by alternately *lifting and replacing* your pencil. For longer distances, you're advised to place small dots at intermediate intervals, as example #53 to #54 indicates. Please, keep in mind that numbers skip between each pair.

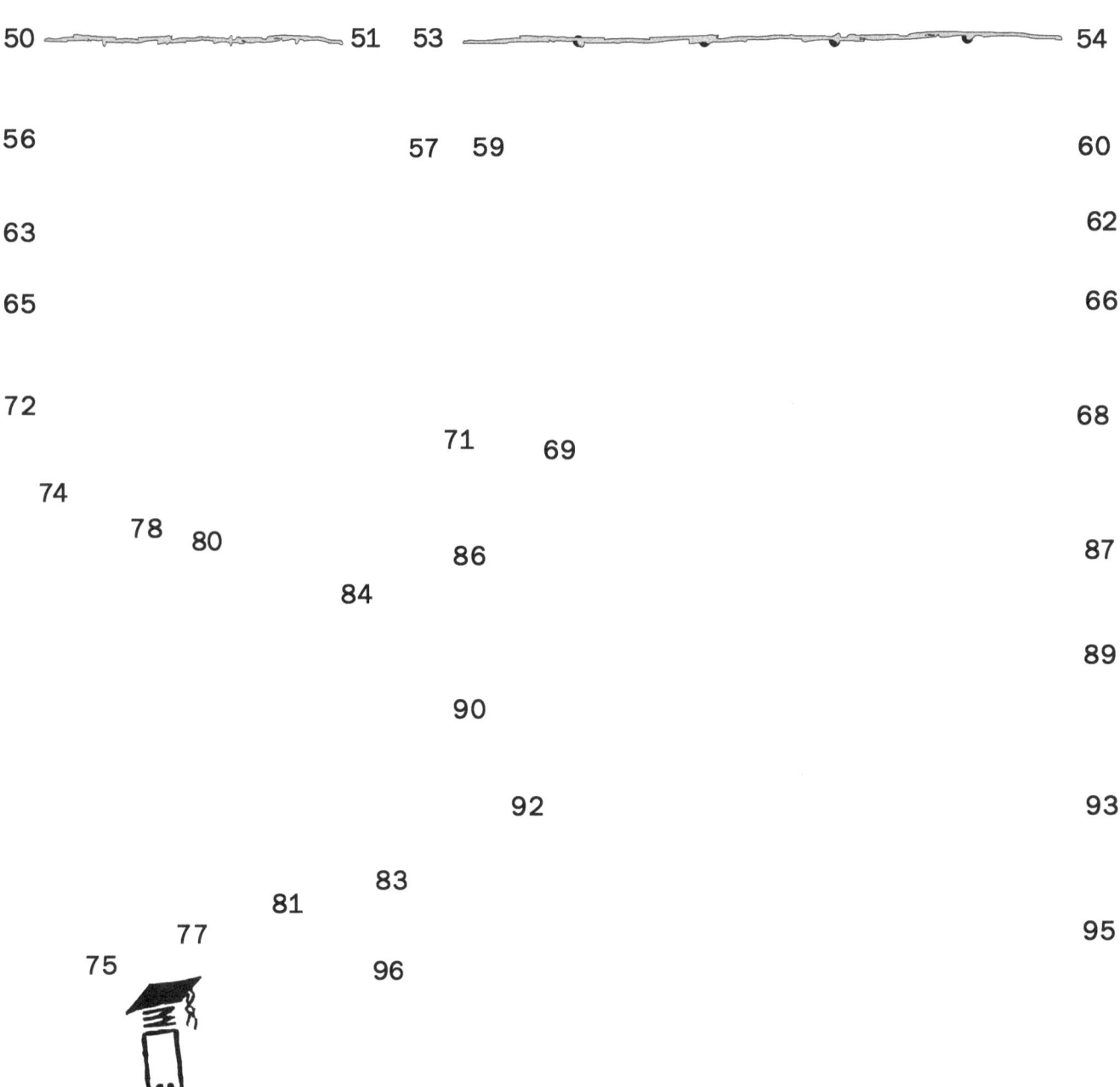

50 ——————— 51   53 ——————————————— 54

56   57   59   60

63   62

65   66

72   68

                        71   69

74

    78   80   86   87

          84

                                                                       89

                    90

                        92   93

                        83

              81

        77   95

    75   96

*Both the continuous and sketch line method
have their uses, don't they?*

HAVE YOU CAUGHT ON YET?

There are MANY types of lines and a multitude of techniques by which to DRAW them. Aside from that, *freehand* lines have character. So, please reject the notion to use a ruler. Sure, a ruler is easy to use. You only have to decide where you intend to START and STOP your line in order to achieve the desired distance. With FREEHAND lines, you need to be aware of the beginning and the ending points, **PLUS WHERE YOU ARE at all times ALONG THE ROUTE.** But, that's the SECRET! Now that you are aware of this worthy piece of information, please erase a couple of your lines to learn another valuable lesson. Should your marks resist, you pressed too HARD! And, even if you found the right intensity (by controlling pressure and momentum), I recommend you practice some more.

Take my advice. On a separate sheet of paper, place random dots, both close together, and far apart. After that, connect pairs; alternating occasionally by applying the *continuous* type of straight line for one set, and the *sketch* method for another. Try going **fast**, and switch to **slow.** Direct your hand **from left to right** for one line. Then, reverse the **direction** for a change. In addition, produce lines at an **incline** (upward slope) as well as at a **decline** (downward slope).

During the procedure, be sure to GLIDE the pencil DELICATELY, with the SIDE of the pencil point, to FEEL the acceleration and pressure. Also, **remember to use a FEATHER TOUCH.** That means hold the pencil like you normally do, but release your "vise grip." Then allow only the weight of the pencil to touch the paper and PULL rather than push it, stroking **GENTLY from the wrist.**

For an alternative, I also suggest that you experiment by keeping your **WRIST LOCKED.** This enables the whole arm to move only *FROM THE ELBOW.* **The technique might feel odd AT FIRST**, but after awhile you'll get the hang of it. Besides, as I said, LINES ARE FUNDAMENTAL TO SHAPE AND STYLE. Strive to navigate with ever increasing skill and agility. By guiding your lines FREEHAND, with and without extra dots, in various lengths, directions and speeds, your eye/hand coordination should gradually improve.

Next, let's get acquainted with yet another contribution to drawing, namely PROPORTION. Yes, I know you're eager to apply the principles you've already learned. Admit it! You're itching to draw the six-sided figure, and for this, I applaud your zeal. But hang in there! After all, shapes generally include proportion, so you need to understand how it works and how to use it.

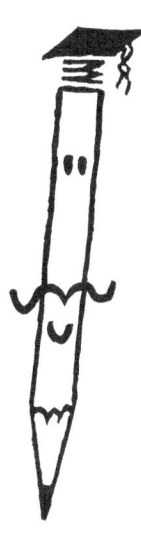

PROPORTION

When it comes to drawing, **proportion** is just a simple **comparison of one size to another size.** You did this on page 2 when you compared the overall *height* and *width* of a shape. Now look at Rectangle A. The *height* is **longer** *than the width*. So that you can *visually* determine *how much* longer it is and thereby **estimate proportion** *(without a ruler),* pretend that an ant walked along the *top* and left a trail like the bold **gray** line. Next, pretend the ant made a turn and walked the **same distance** *downward* (bold **black** line). Since the imaginary ant reached about halfway, it's easy to see the rectangle's estimated **height** is **twice** the **width** (B&C). Using this method, you can draw Rectangle A not only in **proportion**, but also in **any size**, smaller or larger (D thru G.)

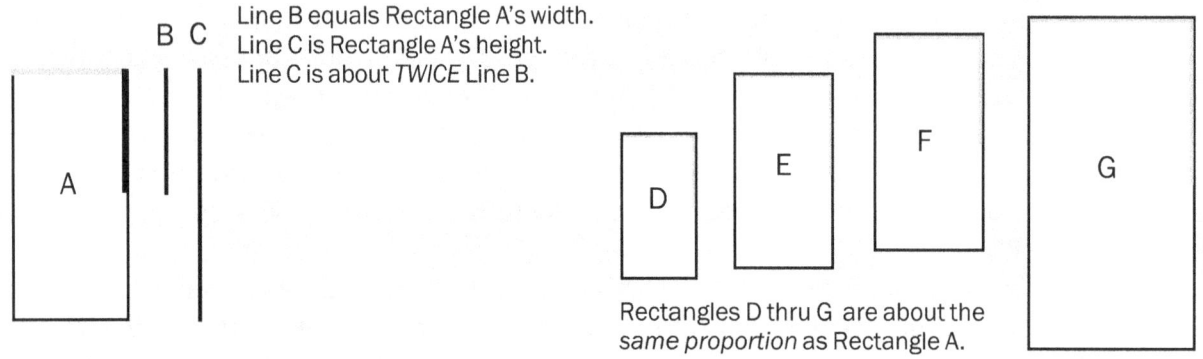

B C
Line B equals Rectangle A's width.
Line C is Rectangle A's height.
Line C is about *TWICE* Line B.

A

D   E   F   G

Rectangles D thru G are about the *same proportion* as Rectangle A.

How could the rectangle be replicated even *bigger* than G? In the *1st stage,* roughly visualize the increased size (light gray field) and draw a *horizontal* line to represent the **top** (1). In the *2nd stage,* estimate *that* distance *downward* and lightly place a dot (2). Then move the *same* span *below* the *first dot* and place another dot (3). **This produces the double distance in height compared to width proportion.** In the *3rd stage,* simply connect the two dots with a line to form the rectangle's right side (4), followed by the *final stage* with lines 5 and 6 which make the left side and bottom. Of course, you could just as easily create a *smaller* version than rectangle D by starting with a **very short** *horizontal top line* to intiate the proportional procedure.

Stages and Steps used to draw Rectangle A *proportionally* larger than Rectangle G.

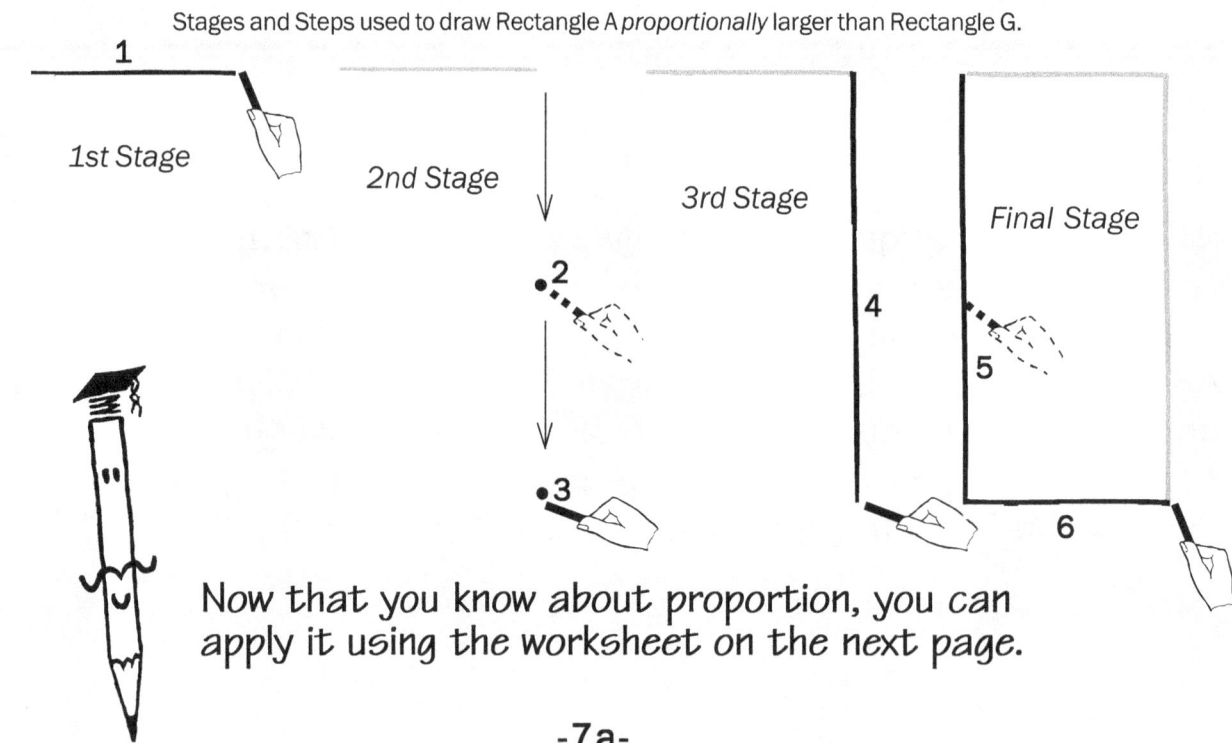

1

1st Stage

2nd Stage

•2

•3

3rd Stage

4

Final Stage

5

6

Now that you know about proportion, you can apply it using the worksheet on the next page.

Worksheet C   Practice ESTIMATING and DRAWING PROPORTIONAL LINES

DIRECTIONS: *ESTIMATE* the PROPORTIONAL relationship of Line A to Line B by EYE (no ruler). Then extend Line D in the *same proportion* to Line C.

EXAMPLE: Line B is roughly TWICE the length of Line A. So, Line D is extended to be about TWICE the length of Line C.

EXAMPLE

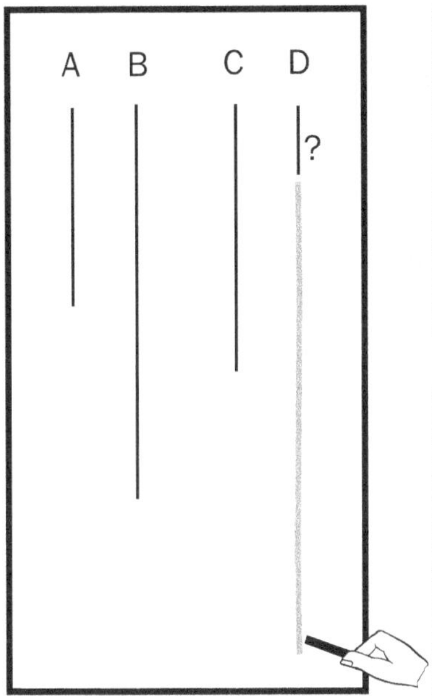

A is to B as C is to D

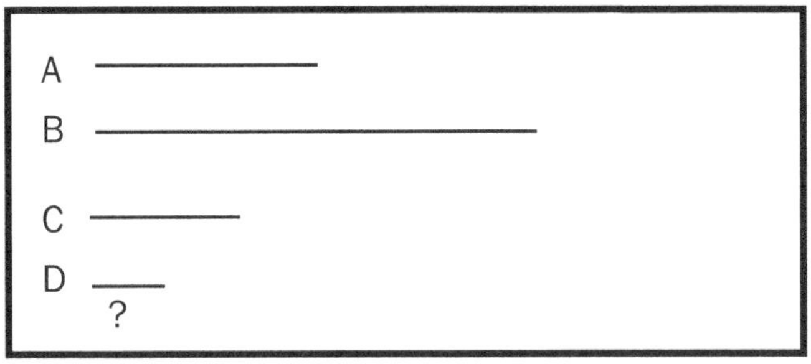

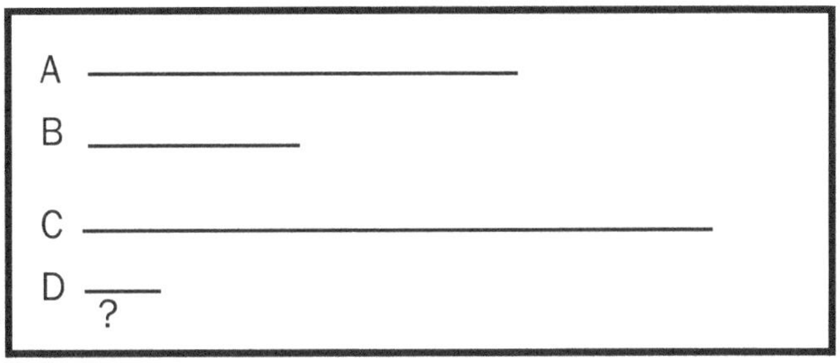

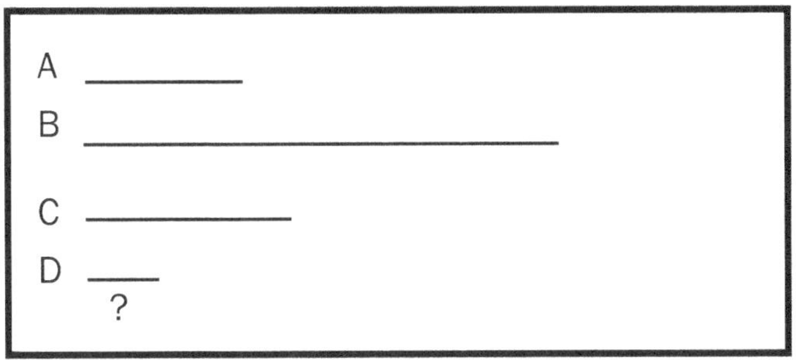

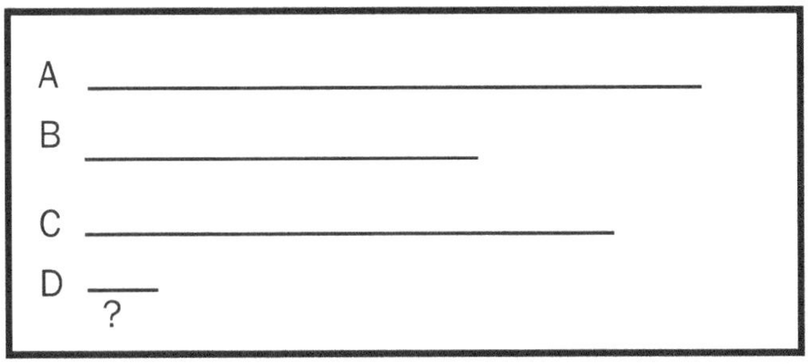

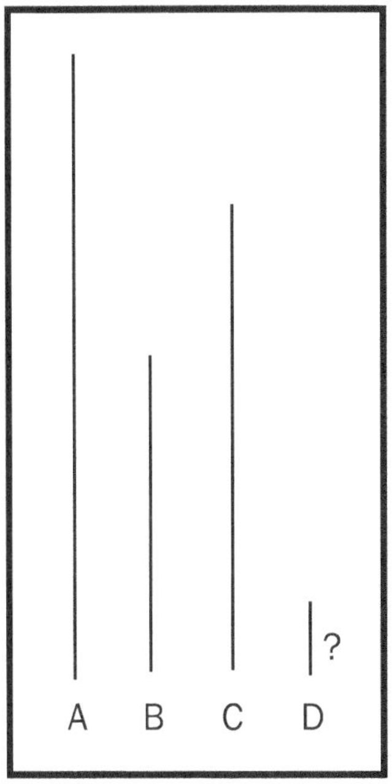

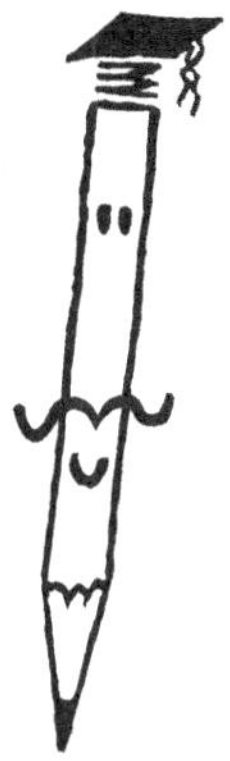

After a break, we can explore ANGLES.

WHAT'S SPECIAL ABOUT ANGLES?

An angle (or diagonal, as it is also termed) is the proper word for a slant. How do we know when there's a tilt? By sight, of course, but what gives it away? The answer is simple. We can be sure an angle exists when it is *NOT plumb* (running *parallel*, or equidistant at both ends, with the SIDES of the paper). We can also be certain there is a tilt when the alignment is *NOT level* (parallel with the TOP/BOTTOM of the paper). How do we determine the *amount* of tilt? Take a look at angle example 1-2, on the left. We can see there is an angle, by comparing it to the edges of the paper. The trouble is, the *rate* of tilt is still difficult to judge. The angle seems to hang in space. Next, survey angle 1-3. It has a unique addition; there is an *imaginary* LEVEL alignment running sideways from the lower end parallel to the bottom of the paper). Furthermore, an imaginary PLUMB alignment connects from the upper end, running parallel with the SIDE of the paper. Combined with the angle, a TRIANGLE is formed. And, as you can tell, it's the specific SHAPE (enhanced by gray) which makes the rate of tilt easier to estimate.

1-2 **WITHOUT visualized** plumb & level lines there isn't any source of reference. This makes it difficult to judge the rate of tilt.

1-3 **WITH imaginary** plumb and level lines *(parallel* to paper edges) a TRIANGLE is formed to provide a reference source.

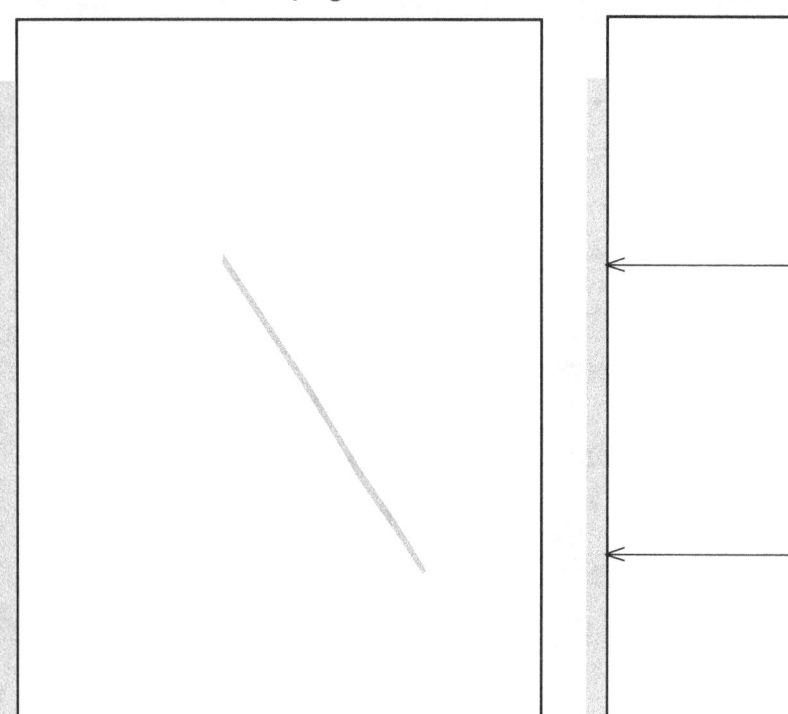
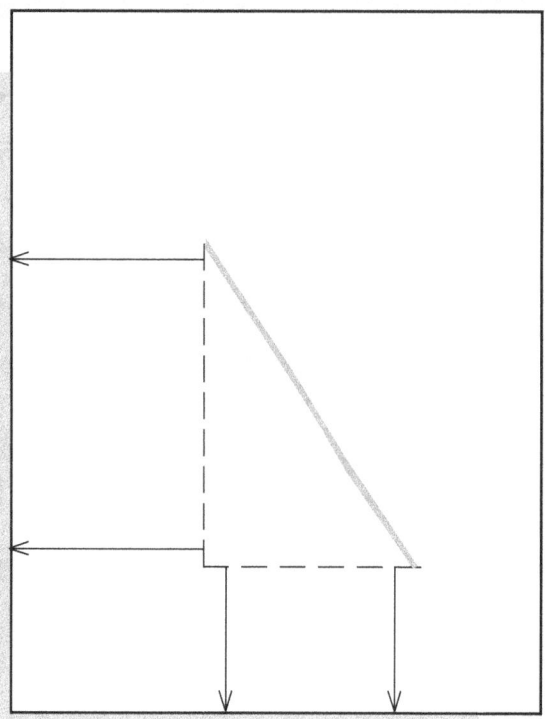

As illustration 1-4 demonstrates, whether right side up, upside down, left direction, or the opposite, angle rate can be estimated more easily with the assistance of PLUMB, and LEVEL alginments. These two *NON-ANGULAR* constants can be envisioned or drawn while you form your angles. **No wonder they can also be considered "GUIDE" lines**.

1-4 Plumb and level guide lines help see an angle's amount of slant.

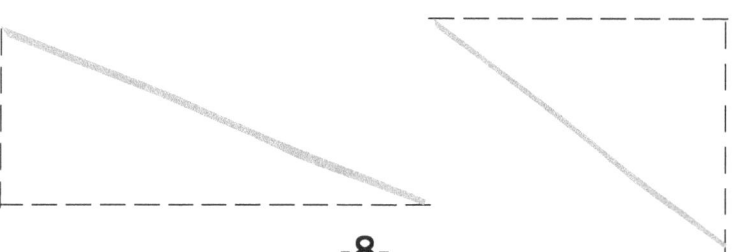

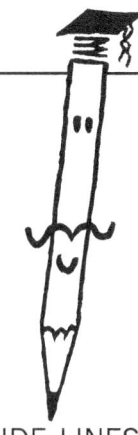

Fine and dandy, you're probably thinking.
However, the ability to judge angles is
one thing and duplicating them is another,
especially at a different size.

Guess what? I have good news. Those same *NON-ANGULAR GUIDE* LINES which make it easy to judge the angle, also help reproduce it. The secret is that angles not only have a length and tilt, but also PROPORTION. The reason is that when you include PLUMB and LEVEL alignments, *both* a vertical and horizontal span exists. These I like to call "EXTENSIONS." Why? Because the RATE of tilt, as well as the angle SIZE, are determined by how far one end of an angle reaches (or *extends*) vertically along an *imaginary PLUMB alignment* and how far the other end extends along an *imaginary LEVEL alignment* .

For instance, take a look at illustration 1-5. Clearly angle "A" has a taller *VERTICAL* EXTENSION than "B." This causes both the size and tilt to be different, even though both angles have the SAME *HORIZONTAL* span. If we want "B" to be as TALL as "A" and also *match* the amount of tilt, we need to *increase* the vertical extension of "B" until it reaches the HEIGHT of "A." On the other hand, if we prefer to KEEP the SHORTER *height* of "B," but match the *angle* of "A," we must *reduce* the HORIZONTAL extension (width) of "B." In that case, the outcome would be "C."

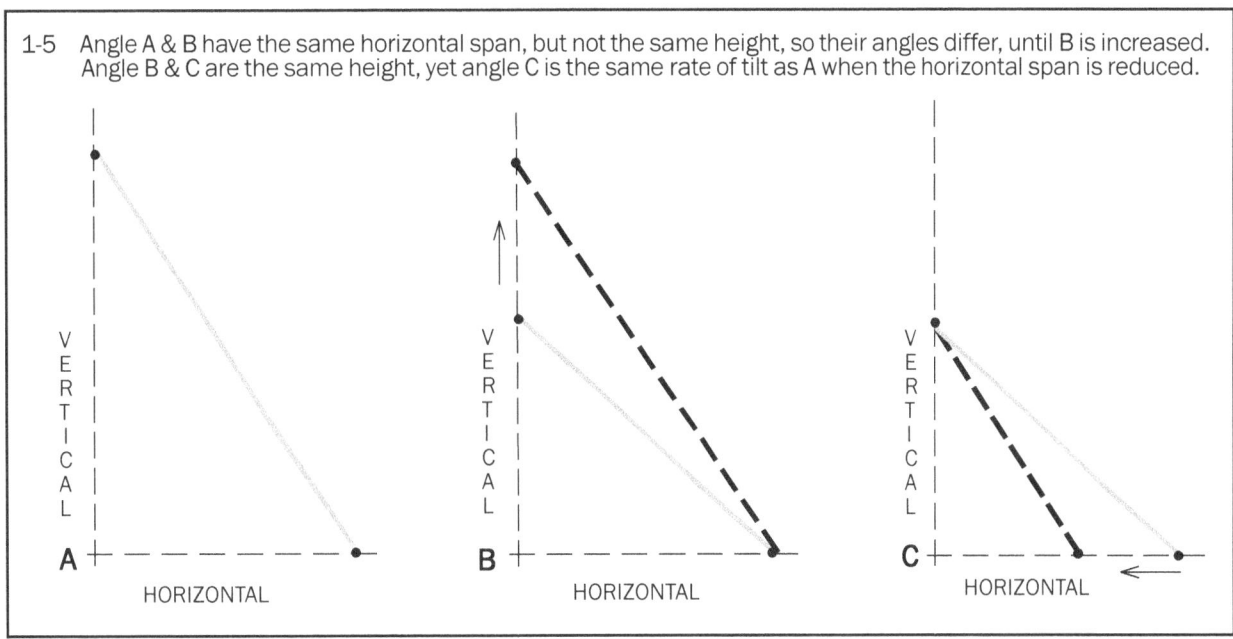

1-5   Angle A & B have the same horizontal span, but not the same height, so their angles differ, until B is increased.
      Angle B & C are the same height, yet angle C is the same rate of tilt as A when the horizontal span is reduced.

Is this technical stuff important? You bet! Many shapes have angles, including the six-sided figure we intend to draw. Therefore, just as I was able to make the *rate* of angle "B" and "C" match "A" (by moving the extensions indicated by broken lines), you need to also learn to match angles at different sizes simply by placing the correct proportional distances along the plumb and level extensions.

It's easy. Test the method yourself.
Turn the page to find out how.

Worksheet D Duplicate ANGLES in a *DIFFERENT SIZE*

DIRECTIONS: Duplicate angles using their identically numbered second set of guide lines ("lefties"may invert the page to clear your view.) ONE reference point is provided at a lesser or greater extent than on the model. The task is to locate the second reference point proportionally, then connect them with a line to match the tilt. Example #1 and its counterpart #1 illustrates. Your turn starts with angle #2, along with its duplicate guide lines. Continue until, one by one, all the angles are done. Fairly close is fine. You need not be exact. If your TRIANGULAR SHAPES (not sizes) are pretty similar to the originals, you've got a winner!

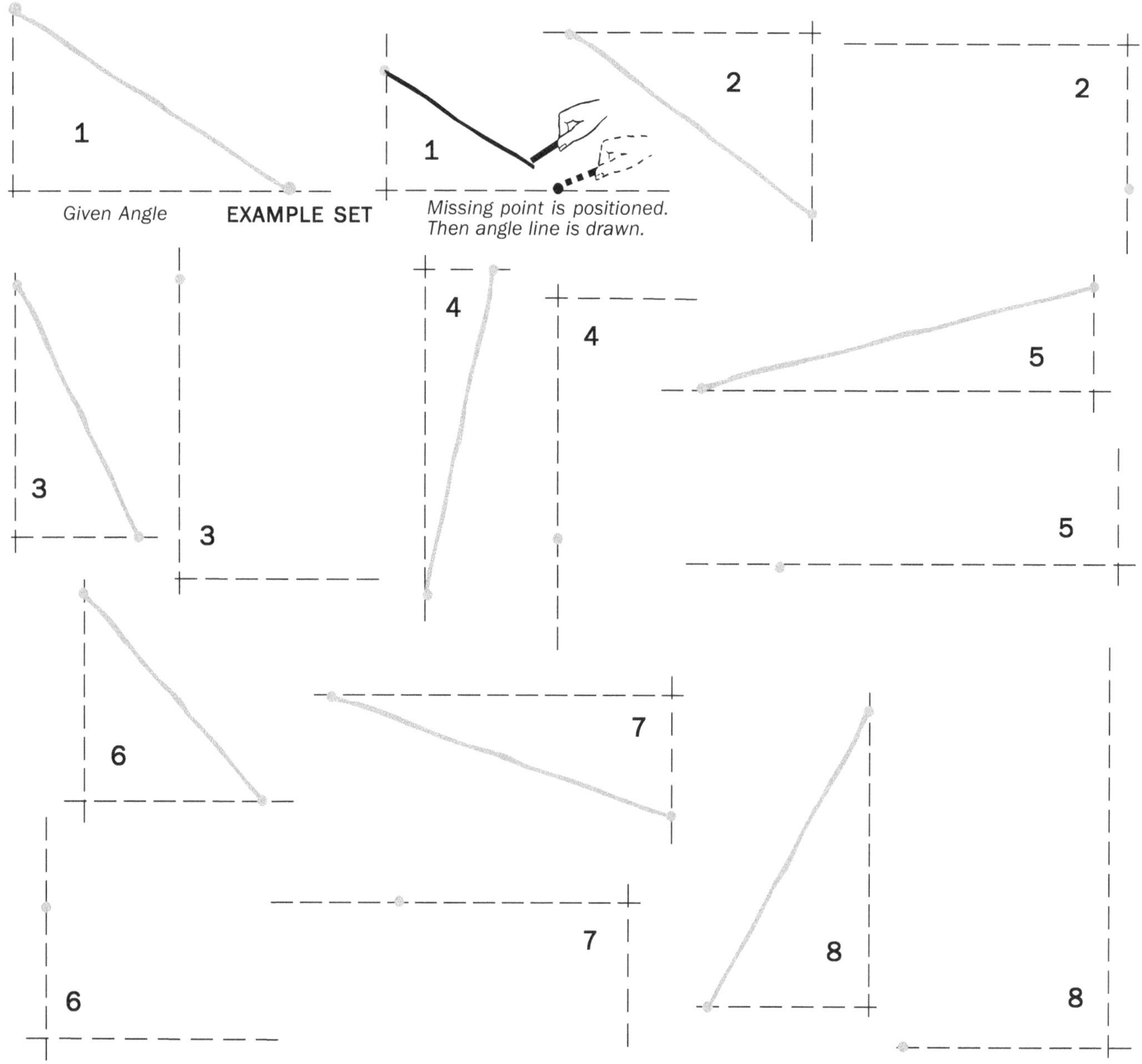

1

Given Angle   **EXAMPLE SET**

1

*Missing point is positioned.
Then angle line is drawn.*

2

2

4

4

5

3

3

5

6

7

6

7

8

8

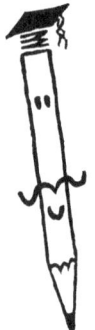

Excellent! You're nearly ready! Since you've had ample practice with STRAIGHT LINES as well as ANGLES and you've become increasingly familiar with REFERENCE POINTS, ALIGNMENTS and PROPORTIONS, you're likely to be on a more secure footing.

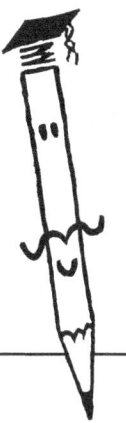

Ya-hoo! We are about to draw the 6-sided figure, but before we do, there are a few VERY IMPORTANT pointers to keep in mind.

1. Each chapter introduces a different method and a simple subject to draw. This enables you to learn and apply advanced concepts and procedures easily. And to make things even easier, clear written explanations, plus hundreds of tips and illustrations, show you what to look for, what to do, how to do it, and when to do each step from start to finish.

2. Always remember to rely mainly on your vision. You may use your pencil readings for assistance, but your eyes and thinking cap should ultimately decide when you are on target.

3. Since you are going to be working FREEHAND (without a ruler), you should not expect your drawings to turn out as accurate, or as neat, as the printed drawings in the book. Fair comparisons are included and, I'm sure you've already noticed, helpful worksheets are also provided from time to time for practice.

Be sure to also get acquainted with the following symbols.

If you see 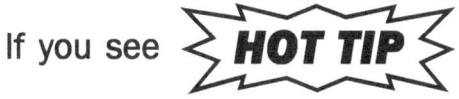 pay special attention.

When you spot these 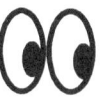 study and observe.

This means 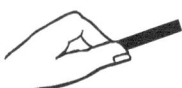 draw.

OK. Now, treat yourself to a break. Have a snack perhaps, and a beverage. Then tune your radio to soft music and flip the page.

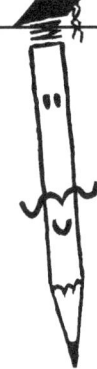

EXERCISE 1

Objective: To Replicate the Six-Sided Figure

I bet you're wondering which way is a good start? What size? Where? Why?

Which approach should you take? These and other related questions are ultimately for you to answer. The trouble is, a blank page staring back at you can be terrifying, and can cause decision making to seem almost impossible, especially when you have no idea what you're doing, right? Well, guess what? It's not as tough as you might think. Like I said at the outset, there are many possibilities. This chapter introduces one easy route. I call it the *overall method* since it initiates with the *maximum* dimensions.

Now, as to the next topic: what size is best? In my opinion, whether you like to work large or small, both are fine, providing your preference works. Translated, you shouldn't pick a size so small you feel cramped. Conversely, you also shouldn't opt for a size so large that you may run out of space. And that brings us to the third and fourth most commonly asked questions.

Where to start and why? Since each situation is different, it all depends. On this occasion, if you ask me, center is safe, simply because there's room to build. So, let's begin to CONSTRUCT our figure, much the way a house is built, from the foundation.

STEP 1　CHOOSE A FOUNDATION

Earlier (on page 2, if you recall), you confirmed that the figure's full extent in both directions, (meaning length and width) was identical. Since that forms a *square*, in this case I suggest *that* would be a good foundation. With regard to a workable size, I anticipate about HALF the SHORT span of your paper should do nicely. Then, reference points can be located in order to map out (or chart) a course for the intended shape. The dots and broken lines here in illustration 1-6 demonstrate. But *it's not time to pick up your pencil yet*. Step 2 will show you *how* to proceed. And if, by chance, you're harboring the notion that you do NOT need guide lines, please reconsider.

1-6　Broken lines show how the figure will eventually develop within guide lines.

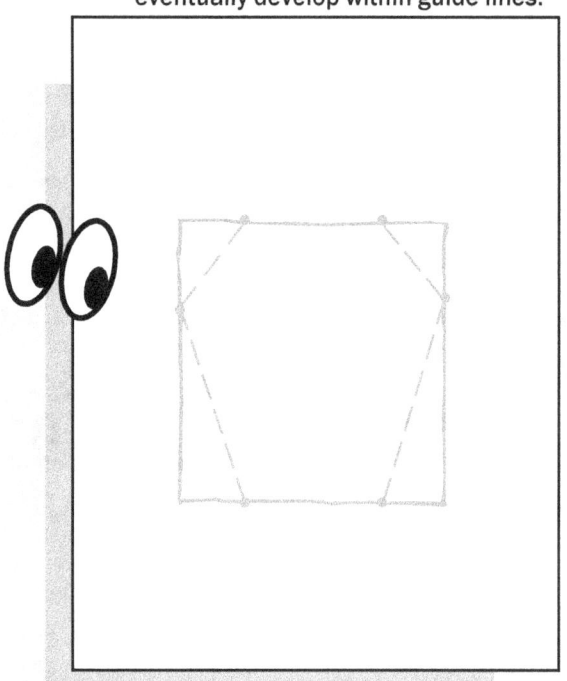

⚡HOT TIP⚡ Don't underestimate the value of GUIDE LINES.

You've seen how guide lines helped estimate angles, and that's just one of their many advantages. Obviously they are not a crutch. Drawn, or visualized, *GUIDE LINES* are an artist's *tool*. I clarify this because it's crucial that you truly appreciate how important they really are. Think of guide lines as flexible and adjustable FORMATS (or templates) which eventually disappear but tend to keep you on track while they last.

On a fresh sheet of paper, take a *HORIZONTAL* pencil check from the UPPER *LEFT* edge to about midpoint, using your subordinate (not drawing) hand (1-7). "Lefties use the *right* edge. Next, center the increment (span of distance) by moving it near the upper middle section. Keep your pencil fairly *level*, but it *NEED NOT be exactly even* from the sides; *approximate is fine.* Once you've found the position, use *ANOTHER pencil and with your drawing hand,* LIGHTLY place one small dot by your thumbnail and one by your pencil tip (1-8). Afterward, be sure to HANG ON TO YOUR PENCIL READING. It will be used again in Step 3.

1-7 Find roughly HALF the *horizontal* span of your paper with a pencil check from about center to the left, or right edge.

1-8 Center your pencil check near the upper portion of your paper and mark the span with two dots.

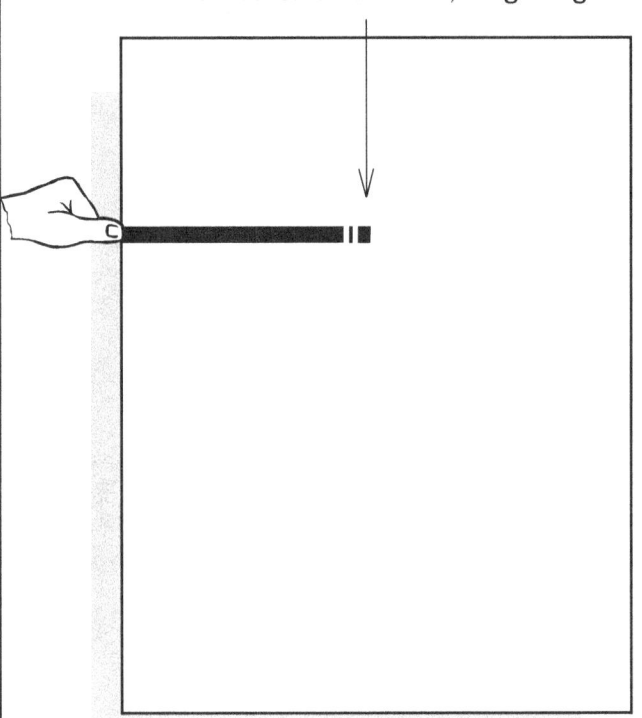

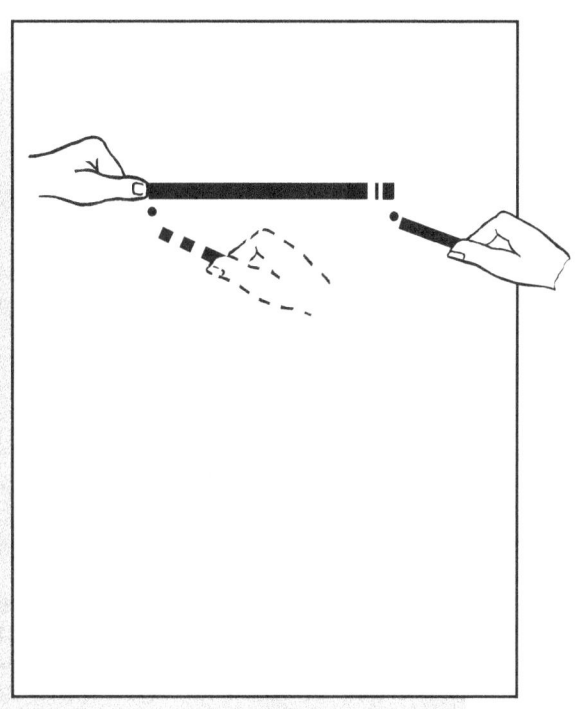

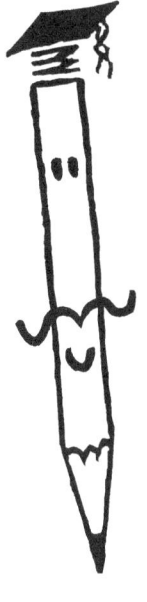

Real or make believe, guide lines may not seem like much. Yet they do so much. You'll see.

STEP 3   ESTABLISH THE *BOTTOM* CORNERS OF YOUR SQUARE

Rotate your *horizontal* pencil reading (held from the previous step) to a **VERTICAL** position. If you accidentally released your pencil check, simply take another reading of your two dots. Next, using the upper *LEFT* dot as a guide, place your eraser tip there, and mark a dot beside your THUMB (1-9). While *STILL HOLDING YOUR PENCIL CHECK*, also use the *upper* RIGHT dot as a guide to position your eraser tip. Then, mark one more spot beside your thumb (1-10). All together, you will have four dots.

1-9   Rotate horizontal distance and align plumb with upper LEFT dot to find & mark bottom LEFT corner.

1-10   Switch to RIGHT upper dot, then repeat procedure to find & mark bottom RIGHT corner.

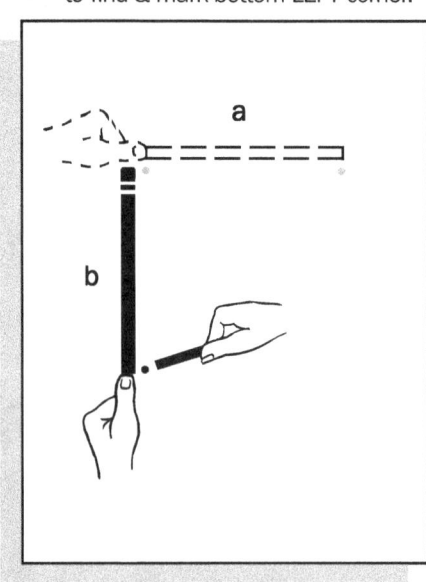

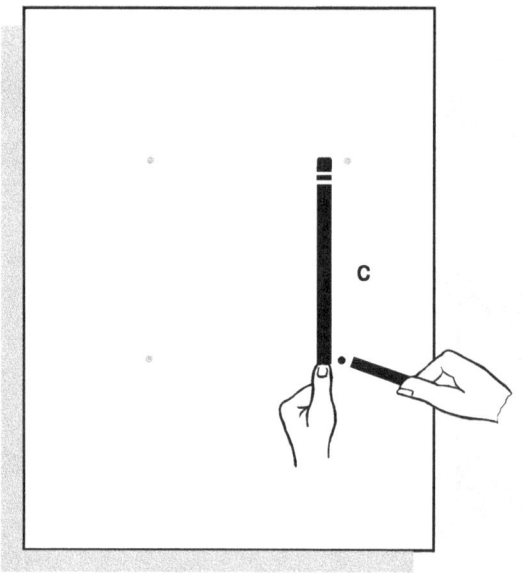

HOT TIP   Raise your paper upright, to eye level and arm's length. Make sure the spaces BETWEEN your pairs of dots appear fairly equal in length, are *not tilting*, (running *parallel* or even with the respective sides as well as top and bottom of your paper). Should adjustment be needed, this is the time to do it. For best results, you may also find it helps to turn your paper *sideways*. What seems correct from one point of view may surprise you from another. If you think these precautionary measures are unimportant, imagine what will happen when lines come in. Your square might become lopsided or go out of proportion. In turn, your figure would be affected. Examples **1-11** and **1-12** illustrate just two of the many adverse (unwanted) possibilities.

1-11   There are 4 dots, but they are cock-eyed. This can bring about a TILTED figure.

1-12   There are 4 dots, but the HEIGHT is too short. This can lead to a BULKY figure.

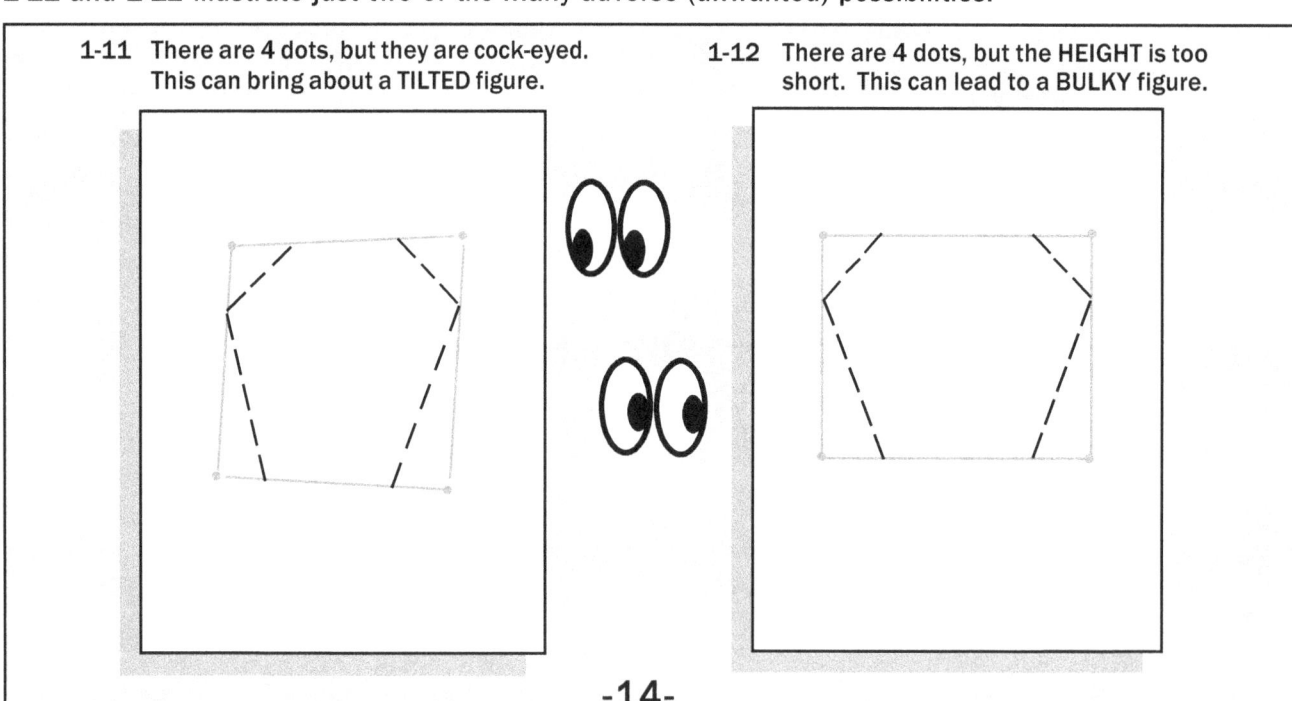

Here's where your earlier practice with straight lines already comes in handy. **LIGHTLY** connect your four dots with the **CONTINUOUS or SKETCH LINE method** (1-13, 14, 15, 16). Once done, you will have formed GUIDE LINES that will serve as a foundation with which to *construct* your figure. That's why guide lines can also be interchangeably referred *to as CONSTRUCTION* lines.

1-13 Link your 2 TOP
Horizontal dots.

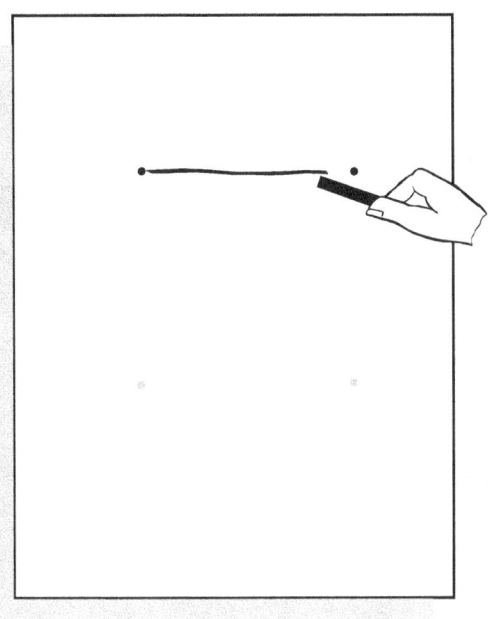

1-14 Link your 2 BOTTOM
Horizontal dots.

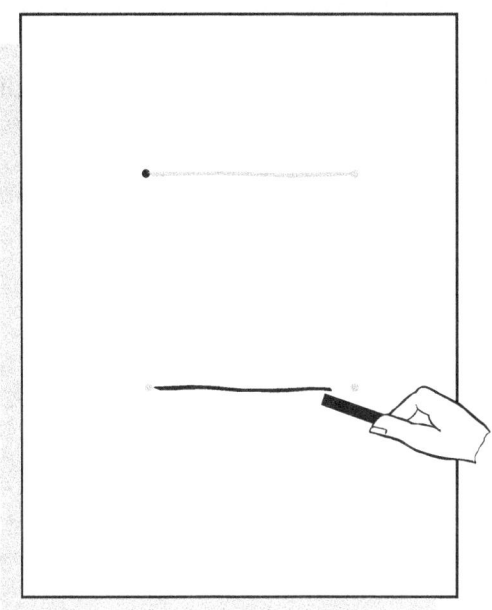

1-15 Link your 2 LEFT
Vertical dots.

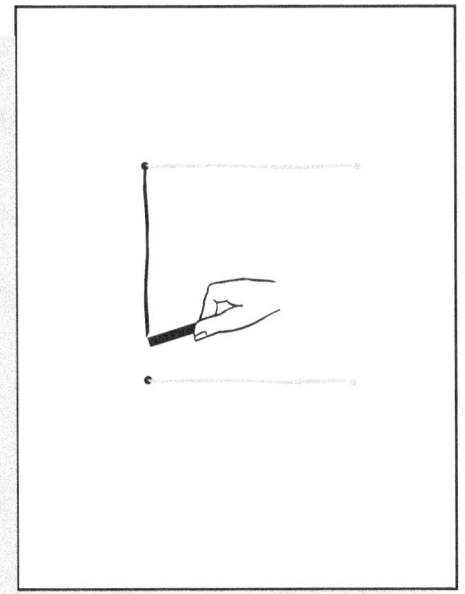

1-16 Link your 2 RIGHT
Vertical dots.

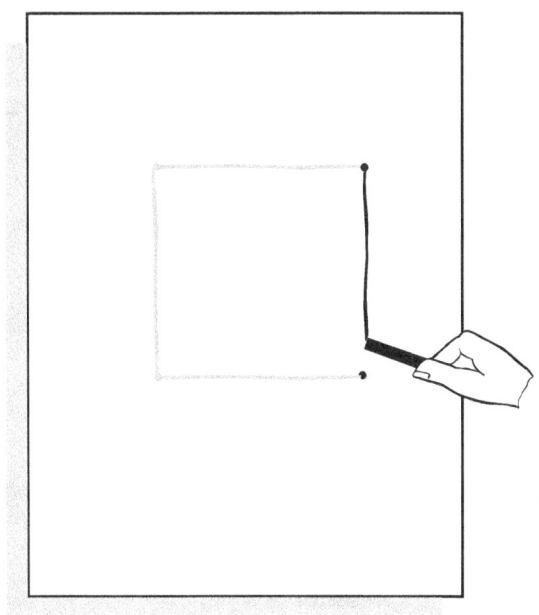

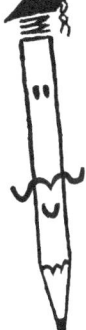

Now that your lines are in, please make sure all four sides of your square are about the same length and they appear reasonably PARALLEL to the respective edges of your paper.

STEP 5 — BEGIN LOCATING REFERENCE PTS. TO CHART A COURSE FOR SHAPE

Notice that the **TOP** and **BOTTOM corners** are inset at a **proportion** rate equal to ONE FOURTH of the entire distance across the figure (1-17). Next, observe that the corner reference points are PLUMB. "Plumb,"as you know, means the alignmen doesn't appear to have any tilt. This is indicated when it runs parallel to the SIDES of the paper. With this in mind, you may now proceed to position YOUR reference points. Begin by locating the *upper* and *lower* CENTERS of your SQUARE. Mark them with dots (1-18). Then, divide each half again to locate the QUARTER distances (1-19).

TIP Sure, you could take a shortcut by folding your paper in order to locate midway points. But please DON'T do that. Once again, I respectfully urge you to exercise your eyes. If desired, verify accuracy with your pencil. However, remember that pencil checks are not foolproof. Use them as a tool, not a crutch. Adjust VISUALLY as needed until things look reasonably correct to you.

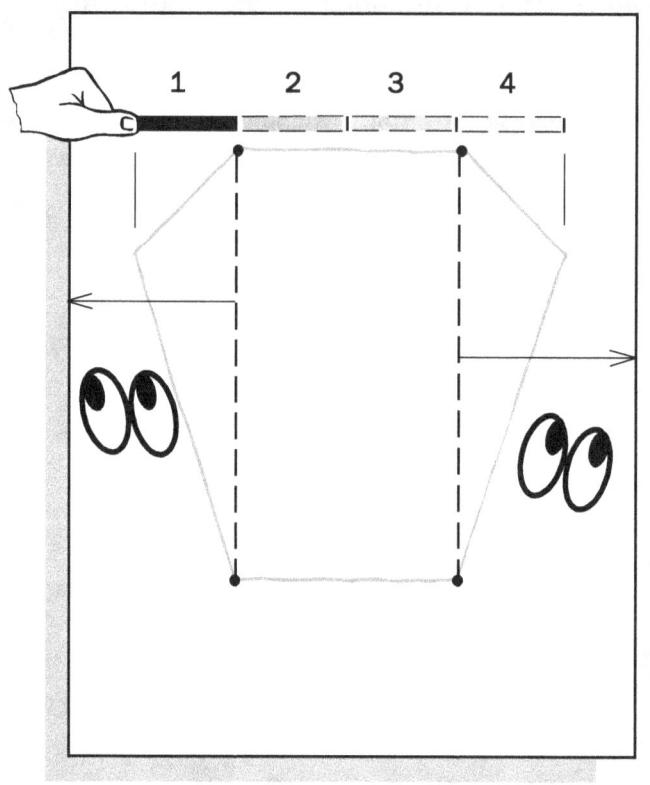

1-17 Top & bottom corners locate at QUARTER distances. Plus, they are PLUMB (parallel with *sides* of paper).

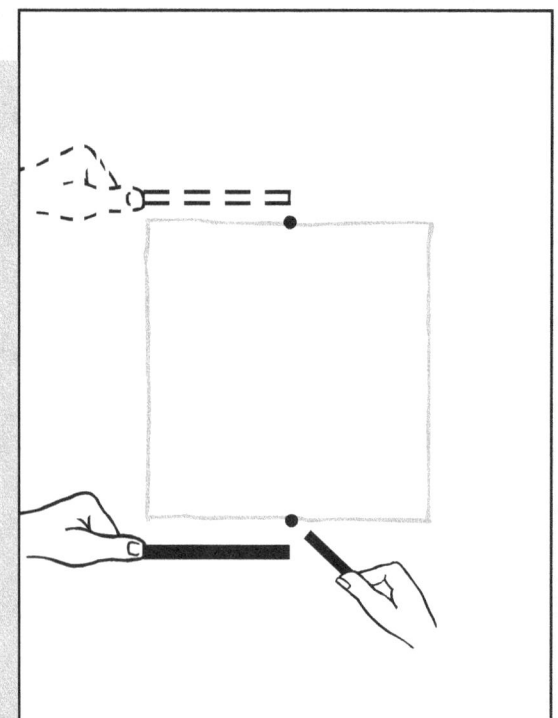

1-18 Estimate the TOP & BOTTOM *CENTER* of your square and mark it with a dot. Pencil check, if needed.

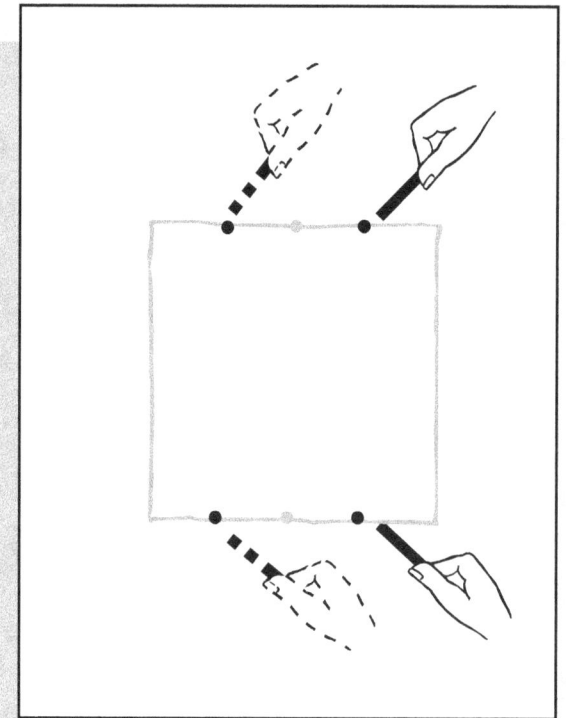

1-19 Sub-divide HALVES to find QUARTERS *VISUALLY,* and mark with dots. Pencil check, if needed.

Drawing 1-20 shows us that the upper **MID-CORNERS** are aligned LEVEL. "Level" signifies that the alignment doesn't have any visible tilt and runs parallel to the TOP and BOTTOM of the paper. Next, please observe that the mid-corner reference points locate ONE FOURTH of the way *DOWN* from the TOP of the figure. That means the remainder is THREE FOURTHS of the overall height. In order to mark those respective reference points *proportionally* on *your* square, first EYEBALL the *CENTER* of both SIDES. In other words, estimate VISUALLY, and pencil check if needed. Next, bisect (divide) both the *UPPER* HALVES into two quarters again with dots. These procedures are indicated by illustrations 1-21 and 1-22.

1-20 Mid-corner ref. pts. locate a quarter down from the top and run LEVEL (parallel to *top & bottom* of the paper) same as upper and lower part of figure.

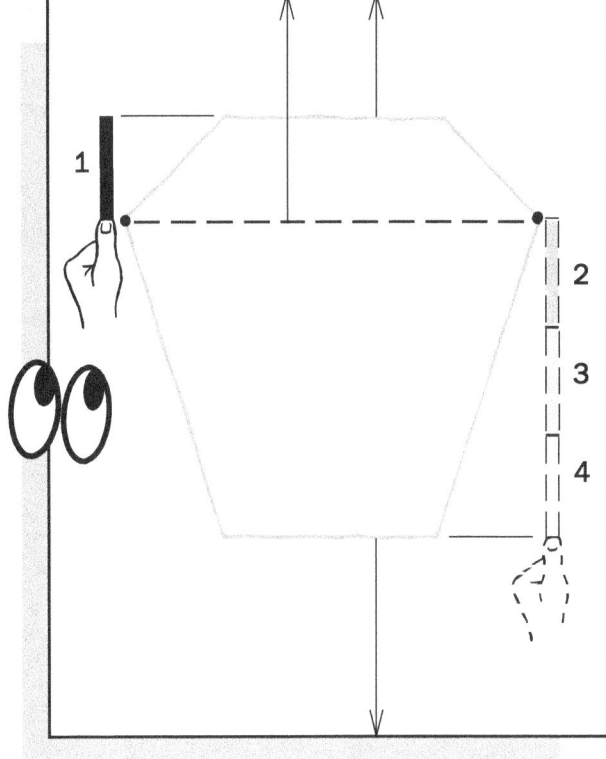

1-21 Divide your SIDES in HALF with dots.

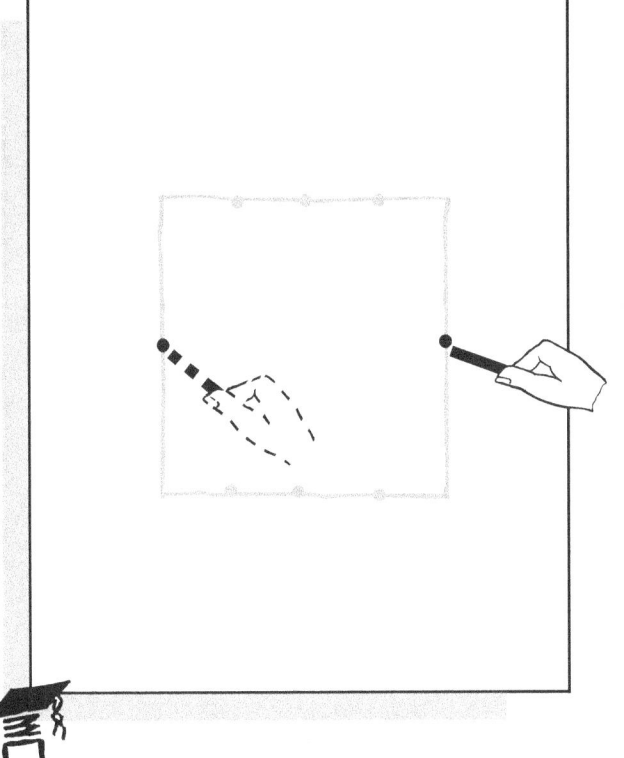

1-22 Divide your UPPER side halves with dots.

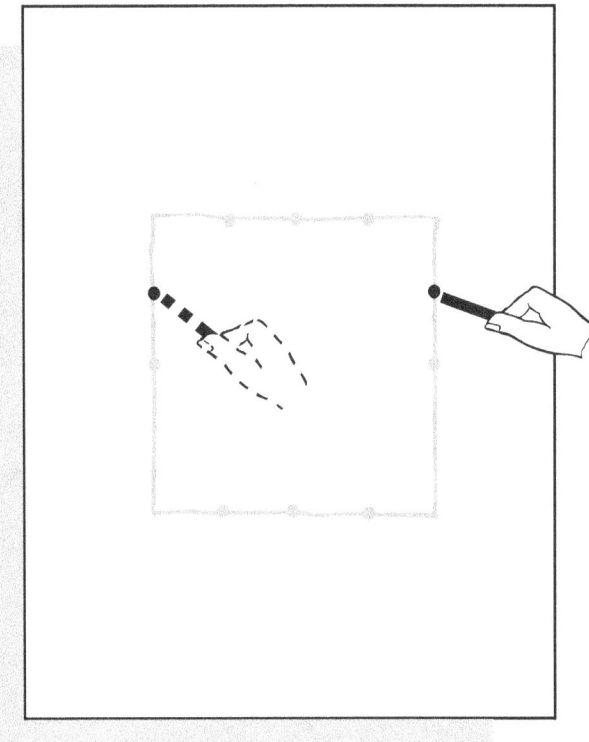

Remember to subdivide only the UPPER halves? Why? Because THOSE are the mid-corner reference points.

STEP 7   ELIMINATE CENTER DOTS

By helping you locate the QUARTER sections, the middle reference points have served their function. Specifically, they helped you set the *COORDINATES* (location) for the sub-proportions, plus the extensions for the side angles. You may now erase the original MIDDLE dots (1-23). Just the six dots, representing ALL the corners, should be left. Once that's done, even though the lines are not drawn yet, you will be able to almost SEE the anticipated 6-sided figure about to take shape (1-24).

1-23   Erase your ORIGINAL center dots.

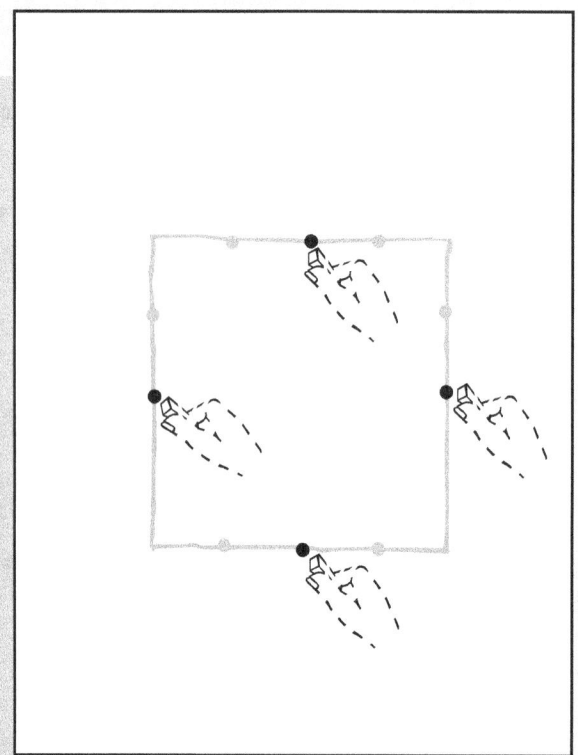

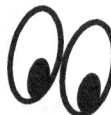

1-24   After your center dots are removed, you can *visualize* the coming shape.

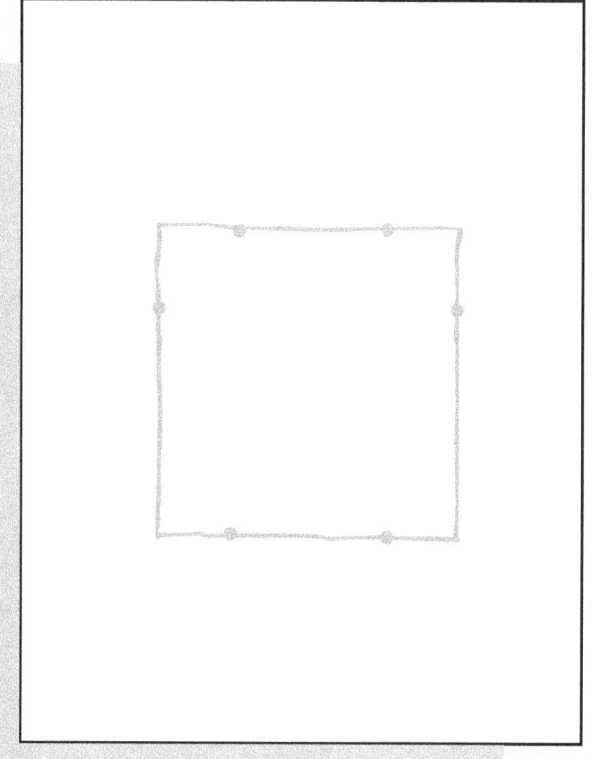

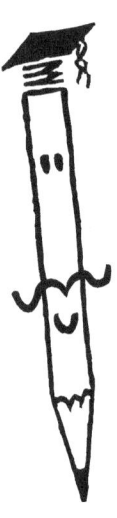

You're doing GREAT. This is an extensive chapter, but well worth it! The structural principles and components you learned about and practiced on your worksheets are paying off now, aren't they? You've already applied many of them.

If any guide lines are still out of place, or any reference points are mispositioned, you can spot them, even before the lines come in to establish the intended figure. For instance, in example 1-25, we can see the base of the square is not level. Plus, the *bottom* left reference point is not aligned plumb with the *top* left reference point. This caused the side ANGLE to tilt too much and distort the figure. Yet with just a simple adjustment, the modification can accurately lead to the desired shape (1-26).

TIP *YOU DON'T HAVE TO STAY STRICTLY WITHIN YOUR ORIGINAL GUIDE LINES.* If they appear out of place, you can always move them or go in or out of your boundaries as needed.

1-25   Example status check reveals a tilted bottom line, plus a dot needs to move left and up.

1-26   Anticipated shape after left *bottom* corner aligned with top, and figure's base is leveled.

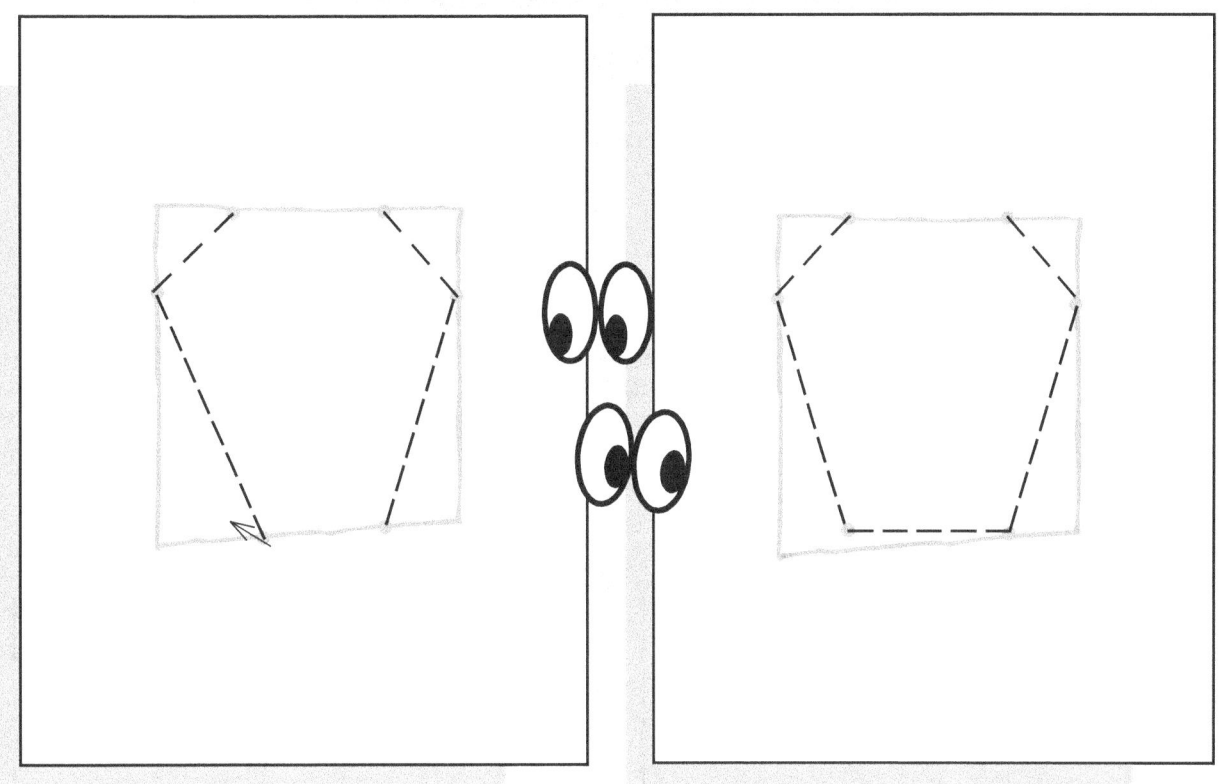

HOT TIP In the event you feel the urge to speed up, please do your best to fight the impulse, especially now. Although you're no doubt eager to finish and see the fruits of your labor, REGULAR, PERIODIC DOUBLE and TRIPLE VISUAL CHECKS are A VITAL PART OF THE DRAWING PROCESS. Just as you made certain that your dots were situated accurately for your square, you must continue to take every opportunity to fine tune as you progress. Never forget: *pencil readings, reference points,* and *construction lines* are **preliminaries** that act like *"THINK" aids,* or **helpers.** Ultimately, you have to judge VISUALLY, *while making sure not to get carried away.*

Accuracy doesn't mean you have to be exact.
After all, drawing is based on ESTIMATES,
and estimating means judging with the naked
eye (without rulers or other artificial devices).
What looks APPROXIMATELY right is fine.

CONNECT THE *UPPER* REFERENCE POINTS TO BEGIN ESTABLISHING YOUR 6-SIDED SHAPE

Once you're certain your dots are accurately positioned, proceed to bring the figure into being. You can choose the SKETCH or CONTINUOUS line technique you practiced earlier. Either way you choose, please DRAW LIGHTLY by following examples 1-27 and 1-28 or *your* preferred sequence.

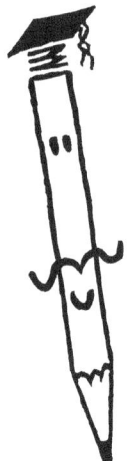

Resourcefulness is encouraged, but try not to be too clever. You just might outsmart yourself.

TIP Let's be honest. We both know, if you wanted to, you could use an artificial device, such as the edge of your book, a ruler, the side of your pencil, or some other shortcut, to help draw your lines. But by now as you no doubt also realize, there is character in your unique marks and these can only come *freehand*. Besides, just as your EYES need to look for reference points and your BRAIN needs to sort out what you've scanned, your HAND also benefits from exercise! It has to, if it's going to keep up. Fact is, all three skills have to develop in order to work well together.

1-27 Draw your UPPER *LEFT* angle.

1-28 Draw your UPPER *RIGHT* angle.

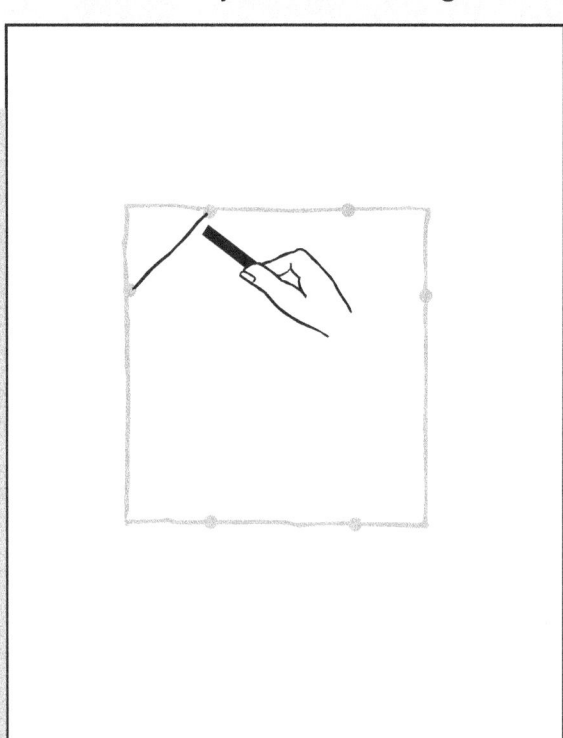

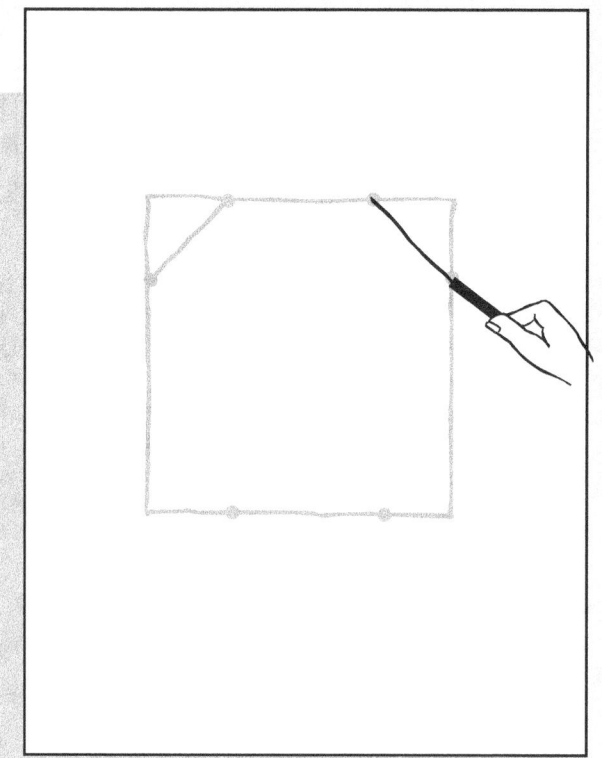

In order to link the remaining dots respectively, you may continue on to diagrams 1-29 and 1-30. Or, if you'd rather, you can complete the sides, using *your* order of preference.

1-29 Draw your LOWER *LEFT* angle.

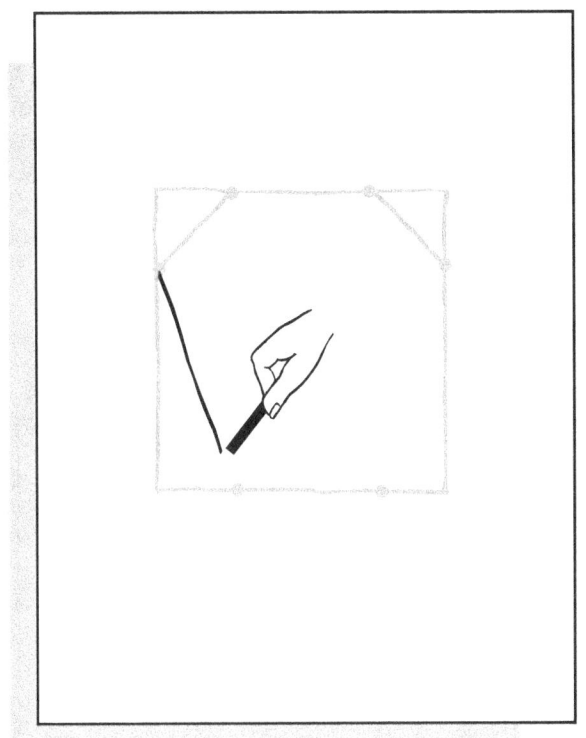

1-30 Draw your LOWER *RIGHT* angle.

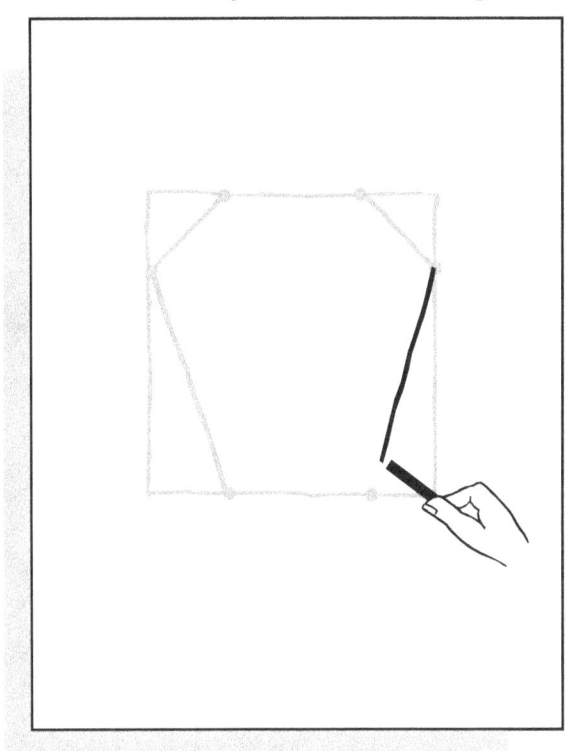

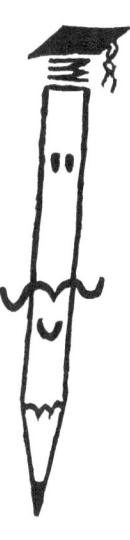

You're not watching TV or talking on the phone, are you? Distractions reduce your potential for learning. If there is a word you don't understand, the glossary in the back of the book can help. Take your time. There's no need to rush. The home stretch is in sight.

STEP 11 ERASE YOUR GUIDE LINES AND MAKE FINAL ADJUSTMENTS

Eliminate the excess lines on your drawing as shown in illustration 1-31. If your result appears a little ragged, like example 1-32, don't fret. Despite your best efforts, you could have accidentally removed more than you intended, or a line may have gone astray. That's where the "finishing touches" come in.

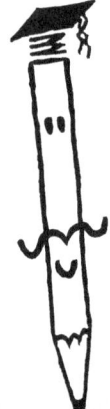

Now, aren't you glad you drew LIGHTLY?

TIP As you complete your refinements, be sure to glance back and forth between your drawing and figure 1-31. That way, you will be less likely to lose sight of the basic shape and possibly change too much. Also, keep in mind that your replica was done FREEHAND. The *UNIQUE* QUALITY of YOUR pencil lines is more desirable than the stiff look of PRINT.

1-31 Erase your unwanted lines.   1-32 Example of a semi-finished figure.

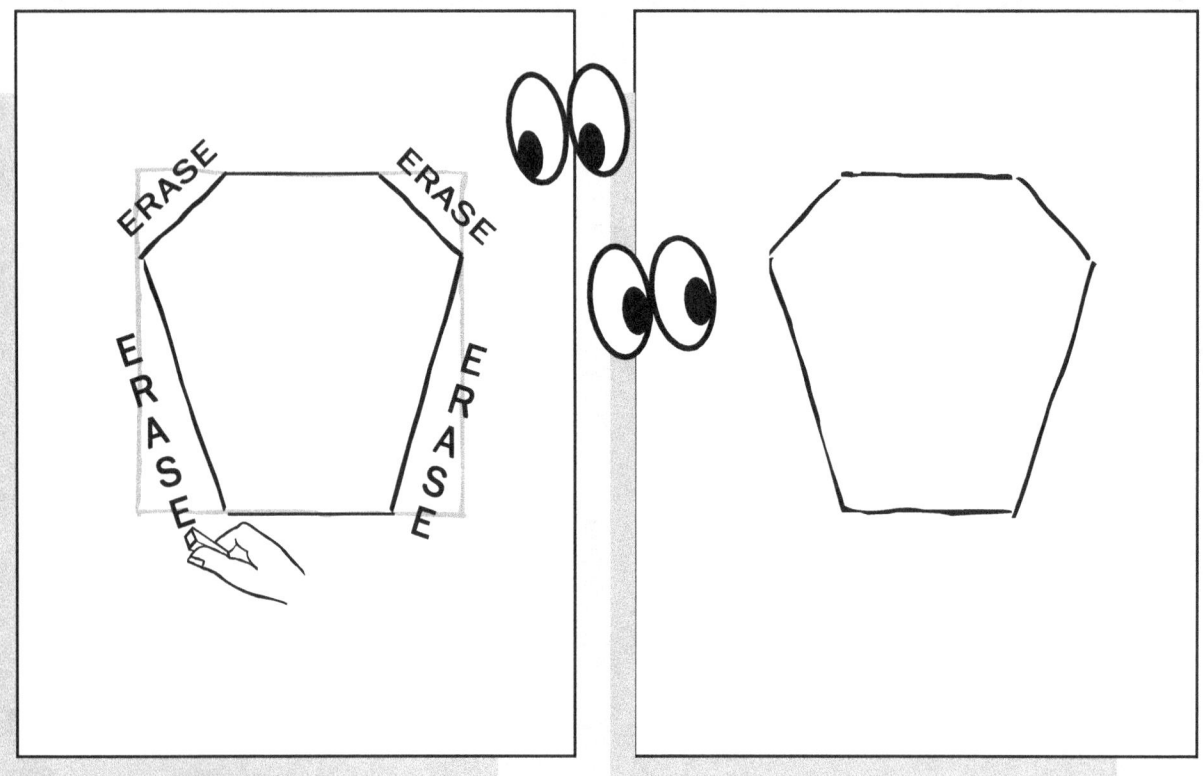

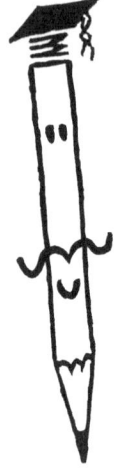

After you've made refinements, see how your fellow students did.
(next page)

EXERCISE 1
MODEL & SAMPLE DRAWINGS

HOT TIP Study the following examples. Compare them and your figure to the MODEL. All the while, please remember that perfection is not the goal, nor is it a contest to see whose picture is the best. Whether you think yours missed the mark, equaled or excelled, what really counts is the wealth of knowledge you gain from your experiences and by observing the works of others.

Model

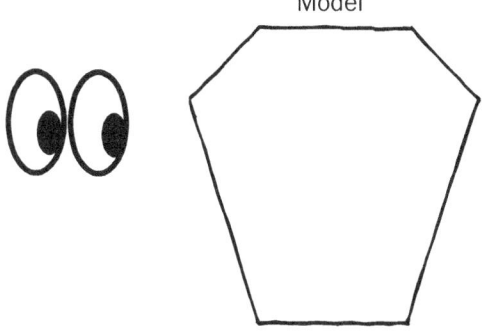

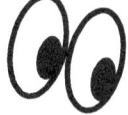

STUDENT EXAMPLES
All three student drawings are fine. I'm sure yours is, too.

1-33

1-34

1-35

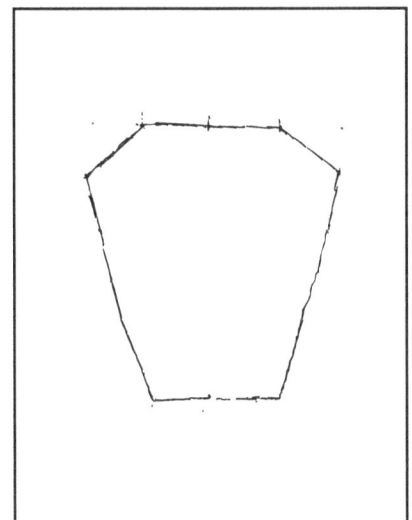

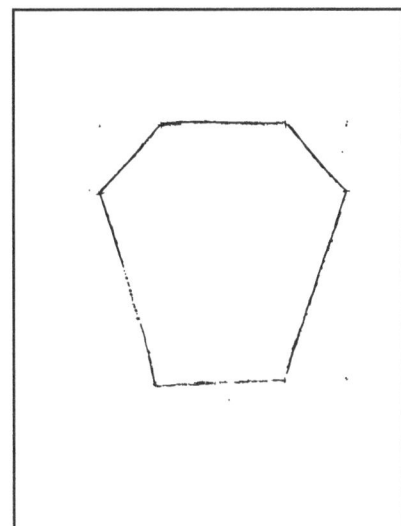

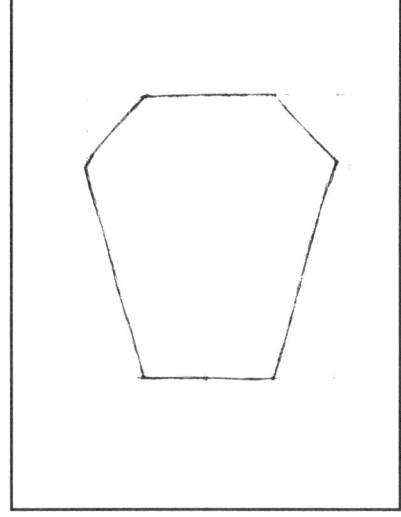

Here are the obvious things I observed. See if you agree.

The *height* of the *upper* angles on drawing 1-33 are *less* than a quarter of the figure's height, aren't they?

Example 1-34 has a bottom which is not level, right?

Version 1-35 is too tall proportionally. It can be widened across or reduced in height.

Having surveyed these works and yours, hopefully you've gathered even greater understanding. Incidentally, be sure to KEEP YOUR DRAWING. YOU WILL NEED IT IN THE NEXT CHAPTER. For the present, please read the FOLLOW-UP.

Chapter 1
FOLLOW-UP

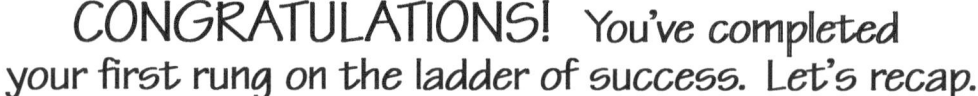

CONGRATULATIONS! You've completed
your first rung on the ladder of success. Let's recap.

1. You discovered that shapes can be taken apart with your eyes.

2. Becoming familiar with your subject BEFORE you begin to draw is very helpful.

3. Much of WHAT you're searching for is right there in front of you, but you have to take the time to look.

4. Drawing is a process which can be divided into manageable stages. With them, you gradually bring shapes into being. Maybe that's one reason this is considered creative.

5. Reference points, alignments, straight lines, angles, and proportions are helpful ways to assess and draw the structural aspects of shape.

6. A pencil is not just a writing and drawing tool, but also handy for checking alignments and proportions. It also helps avoid false impressions.

7. Straight lines and angles can be approached in many ways other than with a ruler. In fact, it's the FREEHAND types that are desirable. They express YOU!

8. It's good to know not only where you should start and end a line, but where you are along the route.

9. Locating reference points prior to drawing the line is a smart practice.

10. Real and imaginary guide lines are a worthwhile means by which to "map out" (or chart) a course for shape because they instill confidence, accuracy, and ease.

All told, this is quite a tally indeed.
Now that you're off to a marvelous start, always remember:

Successful drawing doesn't stem from able HANDS alone.
It also comes from skillful THINKING and OBSERVING.

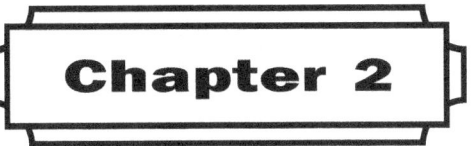

Chapter 2

THE ATTACH METHOD

We're going to make changes...

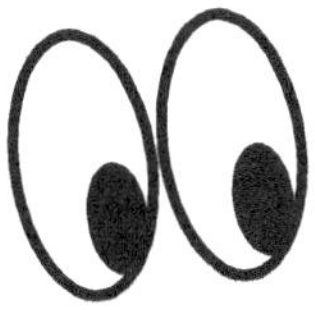

from this...

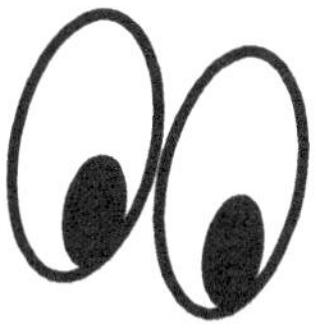

...to this.

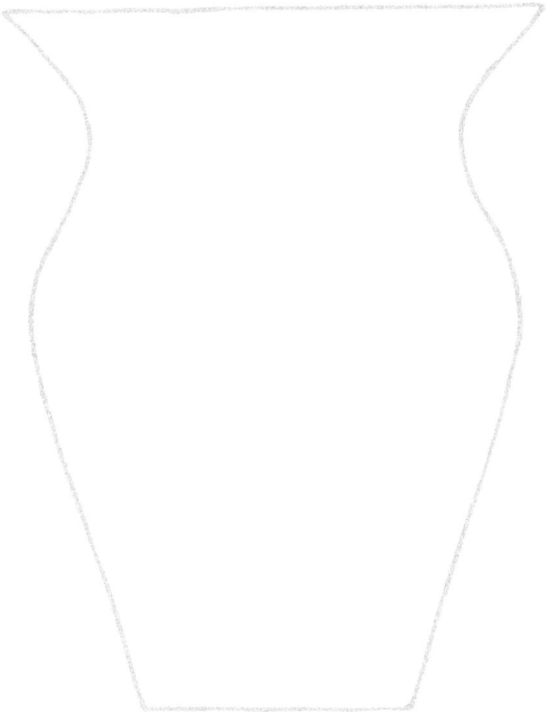

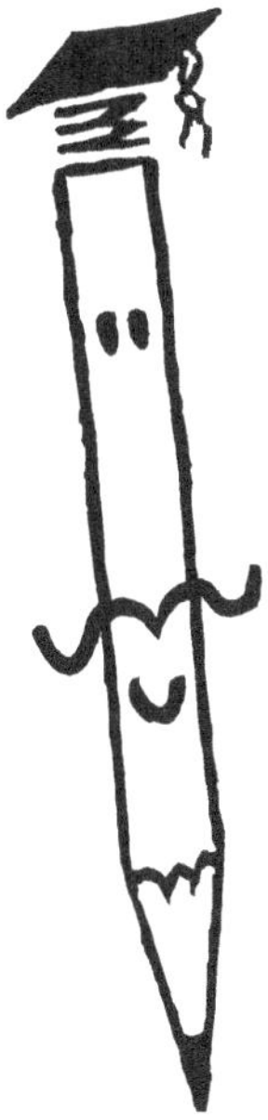

How is such a miracle accomplished?
Read on and you'll discover.

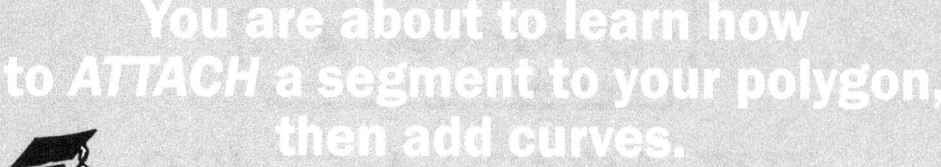

You are about to learn how
to *ATTACH* a segment to your polygon,
then add curves.

For those who are wondering...
a POLYGON is a shape which has at least
3 straight sides. Yours already
has 6, but it's destined for more.

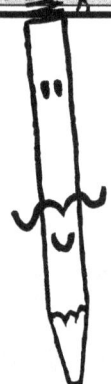

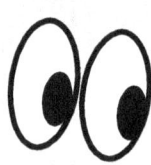

YOUR POLYGON
CURRENTLY

WHERE WE'RE HEADED

STAGE 1
STRAIGHT LINE ATTACHMENT

STAGE 2
CURVE LINE ATTACHMENT

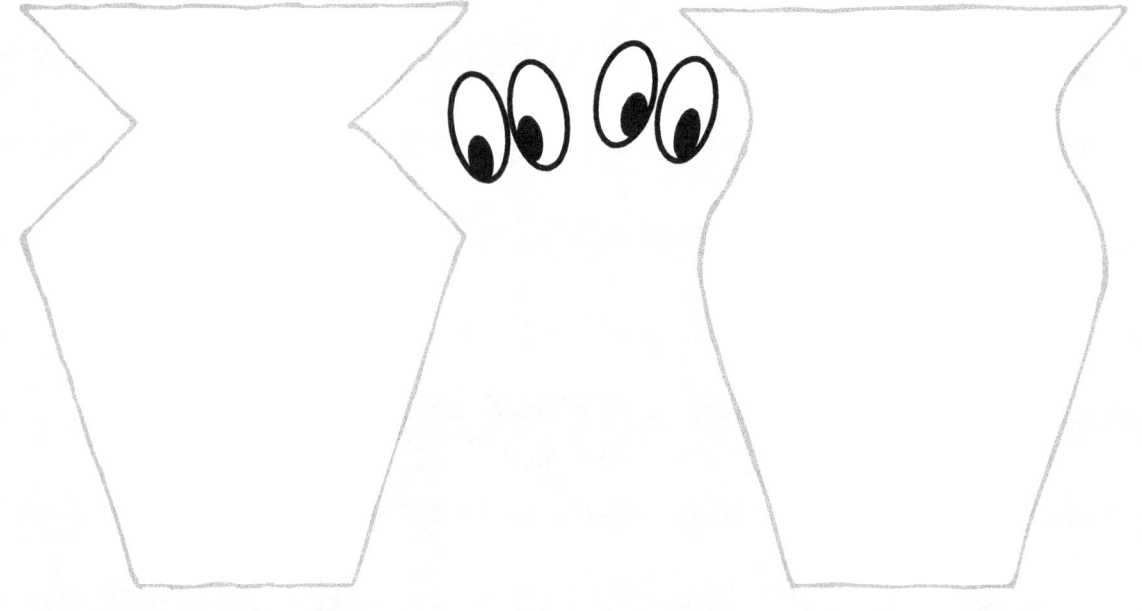

EXERCISE 2   STAGE 1
STRAIGHT LINE *ATTACHMENT*

STEP 1   LOOK
              BEFORE YOU LEAP

Study illustration 2-1. It shows that the intended *addition* connects, or "ATTACHES," to the top corners of the ORIGINAL figure with STRAIGHT lines. These rise diagonally (at an angle) from the previous top until they align *FLUSH (or even) with the maximum expanse* (furthest extent).   As a result, a 2nd shape can be formed, complete with a ***new*** TOP.

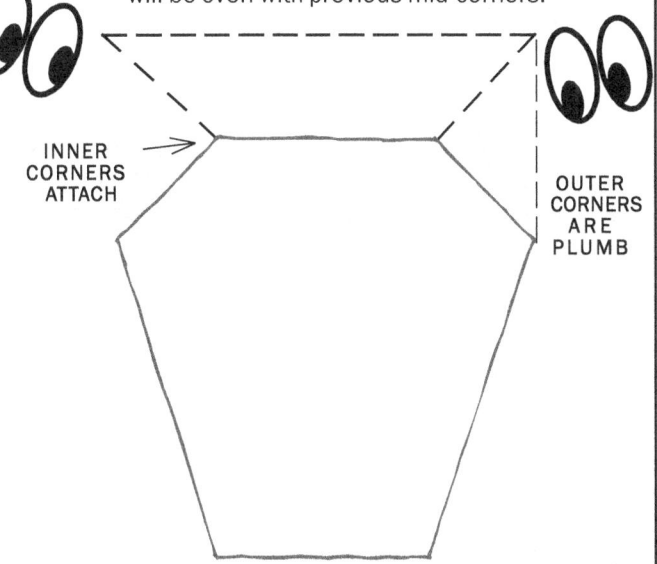

2-1 New upper shape is to be "ATTACHED" to *current* polygon's top corners. *New* top will be even with previous mid-corners.

INNER CORNERS ATTACH

OUTER CORNERS ARE PLUMB

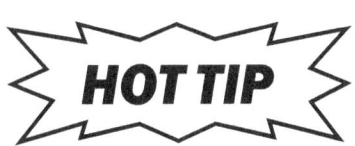

Take the time to observe. The more you see, the easier drawing becomes.

Notice: illustration 2-2 below indicates that the **HEIGHT** from *CURRENT* mid-corner "a" to CURRENT top "b" is the *SAME* as the distance from *CURRENT* top "b" to *eventual NEW* top "c."   Since "a" to "b," if you will recall, is *one fourth* of your *current* polygon's height, and this is the span you will use for your *coming* attachment, please double check your *present status now,* and adjust if needed.

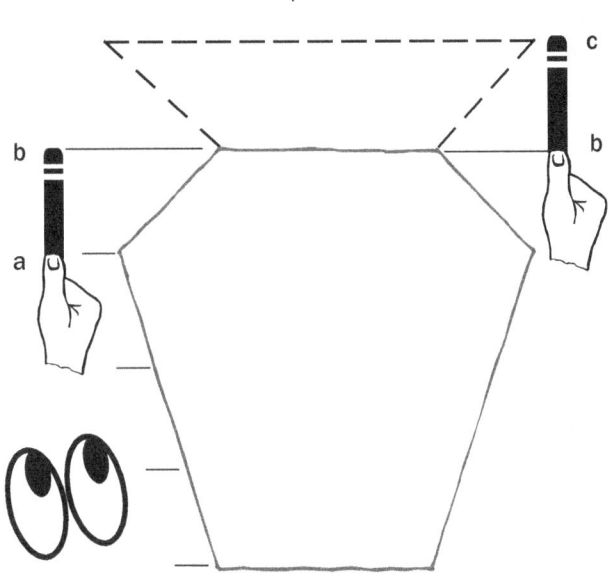

2-2 *Present* mid-corner to the top is one fourth of the distance. *New* shape HEIGHT will be the same.

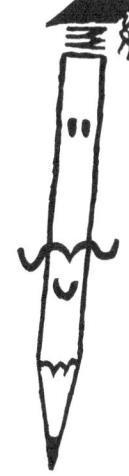

Estimating proportions is NOT DIFFICULT. It's just a simple size comparison of one part to another. And since we've completed our initial survey, we're ready to do the first stage ATTACHMENT.

STEP 2   MAP OUT THE ADDITION

As shown in illustration 2-3, you will need to locate TWO reference points on YOUR drawing. Find them **proportionally** by taking a pencil reading of **the distance of YOUR** polygon from the LEFT MID-CORNER until it aligns LEVEL with the TOP (2-4). Next, while holding your pencil check, move ONE increment (span) up. *Be sure to keep it PLUMB (or even) with the left end.* Then mark a dot near your eraser tip. Next, repeat the process at the **right** side of your figure (2-5). The 2 dots above your polygon will be locators for the coming lines (STEP 3 next page).

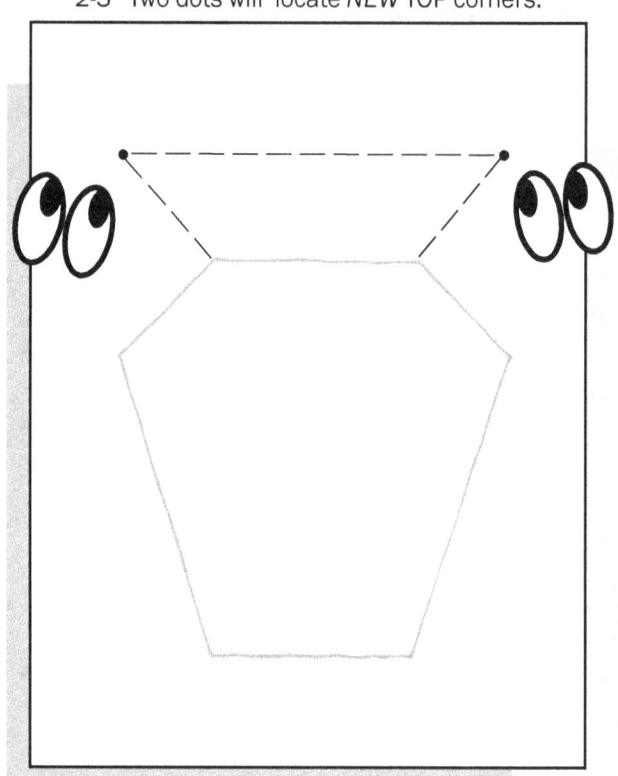

2-4 Take a pencil reading of YOUR polygon from the LEFT MID-CORNER to the top.

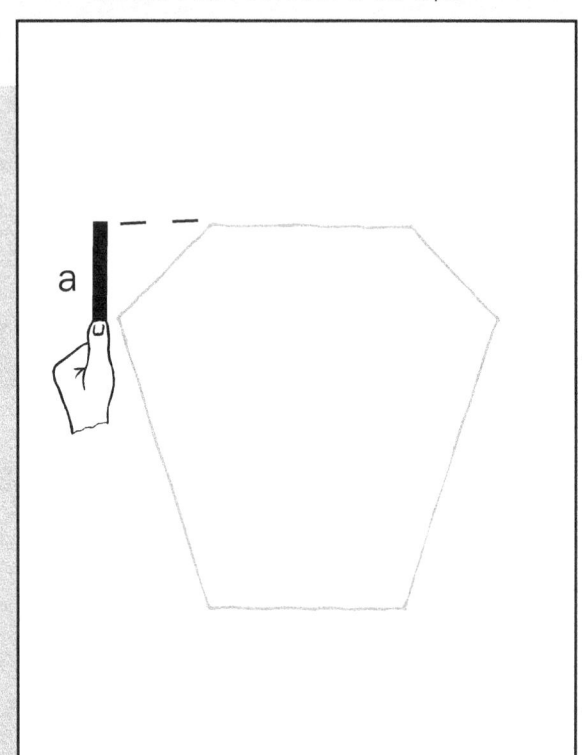

2-5 Move your pencil check one span up. Align it PLUMB with LEFT corner and place a dot. Repeat the procedure at the RIGHT corner.

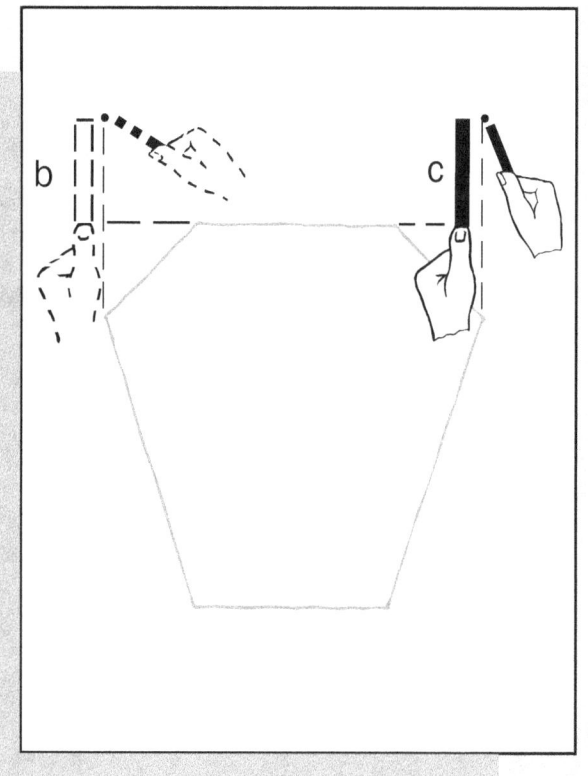

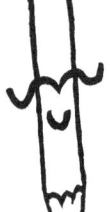

Now you know why I like to call this the ATTACH method. We're "attaching" another segment.

DRAW THE TOP AND SIDES FOR YOUR NEW SECTION

Start by LIGHTLY connecting your two dots with a *horizontal,* continuous or sketch line (2-6). Next, link the left and right ends of the NEW line to the respective CORNERS below (2-7). Then, as illustration 2-8 indicates, erase the MIDDLE line *(previous top)*.

TIP *Compare your results* to the model (previous page) and rely on your eyes, more than your pencil readings. They help you ESTIMATE sizes but are NOT meant to MEASURE *EXACTLY.* If anything APPEARS to be amiss (incorrect), it probably is. Adjust your figure as needed until things seem okay VISUALLY. Look for the same factors you use to draw. These include reference points, proportions, alignments & angles.

2-7 LIGHTLY draw corresponding angle lines from your NEW top ends to PREVIOUS top corners.

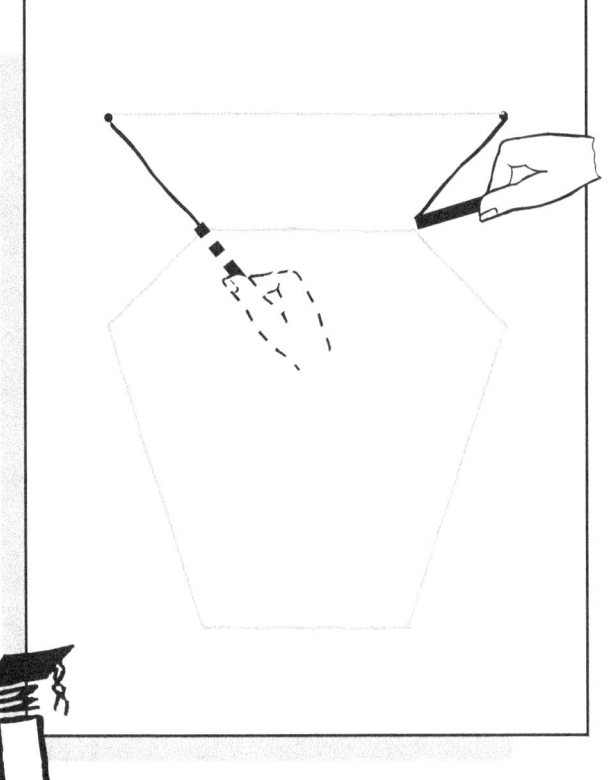

2-6 LIGHTLY draw a horizontal line dot to dot to form a NEW top.

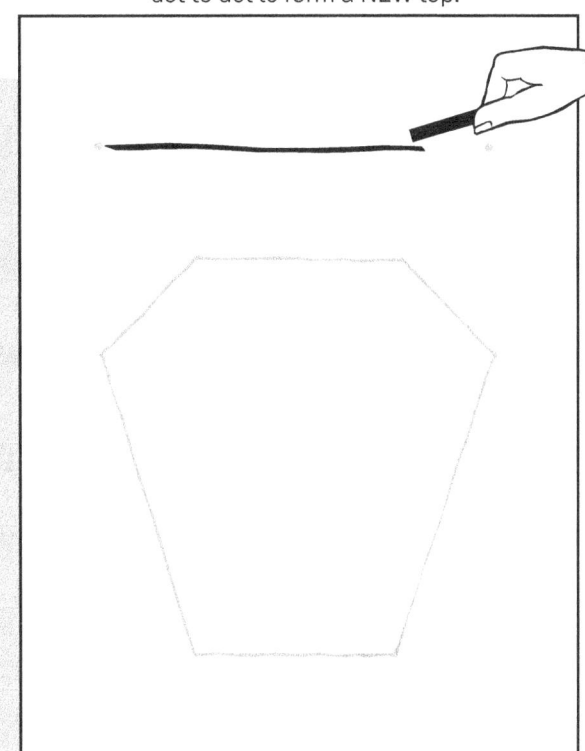

2-8 ERASE your MIDDLE line (Previous Top).

Bravo! Stage 1 is nearly finished. Before moving on to Stage 2, be sure the height of your attachment is one fourth the height of your large shape below it, and the new top is even with the total distance across.

-29-

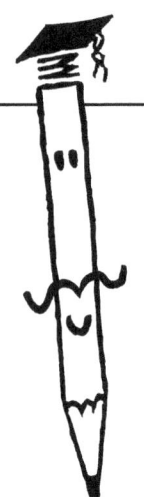

PREPARE for STAGE 2
The CURVES

AS USUAL, DO THE SMART THING...
...SURVEY THE SITUATION.

WHERE WE'RE HEADED

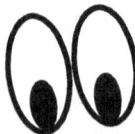

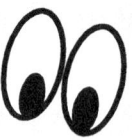

CURRENT STAGE

STAGE 2

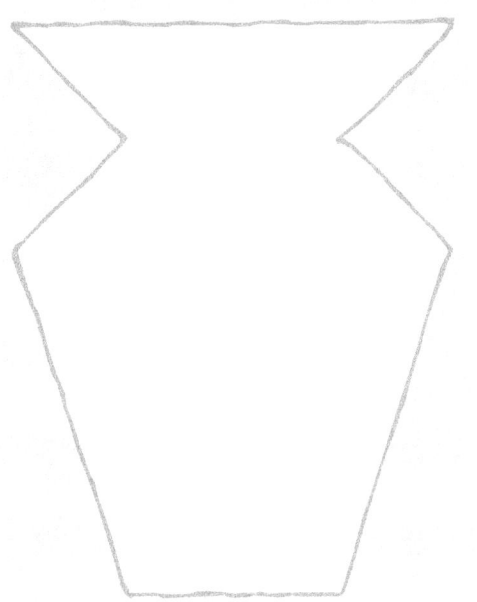

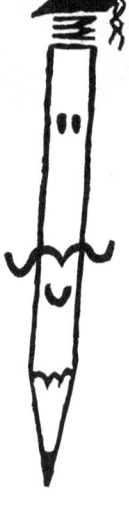

In order for the 2nd phase to work, some preliminary explanation is called for. After all, like straight lines, CURVES ARE ALSO A MAJOR PART OF DRAWING.

THE *IN'S* AND *OUT'S* OF CURVES

Think of a curve (or arc) as a line that BENDS. When this happens, curves have LENGTH and WIDTH, just like angles do. In turn, they also have *proportion*. For instance, there are wide arcs and narrow ones. Examples of these are shown in illustration 2-9.

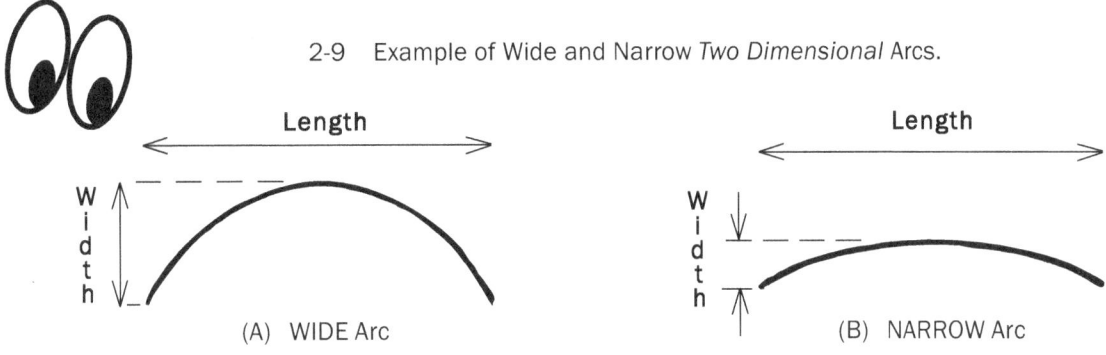

2-9   Example of Wide and Narrow *Two Dimensional* Arcs.

(A) WIDE Arc

(B) NARROW Arc

Another interesting feature is that just as straight lines can be classified according to 2 main types (continuous or sketch), the same is true for curves. The similarity ends there, however. Curves not only fall into two basic categories, but two subdivisions on top of that. First, I will explain the main category that most people are familiar with. It's called the FORMAL, or *more properly* termed, **symmetrical** variety. But, don't let the fancy word scare you. "Symmetrical" simply means evenly distributed. As for the other kind, it's INFORMAL (unevenly distributed) or **asymmetrical.** Next, permit me to also introduce you to the subcategories. Not only can curves appear even and uneven (regular and irregular), they can be **CONVEX** or **CONCAVE**. "Convex" essentially signifies that a curve "flexes" or bends **outward**, like a mound of soil. In contrast, if it sinks **inward,** like a cave, it's identified as "concave." (Hence, perhaps the reason the latter part of the word is termed *"cave."*) In any event, the following two arcs, placed horizontally in illustration 2-10, exemplify all four aspects of curves. Sample "C" is the even, convex arc, and "D" is the uneven, concave arc.

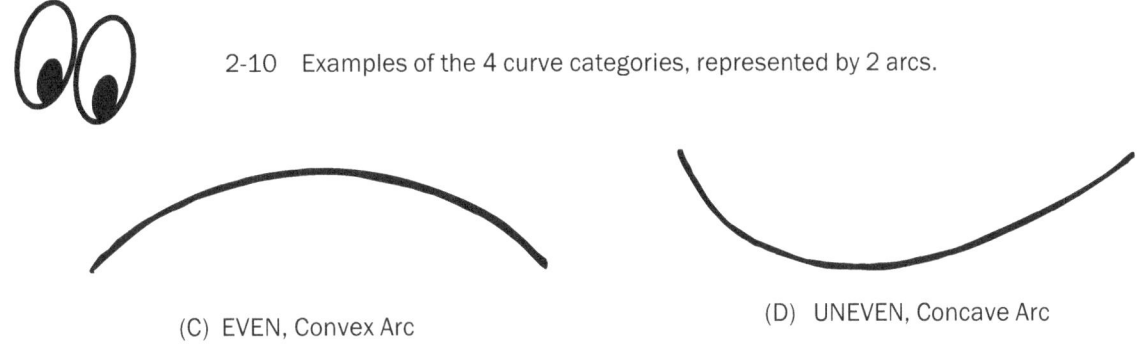

2-10   Examples of the 4 curve categories, represented by 2 arcs.

(C) EVEN, Convex Arc

(D) UNEVEN, Concave Arc

Aside from these examples, arcs can also be positioned vertically or at a slant. Include scale variation, plus combine more than one kind of curve, and the possibilities are virtually endless. So how do you eliminate the confusion and guesswork in order to draw curves? It's not as tough as you might expect. Actually it's easy, once you know the secrets.

Please, continue reading.

JUST LIKE ANGLES, *CURVES CAN HAVE GUIDE LINES TOO!*

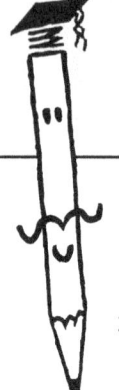

I like to call curve guide lines
BASE LINE, ELEVATION LINE,
SIDE LINES and CORNER LINES.

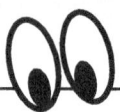

Observe arc 2-11 **WITHOUT** guide lines. Clearly, with nothing to compare it to, the shape just floats in empty space.

2-11 The rate of a curve without a reference source is difficult to estimate, let alone replicate.

BASE LINE

Study an identical curve (2-12). Notice that this one has an *imaginary* line which connects the two ends of the curve. In this way, a closed *shape* is formed which makes the curve's amount of FLEX, or bend, easier to estimate.

2-12 Like a string shows the tension of a bow, the imagined base line helps estimate the curve's amount of flex.

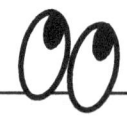

Base Line

ELEVATION LINE

Include a *straight* guide line at the CREST (maximum bend) of the curve, or make believe the line is there, and you have an ELEVATION LINE. With its help, you can see the angles on both ends of the curve, as though it were made by two separate curves. In turn, this makes it possible to estimate the flex of one, then the other, and draw the entire curve with TWO HALVES (2-13). You also have the option to place dots between the start, widest point and ending locations. You may even elect to position them anywhere in between, similar to the method used to direct your straight lines.

2-13 An imaginary ELEVATION LINE at the CREST of a curve helps to see its height, as well as judge the rate of rise and fall. This makes it easier to draw the arc with TWO HALVES, especially with dots along the way.

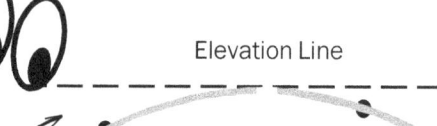

Elevation Line

1   2

SIDE LINES

Add SIDE LINES, or pretend they are there, and the curve becomes "boxed-in" (2-14). This kind of "FRAME OF REFERENCE," as I like to call it, also makes the curve less difficult to estimate. Why? Because, you are able to spot the overall *proportion* (length and width) more easily. Better yet, you can see *all* the shapes the curve creates within the boundaries. Illustration 2-15 shows *one* such area, filled with gray; the others are indicated with arrows.

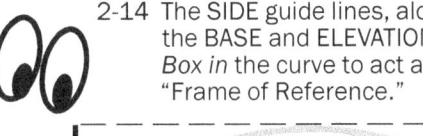
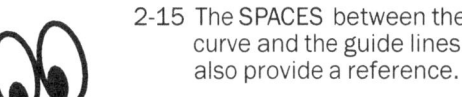

2-14 The SIDE guide lines, along with the BASE and ELEVATION LINE *Box in* the curve to act as a "Frame of Reference."

2-15 The SPACES between the curve and the guide lines also provide a reference.

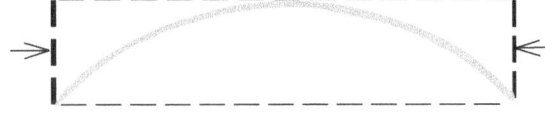
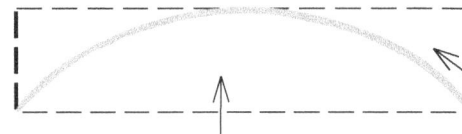

CORNER LINES

When curves are at a *slant,* it's wise to include PLUMB and LEVEL guide lines. Acting like *extensions* used for *angles,* you can create what I like to distinguish as CORNER LINES. Combine them with a BASE LINE, to form a TRIANGLE, and you can estimate the **rate of TILT as well as BEND more easily**. Figure 2-16 illustrates.

2-16 Tilted curve is easier to estimate with the help of a visualized, or fashioned TRIANGLE made by CORNER LINES and a BASE LINE.

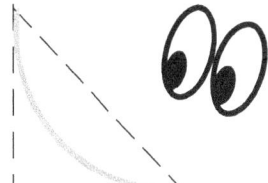

TIP   Apparently, curves are not as challenging as you may have expected, are they? Just as with straight lines, it's important to know where you intend to start, where you are along the route, and where you plan to stop. However, curves require some additional things to watch for. What are these? They are: FLEX, INCLINE, DECLINE, PROPORTION and TILT.

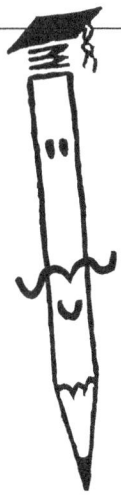

Fear not. With the help of visualized and/or actual guide lines, curves are quite easy to draw. Test this for yourself. Complete the worksheet on the next page.

Worksheet E   Replicate CURVES

DIRECTIONS: Notice there are *paired* sets of guide lines. One set has a curve, the other doesn't. Your job is to match the regular and irregular arcs within the empty boundaries beside each model. Use the **continuous or sketch line** technique. **Draw LIGHTLY as you CONSTRUCT your arcs.** Also, remember to *glance back and forth* between the original and your progressing arc while you STEER your pencil. This gives you the opportunity to adjust as you go. **Do NOT TURN the worksheet** for convenient positions, (although "lefties" may invert the page so your view of the model isn't blocked). The goal is to form curves in a variety of directions, thereby enabling your hand to become increasingly versatile and skillful. The *shapes* you create BETWEEN your curves and guide lines can also serve as a helpful reference. The arrows on example A-1 demonstrate. Sample A-2, 3 & 4 also show suggestions. After you've finished, I also recommend that you draw some more arcs on a separate sheet of paper in a variety of ways, sizes, angles, and types. Then replicate them for additional practice.

Suggested methods to help you draw your arcs.

A-1 Surrounding areas provide reference

A-2 Either direction left or right

A-3 Intermediate dots help guide pencil

A-4 Either direction Two half curves

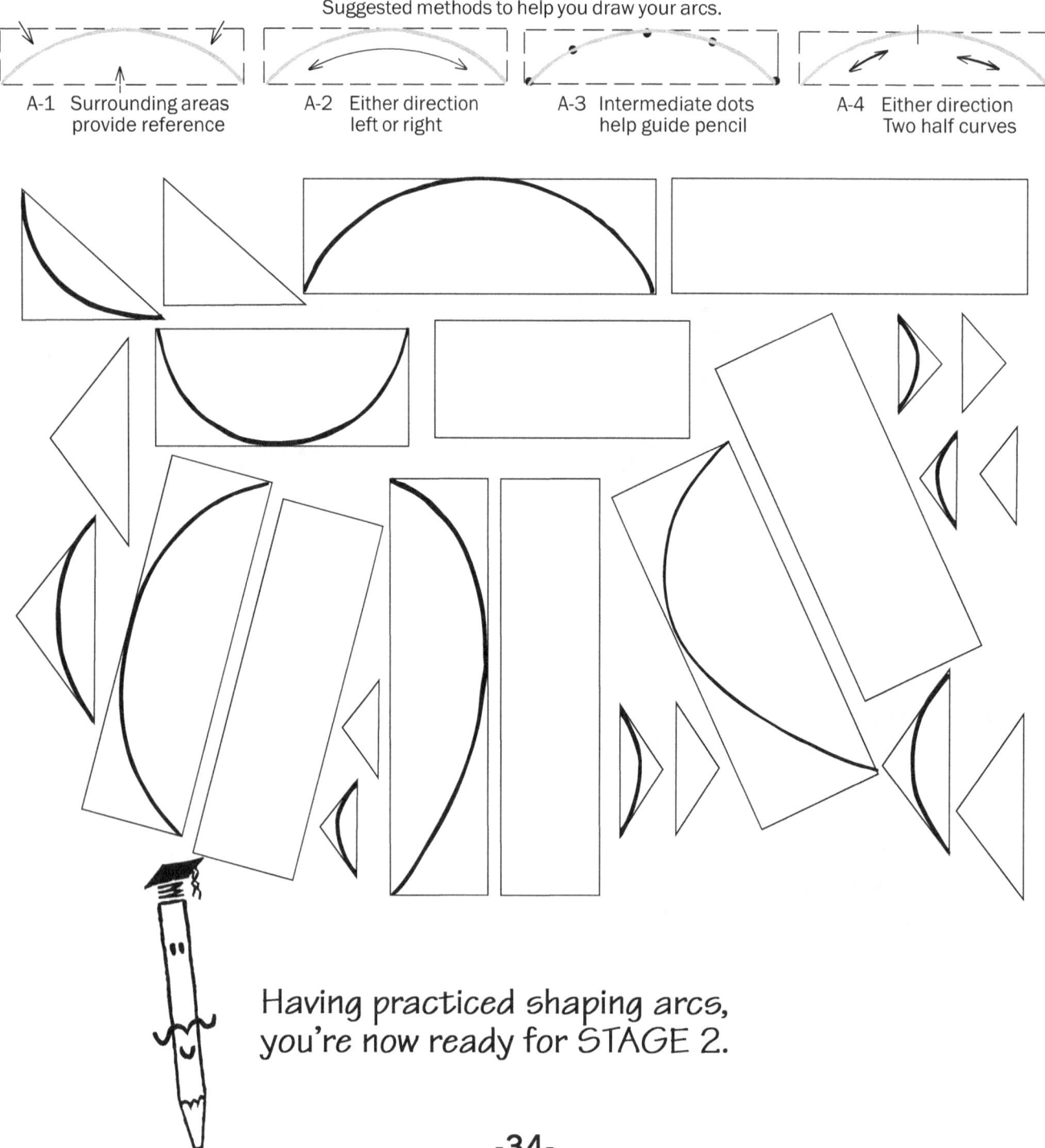

Having practiced shaping arcs, you're now ready for STAGE 2.

-34-

EXERCISE 2 STAGE 2
THE *CURVES*

Please examine illustration 2-17, and pay special attention to the "BOW" of the concave arcs. Note their amount of bend, in relationship to the figure. Next, form your arcs proportionally, ONE by ONE (2-18). Then erase the excess lines (2-19).

HOT TIP Since the arcs are to fit within the area where two straight lines meet, these can work as CORNER GUIDE LINES. For best results however, be sure to make gradual adjustments during your advance and verify accuracy. In other words, *DON'T just draw a QUICK curve FROM MEMORY (or in a way you happen to like), assume it's identical to the book version, then fashion a MIRROR image for the opposite side. INSTEAD, give equal attention to each arc separately, by keeping track of the model as you form one arc at a time.* This will help you create the right amount of "bend." Afterward, *compare each of your curves to the model once again.*

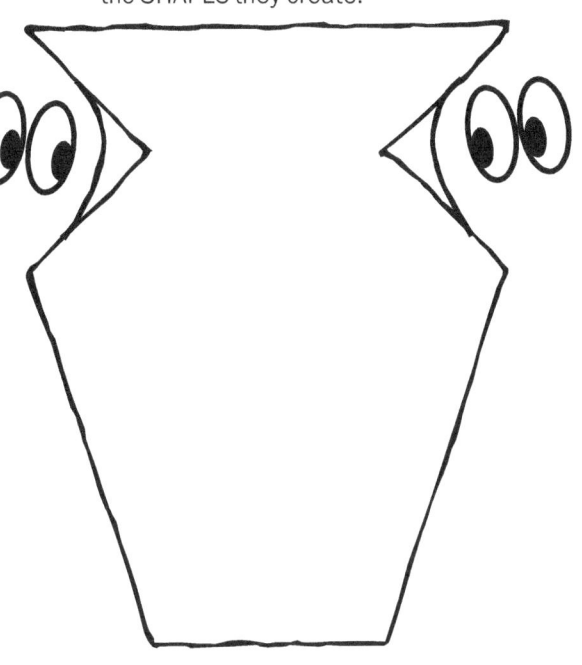

2-17 Study the 2 curves INDEPENDENTLY as two SEPARATE arcs, along with the SHAPES they create.

2-18 Lightly draw one curve, then the other.

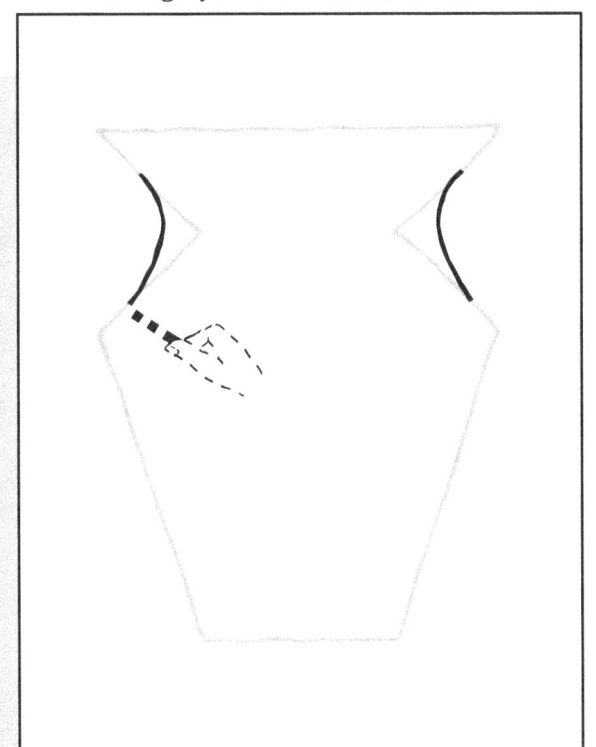

2-19 Erase your excess lines.

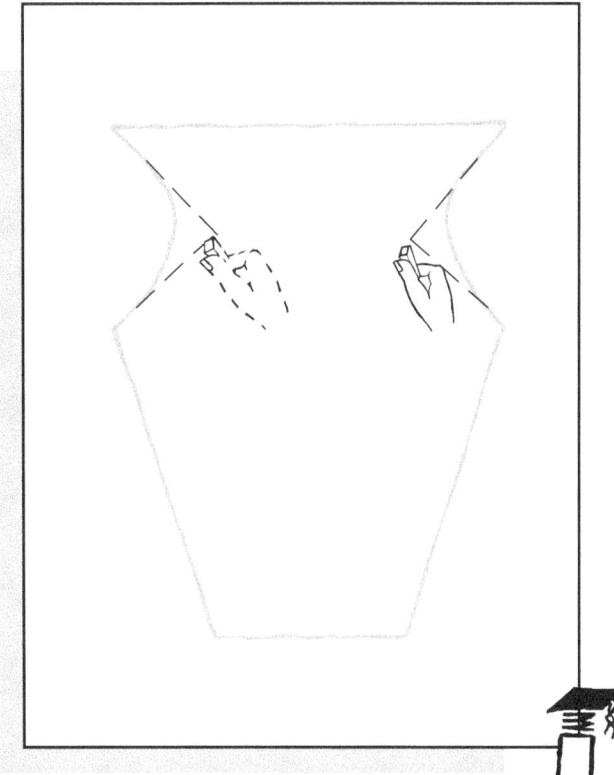

Now, double check your curves. Keeping in mind you're human, find a balance between being too lax or too strict. Should something be obviously amiss, modify but don't over do it. Reworking too much can cause more harm than good. That's why ACCURACY MEANS VISIBLY CLOSE, NOT EXACT.

As you know, it's smart to refer to your model OFTEN. The procedure not only helps prevent your picture from getting out of hand, but also heightens your observational skills, increases your accuracy, and improves your drawing tempo (speed). Let me repeat - this is SO important. **Make it a routine to check your work REGULARLY,** and especially whenever you finish, add, or make changes. At these times, STOP DRAWING and double check your accuracy, *preferably upright at arms length,* with both the model and your work *side-by-side.* When you're busy drawing, your concentration is divided, but during a break, you can evaluate your current situation and spot more because ALL your attention is able to be devoted ENTIRELY TO OBSERVING (back and forth almost simultaneously). Since we're on the subject, please compare the curves on illustration 2-20 to those on drawing 2-21 and 2-22. It's easier to see the differences in the arcs and the impact they have on the shapes with the help of visualized, or actual base lines, isn't it?

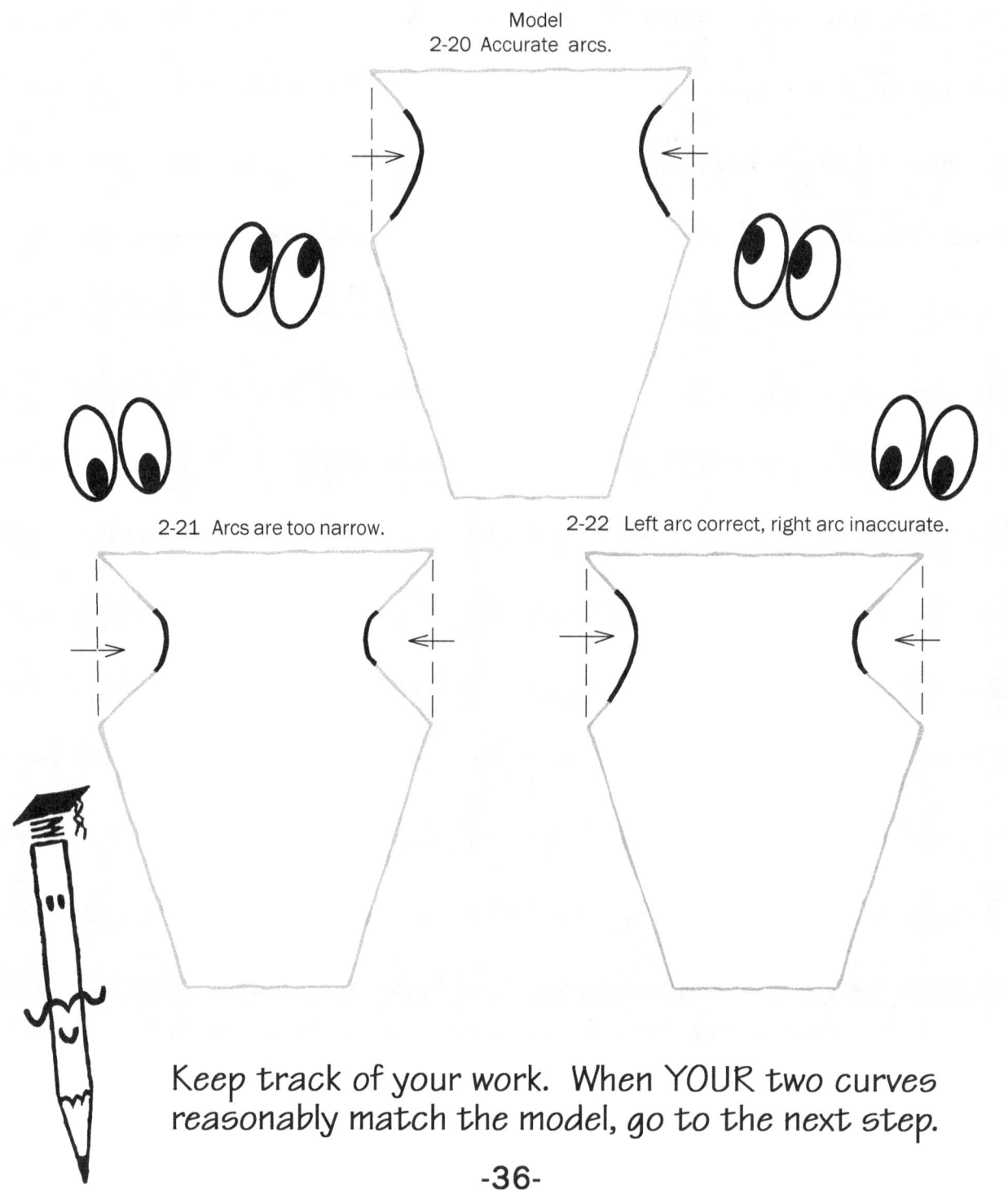

Model
2-20 Accurate arcs.

2-21 Arcs are too narrow.

2-22 Left arc correct, right arc inaccurate.

Keep track of your work. When YOUR two curves
reasonably match the model, go to the next step.

ROUND THE MID-SECTION WITH A PAIR OF CONVEX ARCS

First, please acquaint yourself with the "FLEX" (or bend) of both the lower curves by studying illustration 2-23. Notice how small they are and barely arc. Here too, the corner lines can act as a reference guide. Start by drawing the right or left curve (2-24) but, either way, be sure to keep an eye out for SCALE. That way your arcs will fit YOUR figure. To ensure that the amount of "BOW" (bend) is correct, draw **one arc at a time,** and remember to glance back and forth between the model and your drawing as you direct your pencil. Then CHECK your result by comparing again. Adjust if needed. Once you're sure your 2nd set of curves are fairly accurate, erase the excess lines (2-25).

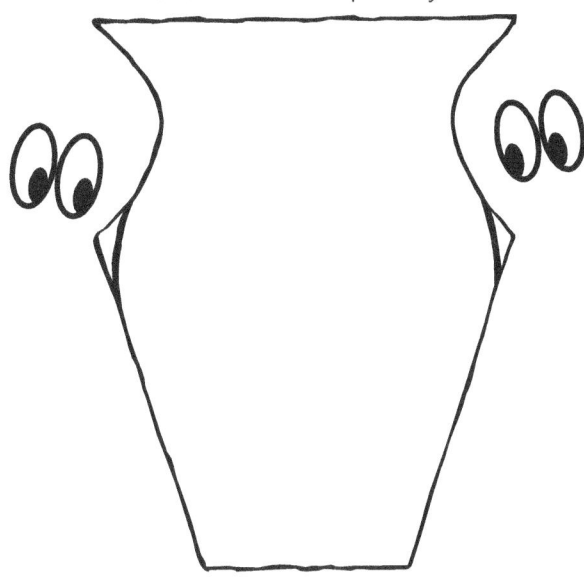

2-23 Study the 2 curves individually, and draw them separately.

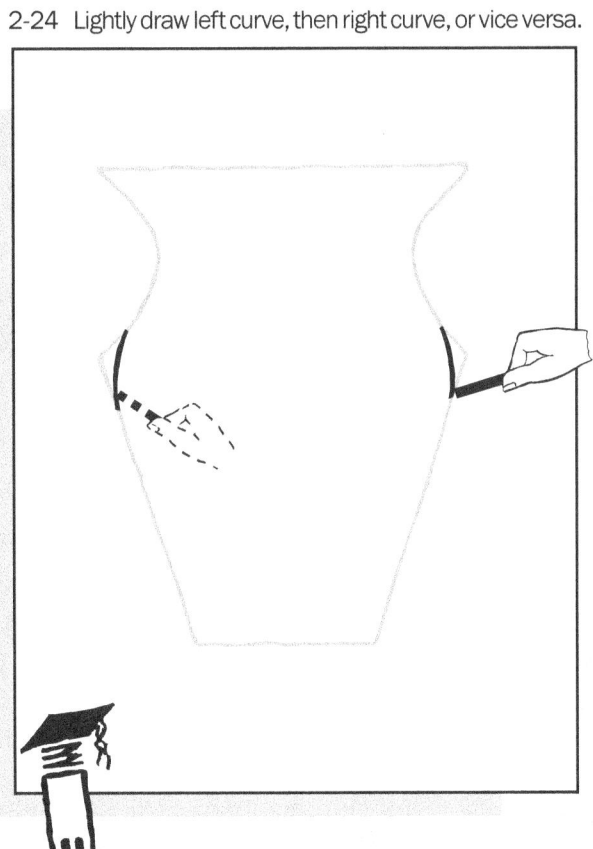

2-24 Lightly draw left curve, then right curve, or vice versa.

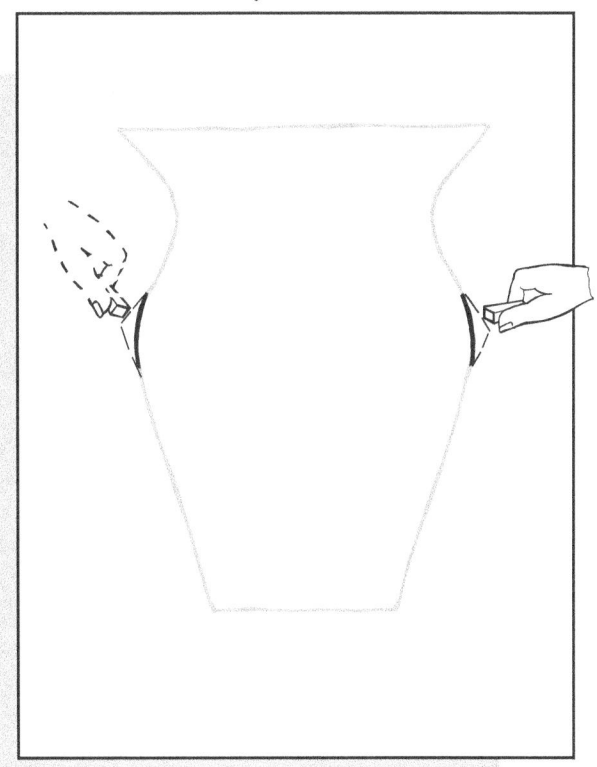

2-25 Erase your excess lines.

Are you thinking about how long the exercise is taking? If so, your thoughts are being distracted. You're not in a race. You and your drawing should both be allowed to take as long as needed.

Compare the two *side curves* on model 2-26 to those on figures 2-27 and 2-28. Notice how they affected the *entire* shape. Then compare YOUR two side curves, and the *overall* result.

Model
2-26 Accurate side curves.

HOT TIP During the many stages your drawing underwent, it may have changed more than you might think. In order to do a thorough once over, compare not only your last two curves, but also the entire figure AS A WHOLE with respect to the model. Be sure to look for the same structural components you applied while drawing. The ones I'm referring to are reference points, alignments, proportions, angles, straight lines, and now, curves. After you've surveyed, and made necessary adjustments, the final transformation from polygon to vase will be complete.

2-28 Side curves bulge.

2-27 Side curves are too small.

P.S. BE SURE TO KEEP YOUR DRAWING. You will need it later, in another chapter. Now take a peek at some student works.

EXERCISE 2
MODEL & SAMPLE DRAWINGS

SUGGESTION: Do not seek to determine whether or not your drawing is the best. The sampling is here for you to learn from, not to compete with.

Model

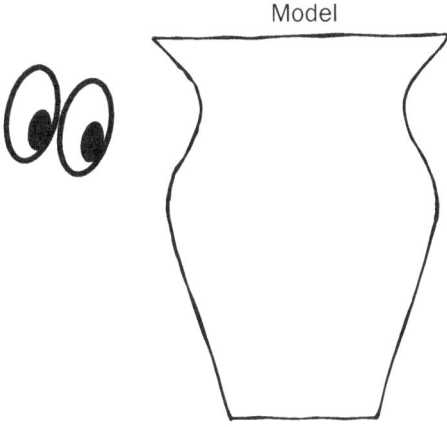

All three of the following student renditions are pretty good. Each is slightly different, of course, and that's to be expected. Compare them to the model to see where they differ the most.

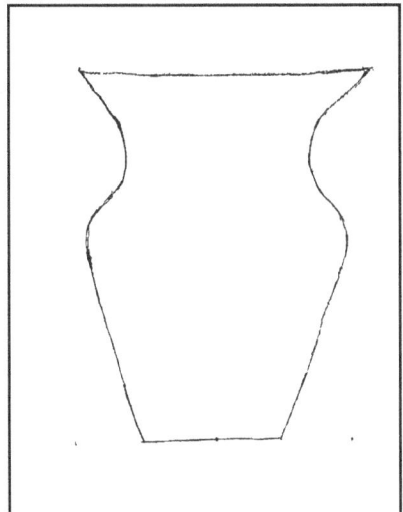
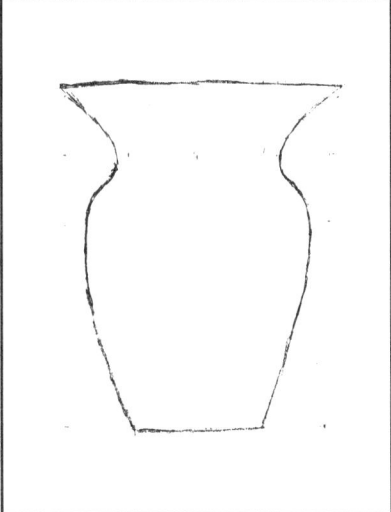
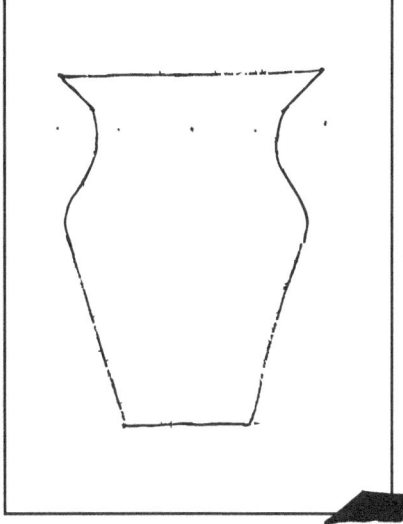

I bet I know what you're thinking. No matter how close your picture resembles the model, because of its perhaps less than striking appearance, you may be feeling as though you didn't really accomplish much. But guess what? You actually did alot! The real achievement is in what you learned. Now it's time to put your knowledge to good use. Curious to find out HOW? Please turn the page.

CHAPTER 2
SUPPLEMENTAL EXERCISE

OBJECTIVE: Replicate Perfume Jar
(in PROPORTION and LARGER than shown)

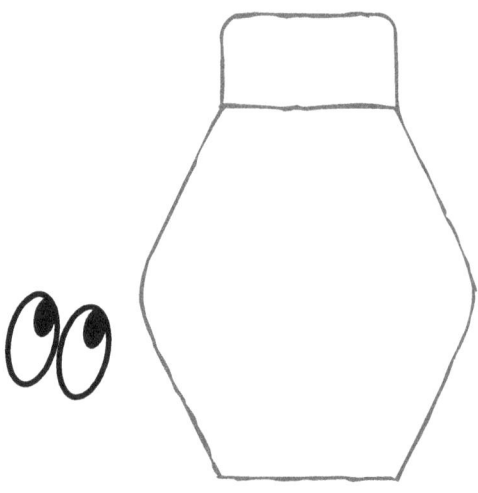

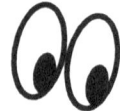

3 STAGES ARE RECOMMENDED

Stage 1	Stage 2	Stage 3
Large Shape	Smaller Shape	Curves

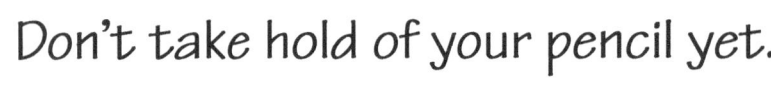

Don't take hold of your pencil yet.

A. Observe that the LARGE portion is composed of 6 sides, but its length and width are the same dimension (2-29). Plus, a smaller section, composed of 3 sides is attached (2-30).

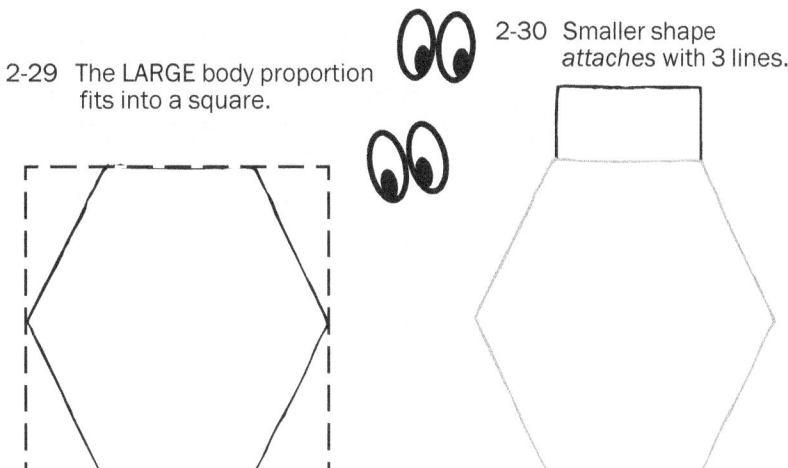

2-29 The LARGE body proportion fits into a square.

2-30 Smaller shape *attaches* with 3 lines.

B. Interestingly, as illustration 2-31 shows, the two sets of SIDES meet at the MIDDLE, but the angle extensions are inset about ONE FOURTH of the way from all four corners. Note, too, that the HEIGHT of the additional piece (or cap) is also ONE FOURTH of the main body. As for the distance across, it's even with the base, and therefore HALF the entire span (2-32). Rounding off the figure are 2 small curves at the corners of the cap. Plus, there are a pair of larger arcs at mid-sides (2-33).

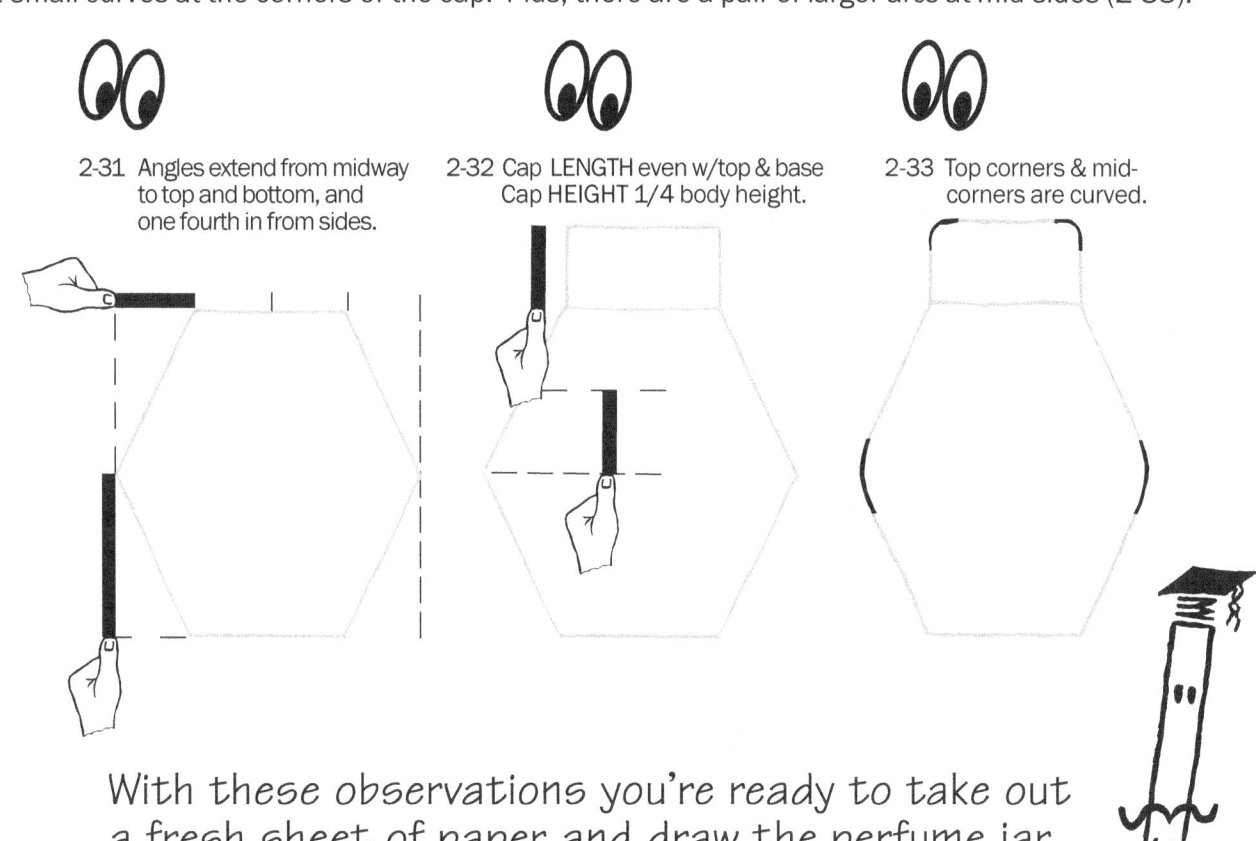

2-31 Angles extend from midway to top and bottom, and one fourth in from sides.

2-32 Cap LENGTH even w/top & base Cap HEIGHT 1/4 body height.

2-33 Top corners & mid-corners are curved.

With these observations you're ready to take out a fresh sheet of paper and draw the perfume jar without further assistance. If you prefer, you may follow along, step by step, on the next two pages.

STAGE 1
THE LARGE SHAPE

STEP 1 ESTABLISH THE FOUNDATION & FORM MAIN SECTION

Since the subject's main body is the same in length as in width, start your drawing by centering a fairly accurate square, about half the short span of your paper (2-34). For reference, flip to Chapter 1, pages 14 and 15. Next, divide all four sides of your square in half with dots (2-35). Then, bisect your HALVES along the top and bottom, again with dots (2-36). After that, erase your top and bottom MIDDLE dots (2-37).

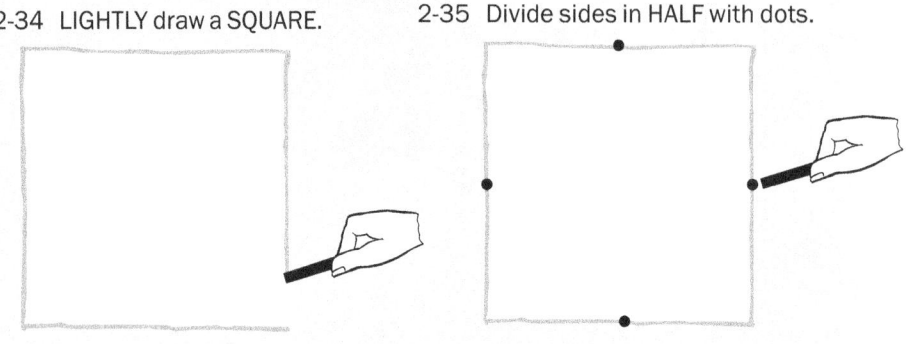

2-34 LIGHTLY draw a SQUARE.

2-35 Divide sides in HALF with dots.

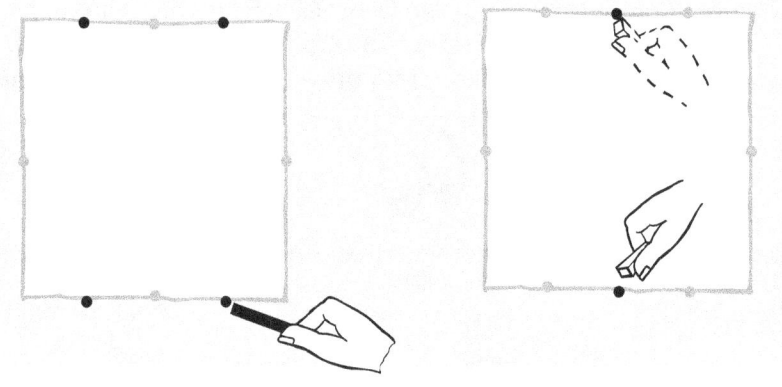

2-36 Divide both halves on TOP & BOTTOM.

2-37 Erase top and bottom MIDDLE dots.

STEP 2 FORM THE 6 SIDES OF THE LARGE PORTION

Lightly connect your dots with continuous or sketch lines (2-38). Then, eliminate the excess (2-39).

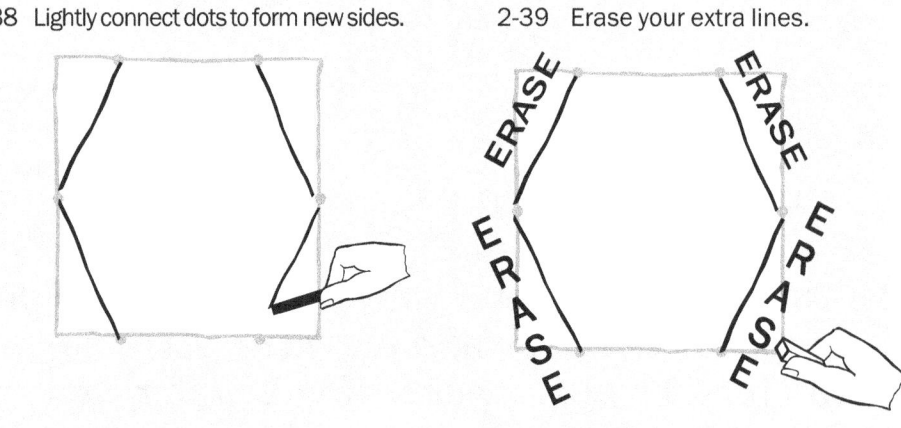

2-38 Lightly connect dots to form new sides.

2-39 Erase your extra lines.

STEP 1 ESTABLISH THE *TOP* OF THE CAP

Locate a span one fourth the height of your figure and mark it with a couple of dots above the left and right corners (2-40).   Lightly connect your two dots with a HORIZONTAL line (2-41).

2-40   Locate 1/4 HEIGHT of your present
figure above top corners with 2 dots.

2-41   LIGHTLY connect dots
with a horizontal line.

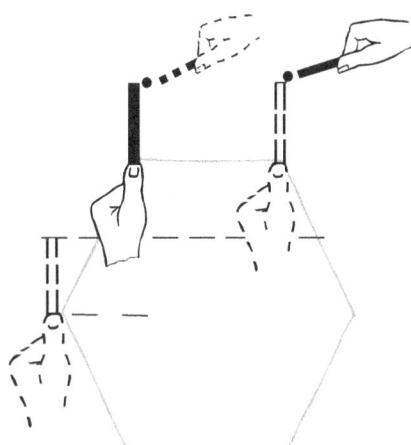

STEP 2 ESTABLISH THE CAP *SIDES*

Lightly draw a **plumb** line from the LEFT end of your **horizontal** line to the **left** corner, below as shown on illustration 2-42. Then repeat by also lightly drawing a plumb line from the RIGHT end of your HORIZONTAL line to the RIGHT corner below (2-43).

2-42   Lightly draw LEFT vertical line.

2-43   Lightly draw RIGHT vertical line.

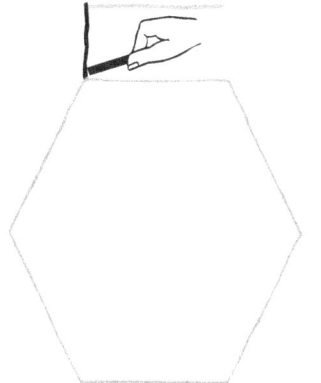
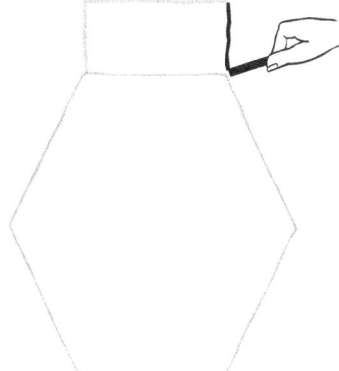

STAGE 3
CURVES

STUDY AND DRAW THE *CAP* CURVES

Observe the amount of bend in the top curves and plan to use your straight lines as guide lines, as shown on (2-44). Begin by LIGHTLY drawing the left corner arc. Make sure it's proportional to the model (2-45). Next, LIGHTLY draw the right corner arc, also in proportion (2-46).

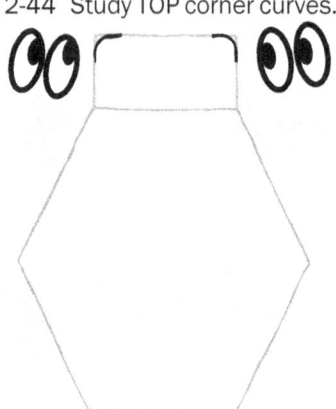

2-44 Study TOP corner curves.

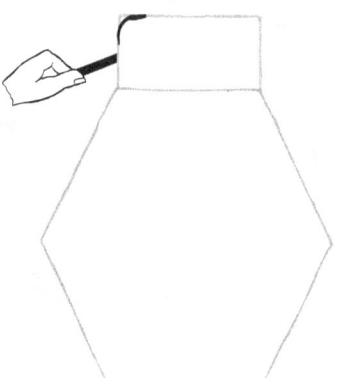

2-45 Draw top LEFT corner curve.

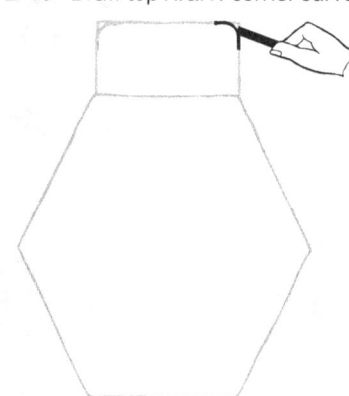

2-46 Draw top RIGHT corner curve.

STEP 2 STUDY, THEN DRAW THE *BODY SIDE* CURVES & CLEAN-UP

Survey the amount of bend (2-47). Next, lightly draw your side arcs, individually and in proportion to the model (2-48). Then, erase extra lines and do some finishing touches, for a result similar to (2-49).

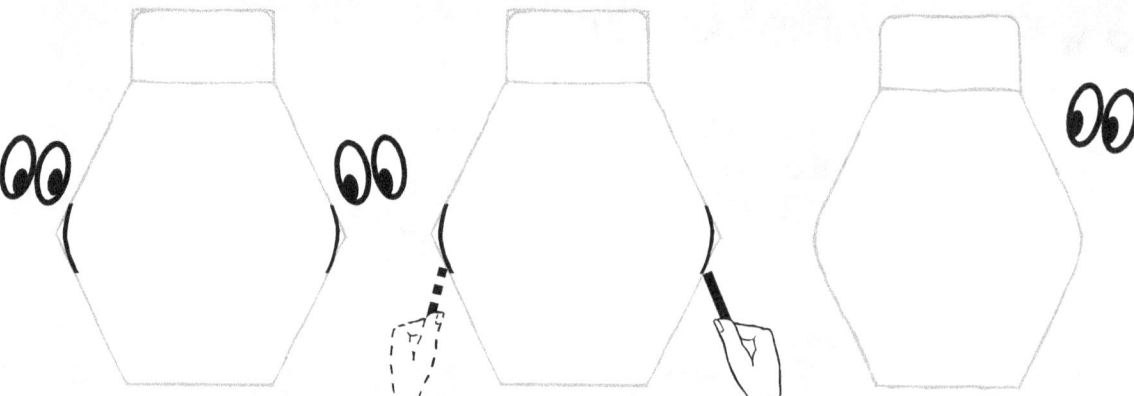

2-47 Study the SIDE curves.   2-48 Draw the SIDE curves.   2-49 Outcome after clean-up.

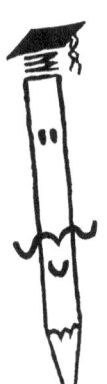

TIP If you erased too much, simply reposition your lines. Make certain that you look at both the model and your drawing during reconstruction. Otherwise, you could go astray. Also, remember to do a final once over, *visually*. Search mainly for things that STAND OUT. Adjust only if absolutely necessary. Don't fuss with minor stuff.

When you're finished with the refinements, you will have completed your supplemental exercise. Next, share the advantage of seeing usual results.

CHAPTER 2
SUPPLEMENTAL EXERCISE
WITH STUDENT EXAMPLES

Model

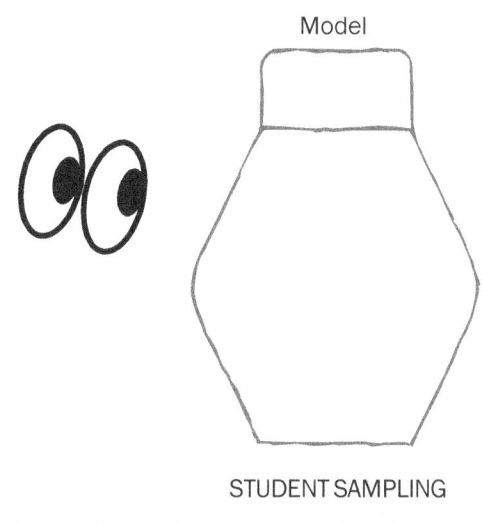

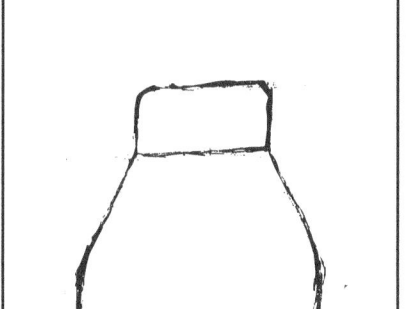

STUDENT SAMPLING

2-50	2-51	2-52

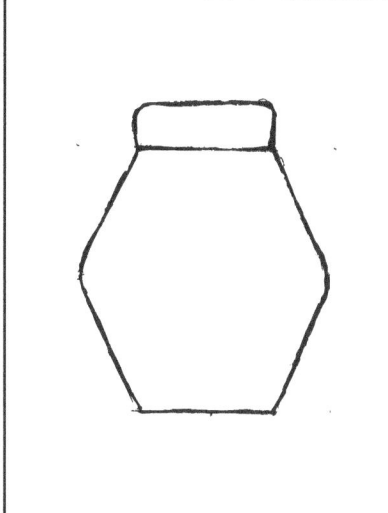
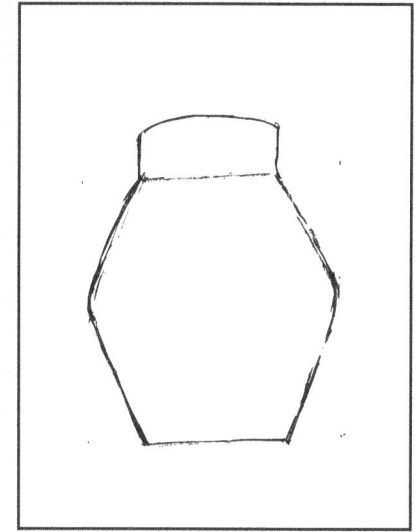

What obvious variations do you detect between the model and the sampling?
See if your findings agree with mine.

Example 2-50 seems to have exaggerated side curves, and the body is slightly lopsided, isn't it?

Example 2-51 has a top that should be a little taller, wouldn't you say?

Example 2-52 has a rounded top instead of being flat in the middle, don't you think?

Having studied the examples, I trust you gained from them. You see, the true measure of your achievement is not how well, or not so well, you think your drawing turned out. It's what you learned that counts. The follow-up explains.

Chapter 2
FOLLOW-UP

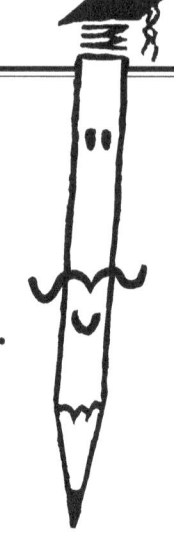

Give yourself a round of applause.
You've earned it!

Aside from performing absolute wizardry, you've discovered more about the benefits of construction lines. Whether visualized, or temporarily drawn, they help establish the foundation and pave the way for additions, including curves, don't they?

Too much or too little, you realized, does greatly alter shape. Because of this, hopefully you also gathered it's wise to start with straight lines, then bring in the arcs. They're certainly easier to handle separately. After all, as you know, drawing is meant to be performed in stages and to undergo changes. You've already seen many of them right before your very eyes. What started with dots became squares, then turned into six-sided polygons. Next, with a simple attachment and a few well positioned arcs, more amazing things happened. One figure emerged to resemble a vase and another, a perfume bottle. If you stop and think about it, that's quite an incredible feat and some hefty magic.

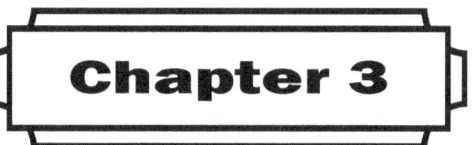
THE SIDEWAYS APPROACH

Parts and pieces, *pieces and parts*.

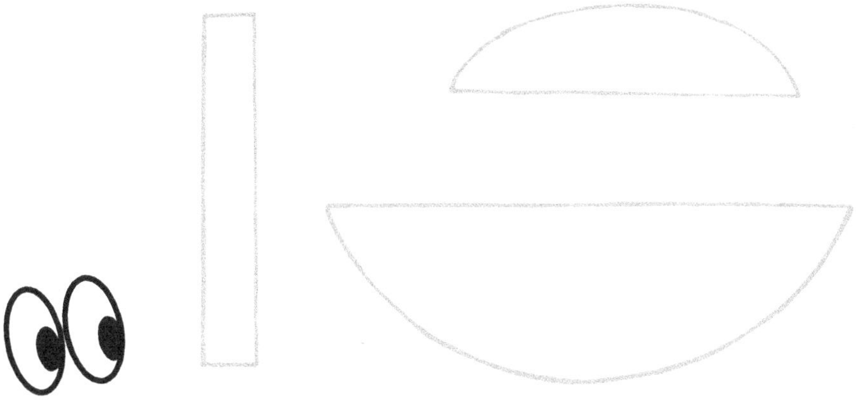

Connect them and they become *THIS*.

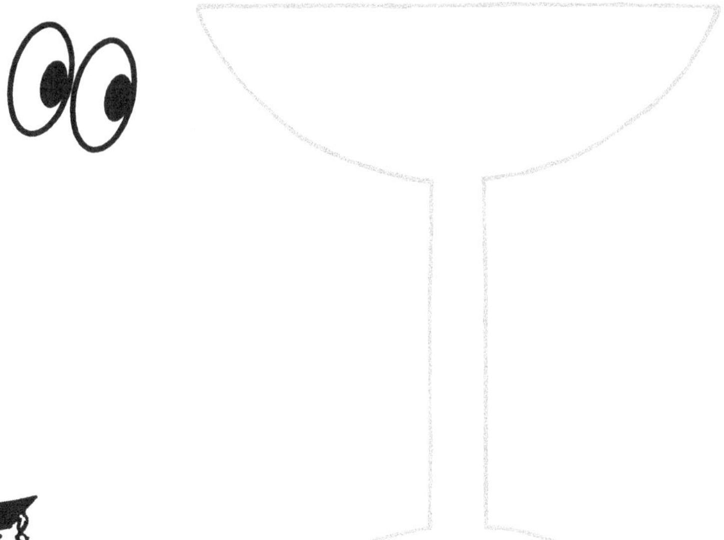

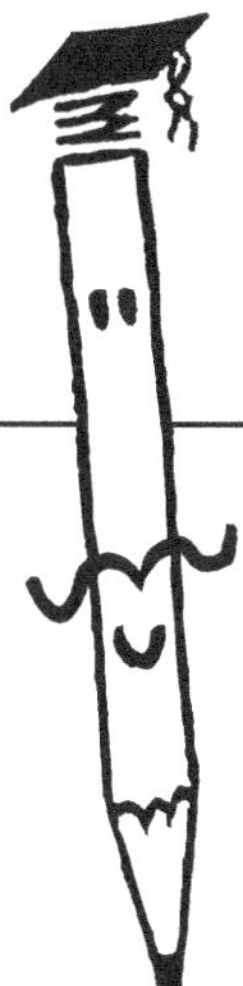

There's just one catch. Intrigued?
Good! Keep going.

We are going to replicate the figure *THIS* way.

...and, not just yet.

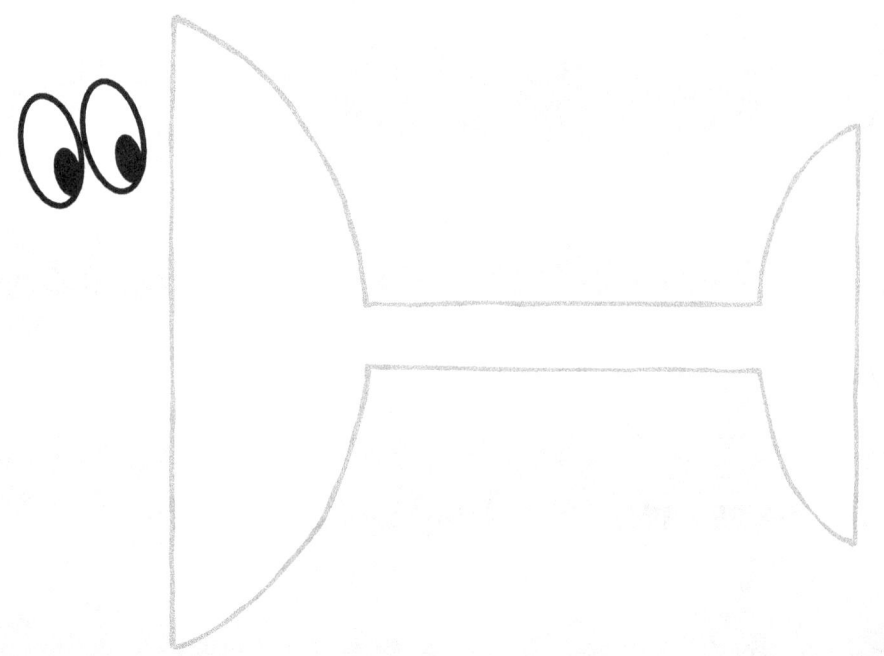

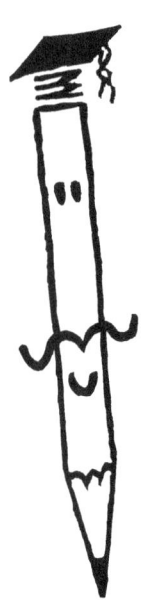

Why draw the subject
on its side, you ask?
Read on to continue
unraveling the mystery.

Look at the next illustration.

What do you see?

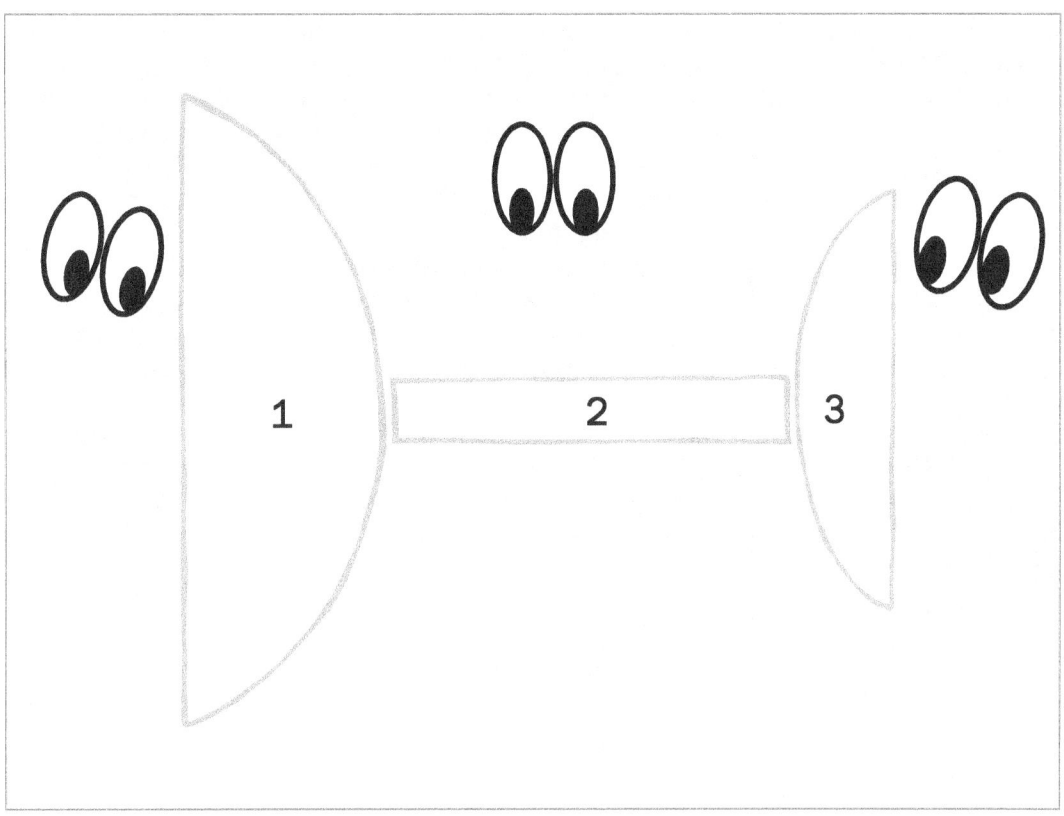

This is basically the same drawing as the one on the previous page, except the shapes are separated and numbered, aren't they? Because of this, perhaps during your second take, you noticed *individual* pieces, instead of one entire object. And, since we usually read left to right, and in sequence, it's likely you first spotted the large convex arc marked "1." Next, I bet your focus switched to the long, middle rectangle designated "2." That is, until, your attention was probably caught by the smaller concave arc, located on the other end, marked "3."

One shape is apparently made of three, wouldn't you agree? And whether you scanned sections as I did, the point is you scanned. Do that whenever you observe.

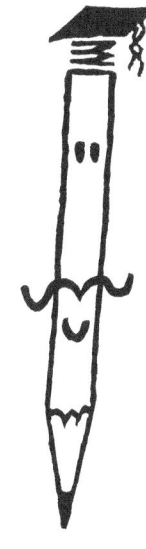

DON'T JUST LOOK FOR THE WH<u>OLE</u>
LOOK FOR THE *PARTS* AND
THEIR *RELATIVE* PROPORTION

In this chapter, there are three sections which make up the figure. In order to draw a fair likeness, we need to determine not only the OVERALL proportion, but also the scale of *individual piece*s as they RELATE *to one another.* That's why I like to call these assessments, *RELATIVE* PROPORTION. For example, as illustration 3-1 shows, a visual and/or pencil reading of the big arc, taken *horizontally* and rotated *vertically,* confirms it fits into the *height* three times. Next, observe what happens when we compare that same reading to the MID-SECTION *length.* Instantly, we learn it fits *twice.* Continuing to move along, we also see that the end piece has a horizontal span equivalent to about *half the width* of the big arc.

Presto! That easily we have determined the *overall scale,* and most of what we need to know about the contributing segments. Surprised how simple that was? You shouldn't be. The process is much like standing with your hands at your side and observing yourself in the mirror. If you see that your hands are about *halfway* to your thighs, you are making a proportional comparison of your arm length in relationship to your body. No matter what size you chose to draw yourself in that position, your hands would always have to reach the middle of your thighs. Actually, you have already applied this principle many times. For instance, in Chapter 1 you sub-divided the six-sided shape to locate its quarter distance sub-proportions. In Chapter 2 you attached a section to the upper part to help form both the vase and the perfume bottle, *proportionally.* And guess what? That rule applies to just about all situations, including our current subject and *its* parts.

3-1 Distance comparisons help determine overall scale and relative proportions.
The BIG arc width is one third the height and fits twice across the mid-section.
The SMALL arc width is half of the big arc width.

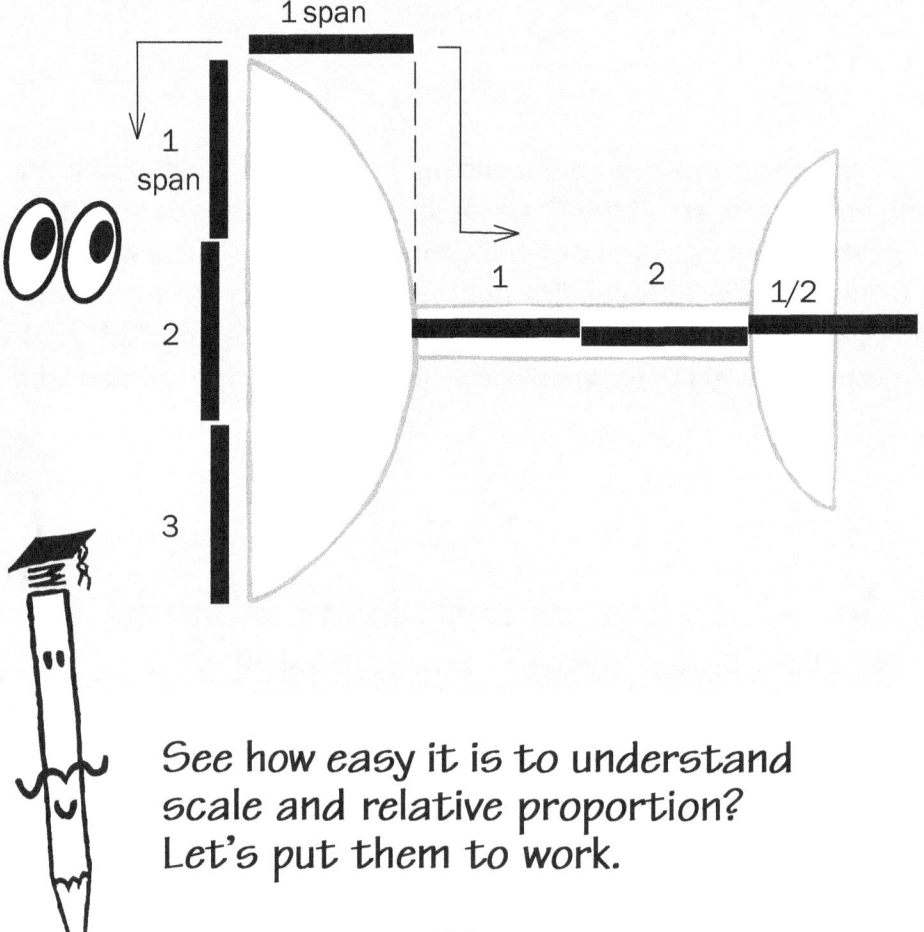

See how easy it is to understand
scale and relative proportion?
Let's put them to work.

EXERCISE 3

OBJECTIVE: Replicate the three piece figure on its side.

STEP 1 TAKE A FRESH SHEET. IT'S TIME TO DRAW

I suggest we begin with the BIG arc. Why? Because it's usually easier to work from large to small. And since our survey revealed that the rest of the figure requires two and a half times the short span of the big arc (toward the right), in this situation it makes sense to begin near the *left* side of your paper. With this in mind, LIGHTLY draw a short, HORIZONTAL line in the upper left quadrant. A span about half the length of your thumb will do nicely to *represent the big arc's WIDTH*. Then, if you *visualize* two and a half times more than that distance across (shown by short vertical lines) you can test how far the other two parts would extend. Such pre-planning can ensure there's room for the coming figure, and its placement (3-2).

3-2 Horizontal line, approximately ½ the length of your thumb, stands
for the *horizontal* span for the LARGE arc. Place it near the top left
left corner of your paper to reserve space for the rest of the parts.

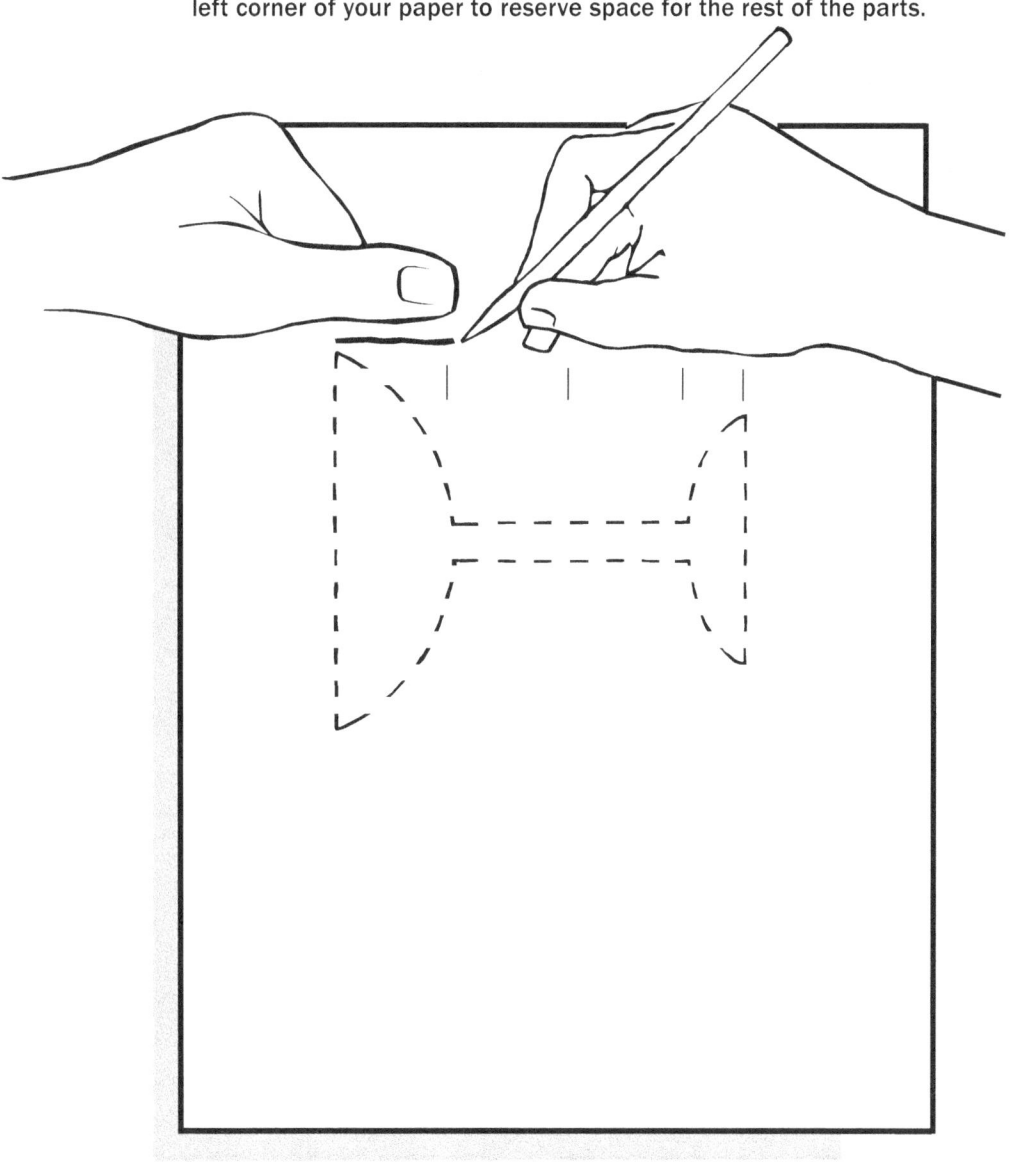

PLOT SCALE FOR YOUR LARGE ARC

On page 50 we observed that the large arc's height is three times its width. Since you already have a width (represented by your horizontal line), all you have to do is stack that span *three times vertically* to get the right proportional height for *your* figure. Start by taking a pencil reading of your horizontal line. Then, align the eraser tip plumb with the LEFT end of your horizontal line and mark a dot by your thumbnail (3-3). Repeat the procedure two more intervals down, one at a time (3-4, 3-5).

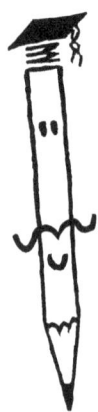

Don't be spooked by seemingly technical stuff. We're simply reproducing the ONE span width to THREE span height with the help of pencil readings.

3-3 Take a pencil reading of YOUR line, turn the span vertically, and mark the distance.

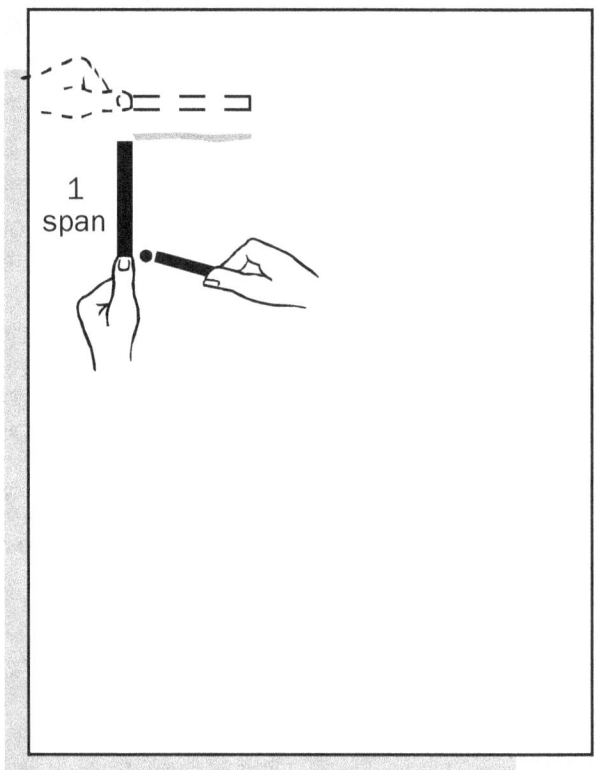

1 span

3-4 Move your span one interval down and mark it with another dot by your thumb.

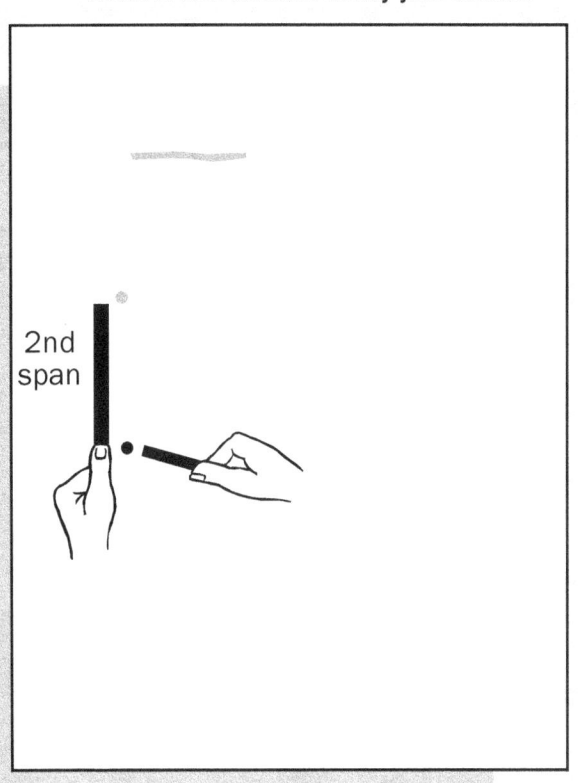

2nd span

3-5 Move your pencil reading one more span down. Mark it with a dot. This gives the 3 to 1 scale.

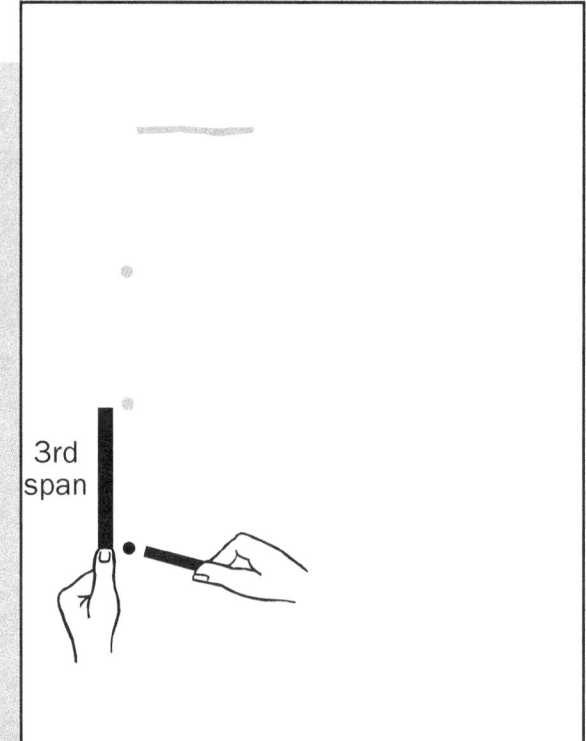

3rd span

You now should have 3 spans down and one span sideways. This is the *correct proportion* needed for the large arc (as shown by the broken lines in illustration 3-6). Those of you who started with a smaller horizontal line will end up with a smaller arc. Those who started with a longer line will have a larger arc. Either way is fine, providing YOUR scale is in correct proportion.

3-6   At this stage the large arc is ready to be formed
within the 1 to 3 three span proportion.

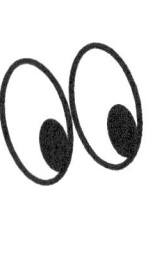

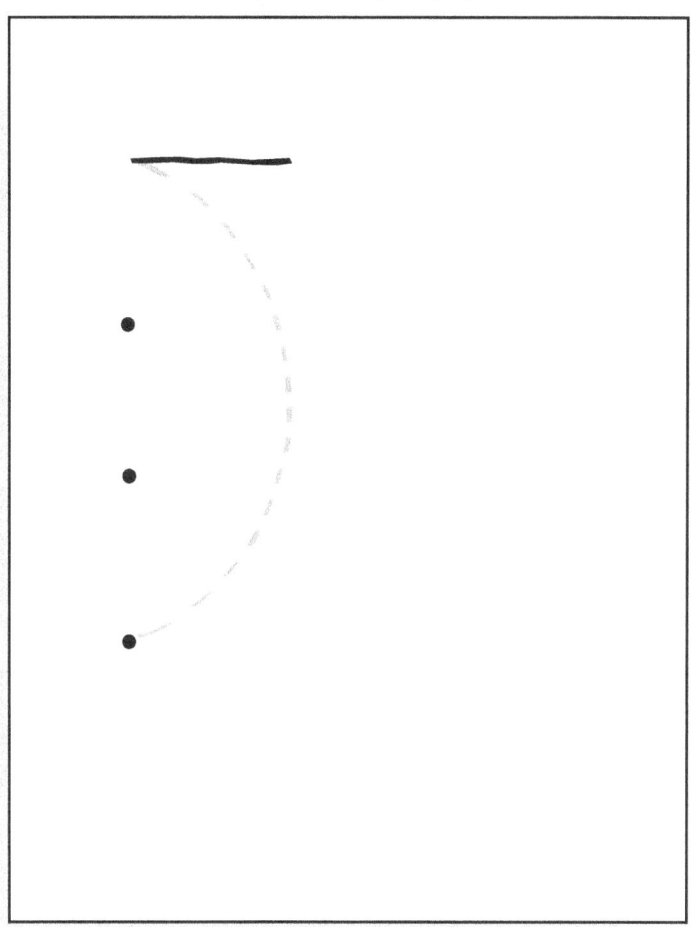

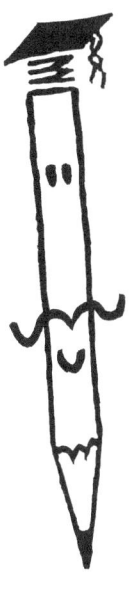

Double check your sizes VISUALLY. After all, even though pencil readings are useful, they are not foolproof. If you've created a HEIGHT that doesn't appear to be about three of your horizontal lines placed vertically, please make the adjustment now, prior to moving on.

If you will recall, in Chapter 2 you learned it helps to form curves with guide lines. Illustration 3-7 shows how to put this knowledge to use here. Start "boxing-in" your large arc by *LIGHTLY* linking a plumb line through YOUR dots (3-8). Also draw an even, parallel line, starting from the *RIGHT end of your TOP line* (3-9). To finish your rectangle, connect the bottom with a horizontal line (3-10).

3-7 Visualize your intended curve "boxed-in.

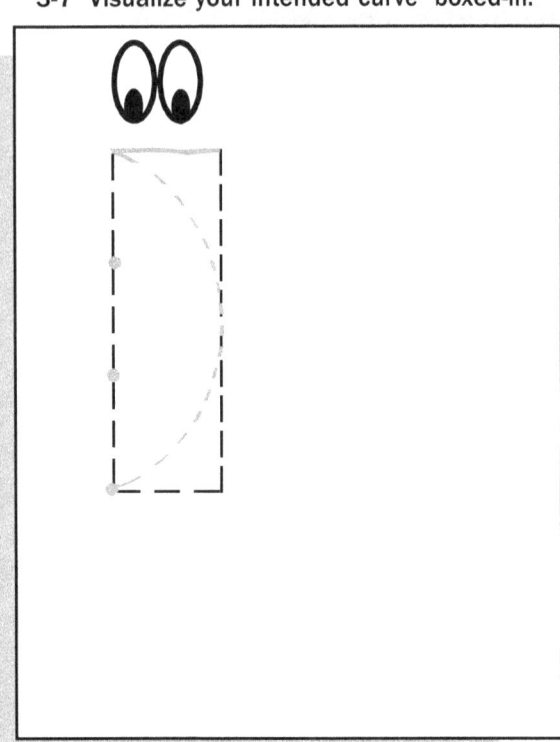

3-8 LIGHTLY draw a vertical line through your dots.

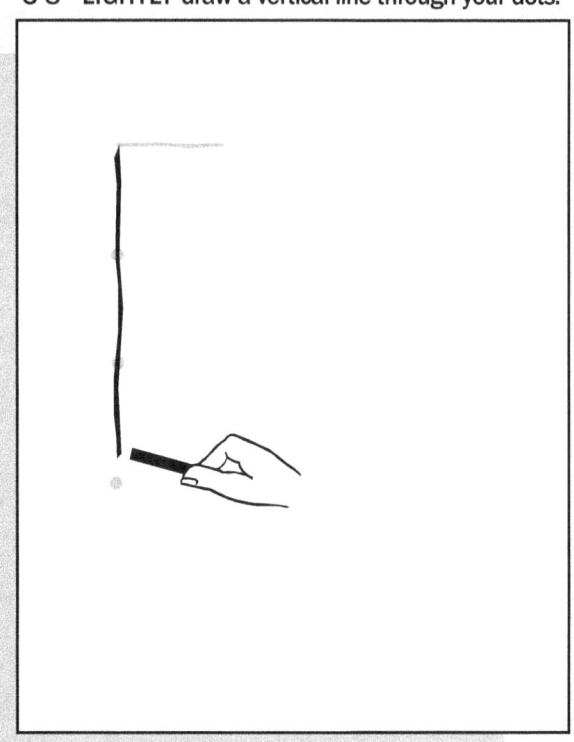

3-9 LIGHTLY draw another vertical line parallel and even with your previous line.

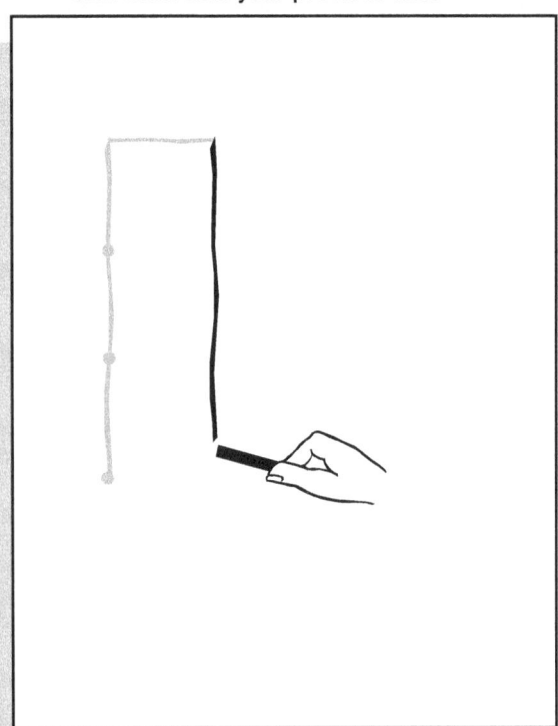

3-10 Finish "boxing-in" your rectangle. The lines will serve as guide lines for your curve.

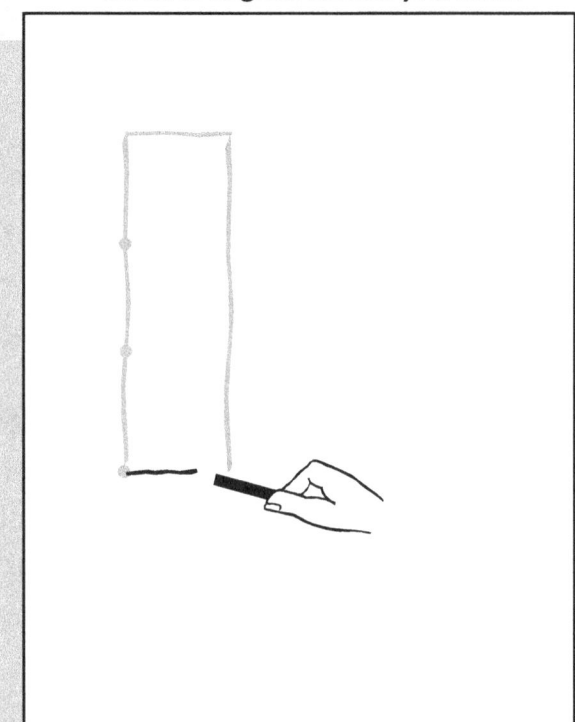

STEP 5 FASHION YOUR LARGE ARC

Now, I call your attention to illustration 3-11 below. Notice the rate of bend on the BIG arc. Next, as you glance back and forth between your drawing and the illustration, proceed to replicate the curve inside YOUR rectangle (3-12). *Remember to watch for the SHAPES that are being created between your arc and the guide lines. By comparing your version to the model, it's easier to form the right amount of curvature.* Afterward, you may erase the excess lines (3-13).

3-11   Notice both the curve and the
       SHAPES created within the box.

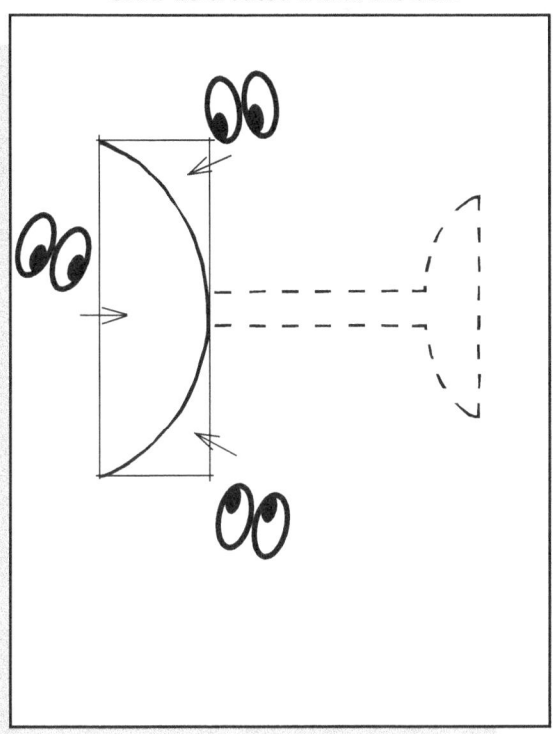

3-12   You can form your large curve
       with two smaller curves.

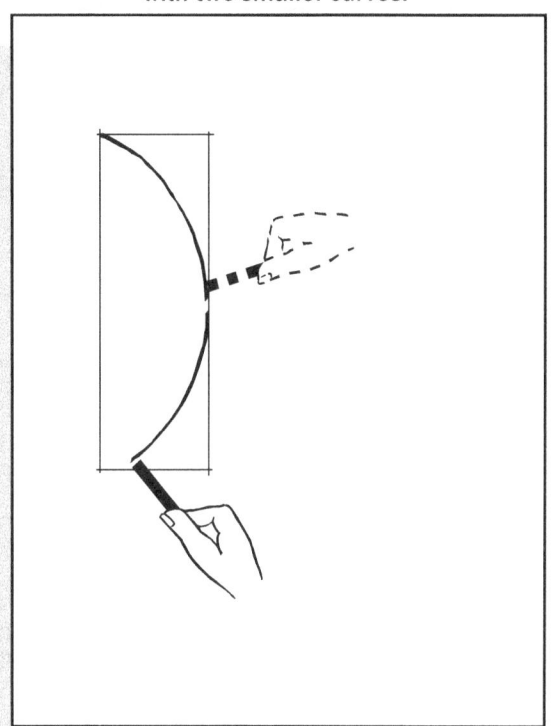

3-13   Eliminate your excess lines.

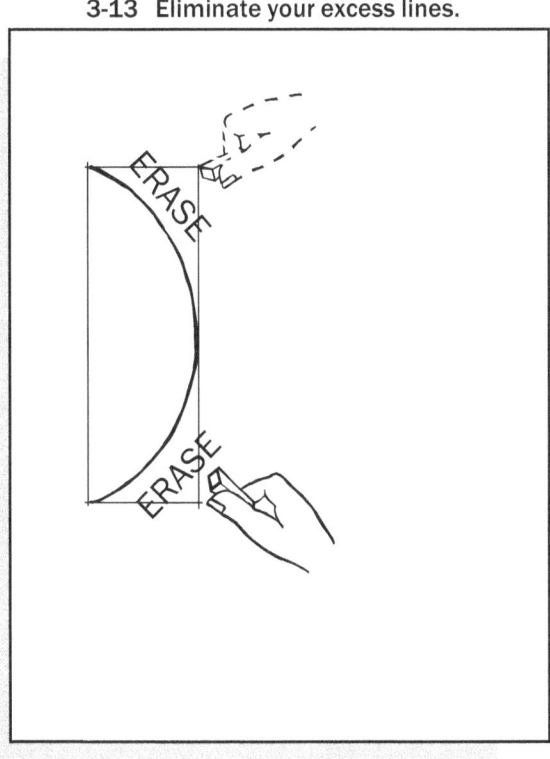

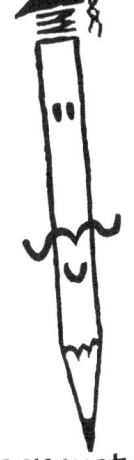

Have you been watching the flex of your arcs, as well as the shapes they make beside them? EXCELLENT! The first piece of your figure is done. Simple, wasn't it? By all means, keep going.

Observe that the *"thickness"* of the middle piece is equal to **one third** of the LARGE CURVE'S *horizontal* span (3-14). To find that scale to fit YOUR drawing, take a pencil check, one third across **YOUR** arc. Next, CENTER that distance **vertically** and mark it with a couple of reference points. One dot should be by your thumb and the other by your pencil top (3-15).

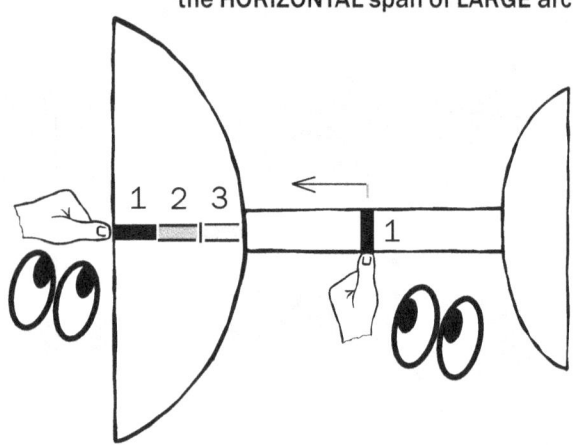

3-14 MID-SECTION *HEIGHT* is ONE *third*
the HORIZONTAL span of LARGE arc

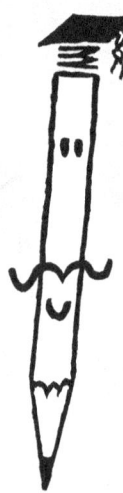

The more you observe
your subject...
the easier it is
to draw.

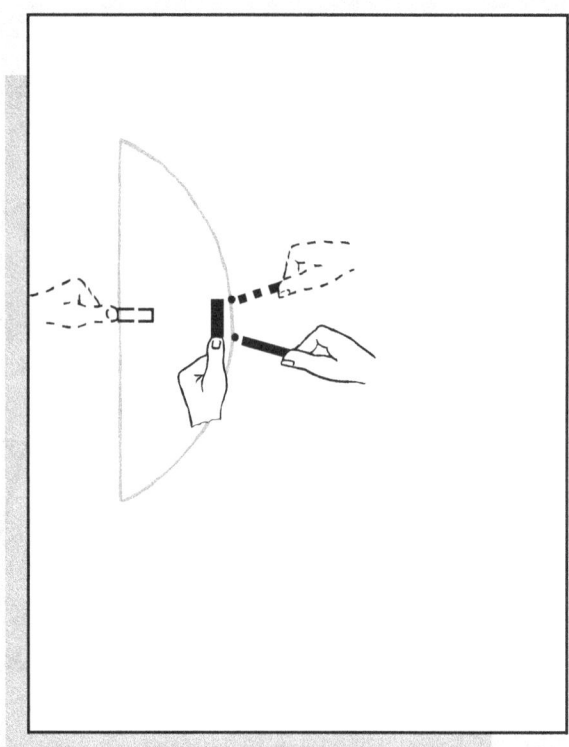

3-15 ONE *third* span across YOUR arc
centered **Vertically,** *MARKS* the mid-
section HEIGHT, PROPORTIONALLY.

LOCATE THE *LENGTH* OF THE MID-SECTION FOR YOUR DRAWING WITH REFERENCE POINTS & ESTABLISH THE SEGMENT WITH LINES

Notice that the HORIZONTAL distance of the *center* piece is TWICE the short span of the large curve (3-16). To locate that in scale, take a HORIZONTAL reading of YOUR large arc at its widest expanse. Shift the measure over, so your thumb is even with the mid-section's **LOWER** dot. Mark a reference point by your eraser tip (3-17). Next, move over one equivalent interval and place another dot (3-18). Link your **LOWER** dots with a line. Then draw a horizontal *parallel* line, starting from your **UPPER** dot (3-19).

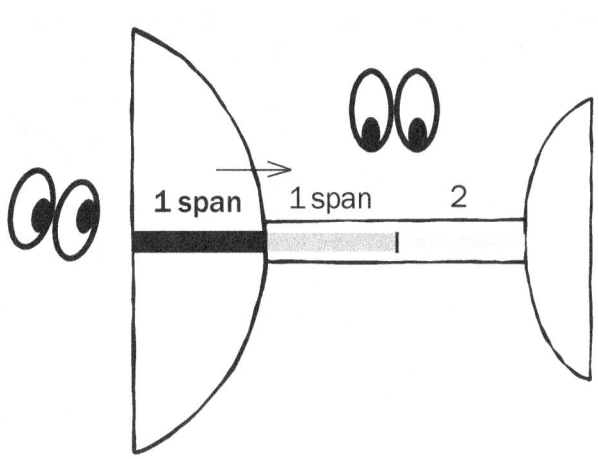

3-16 MIDDLE SECTION is about TWICE the large arc span, checked HORIZONTALLY.

1 span 1 span 2

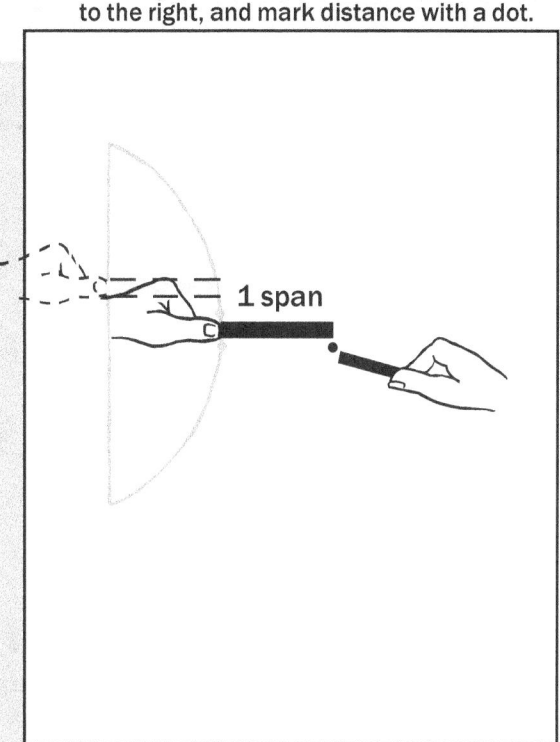

3-17 Take a pencil reading of your large arc sideways, shift the span OVER one interval to the right, and mark distance with a dot.

1 span

3-18 Shift one more span over and mark it with a dot.

2nd span

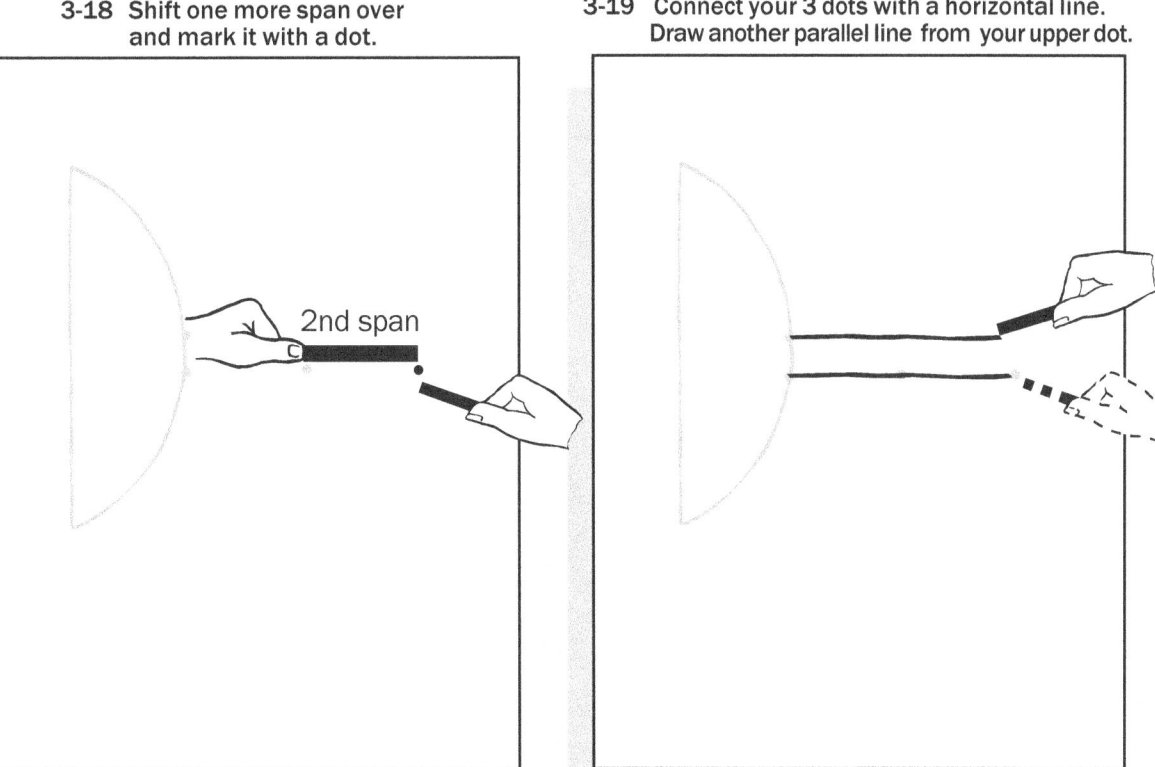

3-19 Connect your 3 dots with a horizontal line. Draw another parallel line from your upper dot.

STEP 8   FIND THE PROPORTIONAL *HEIGHT* FOR YOUR SMALL ARC

Take a look at illustration 3-20. It reveals that the **small** arc is about **one third SHORTER** than the large one. To locate that proportion on your drawing, take a pencil check **TWO thirds** the **vertical** distance of YOUR big arc. Then, center the span to the right of the mid-section and mark 2 dots-one by your eraser tip, the other by your thumb (3-21).

HOT TIP   Remember to rely mainly on your eyes. After all, your assessments and pencil readings are ESTIMATES, not EXACTS. If something doesn't appear right on your drawing, chances are, it isn't. Your job is to find the area that doesn't seem to fit well. To do that, compare your present status with the model. If you discover that you must alter a segment, don't fret. It doesn't mean you made a mistake. It's a sign your observational skills are expanding. And when you make an adjustment, don't expect to position your new lines accurately on the first try. Your hands also need training. That's why you should continue to proceed lightly. *Drawing is meant to be a changeable* process.

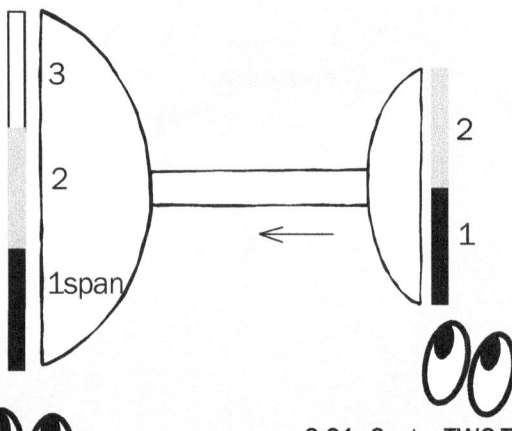

3-20   Small arc height appears to be TWO THIRDS of large arc HEIGHT.

All this proportional mumbo-jumbo may seem like a chore now, but after awhile you will see that the wealth of knowledge it provides will not only improve your accuracy but also boost your confidence.

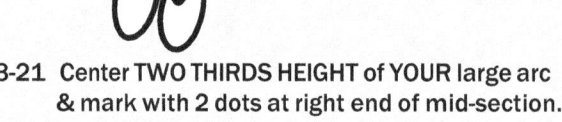

3-21   Center TWO THIRDS HEIGHT of YOUR large arc & mark with 2 dots at right end of mid-section.

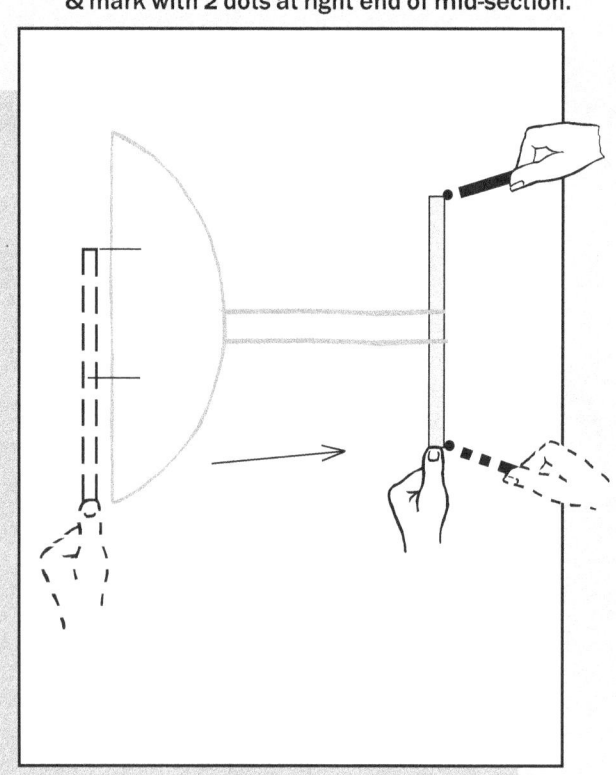

STEP 9 — DETERMINE THE *WIDTH* FOR YOUR SMALL ARC, TO SCALE

Illustration 3-22 reconfrims that the SMALL arc is equal to HALF the **HORIZONTAL** span of the LARGE one. In order to locate that size in scale, take a sideways pencil reading across YOUR big arc, to *midway*. Next, move that unit to the right side of your figure and place your thumb even with your upper dot. Mark one reference point by your eraser tip (3-23). Then repeat the procedure at the *LOWER* dot (3-24).

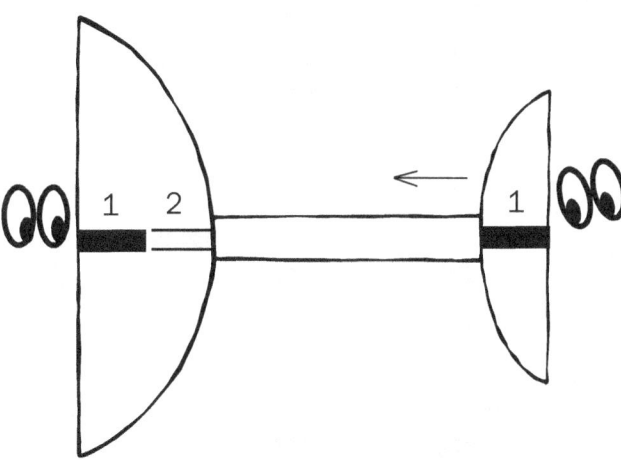

3-22 Horizontal span of small arc is half the large arc.

3-23 Transfer half horiz. distance of YOUR large arc to upper dot and mark with another dot.

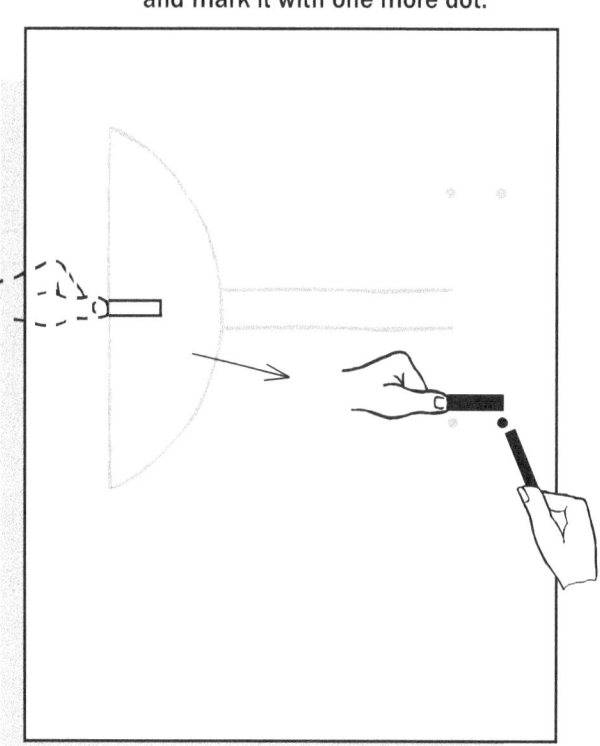

3-24 Transfer span to your LOWER dot and mark it with one more dot.

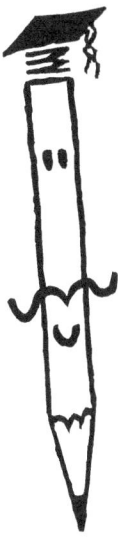

From time to time, you're stopping to make sure your figure is in proportion and isn't tilting, aren't you? And you're not thinking about how long the process is taking, or eager to finish, so you can see the end result, right? Each step performed well is bound to yield a more desired outcome.

LOCATE GUIDE LINES FOR SMALL ARC, THEN DRAW IT

3-25 Visualize your intended curve with guide lines.

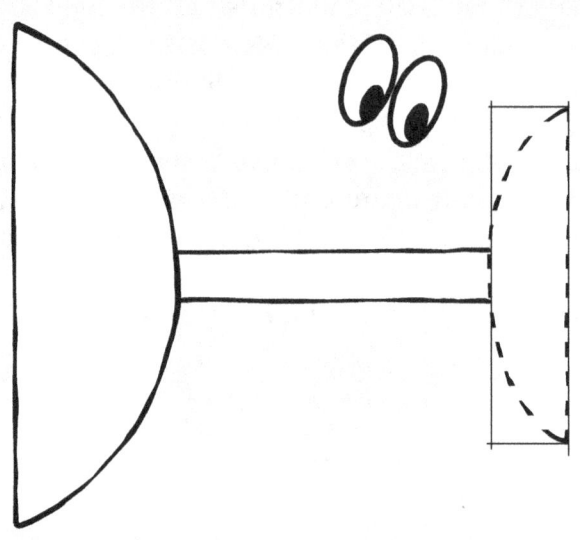

Notice that in illustration 3-25, the SMALL arc is boxed-in. With such guide lines, the "bow" can be drawn more easily, right? For this reason it may be wise to close up the reference points on YOUR drawing (3-26). Then fashion your small arc the way you did the large one (3-27).

HOT TIP Look at the illustration here on the right. It's a useful reference to help you fashion your arc more accurately. Try not to go overboard, though. By attempting to be too precise, you may accidentally change the appearance and possibly the size of your arc to the extent it no longer resembles the model. For example, your version may end up bowing too much or too little. The obvious sign that you are overworking is that you look more at your drawing and hardly (or not at all) at your model, *after* your basic shape is formed. You also do a lot of erasing and redrawing.

3-26 LIGHTLY connect your 4 dots to help BOX-IN your small arc.

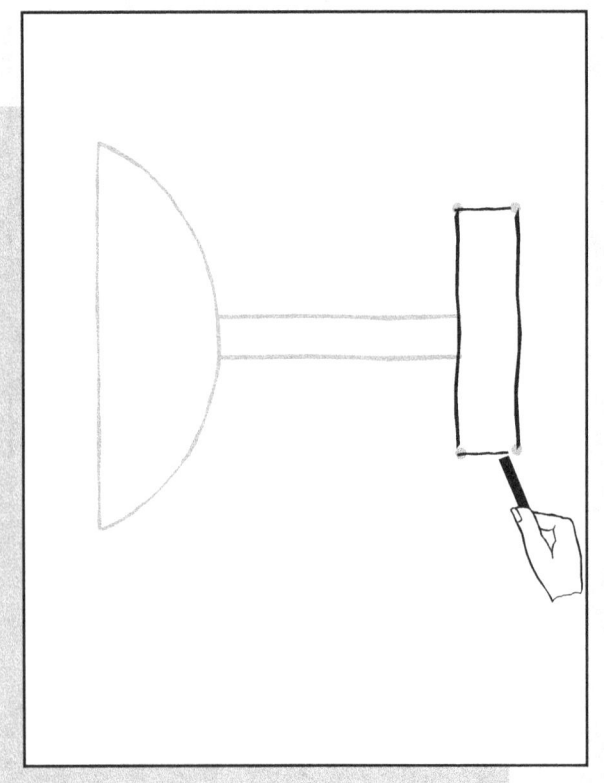

3-27 LIGHTLY form your small arc at roughly the same PROPORTION & BOW as the MODEL.

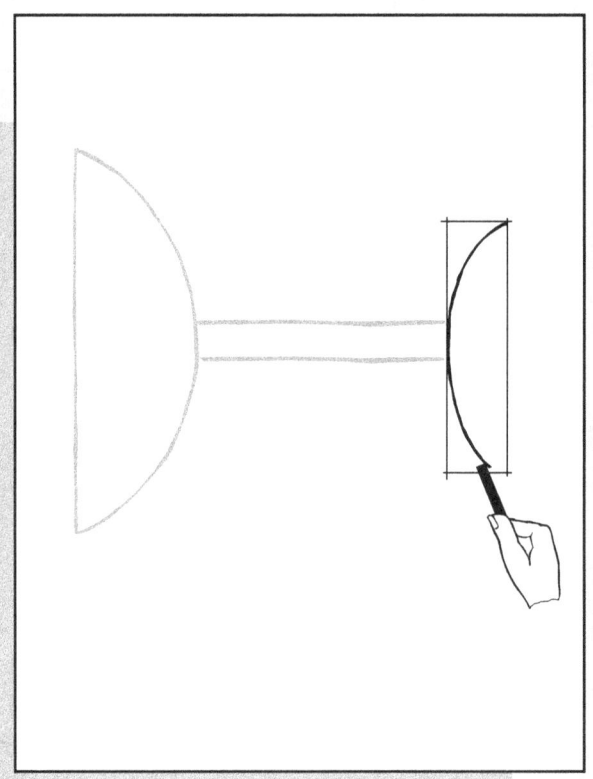

Eliminate the unwanted guide lines and connections (3-28). Next, compare your drawing to the book version. Be sure to double check whether your individual parts more or less match proportionally. Also verify that your curves bend similarly to the model. Look for the OBVIOUS first. For instance, take a look at example (3-29). The figure was originally correct but during the cleanup stage, overworking caused the small arc to shrink below the desired height and the large arc to become too narrow. The broken lines show where the curves should be.

TIP Do a "DOUBLE CHECK" the way you learned in Chapter 2, page 36. If you find something needs adjusting, it doesn't mean you goofed. You're merely taking advantage of the opportunity to improve on what you've already done. As you modify, however, don't lose sight of the model and don't get carried away. Overworking usually causes more harm than good.

3-28 Erase your connecting lines and guide lines, then refine as needed.

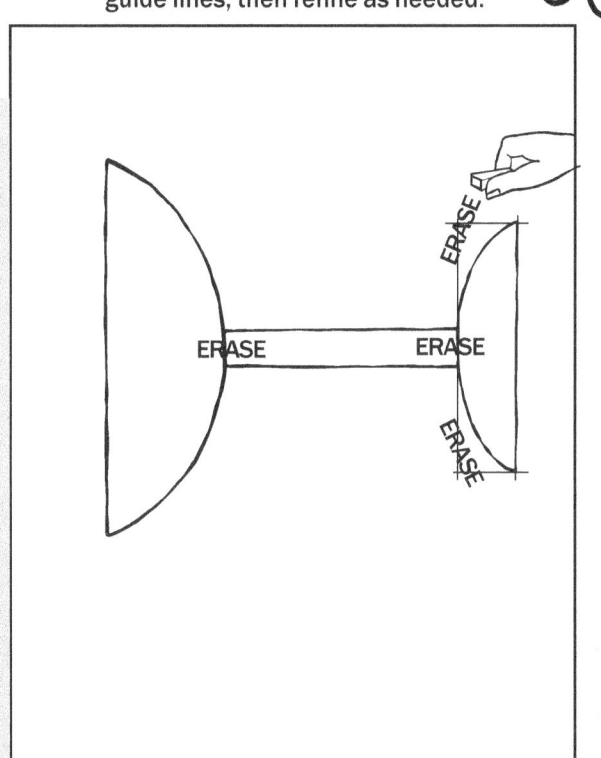

3-29 In this example, excessive correction caused the large curve to become too narrow and the small curve to shrink in height.

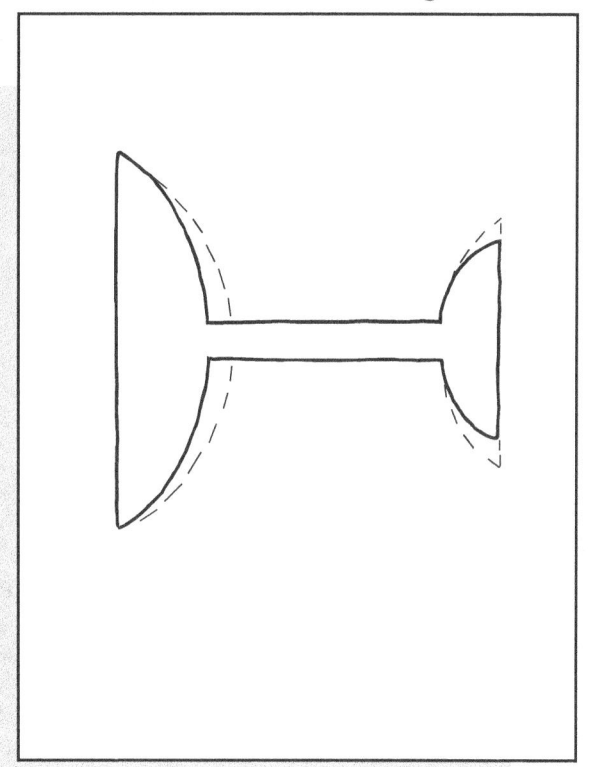

After you've completed your refinements, feel free to rotate your paper and view your drawing upright. As you do, please keep in mind, it's what you experienced by having completed the assignment that matters, not whether your finished piece is ready for framing. Remember, you're learning, so study your work and the student examples displayed on the next page, mainly to help advance your skills.

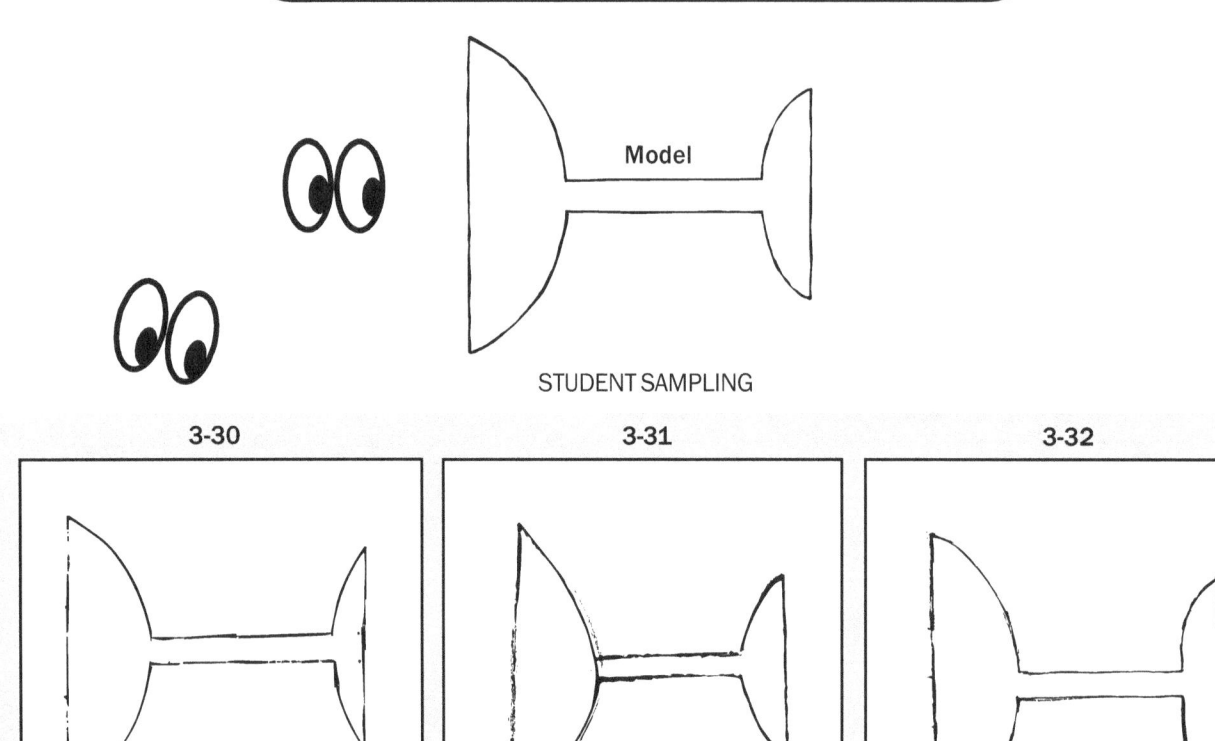

Model

STUDENT SAMPLING

| 3-30 | 3-31 | 3-32 |

These student drawings look terrific, wouldn't you agree? They definitely resemble the model, but figure 3-30 would be better if the *small* arc was wider. Next, let's look at figure 3-31. In my opinion, both of its arcs could use a bit more *gradual* rounding. As for figure 3-32, the *small* arc appears slightly flat at the crest. Isn't it interesting that *little* arcs generally seem to require more adjustment than the large ones? Are you wondering why? My guess is that by the time students get to the small arc, they are in a hurry to finish so they can see the end result. Or maybe they think the big arc is more important, hence they tend to pay less attention to the little arc. Get the message? ***All parts deserve equal care.*** And now that you realize this, you should check YOUR figure for one more follow through. You don't have to do any further changes. Just make a mental note of what you learned from your observations.

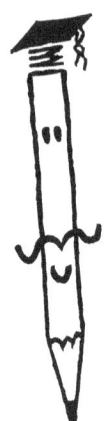

The supplemental exercise awaits.
Take a break, then go for it.

CHAPTER 3
SUPPLEMENTAL EXERCISE

OBJECTIVE: Replicate the following figure
(in PROPORTION and LARGER than shown)

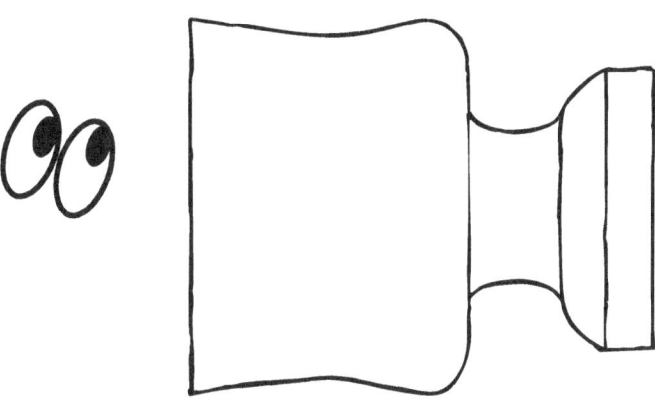
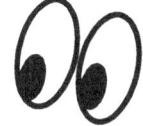

TWO STAGES ARE RECOMMENDED

Stage 1 - STRAIGHT LINES

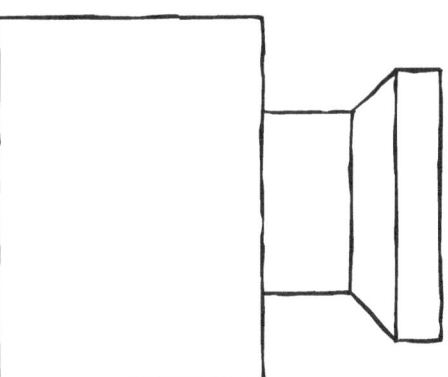

Stage 2 - CURVES

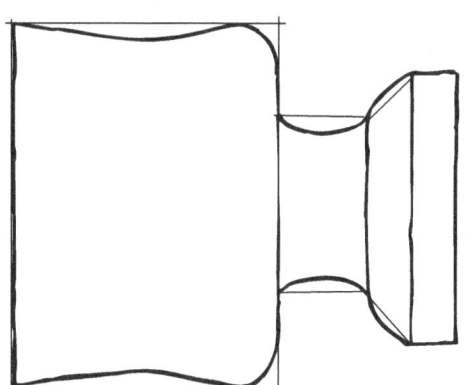

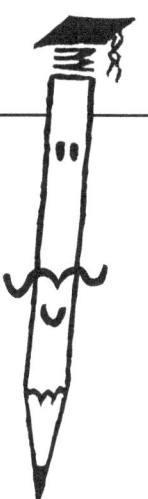

Nope. It's not time to reach for your pencil yet. Please turn the page and study the subject in detail.

3-33

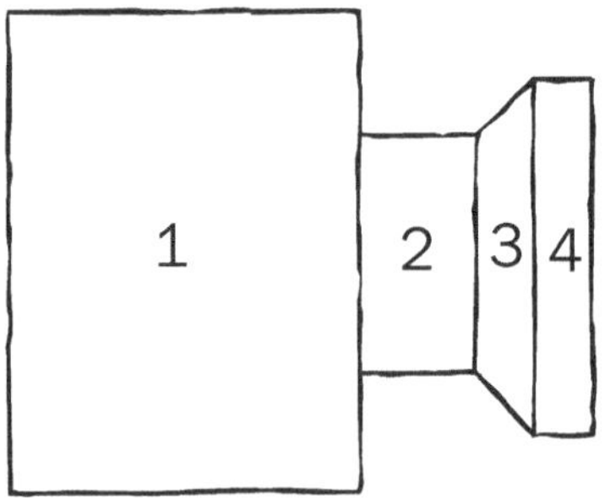

1 | 2 | 3 | 4

3-34

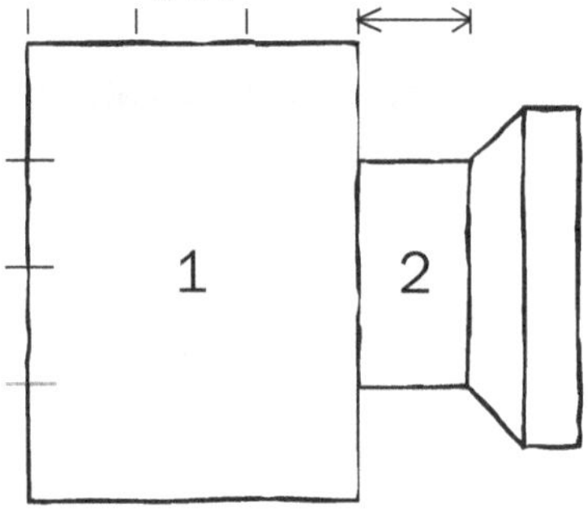

1 | 2

3-35

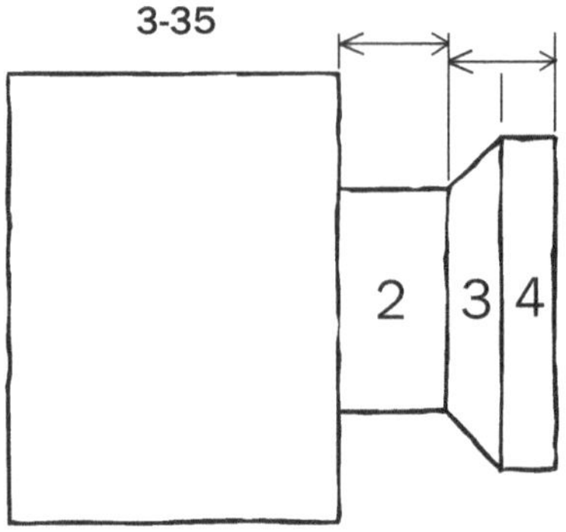

2 | 3 | 4

3-36

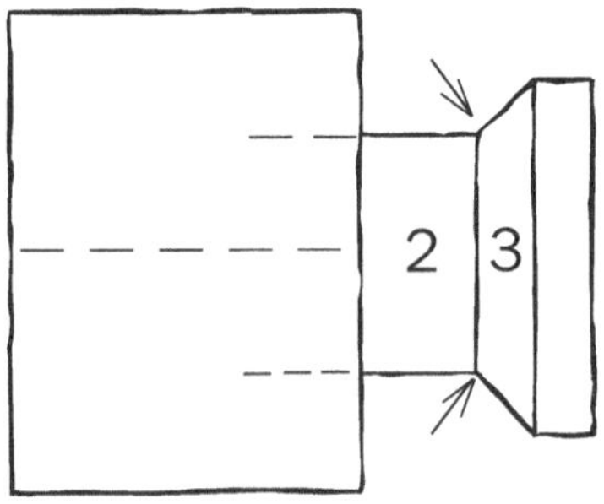

2 | 3

3-37

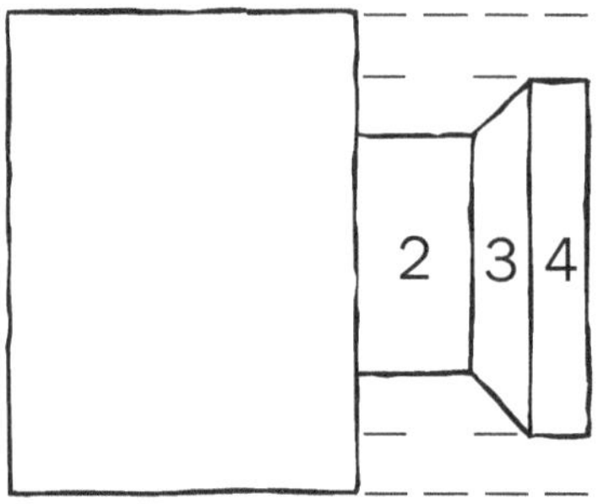

2 | 3 | 4

3-38

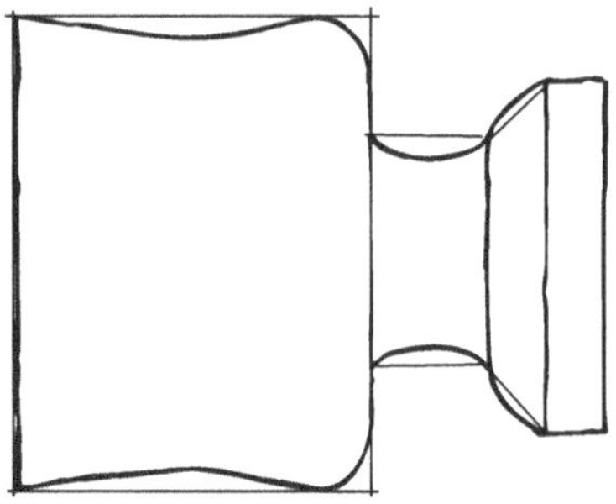

- Illustration 3-33 shows us that the figure consists of FOUR (numbered) sections.

- Illustration 3-34 demonstrates that the COMBINED horizontal spans of parts #1 & #2 are the same as the height of the figure, and form a square. The width of section #2 is one fourth of that square.

- Illustration 3-35 indicates sections #3 and #4 are equidistant across, and TOGETHER they are the same width as section #2.

- Illustration 3-36 reveals that the *HEIGHT* of section #2 is HALF the figure's *overall* height and is centered between the top and bottom. Also, notice that section #3 is linked to section #2 at the right corners by a pair of diagonal lines.

- Illustration 3-37 shows that section #4 is *centered* half way between section #2 and the top as well as bottom of the figure.

- Last, but not least, illustration 3-38 depicts the curves. Study their various amounts of bend.

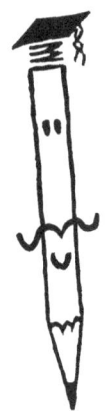

With these important sightings, we're ready to draw. The steps begin on the next page.

STEP 1 On a new sheet, LIGHTLY draw a square (3-39). Center it roughly between the top and bottom of your paper but *closer* to the LEFT side. This will leave room for the additions.

3-39

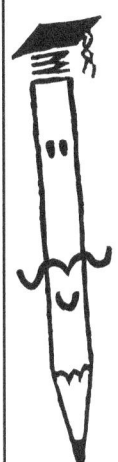

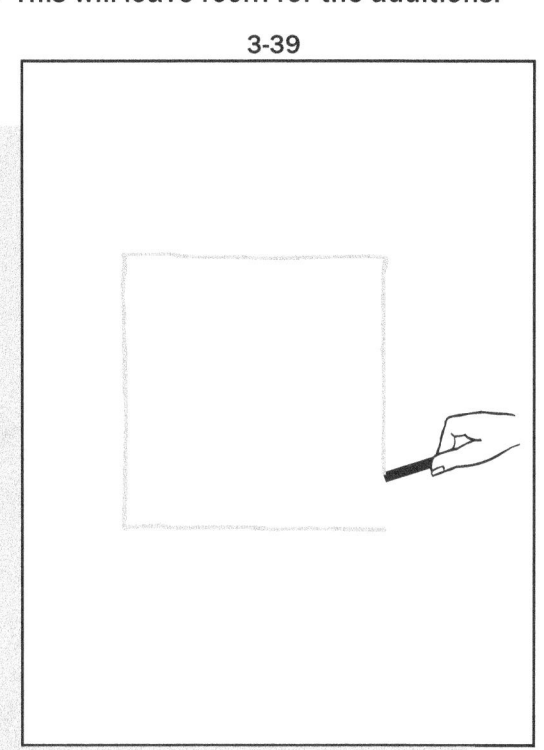

Remember to choose a size and position for your square that will work. That means, it should be big enough so you don't feel cramped, but small enough so there will be space to add the rest of the sections to the right.

STEP 2 Divide the TOP and BOTTOM of your square in HALF with dots (3-40). After that, bisect (or sub-divide) ***ONLY the RIGHT upper and lower HALVES with two more dots.*** Then, LIGHTLY connect the 2nd set of upper and lower dots (between middle and right side) with a vertical line (3-41).

3-40

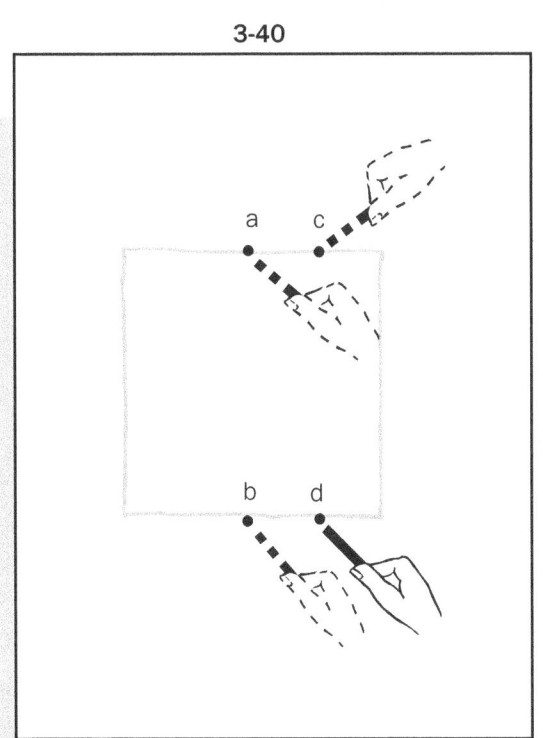

3-41

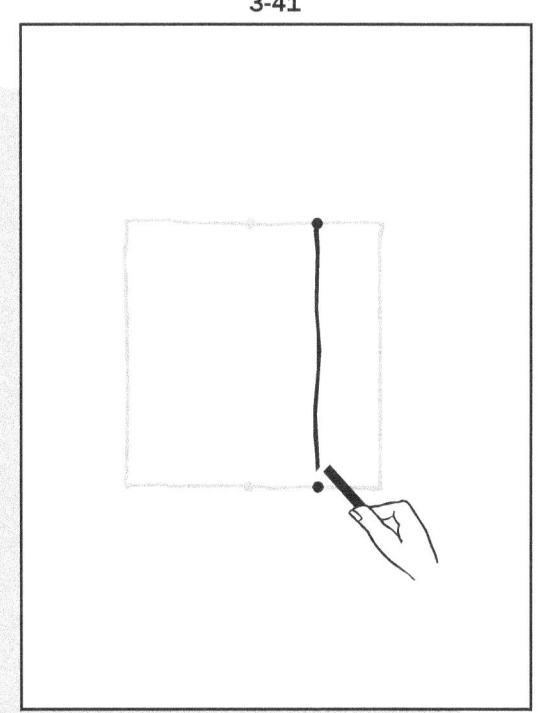

STEP 3 Attach a section *equal* to your *narrow*, previous piece (3-42). Then, divide that segment in half VERTICALLY with a line to form a shape that's even more narrow (3-43).

3-42   3-43

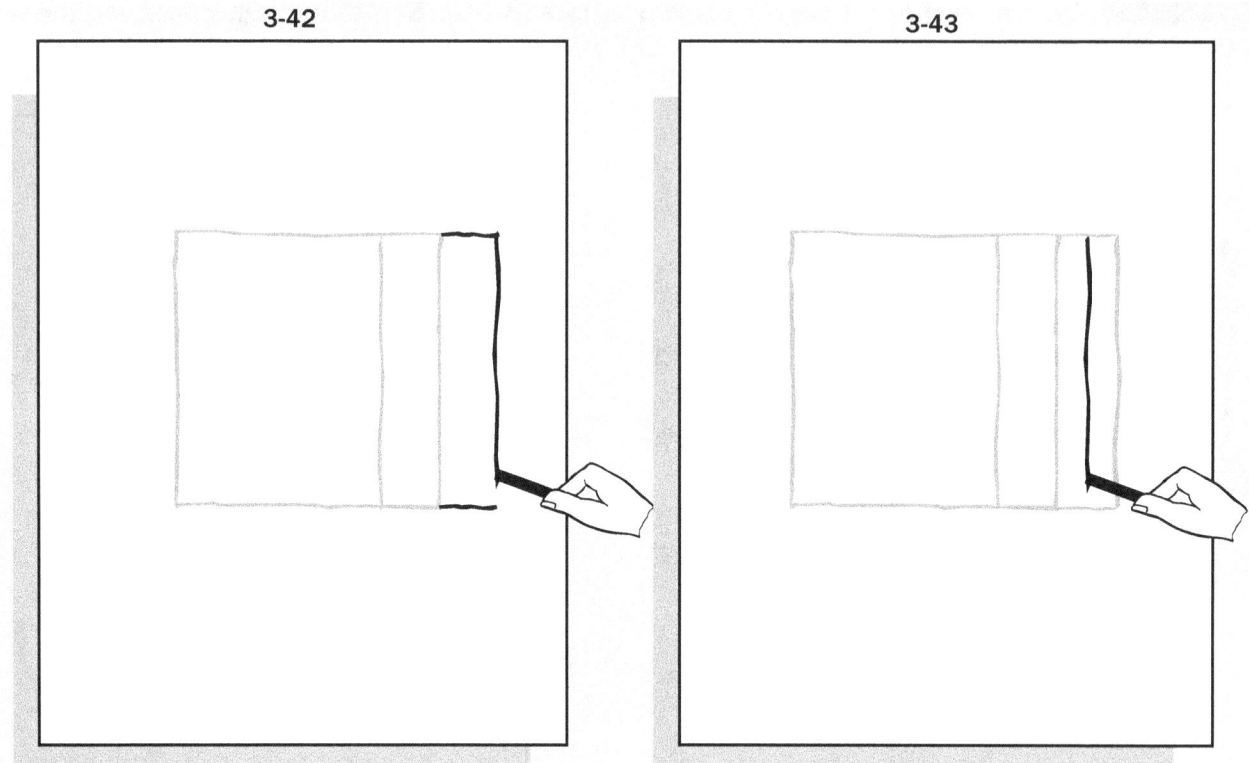

STEP 4 Divide your *2nd VERTICAL line from the LEFT* into FOUR equal parts with 3 dots by estimating the center visually and by subdividing the halves (3-44). Then, lightly draw a couple of *horizontal* lines from your upper and lower dots until they reach the *next* vertical line to the right (3-45).

3-44   3-45

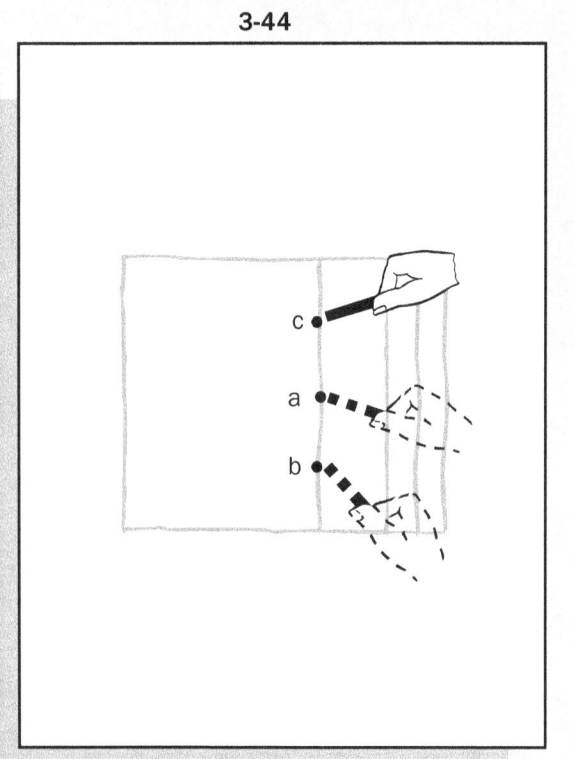 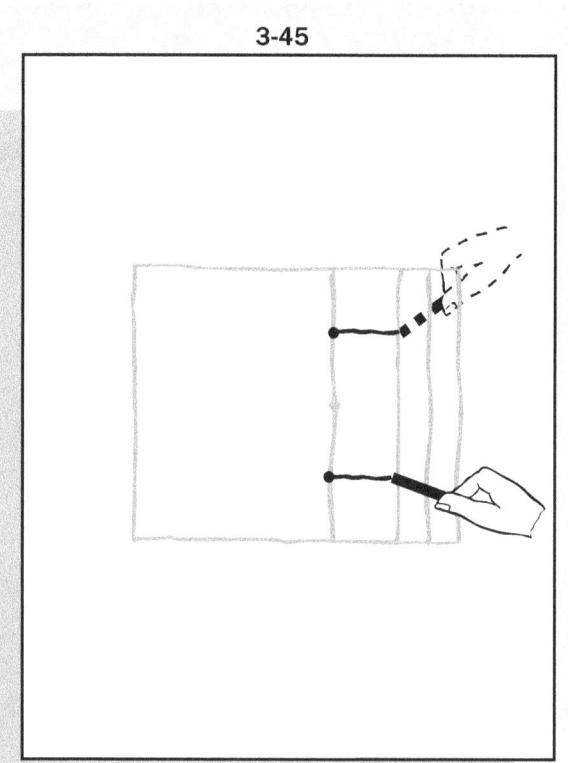

STEP 5   On the *next* to the last line, place a dot MIDWAY between your UPPER *HORIZONTAL* line and the TOP. Then repeat with a dot midway between your LOWER HORIZONTAL line & the BOTTOM (3-46). Next, lightly draw HORIZONTAL lines, one at a time, from each of your two dots to your *last* vertical line (3-47).

3-46

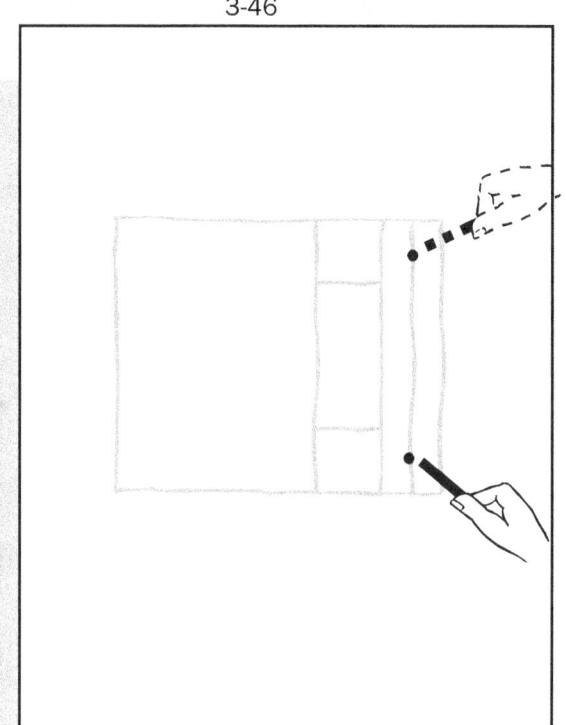

3-47

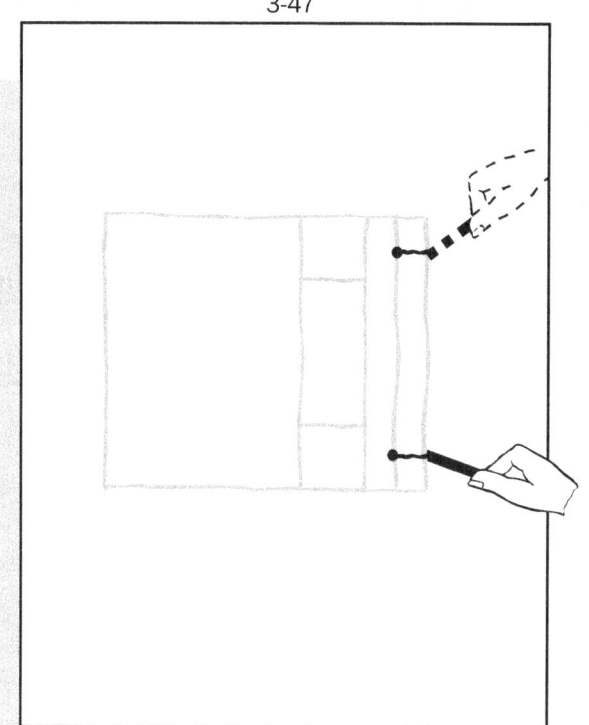

STEP 6   Lightly draw a couple of diagonal lines, as shown in illustration 3-48.

3-48

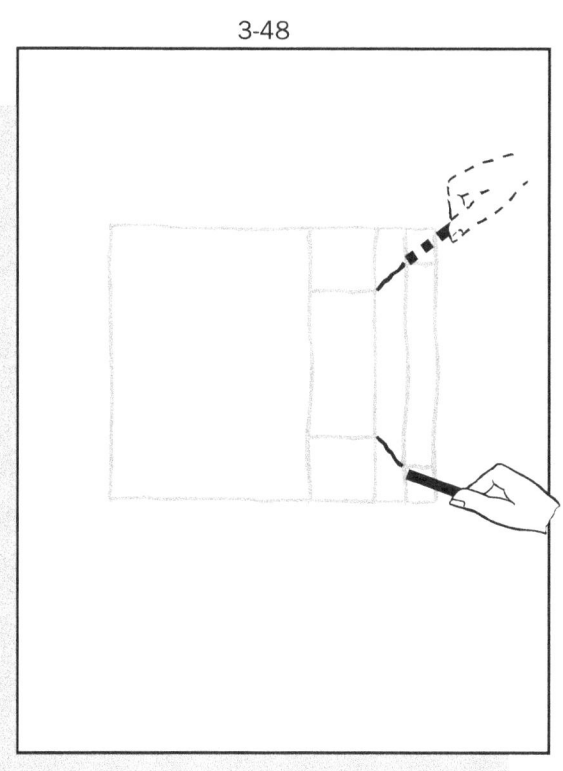

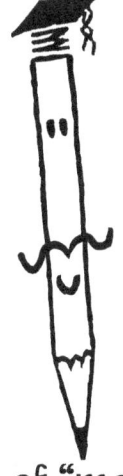

The process of "mapping out" your drawing makes things easier; doesn't it? You can "construct" your figure in sections and watch the shapes practically fall into place.

Stage 2 - CURVES

STEP 7 Draw your curves one at a time (3-49). Erase your excess lines as shown in illustration 3-50 marked with an "X." Then do a little cleanup.

TIP While forming your curves, remember to watch for the spaces as well as the amount of bend you create. Your straight lines can double as guide lines.

3-49

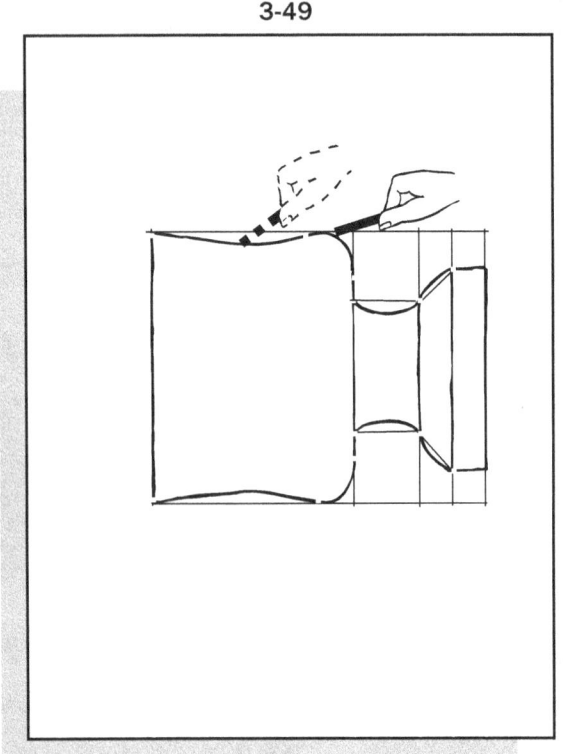

3-50

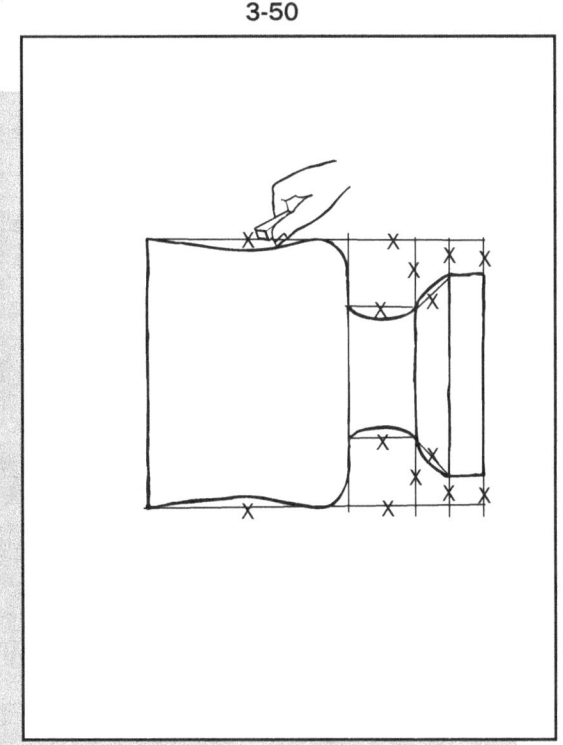

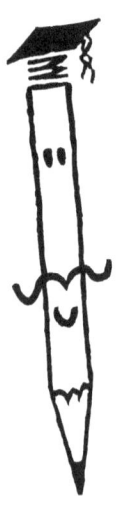

After you've done your finishing touches, your drawing will be complete. Now, think back to the way it developed. How big you chose to make your square, plus where you positioned it, had a strong influence on the outcome. The same was true for the student samples shown on the next page. See for yourself.

CHAPTER 3
SUPPLEMENTAL EXERCISE
WITH STUDENT EXAMPLES

Model

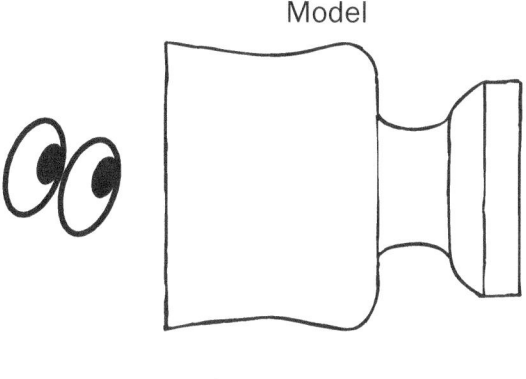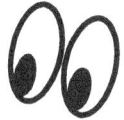

STUDENT SAMPLING

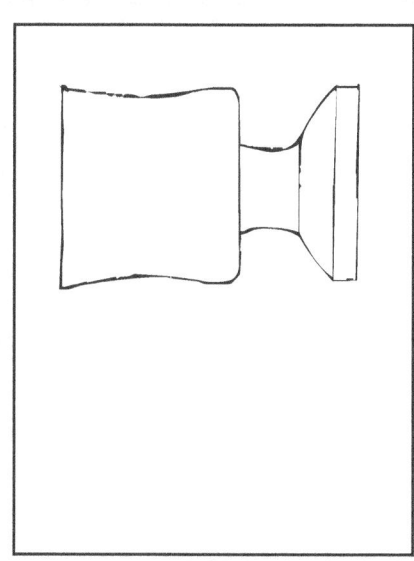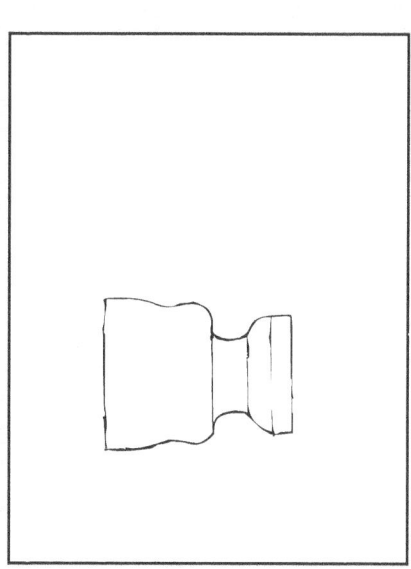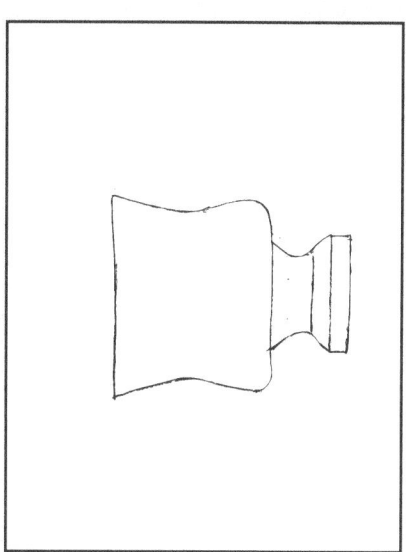

These student works are skillful renditions of the model, don't you think? Yet each ended up being different in size, shape and location. This was mainly due to relative proportions and choice of placement. Those who started with a larger square, closer to the top of the page, probably ended up with a bigger finished version of the figure, similar to the first example above left. Individuals who began with a small square, near the bottom, no doubt achieved a completed figure roughly the size of the middle example. And people who began from center most likely finished with a figure like the last example. Be that as it may, however, there's something else going on. All three have additional qualities which set them apart for another reason.

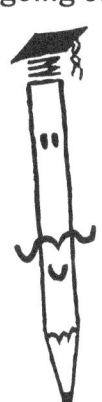

The follow-up reveals a secret. Don't miss it!

Chapter 3
FOLLOW-UP

Once again, you covered a great deal of territory, didn't you? Having completed the exercises as though the figures were made up of fragments has given you plenty of food for thought, hasn't it? For instance, you've no doubt realized proportion is even easier to manage in sections, especially in gradually developing stages. In this light, I'm confident your latest expedition also furthered your understanding that a *quick peek*, before you proceed, *is definitely not enough*. You really do need to *study* your subject carefully and refer to it often. And that brings me to another point. I had a very important purpose for tilting my illustrations of the *champagne glass* and *goblet*, yet being careful not to call them by name until now.

Truth be told, typically when we see something we know, we seldom pay close attention from then on. Aside from that, we have powerful impressions and tend to interpret the way we see fit. This is especially evident when we draw. Whether we find the theme interesting or not, we immediately aim for a likeness that's RIGHT. Commendable yes, but the question is: what's RIGHT? How the subject appears, or how we EXPECT it to appear?

Broadly speaking, people have a generalized notion of everything familiar. Four wooden legs and a flat top usually means *table*. Apply such thinking to drawing and you may be in for a surprise. For example, when I placed a vase in front of several students, deliberately at eye level, many drew a version, *including the opening on top, even though they couldn't see that portion from their seats*. After I pointed this out, they were more amazed than I was. *That's the way they THOUGHT the vase looked, they explained.*

Fascinating, wouldn't you agree? Apparently there's even more going on than meets the eye, isn't there? In Chapter 1, if you will recall, I mentioned a lot can happen between what you observe and what eventually materializes on your paper. The underlying message is that things can get lost in the translation. Usually, the reason is that we are tempted to see (or register) what we *expect* to see. Hence, it's very easy to alter traits, often without knowing you're making changes. Casually reduce a curve here, extend height there, maybe add a few extras, and your picture can quickly get out of hand. That's why I provided you with the opportunity to draw a couple of objects at an *unconventional view*.

Hopefully, from this experience, you can appreciate that it's wise to take shapes at face value. And while obviously things can't always be placed sideways, there IS an alternative. What's the secret? *Simply keep an eye on your subjects as much, if not more, than on your paper, and try to see them as though FOR THE VERY FIRST TIME.* In other words, whenever possible, look at everything differently than ANTICIPATED, and do a lot of comparing between your drawing and your model. This will help remind you to consider the parts, as well as the whole, not just so that you can depict accurately, but also so you will become ever increasingly more observant.

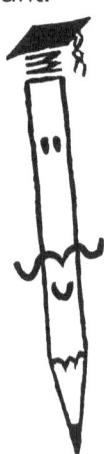

Remember: the more you observe, the more your drawing ability will improve.

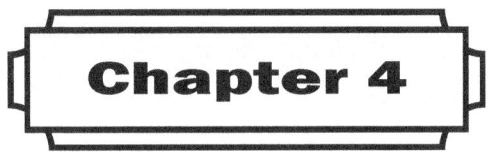

THE INVERSE METHOD

Can you draw TWO Sections of a Jigsaw Puzzle...

...that fit together?

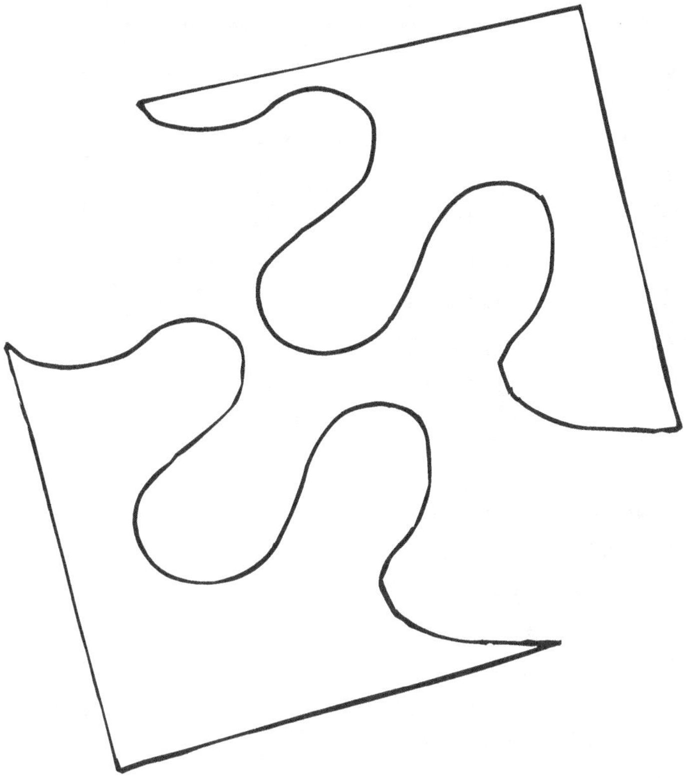

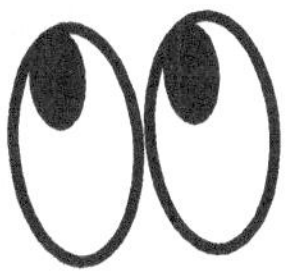

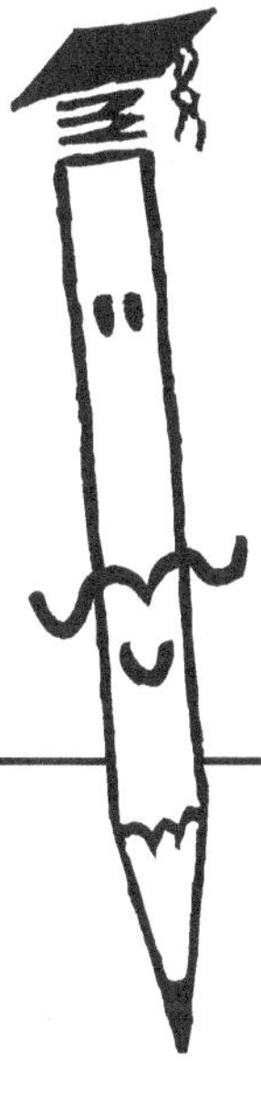

Too DIFFICULT?

It's easy, if you know the SECRET.

TRY THIS! On a piece of paper, draw a rectangle or square. Then, form a wavy line somewhat like mine. Yours can be different, providing it starts in one corner and ends *diagonally* at the opposite corner.

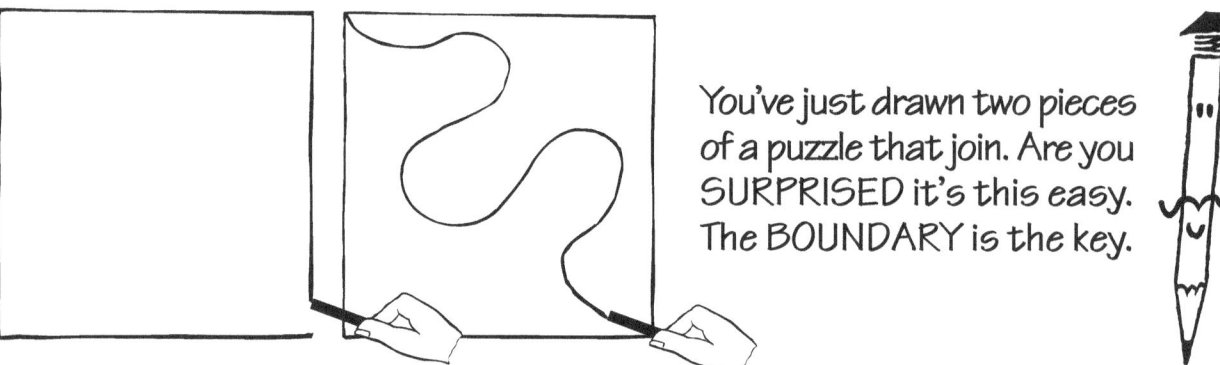

You've just drawn two pieces of a puzzle that join. Are you SURPRISED it's this easy. The BOUNDARY is the key.

CHECK THIS OUT! I've darkened the right portion of my square. But could you tell if you didn't know that? I could have just as easily started with a DARK square and erased a segment to form the white piece. For that matter, do you know which shape was *intended* and which was the *displaced* counterpart? You'd need a crystal ball to answer that. And there's something else to think about.

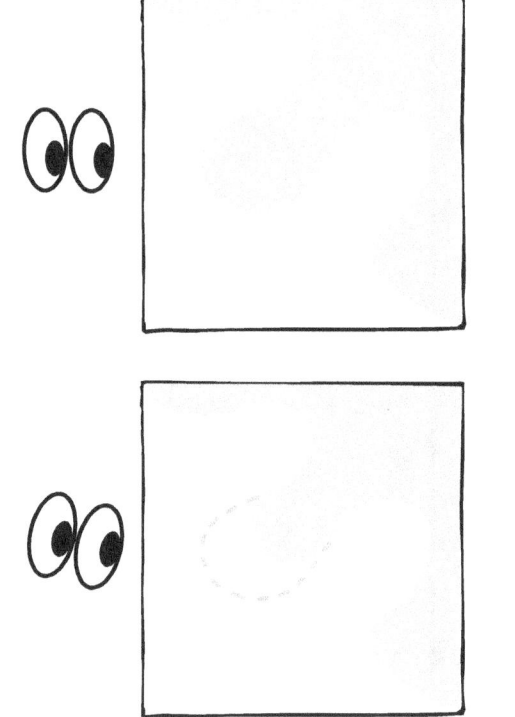

LOOK WHAT HAPPENED! When I *DECREASED the size of my dark MIDDLE portion,* the WHITE *section simultaneously ENLARGED* to fill-in where the dark part used to be (indicated by broken lines). Since one shape changed, so did the other Useful as this is, many students underestimate the value. *Three factors actually come into play the moment you draw a line.* Let me introduce them to you. They are...

FORM, SPACE and EDGE.

What is **FORM**? It's a shape usually associated with things that are tangible (like solid objects).
What is **SPACE**? It's the shape unoccupied by form.
What is **EDGE**? It's the boundary, or separation, between form and space.

*Complete the next exercise to see how
form, space and edge operate.*

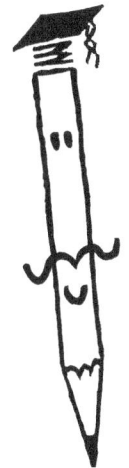

EXERCISE 4

OBJECTIVE: Create a specific shape
by drawing the area beside it.

Impossible? NOT Impossible!
Trust ME. You CAN!

STEP 1 Take out a fresh sheet of paper. LIGHTLY place a *plumb* line to the right of center, about a *third* of the way down from the top and side. The height I recommend is about the extent of your index finger (4-1).

4-1 Draw a plumb line near the right upper section of your paper, approximately one third of the distance from the edges.

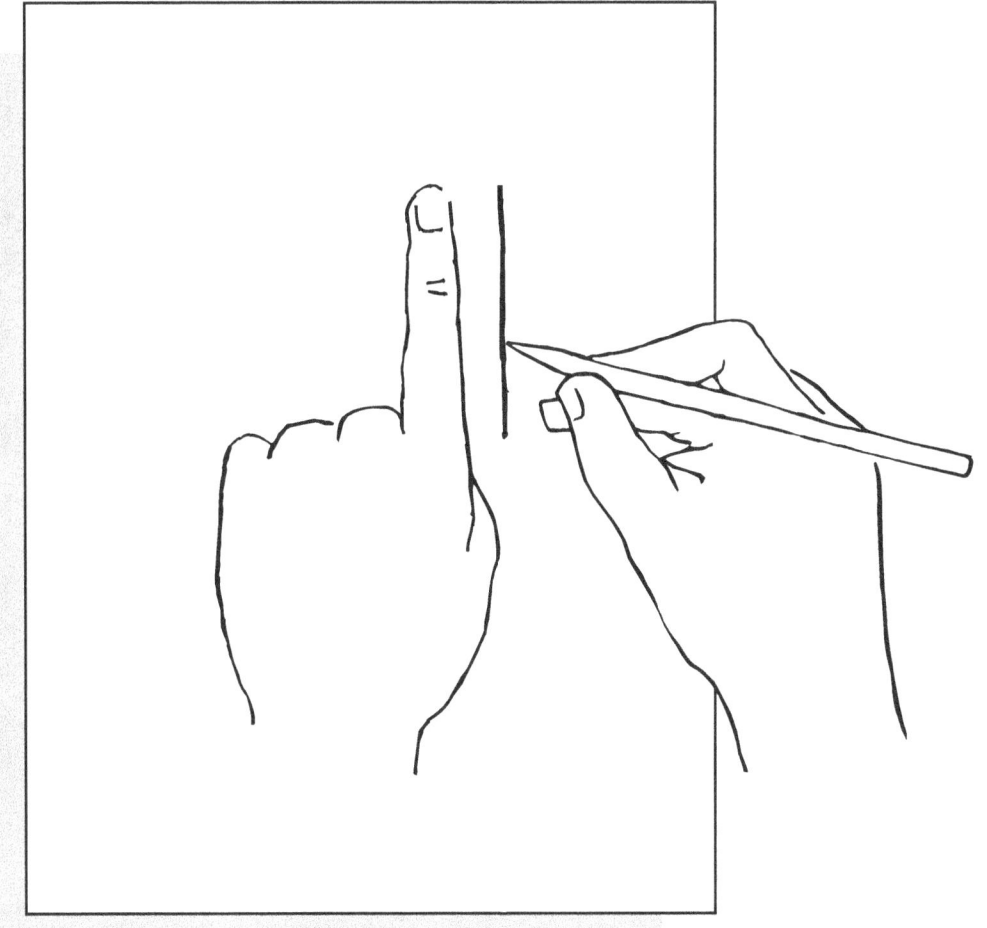

STEP 2 Divide the vertical line you drew in HALF with a dot (4-2). Next bisect *JUST* the *LOWER* half with a dot (4-3). Then repeat the procedure by "subdividing" ONLY the lower half again (with TWO more dots). This will form QUARTER spans (4-4).

4-2 Divide your line in half with a dot.

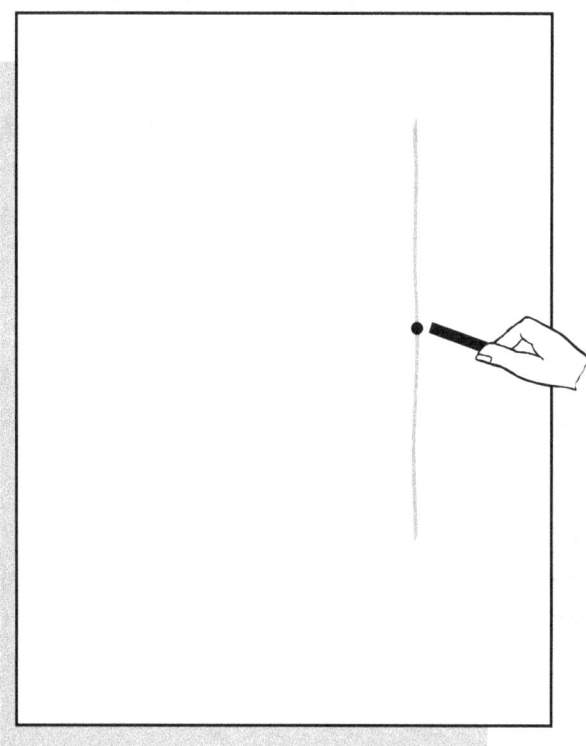

4-3 Divide your LOWER half with a dot.   4-4 Divide LOWER half into FOURTHS with 2 dots.

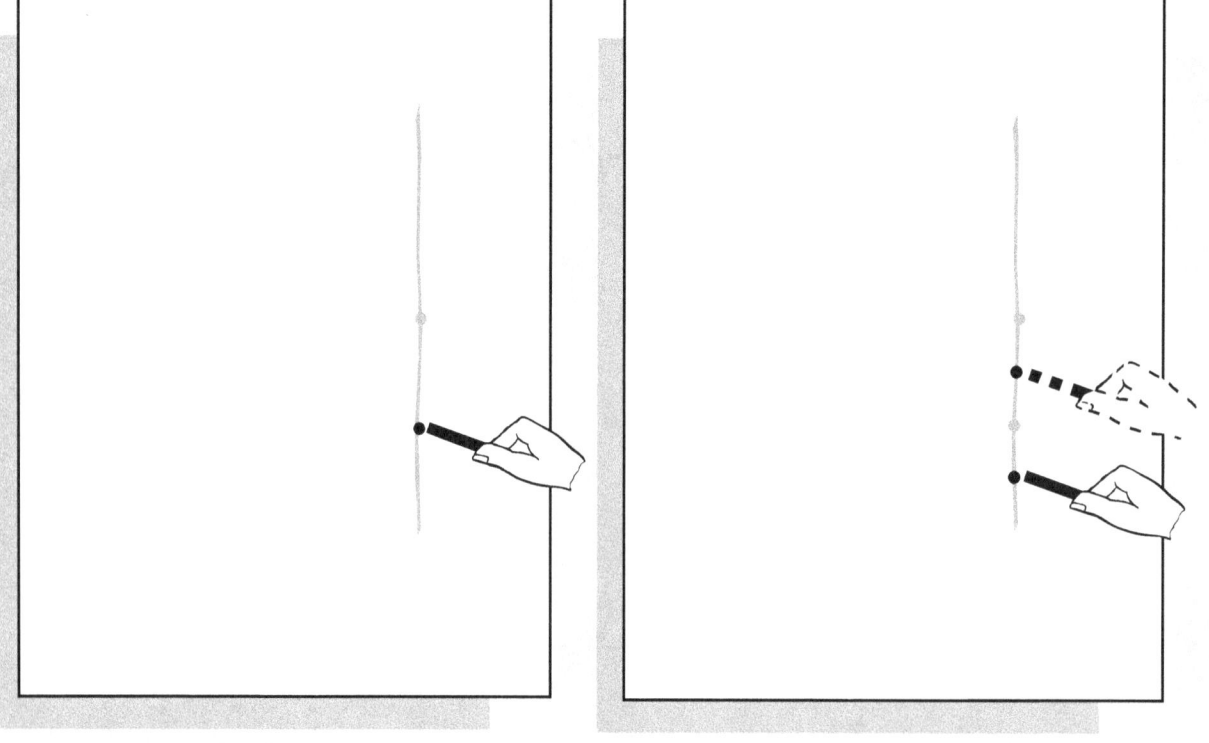

STEP 3 Take a distance check between 2 of your consecutive dots (4-5). Next, as indicated by illustration 4-6, rotate the pencil reading HORIZONTALLY, making sure your eraser tip touches the **top** of your line. Then, from your thumbnail, LIGHTLY draw a ***parallel*** line downward until it reaches MIDWAY (4-6). After that, using the space between your two lines, attach an *even* **CONCAVE** arc equal to **HALF** the height of your *first* line. Proceed left from the top and return at the middle (4-7).

4-5 Take a reading between two of your consecutive dots.

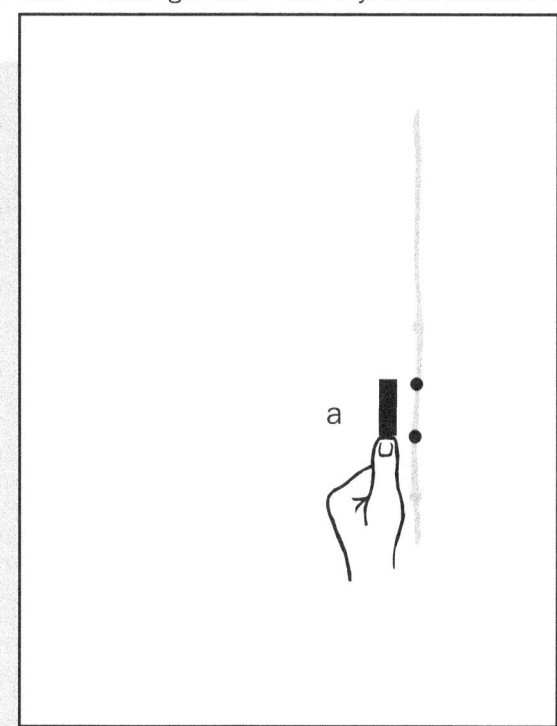

TIP Box-in the area for the curve and/or mark the center for your curve's crest with a dot.

4-6 Use your reading to position a parallel line to the left of your original line, and draw the new line 1/2 way down.

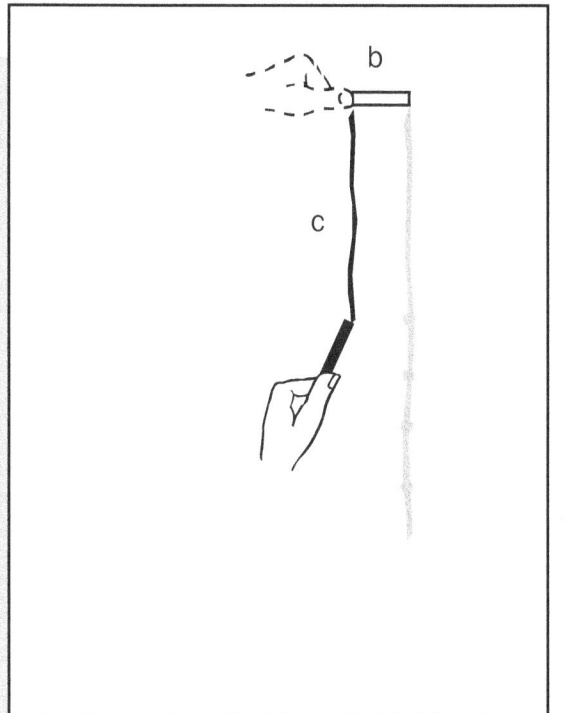

4-7 Box-in upper half, then draw an even concave arc.

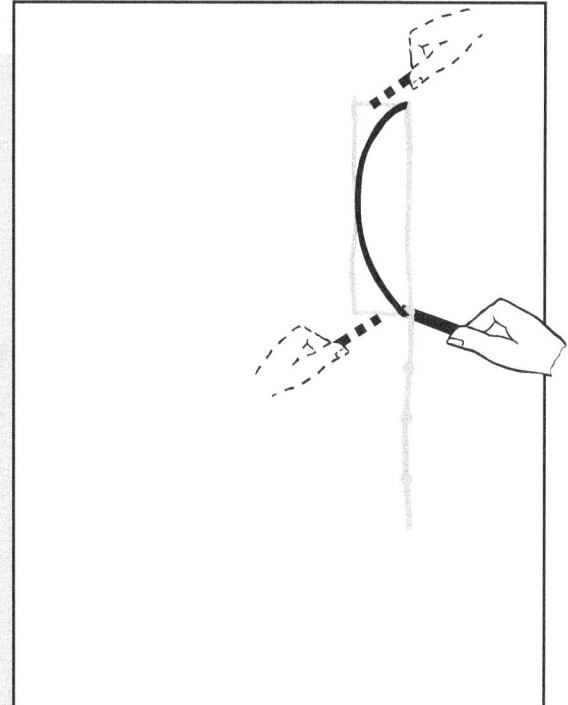

STEP 4
Connect a CONVEX arc to the bottom of your *concave* arc (equal in size to your previous curve). Since, you're **continuing from MIDPOINT,** and simply forming a **"mirror version"** try to draw your 2nd curve **without** guide lines. Begin from the **middle** of your line, advance to the **RIGHT,** and return **at the bottom** (4-8). Then, erase your **straight** lines and reference points to produce the shape of a figure "S" (4-9).

4-8 Draw a reverse image of your first arc from midline to the bottom.

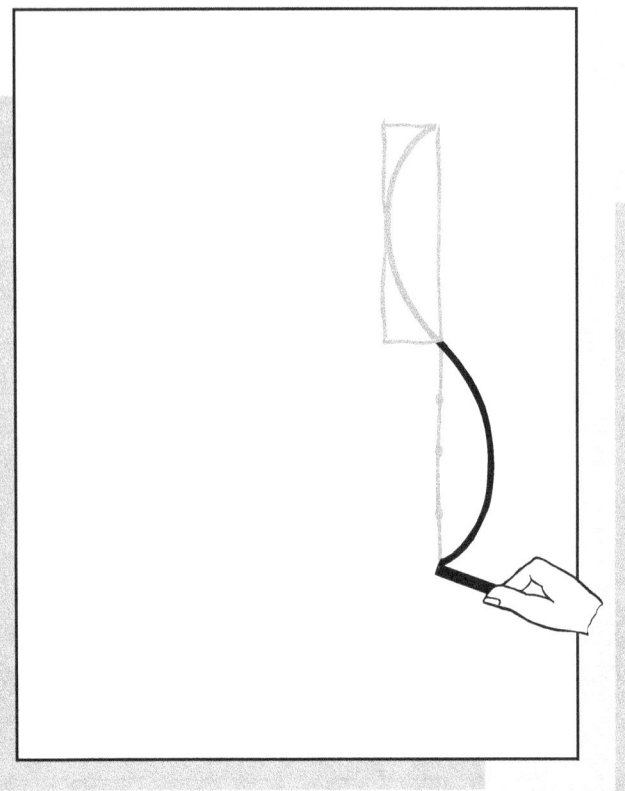

4-9 Erase your straight lines and you will have a figure "S."

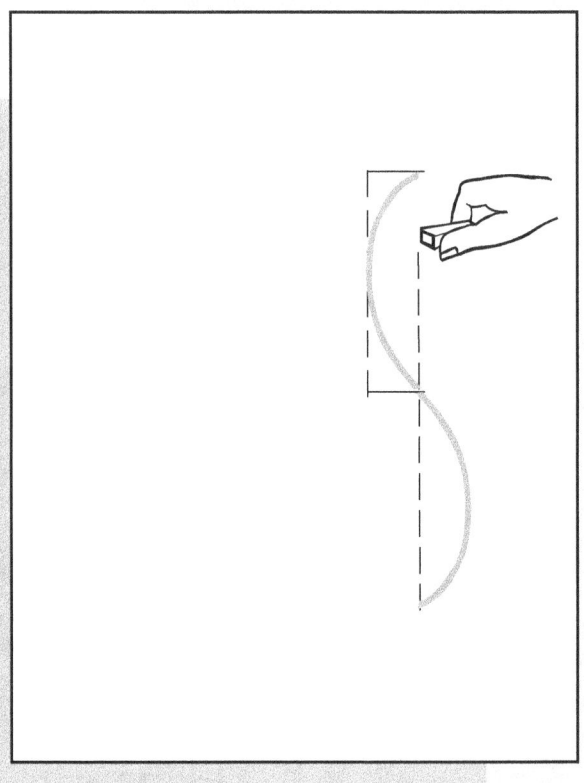

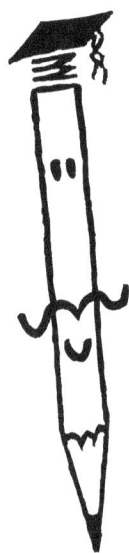

Please DON'T get too DEPENDENT on reference points and construction lines. Use them wisely. YOUR EYES SHOULD BE YOUR ULTIMATE GUIDE.

STEP 5 *LIGHTLY* draw a **plumb** line against the right edge of your lower curve, even with your entire figure "S" (4-10). Two shapes will appear, one above, and one below. Fill them in so they create fields of gray (4-11). Then, draw another FULL LENGTH parallel line. Position it LEFT of your previous plumb line, at a distance equal to HALF the HEIGHT (4-12).

4-10 Draw a plumb line against
your bottom curve's crest.

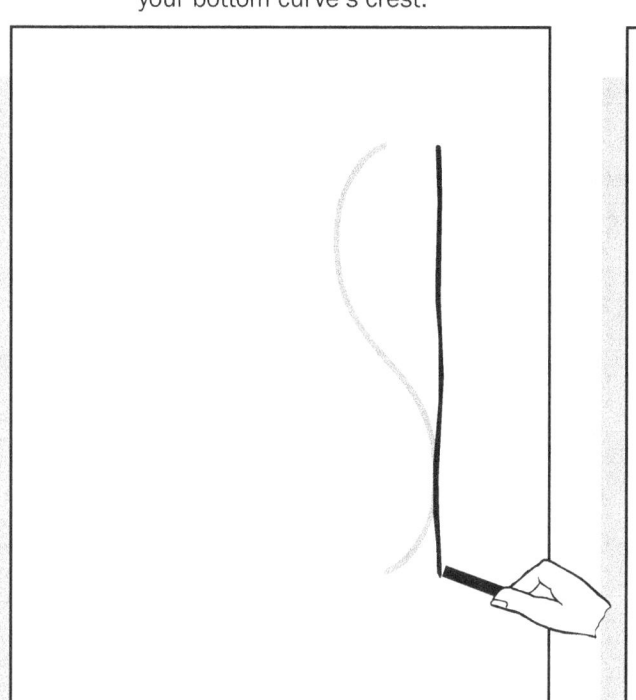

4-11 Fill-in your top and
bottom shapes evenly.

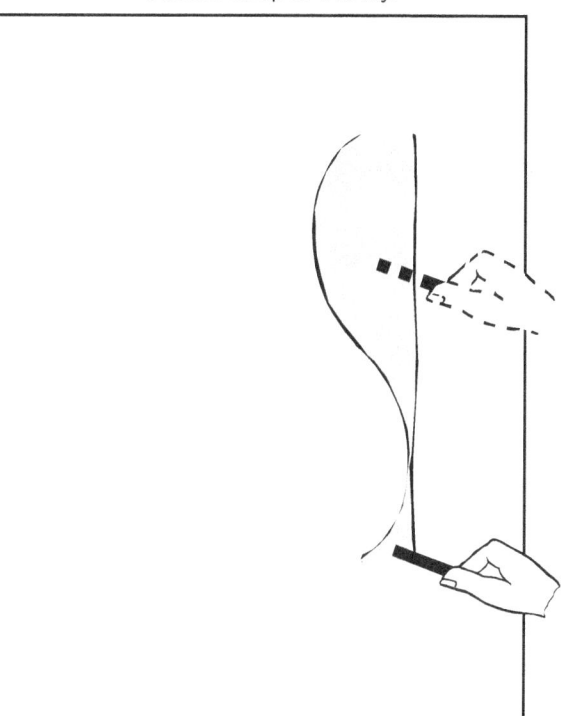

4-12 Locate HALF the length of your RIGHT edge
to the left of it and draw a parallel plumb line.

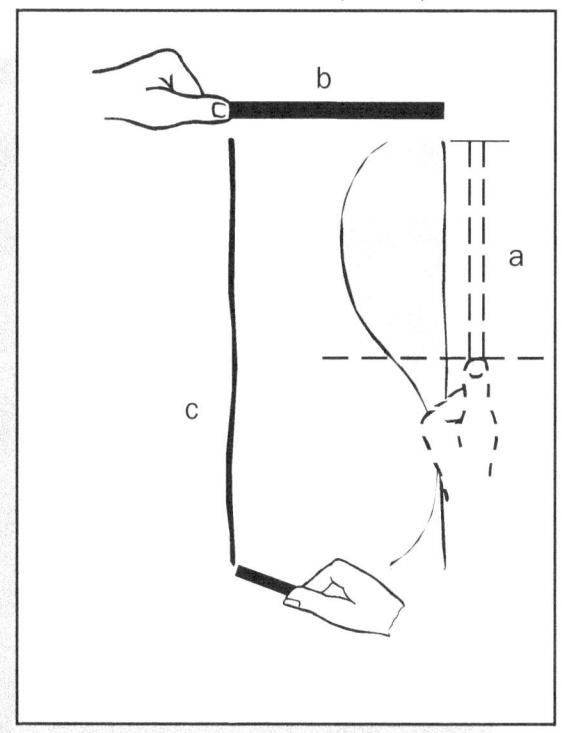

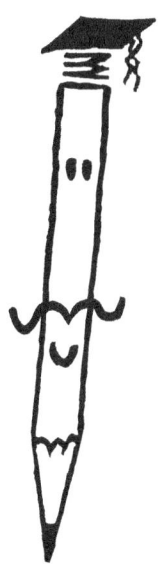

Wondering where we're
headed? Stick with me.

STEP 6 Using your new straight line as a guide line, draw another CONCAVE arc of *equal bend* as your other arcs. Start at the *top*, go **RIGHT** and finish MIDWAY (4-13). From there, place a CONVEX arc on the bottom half with the same amount of bend as your upper arc. Begin at the *middle*, move **LEFT** and return at the base (4-14). Then erase your *straight* line. Your outcome will now be a *backward* "S" (4-15).

4-13 Draw a concave arc at *TOP* ½ of your line.

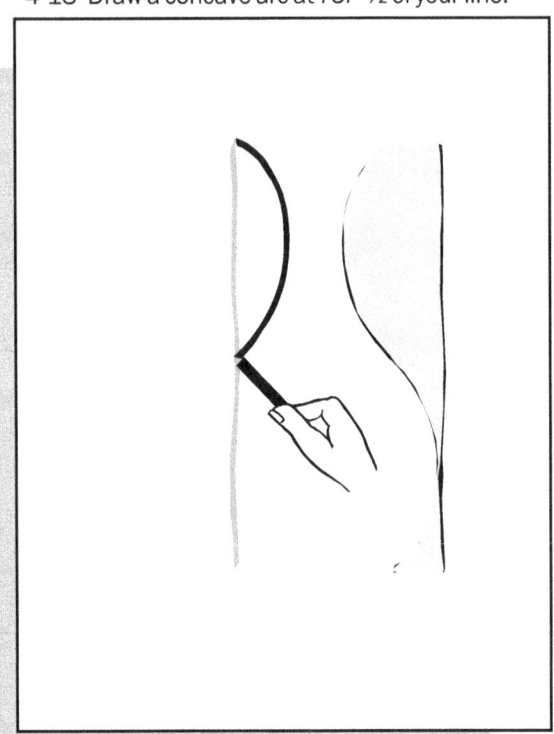

4-14 Draw a convex arc at *BOTTOM* ½ of your line.

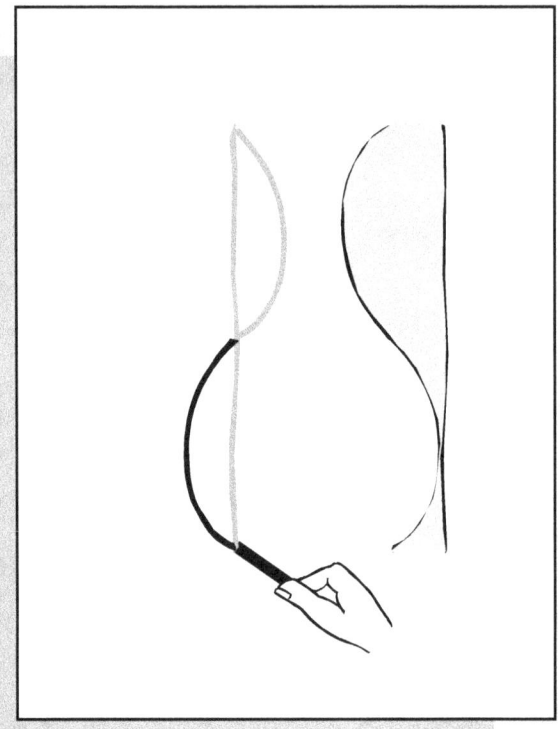

4-15 Erase your guide line and you have a backward "S."

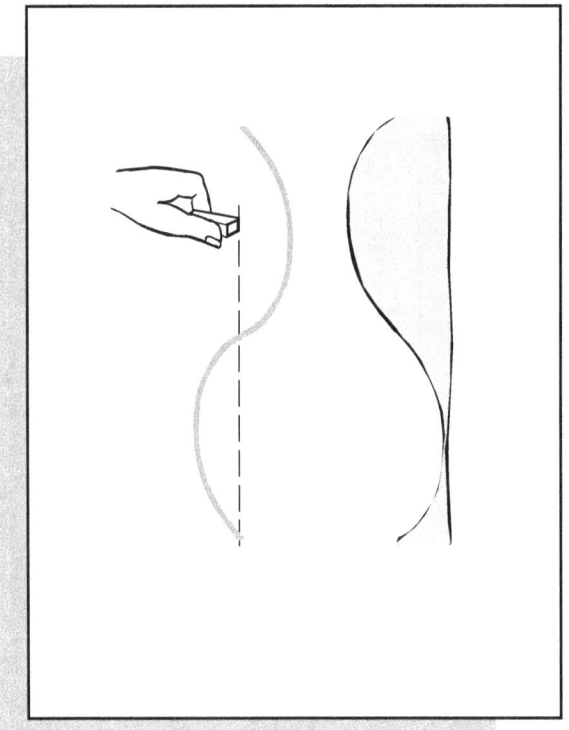

STEP 7 Draw one more vertical line. Position this one against the LEFT side of your BOTTOM arc as shown in illustration 4-16. Then fill in the spaces again. Miraculously, a vase will appear between the two dark, contrasting shapes (4-17). You don't even have to place a line at the top and bottom. Your imagination does it for you, because you expect the boundaries to be there. This is made possible by a process called the "closure principle." Quite some magic, eh?

4-16 Draw a plumb line against
your lower LEFT curve.

4-17 Fill-in upper top and
bottom shapes evenly.

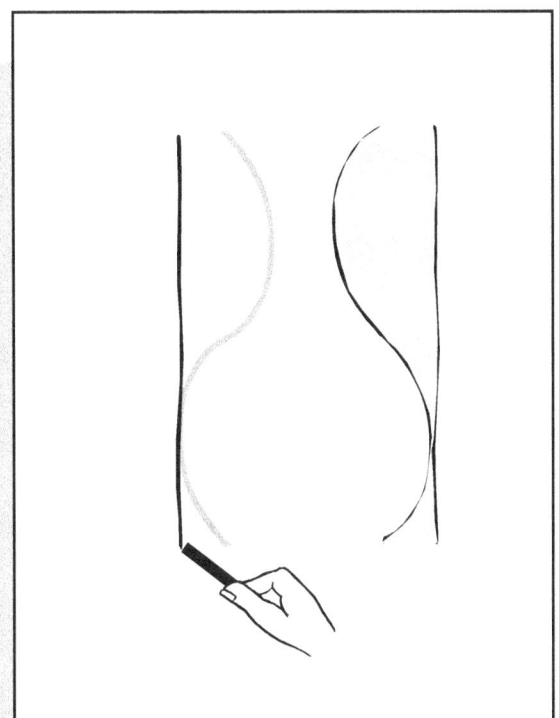

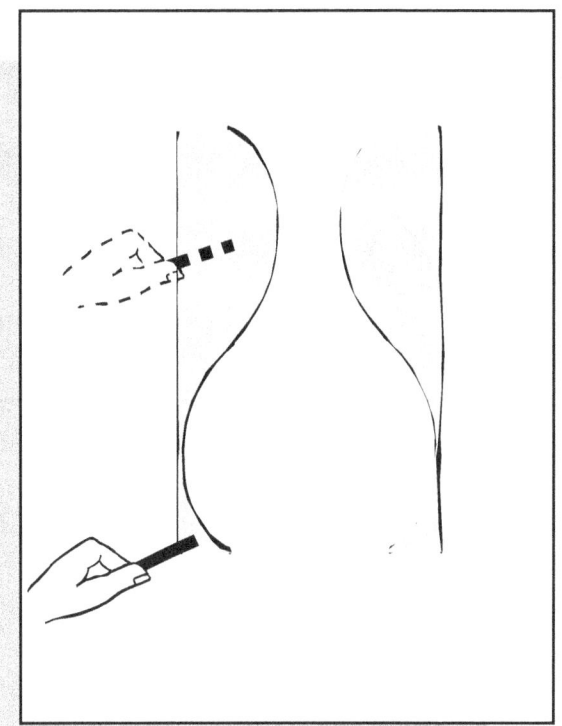

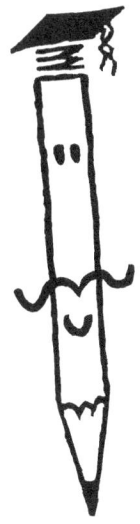

Amazing, isn't it? A white vase has emerged, made visible by the two gray fields. Are you positively thrilled? If not, you certainly should be. There's a marvelous concept going on here that's simple in appearance, yet packs a wallop.

Whether your middle figure closely matches the book's version or it doesn't, and whether it's symmetrical or lopsided, your focus should be on the bigger picture, namely on *how* and *why* it came about the way it did. Confused? Perhaps the student examples on the next page will clarify.

MODEL

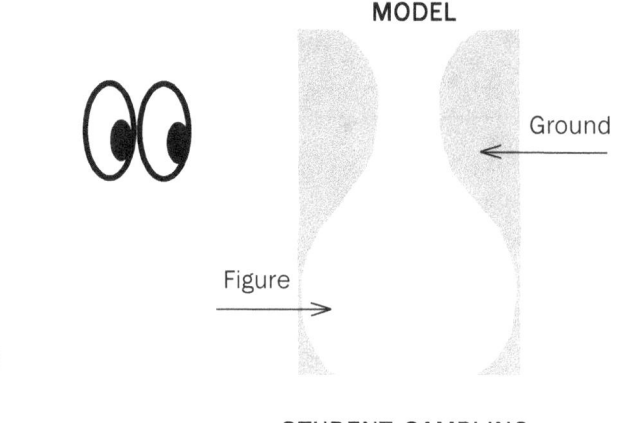

Ground

Figure

STUDENT SAMPLING

4-18	4-19	4-20

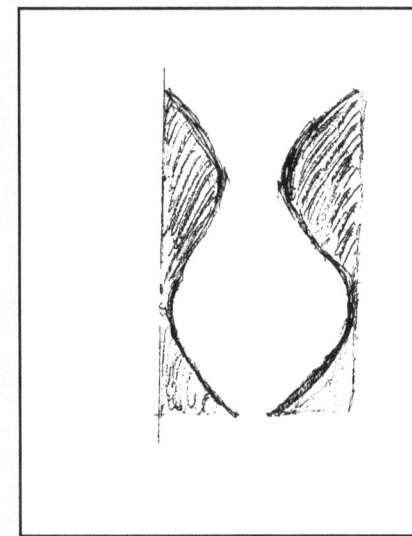

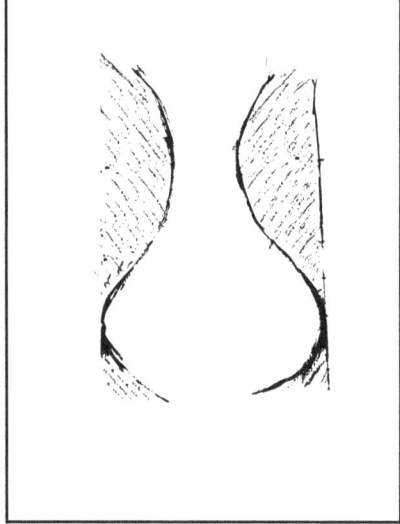

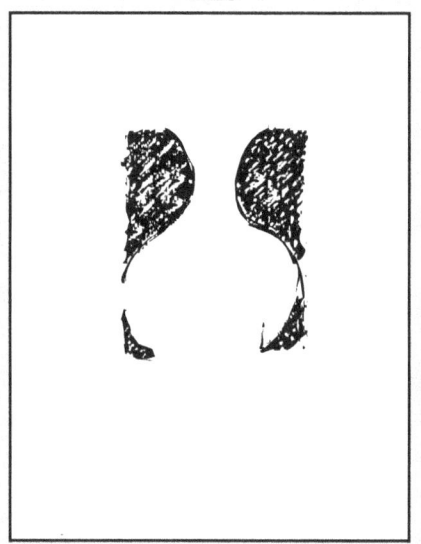

Each of the student examples resemble the model, but they are all quite different, aren't they? And do you know what? That's the point. The way the outer sections emerged affected the shape between them. As I mentioned at the beginning of the chapter, three forces are at work the moment you create boundaries. These are FORM, SPACE and EDGE. The *EDGE* fashioned by your curves established the borders which separated FORM (or figure) from SPACE (or ground). The GROUND areas were darkened to create CONTRAST, so that *both* the *intended* shape and the *space* beside it would stand out.

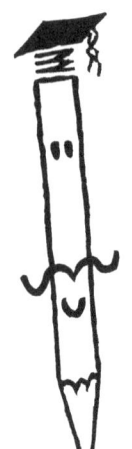

Figure 4-18 appears as it does because the curves (or edges) are fairly straight.

Figure 4-19 has taller upper curves than lower curves. This changed the *desired* shape.

Figure 4-20 has wide curves. That's why the resulting mid "form" turned out bulky.

When all is said and done, what this means is that the BACKGROUND CREATED THE FOREGROUND. Now that you understand the concept and its influence on shape, check the darkened portions which formed YOUR figure again. Then practice "inverse drawing" some more.

CHAPTER 4
SUPPLEMENTAL EXERCISE

DIRECTIONS: Place your pencil point on the dot indicated. "Lefties" may invert the page to provide a clear view. Outline a **mirror image** of the gray shape, FREEHAND, and darken it. A white figure will appear in between. Then, one by one, complete the other two shapes. Do not use a ruler. Your portion is not expected to be as precise as the printed sample. It's your understanding of the principle that counts.

Your pencil point starts here.

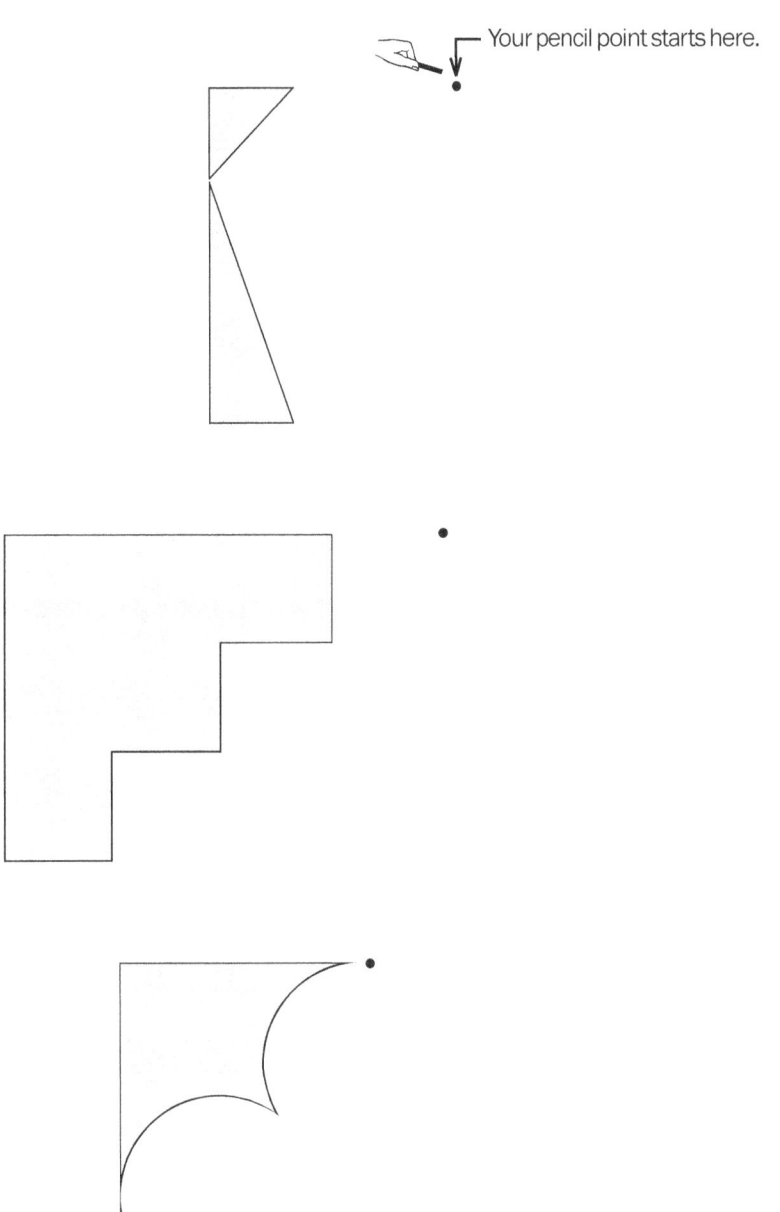

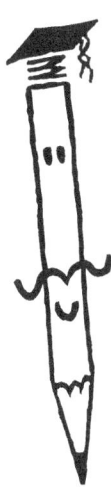

It IS possible to draw shapes INDIRECTLY, isn't it?
The follow-up explains why this is important.

Chapter 4
FOLLOW-UP

---

1 plus 1 CAN make 3
Incredible as this sounds, it's true. *Seeing is Believing*.

The *darkened* side portions, which helped make your middle figures stand out, are usually referred to as NEGATIVE space. I prefer to call them REVERSE space because the word "negative" suggests something undesirable. Yet "opposites," the kinds I'm talking about, are anything but unwanted. After all, where would words be without pauses? For that matter, where would musical notes be without intervals? Interesting question, wouldn't you agree? And the same goes for forms without spaces.

Form and space, or figure and ground, are *equally* important. Sure, we normally pay attention to solid objects we can bump into and trip over. But when it comes to drawing, the area around things (displaced spaces created by forms) deserve just as much recognition. You've been proving this all along. For example, think back to Chapters 1, 2 and 3. The adjoining sections (bordered by guide lines) which you used to duplicate angles and curves (in order to form desired shapes) were actually achieved with the help of REVERSE spaces. An eye-opener, wouldn't you agree?

Always remember, if the *surroundings* you drew are accurate, your figure is too. On the other hand, if the border (or edge) of the adjacent region does NOT appear correct, the shape you are trying to replicate CAN'T be either. DIRECT and INDIRECT space, as I also call them, are intertwined and practically inseparable. THEY *SHAPE* EACH OTHER. So, LOOK for BOTH. Add them to the list of components with which you draw, and believe it or not, your skill will just about double.

Here is your chance to see the figure and ground duo in action, right now. Below are the COMPLETED shapes from the supplemental exercise. Compare them to yours to determine where and why your white middle pieces match and/or differ.

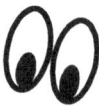   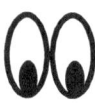   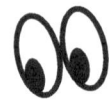

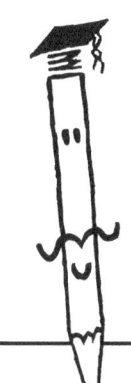

THE STREAMLINE APPROACH

Generally it's easier to start with straight lines, followed by the curves, isn't it?

But what if a subject is virtually all curves? What then?
Take the following ivy leaf, for instance.
There isn't a straight line anywhere...

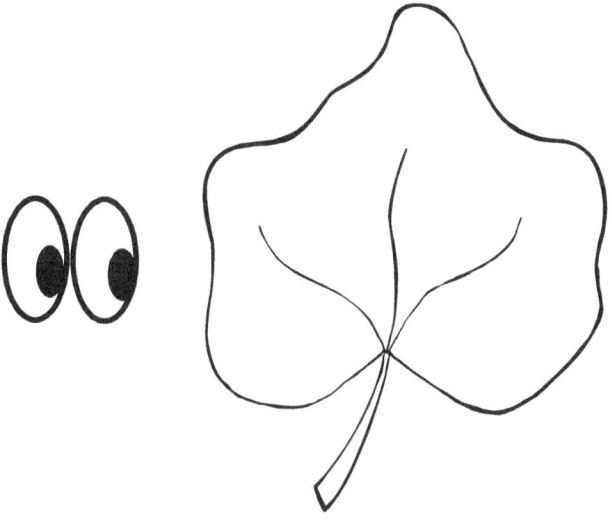

...or is there?
Here's the same figure, STREAMLINED.

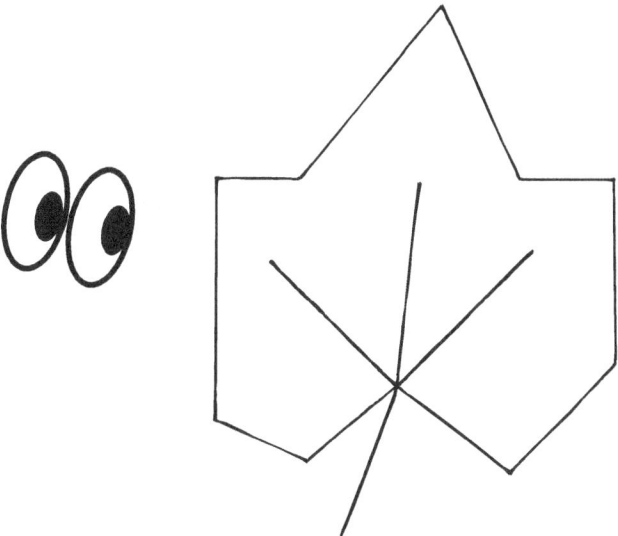

STREAMLINE? WHAT'S THAT?

Streamline is a term I use to describe when shapes are simplified. This makes them easier to start with. How?

Take any shape and change it to a minimum (least amount) of straight lines and presto! You have a STREAMLINE. Actually, you've already been using streamlines. The vase, perfume bottle and goblet (Chapters 2 & 3) began with a square which served as a basic foundation or primary streamline. Next, by locating and connecting reference points, you created a more advanced streamline. When curves were added, the final shape was formed.

Why didn't we just combine all these procedures to save time, you ask? The answer is simple. Think of it this way: just as it's the FRAMEWORK that helps support a house, STREAMLINING does the same for drawing. When each phase is on a secure footing, you can proceed confidently and efficiently toward a dependable outcome. Conversely, if you try to do too much at once, you could overload yourself, and miss important factors. Fair warning as this may be, the problem is that the benefits of streamlines (like construction lines) are generally underestimated and often skipped or rushed.

Regrettably, many students fall into this trap and suffer the consequences. Take a look at streamline 5-1 below. Then study illustration 5-2, showing how the figure ended up. Granted, it's an ivy leaf, but it was *supposed* to resemble figure 5-3.

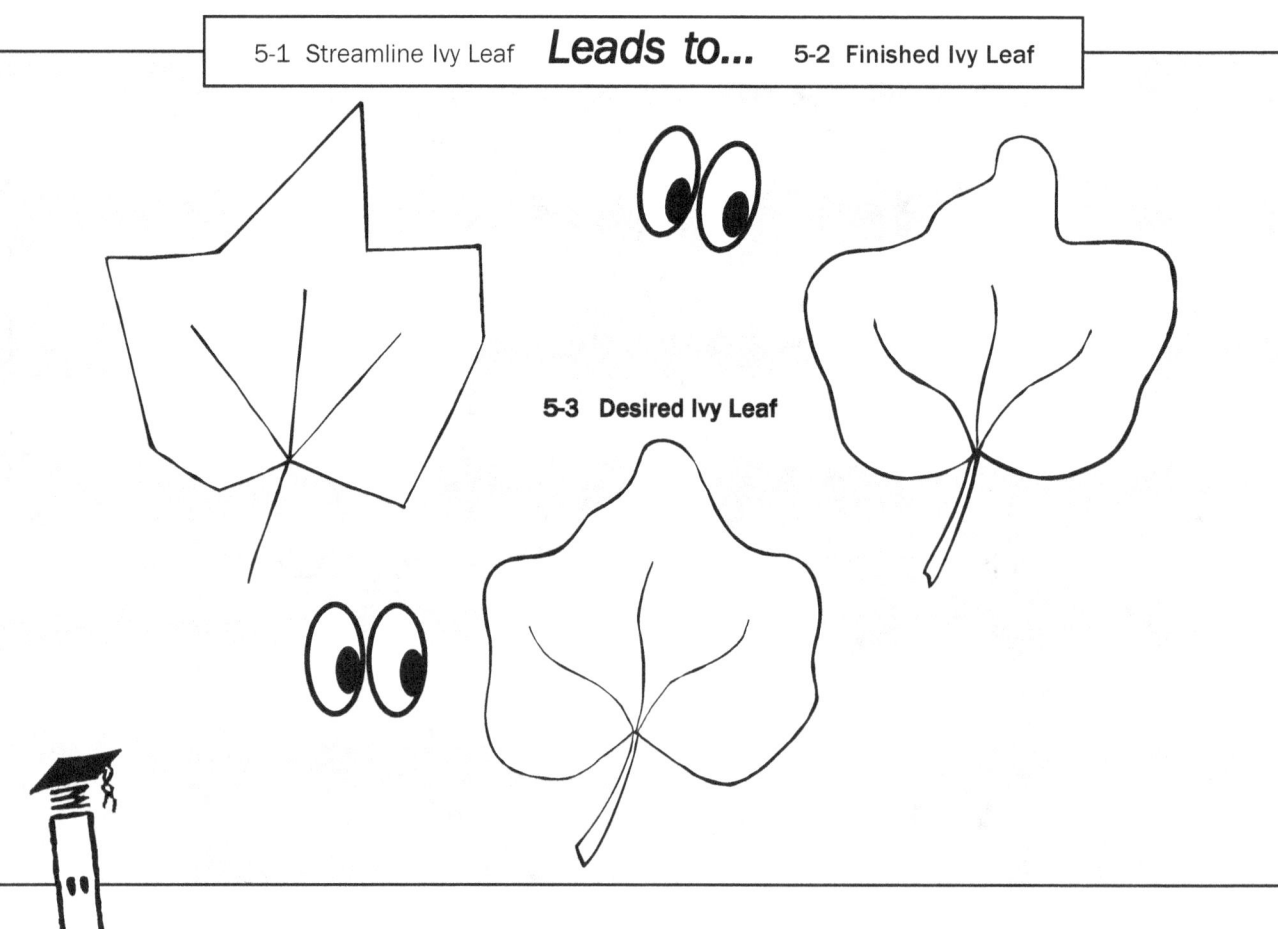

| 5-1 Streamline Ivy Leaf | **Leads to...** | 5-2 Finished Ivy Leaf |

5-3 Desired Ivy Leaf

Can you *see* a difference between the two COMPLETED leaf drawings? With a little detective work, and by using the process of elimination, we can determine why one version turned out as desired, and the other one did not.

CHECK ALIGNMENTS

Observe that the LEFT *SIDE* on the ACCURATE streamline is PLUMB. When the curves were added, the finished ivy leaf turned out correctly (5-4). Next, compare the effects when the same area became *TILTED* on another streamline. The distortion carried over to the curve stage (5-5).

5-4 ACCURATE streamline with PLUMB *LEFT* side	**Leads to...** ACCURATE finished LEFT side

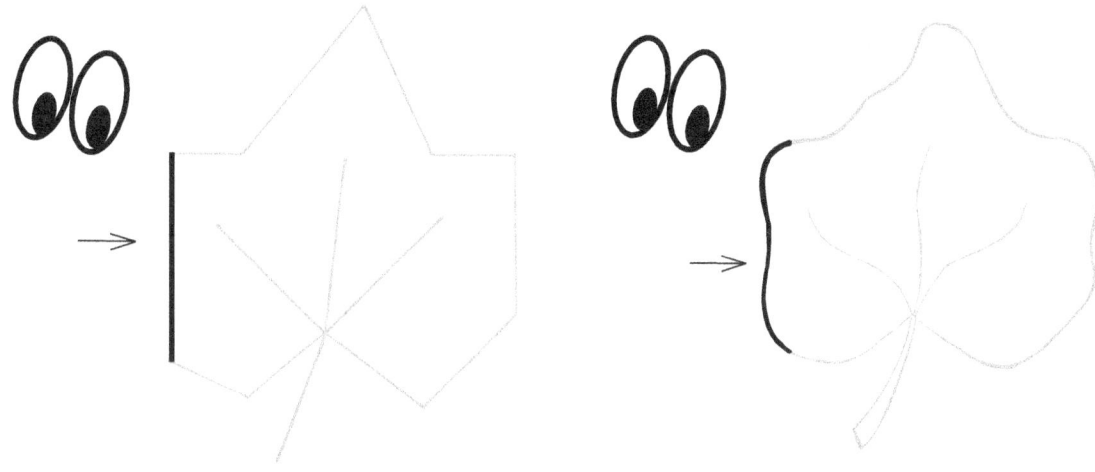

5-5 INACCURATE streamline with a TILTED *LEFT* side	**Leads to...** INACCURATE finished LEFT side

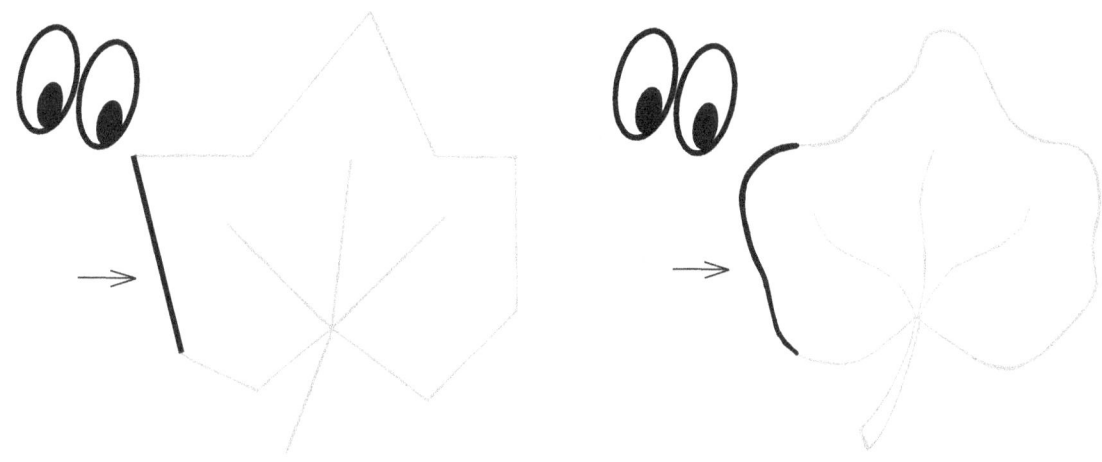

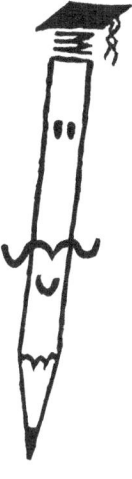

Are you beginning to get the picture?
Fabulous! Let's investigate some more.

CHECK REVERSE SPACE

Please focus your attention on the gray area, in the upper right quadrant of the following streamline. It's depicted accurately. When the curves were added, the top portion came out correctly (5-6). Next, take note that the SAME *area* on the streamline below has less angle (5-7). In turn, the *finished* top portion was also affected. Compare the difference between the tops of the two finished leaves.

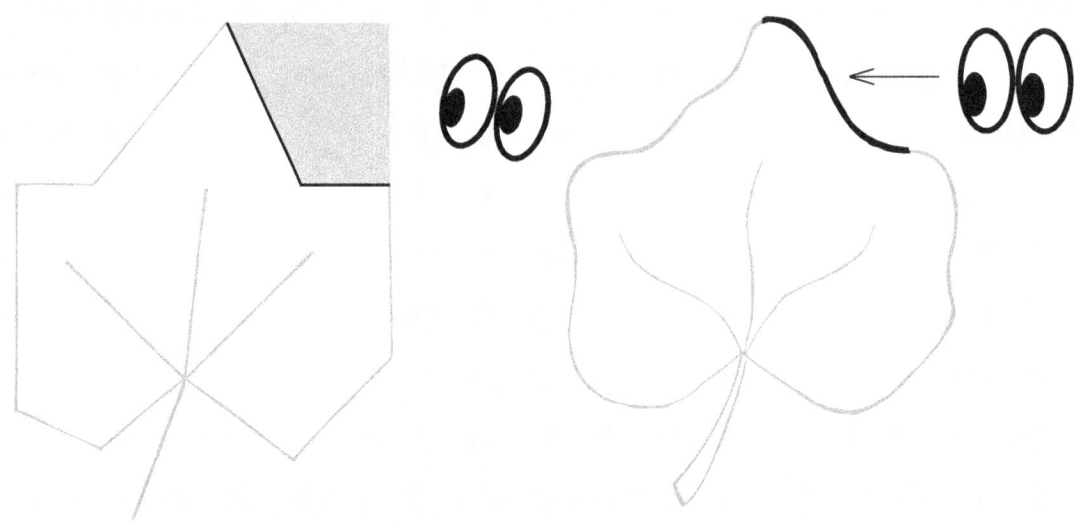

5-6 ACCURATE reverse space **Leads to...** ACCURATE finished RIGHT *TOP* section

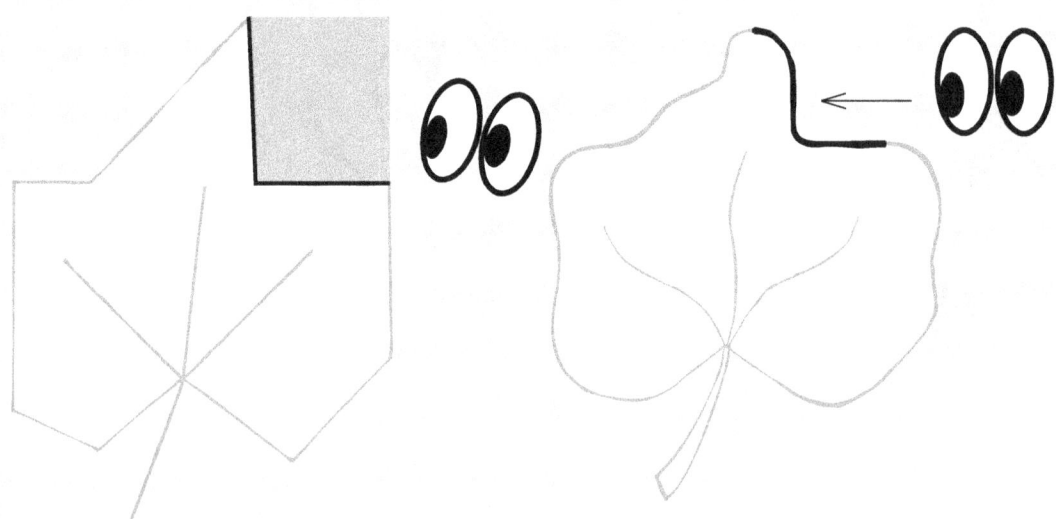

5-7 INACCURATE reverse space **Leads to...** INACCURATE finished RIGHT *TOP* section

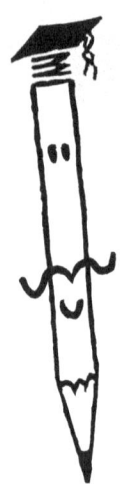

Look at the top section of the ACCURATE finished leaf and compare it to the top portion of the INACCURATE leaf. There's a big difference, isn't there?

CHECK SUB-PROPORTIONS

Notice that the RIGHT *SIDE* of the *accurate* streamline is nearly the same height as the left. That aspect helped bring about the desired finished product when the curves were added (5-8). Next, study the RIGHT SIDE of the *"inaccurate"* streamline and the way it influenced the outcome (5-9).

5-8 ACCURATE streamlined RIGHT *SIDE* **Leads to...** ACCURTATE finished RIGHT *SIDE*

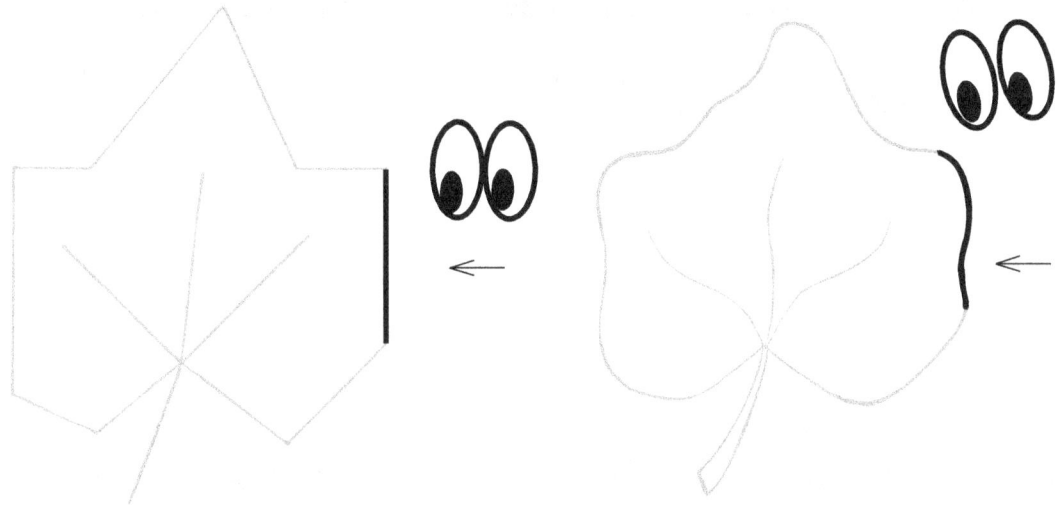

5-9 INACCURATE streamlined RIGHT *SIDE* **Leads to...**INACCURATE finished RIGHT *SIDE*

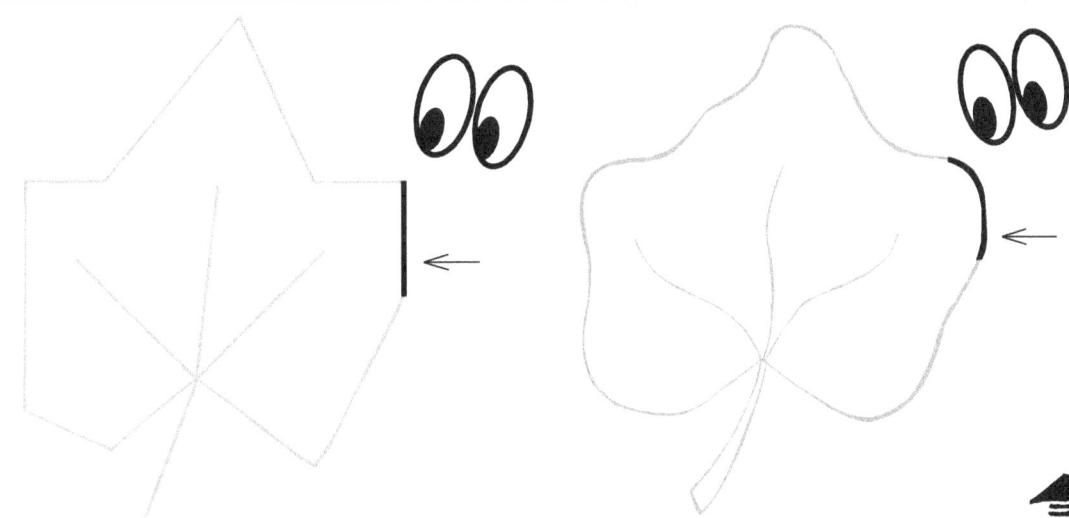

Have you figured it out yet? ALL THREE streamline defects caused the changes on the undesired ivy leaf. Is this a catastrophe? Are we doomed to live with distortion? Not at all. As you know, pencil checks and visual assessments are ESTIMATES. It stands to reason then that you should *expect* to make adjustments.

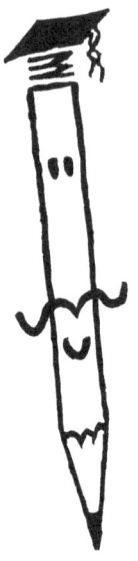

But a LEAF is just a LEAF, right?
Not REALLY! There are leaves
and then there are LEAVES!

If you intend to draw a **PARTICULAR** leaf (or a **SPECIFIC** shape, for that matter) you should **LOOK** for its **UNIQUE** features and **SPECIAL** qualities. And, to make things easier, you might as well start with a *streamline*. While in a simplified state, required adjustments are easier to spot and handle. Then the curves can go in smoothly and with a great deal more certainty. Test this for yourself by completing the next exercise.

EXERCISE 5

OBJECTIVE: Add CURVES to the given streamline.

DIRECTIONS: With the model as your reference, replicate the arcs proportionally, by drawing them one at a time, *directly* on the provided streamline. Start anywhere, go clockwise or counter clockwise. Move slowly and carefully. Every curve makes a difference.

TIP Use the straight lines to help draw your arcs. Watch for BOTH your advancing curve and REVERSE SPACE it creates. This will help you steer your lines and stay on course. After each curve is done, compare the SHAPE of *your* reverse space to the *corresponding section on the model.* I've darkened the tip merely just to show you the kind of shape I'm talking about.

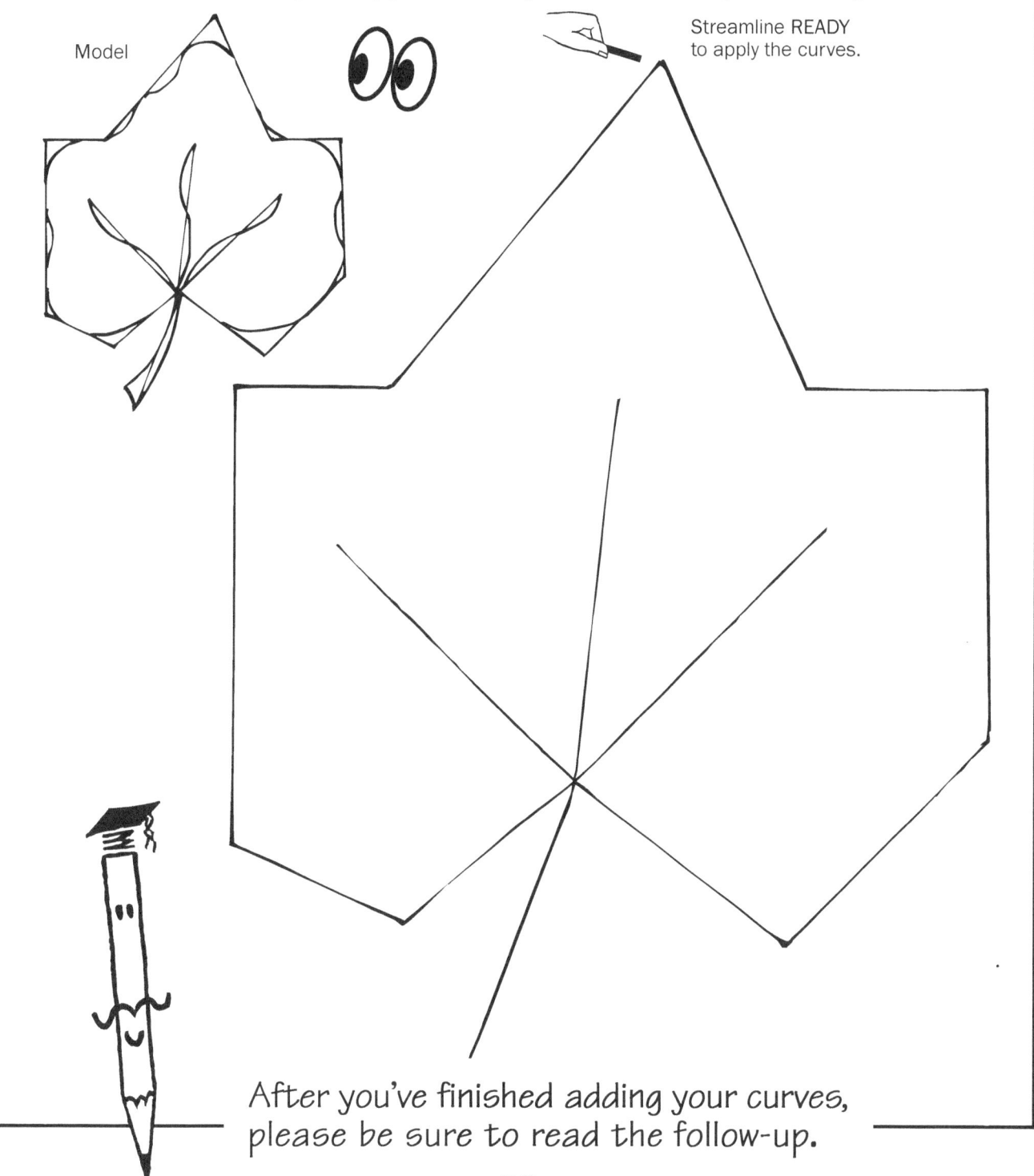

Model

Streamline READY
to apply the curves.

After you've finished adding your curves,
please be sure to read the follow-up.

-89-

Chapter 5
FOLLOW-UP

Generally, when art instructors say, "block-in the form," or they advise you to "*construct* the figure," they are telling you to disregard the fancy stuff. Without them you can see the foundation, steer a clear course, and predict where you're heading. The lesson of the ivy leaf is a prime example. You saw how just a few basic checks during the fundamental phase helped find where modifications were needed, BEFORE any details were added. It's fair to conclude, then, that such precautions can prove to be useful. Permit me to explain.

As you know, the drawing process undergoes many developmental stages. In light of this, it's not wise to be impatient or hurry so you can savor the end result. Instead, it's smart to take all the necessary steps that get you there successfully. Remember you're learning. Be willing to start with straight lines, then proceed to the curves. If they are done together and something goes wrong, you need to backtrack TWICE as much.

Above and beyond that, consider this: to draw, in a sense, you take shapes apart with your eyes, then *reconstruct* their likeness with pencil and paper, right? Therefore, key *structural* components, including STRAIGHT LINES and CURVES, plus REFERENCE POINTS, ALIGNMENTS, PROPORTIONS, ANGLES, as well as REVERSE SPACE, certainly come in handy, wouldn't you agree?

These tools, I like to call the **TRUSTY SEVEN.** Please *memorize* them and take full advantage of their contribution to shaping, not only when you draw, but also when you stop to check your bearings. They will help you stay on track, whether or not you choose to *simplify* your subject. You see, streamlining isn't always necessary. However, it usually makes things less complicated, especially in elaborate situations. Besides, the method sure can save a lot of extra fuss and bother in the long run.

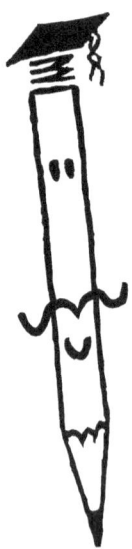

Don't just accept my word. After a brief interlude, prepare to apply the benefits of streamling, and more!

THE CRISSCROSS METHOD

Please take a look at these butterfly wings.

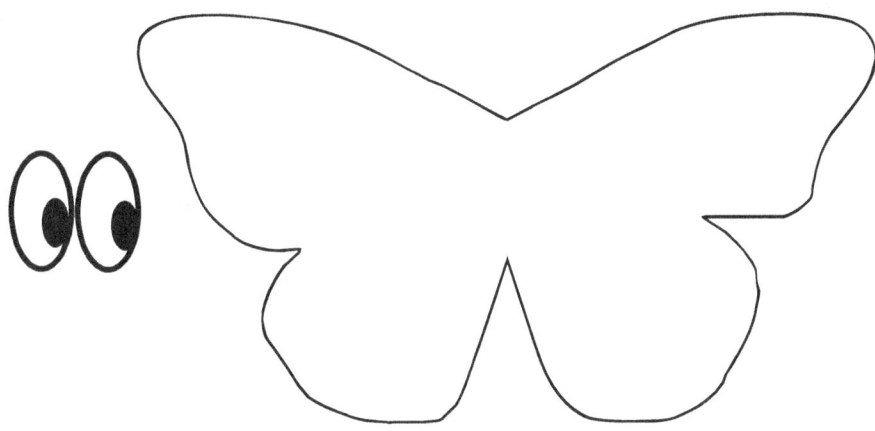

Here they are CRISSCROSSED.

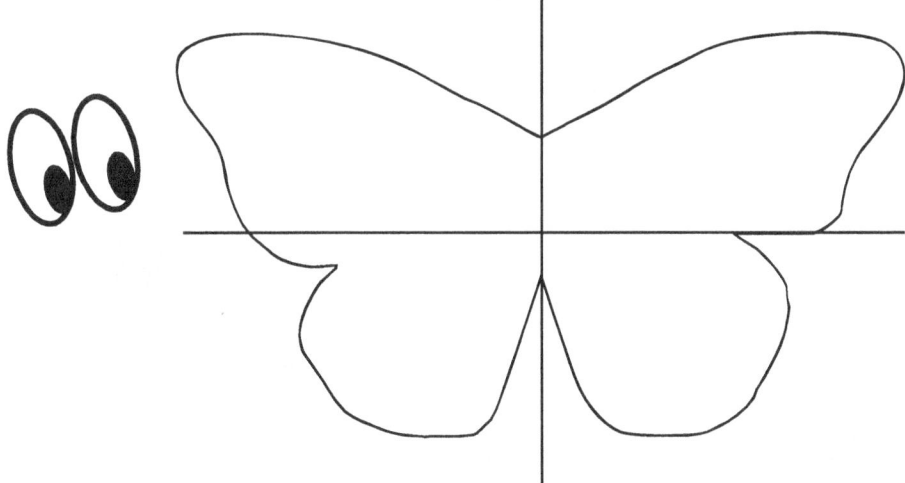

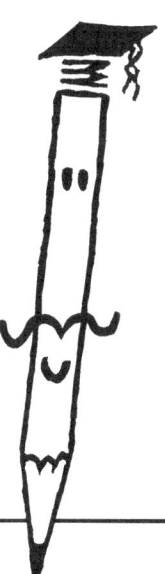

Why is the shape crisscrossed? Sometimes it's easier to draw this way. Read on and find out WHY.

"Divide and conquer," encouraged Napoleon. Little did he know, someday his battle cry would be useful in drawing.

To understand what I mean, let's flash back momentarily to Chapter 3. If you'll recall, we saw a champagne glass composed of three parts (two curves plus a rectangle). In this chapter, we only have ONE shape but it can also be separated into sections. Take a gander at illustration 6-1 below, for instance.   Notice that a *vertical line* divides the form down the middle, and suddenly there are **TWO segments***;* one on the LEFT, the other on the RIGHT. Likewise, if we bisect the figure with a *horizontal line,* we also have two segments, except they fall ABOVE and BELOW the line (6-2). So you see, by dividing either way, we can draw in halves, and make our task twice as easy.

6-1 *Vertical* bisect divides 2 parts, *sideways* .   6-2 *Horizontal* bisect divides 2 Parts, *up and down.*

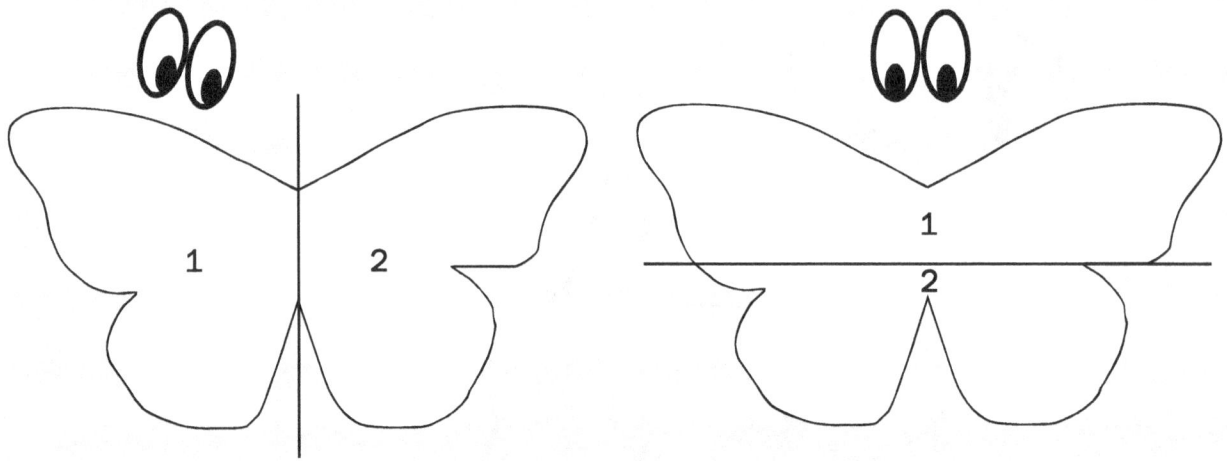

Now study illustration 6-3. With **BOTH** a *vertical* and *horizontal* line, there are **FOUR parts, right?**

6-3 **Vertical** and **horizontal** bisects divide the shape in to **4 segments.**

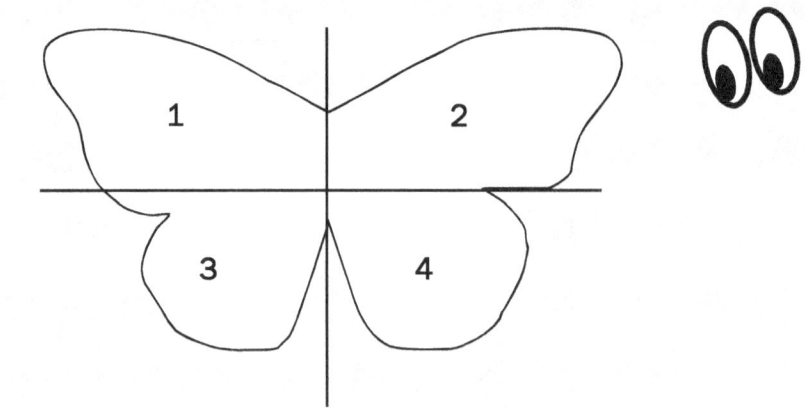

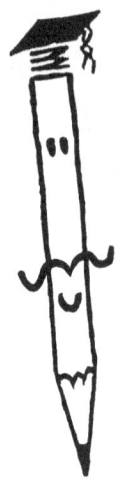

By having 4 sections, wouldn't the drawing approach be four times easier? Sure makes sense, but let's see.

Visualize the figure STREAMLINED, and crisscrossed (6-4). In this fashion it's easier to determine the *overall* proportions. As you can tell, the base is equal to the height, whereas the TOP is equal to the base and height COMBINED. Next, let's look at the subsections on illustration 6-5. They appear as four separate *triangles,* don't they? I've designated them as the "left," "right," as well as "upper" and "lower tapers" (6-5). For those of you who would like to know, a *taper* is a word used to describe a shape made by lines that converge (come together) to provide reference points.

6-4 Crisscrossed streamline helps determine OVERALL proportions.

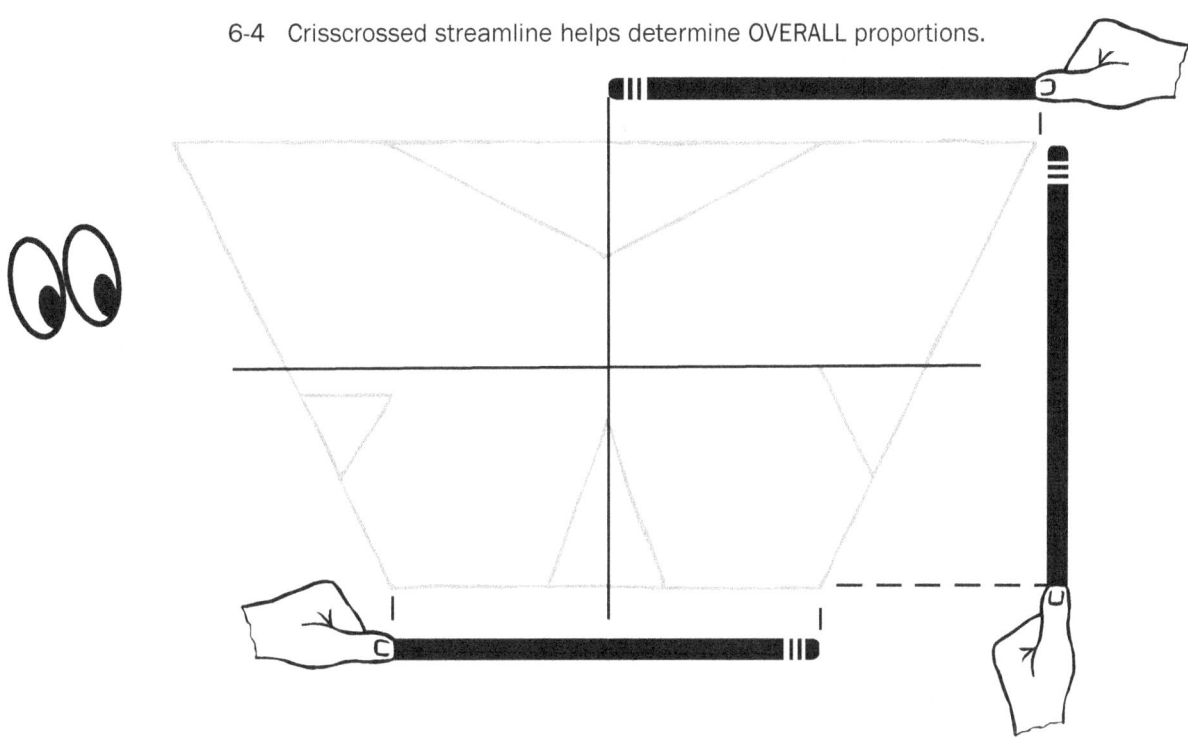

6-5 Crisscrossed streamline helps see there are 4 TRIANGULAR tapers, each with 3 REFERENCE POINTS.

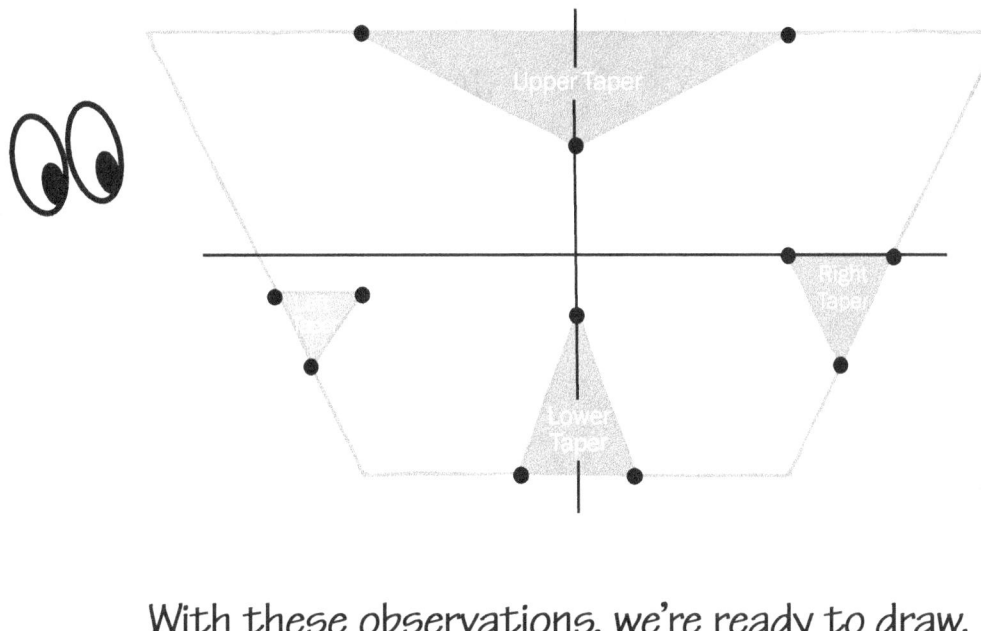

With these observations, we're ready to draw.

OBJECTIVE: Replicate the butterfly wings in **3 CRISSCROSSED** stages.

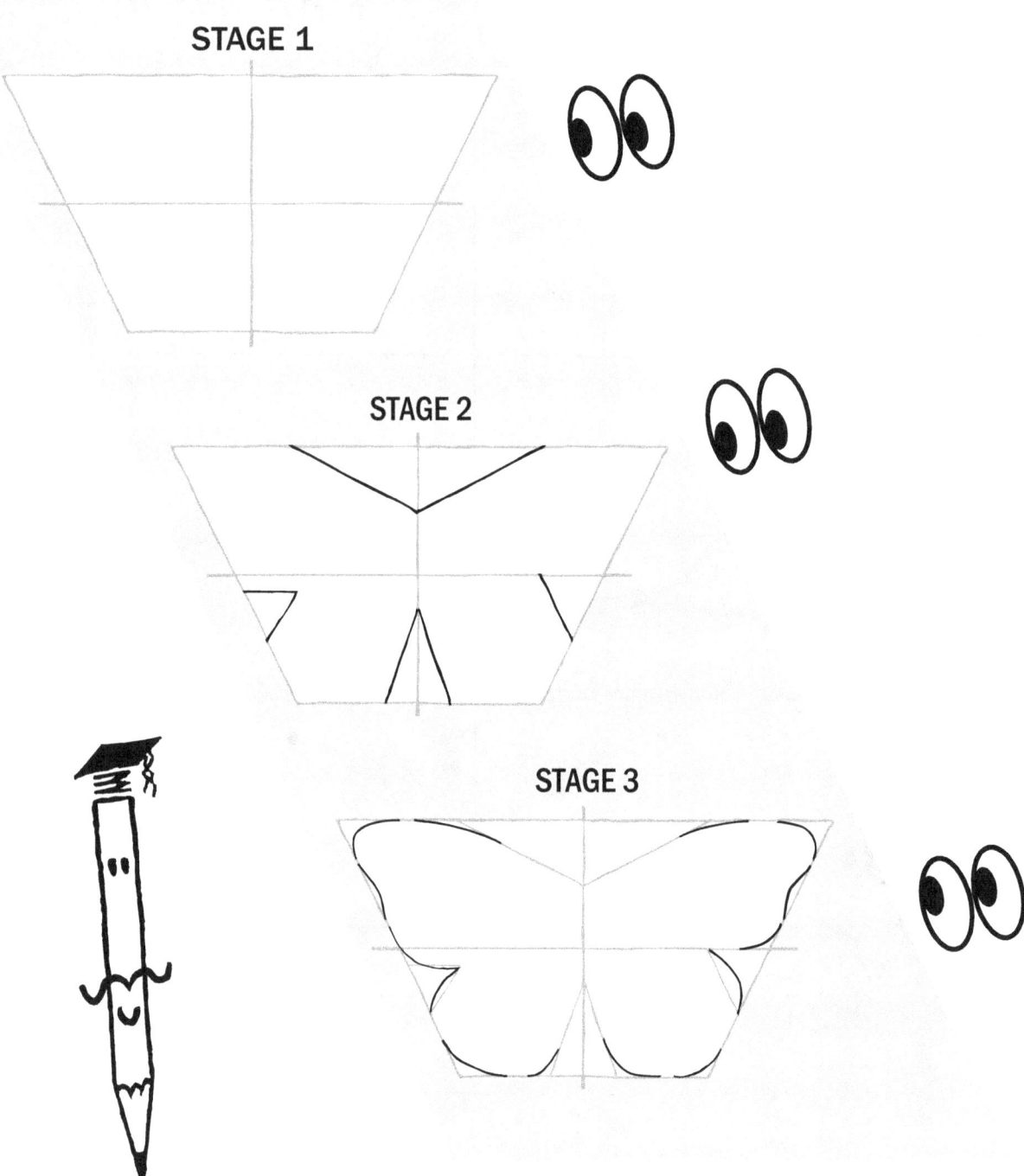

STAGE 1

STAGE 2

STAGE 3

Organizing your steps into stages, plus subdividing your figure, can make the drawing process even easier.

STEP 1   A LOGICAL START

Since we're applying the *crisscross* method, first we need to draw the bisects. On a new sheet of paper, *LIGHTLY* **center** a fairly **LEVEL** *HORIZONTAL* line from nearly side to side. Next, locate the middle of your line, and divide it with a fairly **PLUMB,** *VERTICAL* line. Make the size about the same as your horizontal line. Combined, they form a "plus" symbol or "cross," as shown in illustration 6-6.

Those of you who might be thinking about folding your sheet to find the centers...please don't. Estimate distances by eye. You will benefit much more by exercising your peepers.

6-6 LIGHTLY center a horizontal line on your paper.
Then bisect it with a vertical line.

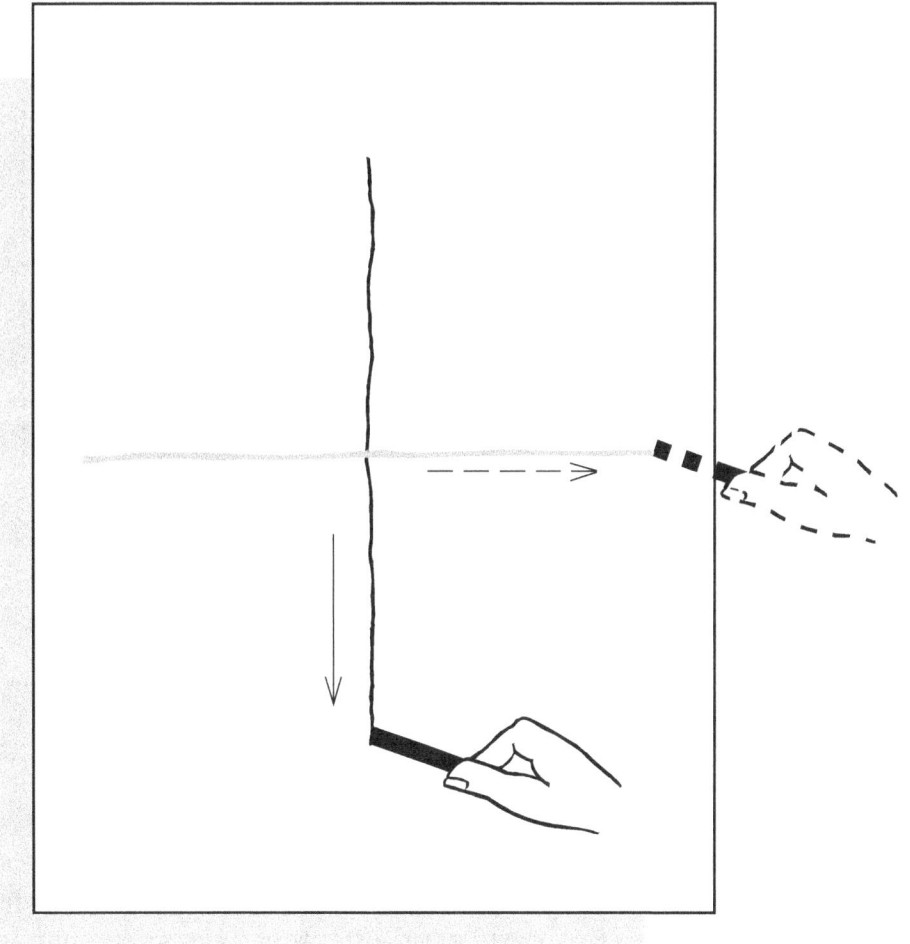

CHOOSE A HEIGHT THAT IS FEASIBLE (WILL WORK)

Being that our survey on page 93 (illustration 6-4) revealed the figure's TOP is TWICE its height, we must make sure the height we select for OUR drawing doesn't exceed TWICE the short span of our paper (6-7). Why? Because without such careful consideration, when the time comes to draw the top of the figure, we could run out of room. As you can see, this is one of those situations where, again, it pays to think ahead.

6-7 The 2 dots *centered* on the HORIZONTAL bisect line represent the figure's height. That distance doubled from the VERTICAL bisect (for the TOP) checks whether it will fit on our paper.

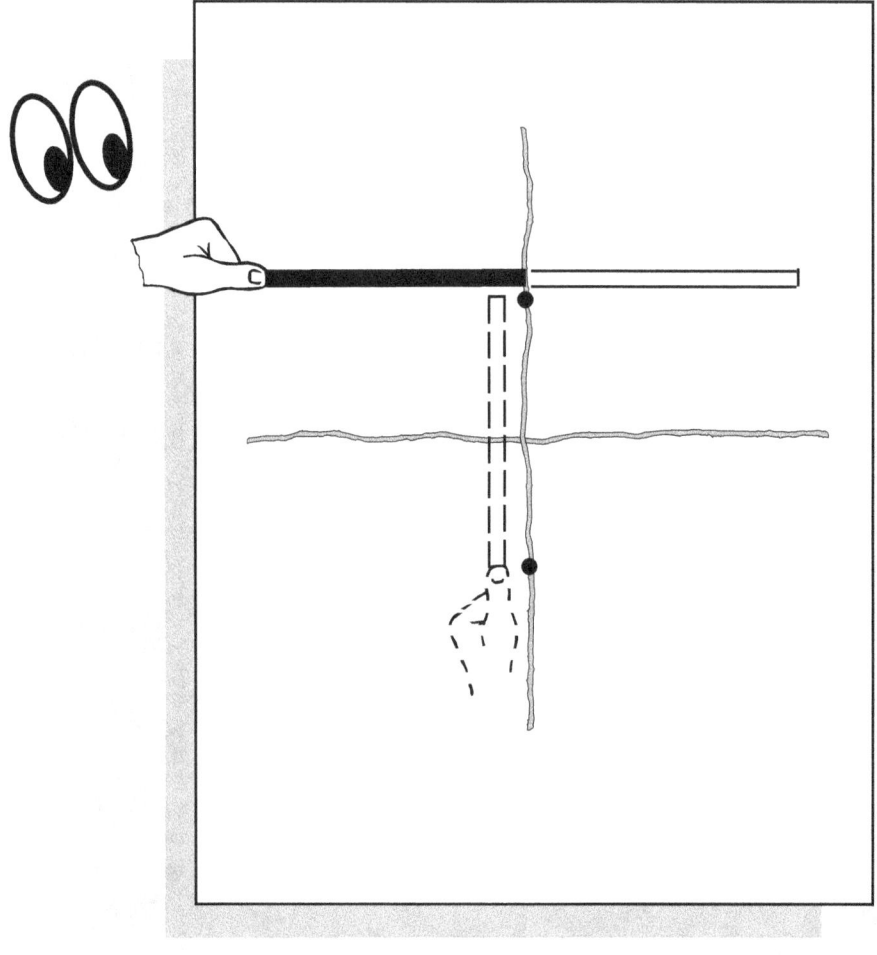

LOCATE THE HEIGHT FOR *YOUR* FIGURE WITH 2 REFERENCE POINTS

Bearing in mind that the crisscross method is being utilized, *HALF the height* will need to be centered on the VERTICAL bisect line, *above* the HORIZONTAL, and the *other HALF below*. For a workable size, I recommend that you place a dot about *midway* up from your *horizontal* line as shown by illustration 6-8 (next page). After that, take an upright pencil reading of that distance (6-9). Then, move it *down* by aligning your *eraser tip* with your horizontal line. Where your *thumb* is, place another dot (6-10).

6-8 Mark a dot ABOVE your *horizontal* line to represent *upper* HALF of the height.

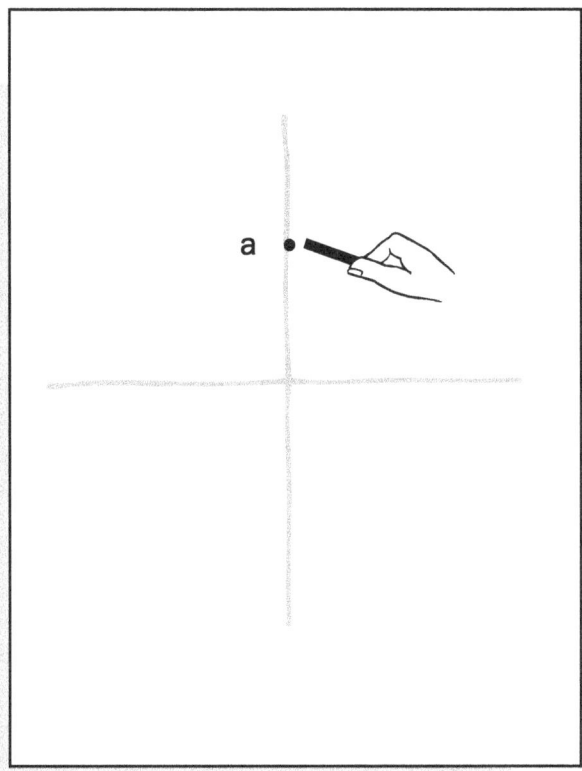

6-9 Take a pencil reading from your dot to your *horizontal* line.

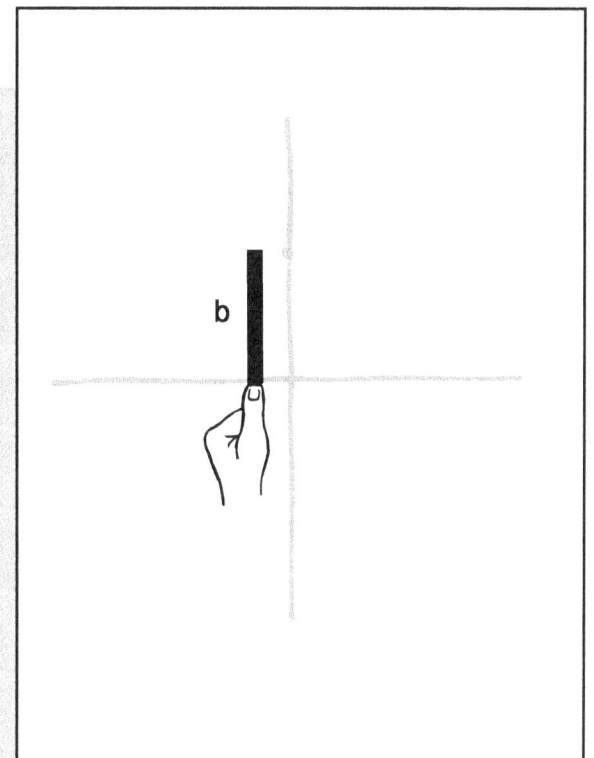

6-10 Mark a dot BELOW your horizontal line to represent the lower HALF of the height.

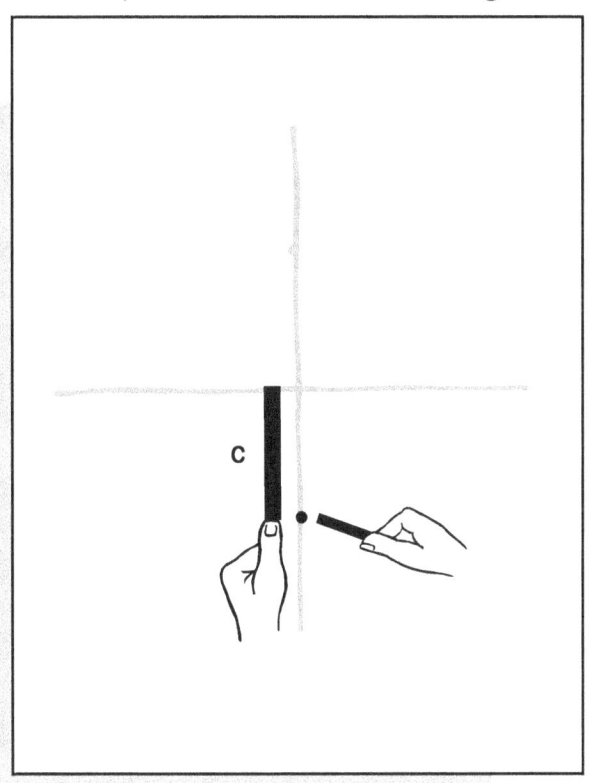

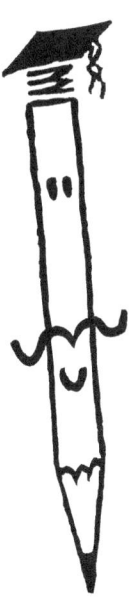

HOLD on to your pencil check. You'll need it for the next step.

During our initial survey (page 93) we learned that the base of the figure is equal to the height. Your pencil check (held over from your previous step) already provides half that. *If you've released the reading, simply take another one* **from the HORIZONTAL bisect, to EITHER your top OR bottom dot.** Next, turn your pencil **sideways.** After that, place the eraser tip on the **lower CENTER dot** and mark a reference point by your thumb (6-11). Then repeat the procedure by moving the increment once to the **right** (6-12). Adjust your dots *visually* as needed and **LIGHTLY** link them with a LEVEL line (6-13).

6-11 Locate LEFT corner reference point.

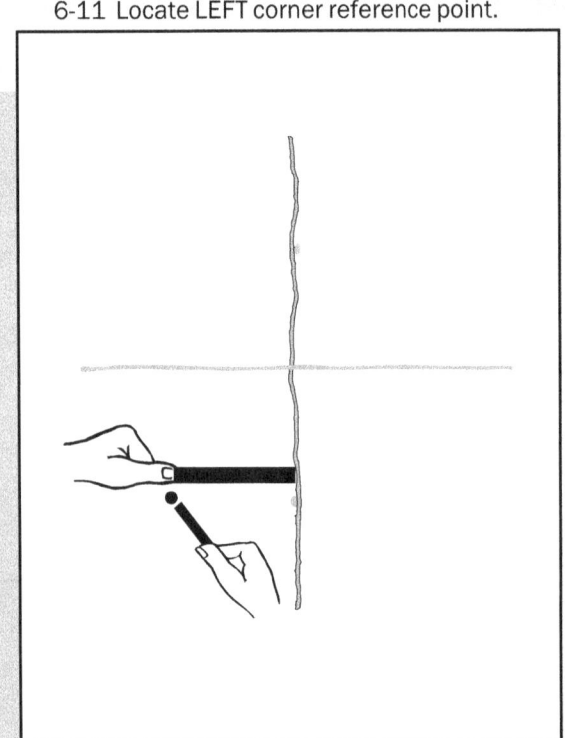

6-12 Locate RIGHT corner reference point.

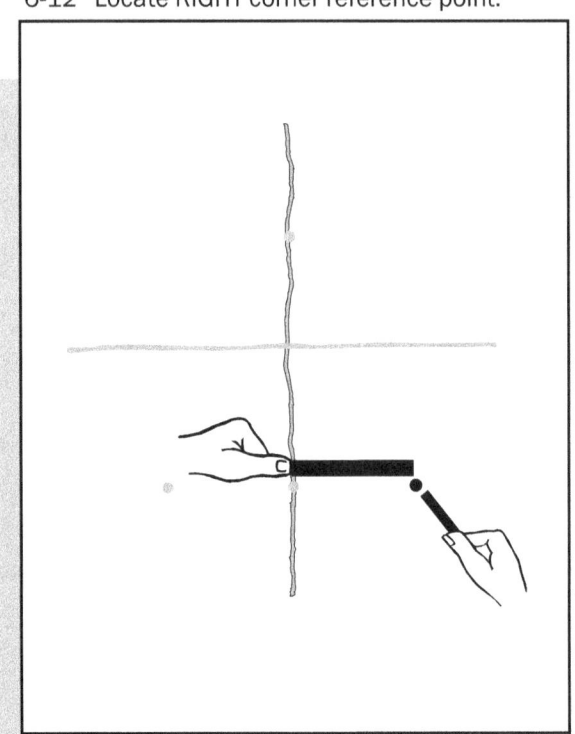

6-13 *LIGHTLY* connect dots with a line to establish base.

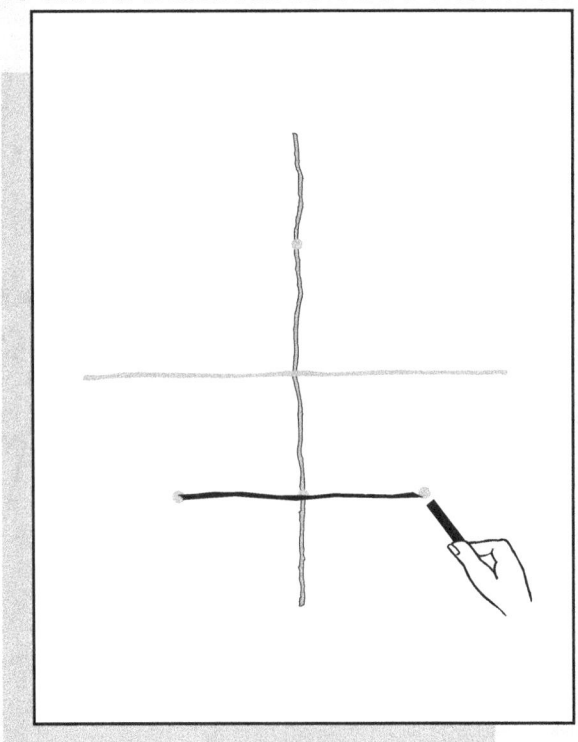

STEP 5 ESTABLISH THE STREAMLINED TOP & SIDES

Our earlier observation (page 93) showed the wing TOP measured DOUBLE, compared to the base. To locate those proportional reference points for YOUR drawing, take a *horizontal* pencil check of YOUR bottom line. Next, move the span to the **UPPER** dot. Be sure the *eraser tip* touches it. Then place a dot **by your thumb,** to locate the **LEFT** corner (6-14). For the *right* corner, move one interval over, in that direction, and mark a dot by your *eraser tip* (6-15). Afterward, adjust VISUALLY and connect your dots with a LEVEL line for the *top* (6-16). Then link your upper and lower respective corner dots with a line for the *sides* (6-17).

6-14 Take a pencil reading of the base length, transfer it to the top LEFT side of *vertical* bisect, and mark a dot.

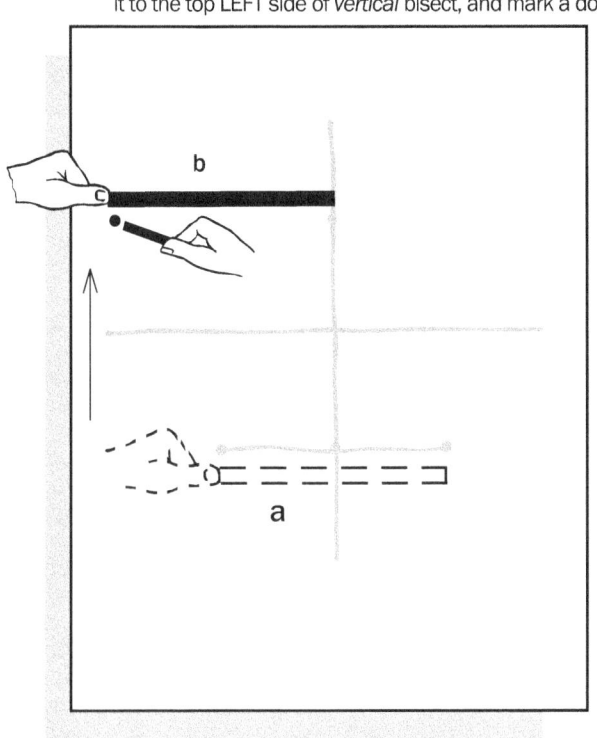

6-15 Move one interval to the right and mark with a dot.

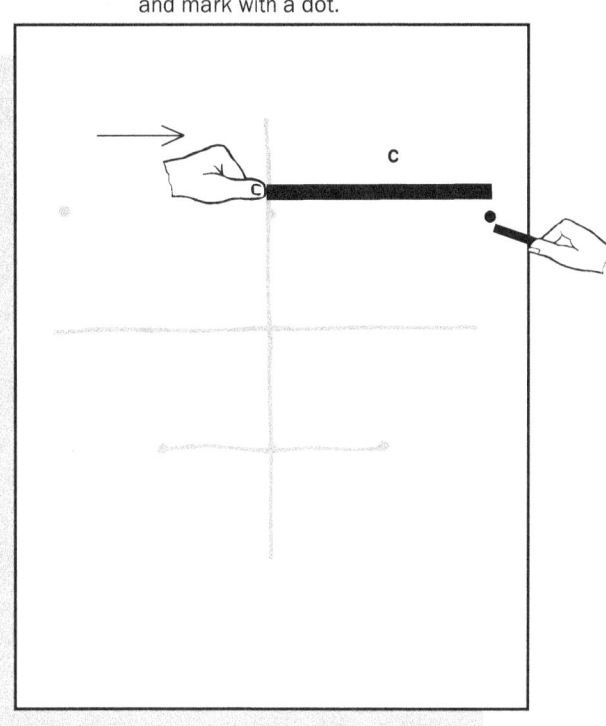

6-16 Link upper dots with a LEVEL line to establish the top.

6-17 LIGHTLY connect respective corners with lines to establish sides.

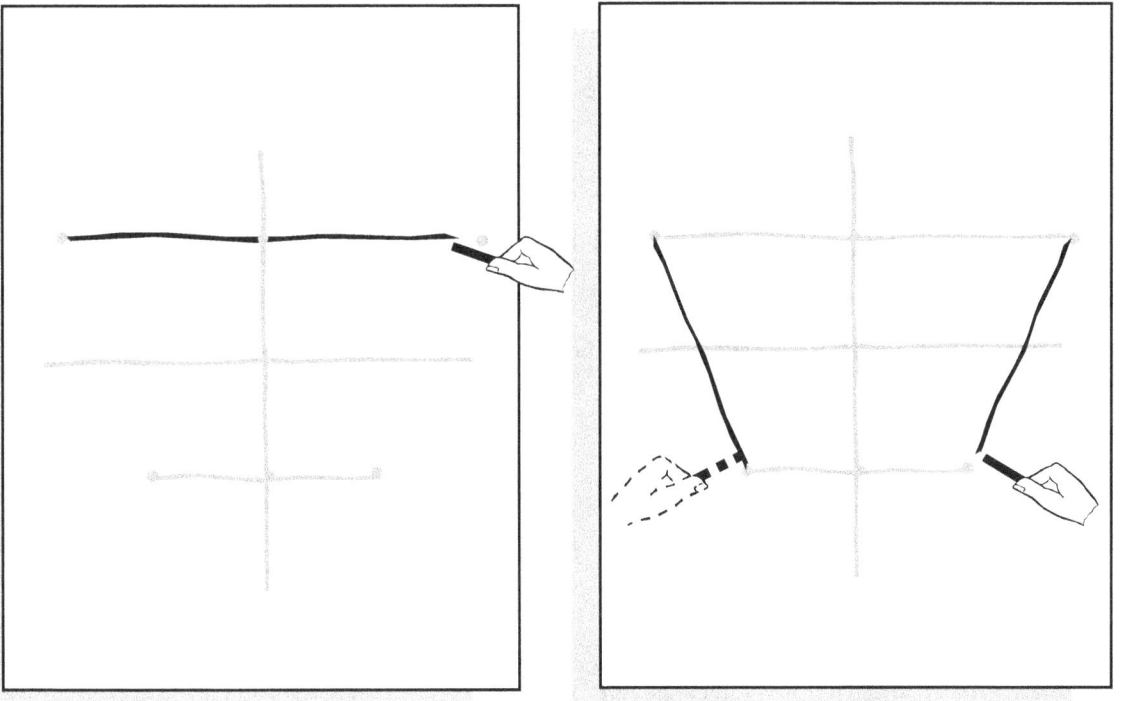

STEP 1 STUDY THE *UPPER* TAPER, THEN REPLICATE IT ON YOUR STREAMLINE

Observe that three reference points form the UPPER TAPER. As illustration 6-18 shows us, two of the points along the top span *half way* from the **VERTICAL** bisect. Plus, they align plumb with the bottom corners of the figure. As for the 3rd point, it's located DIRECTLY on the vertical bisect, *half way* between the *HORIZONTAL bisect* and the top.

6-18 TWO upper taper reference points locate one quarter in from each corner or half way from VERTICAL bisect, in each *lateral* direction. The third point locates midway VERTICALLY between HORIZONTAL bisect and the top.

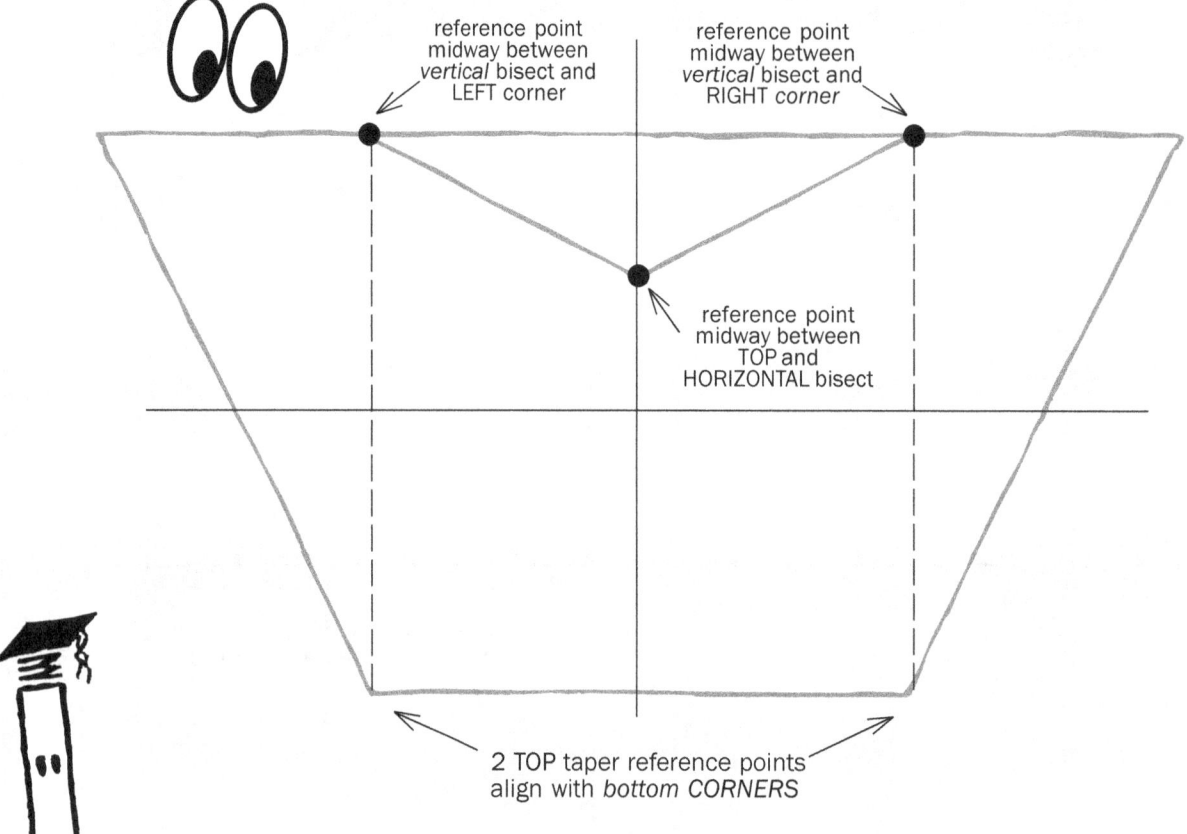

reference point midway between *vertical* bisect and LEFT corner

reference point midway between *vertical* bisect and RIGHT *corner*

reference point midway between TOP and HORIZONTAL bisect

2 TOP taper reference points align with *bottom CORNERS*

Please, DON'T BE FOOLED BY TECHNICAL APPEARANCES. Like finding coordinates on a map, we're merely surveying REFERENCE POINTS in order to plot a course for shape.

To help find the coordinates on YOUR drawing, you can go by illustration 6-18 (above) or follow the steps shown on the next page. Begin by *imagining* there is a **PLUMB** line from the bottom LEFT corner to the **TOP** of YOUR figure. Where it meets, mark a dot (6-19). Repeat the procedure from the lower RIGHT corner, as well (6-20). Next, place the 3rd point *midway* along the upper portion of the VERTICAL line. *Estimate* the distance visually, or pencil check between the **top of YOUR figure** and the **MIDDLE HORIZONTAL line** (6-21). Then LIGHTLY connect your dots with a pair of diagonal lines (6-22).

6-19 Vertically align TOP with BOTTOM
      LEFT corner and place a dot

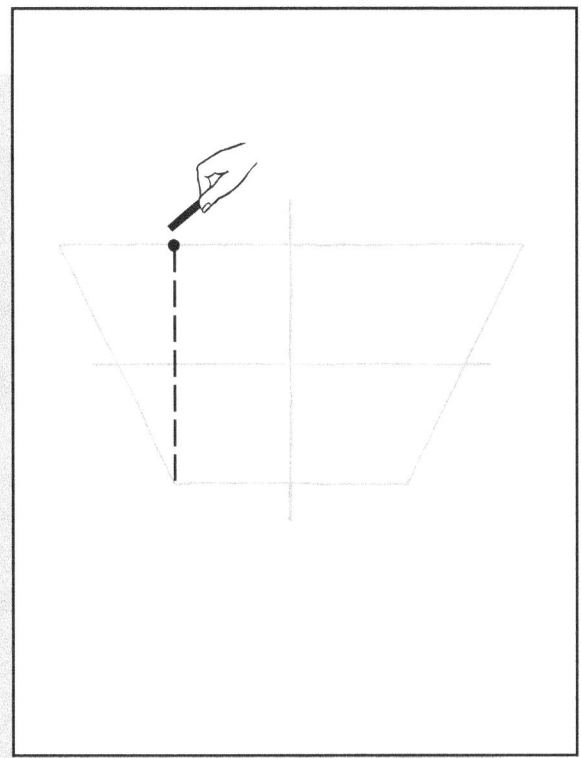

6-20 Vertically align Top with BOTTOM
      RIGHT corner and place a dot.

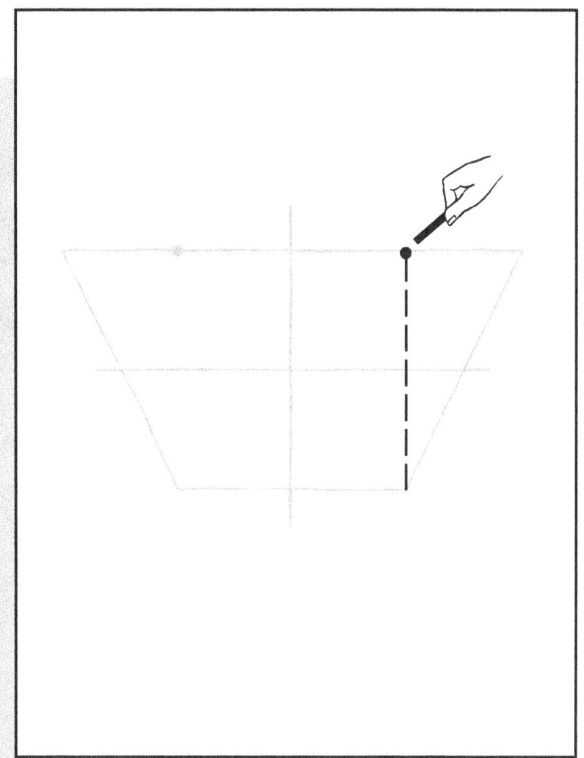

6-21 Locate third dot HALF way between
      top of figure and *HORIZONTAL* bisect.

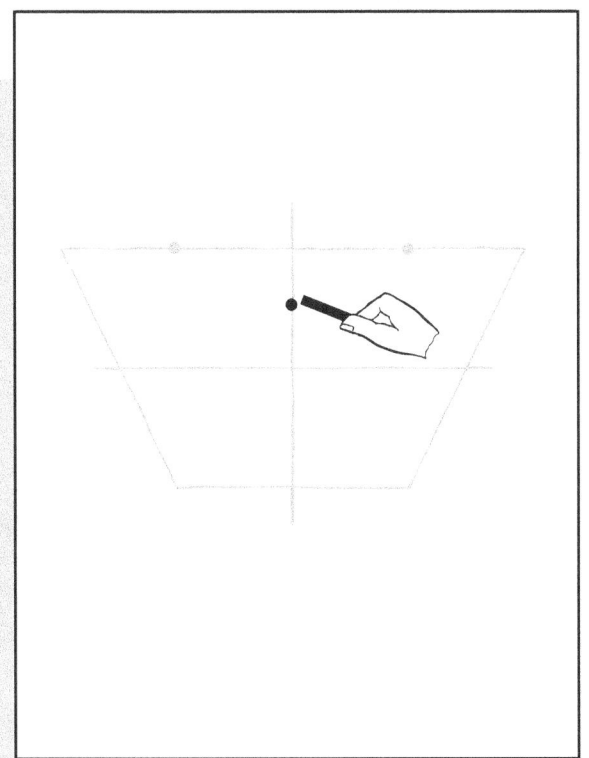

6-22 LIGHTLY connect dots with 2 lines
      to establish your upper taper.

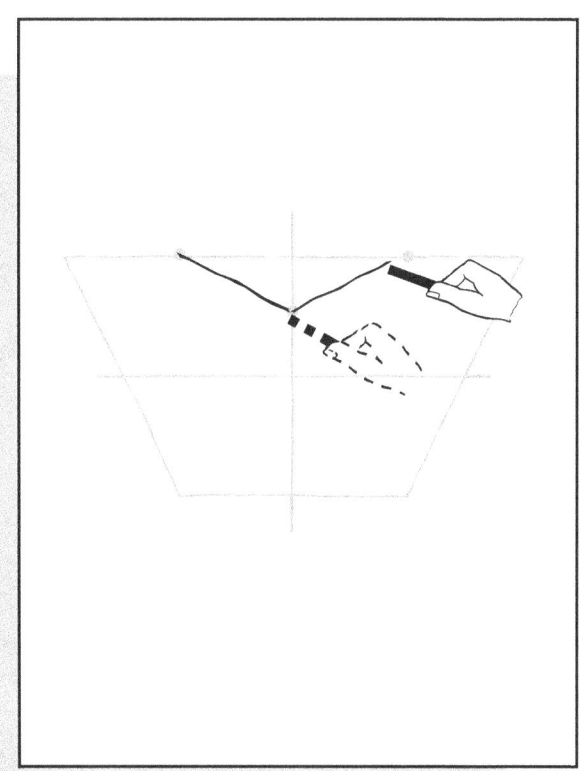

Illustration 6-23 (below) inicates that two reference points fall on the BASE line and only stretch a **quarter** of the distance from the VERTICAL bisect, in both directions. In contrast, the *"TIP"* falls directly on the vertical center line, about a *QUARTER* of the way BELOW the HORIZONTAL bisect.

6-23   Two reference points lie on the base line, one fourth of the way from the VERTICAL bisect.
        The TIP is located on VERTICAL bisect, one fourth of the way from *the HORIZONTAL* bisect.

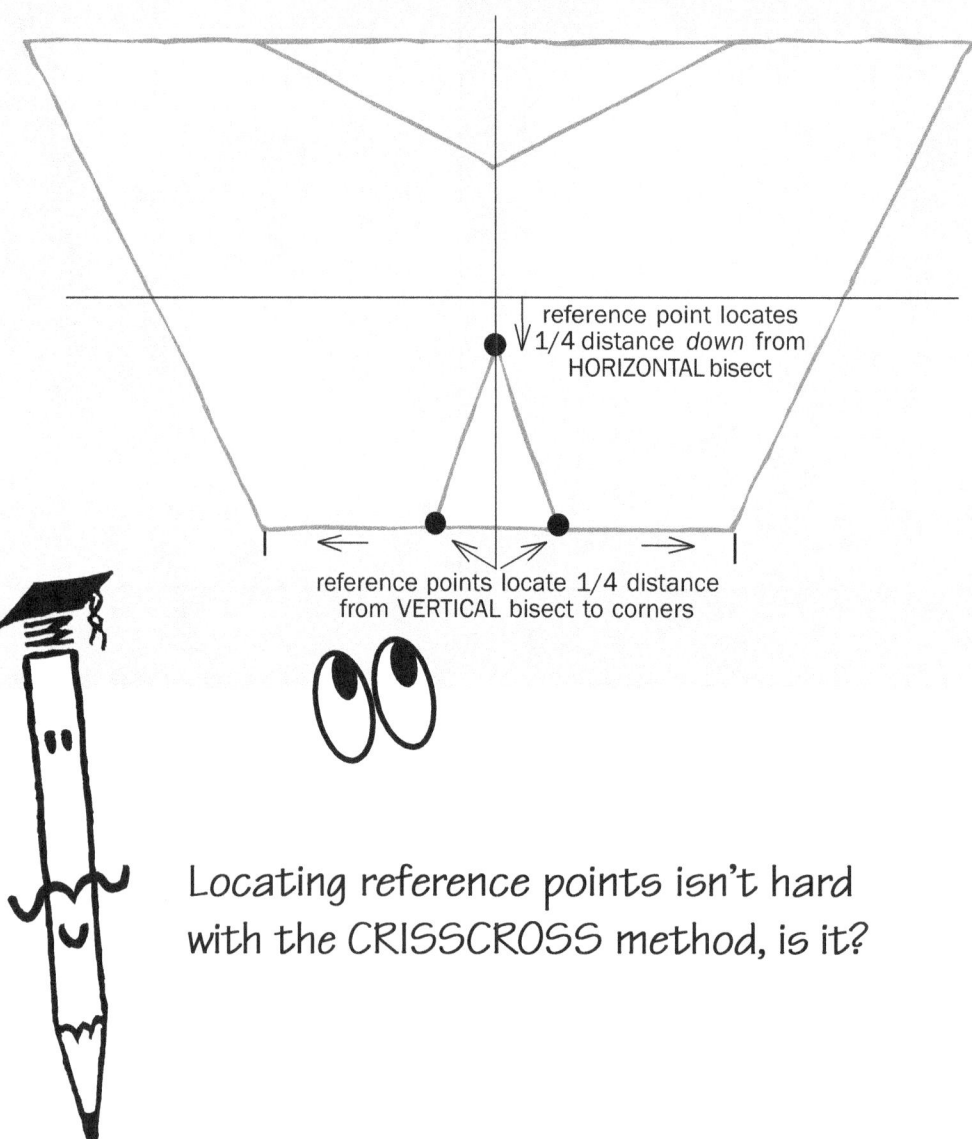

reference point locates
1/4 distance *down* from
HORIZONTAL bisect

reference points locate 1/4 distance
from VERTICAL bisect to corners

Locating reference points isn't hard
with the CRISSCROSS method, is it?

To find YOUR lower taper position in SCALE, continue to estimate by eye and mark reference point locations with dots. The next page shows how. Begin by placing the first dot on the bottom line, a quarter of the way from the VERTICAL bisect to the left corner (6-24). Once that's done, repeat the step to the right (6-25). Next, locate a dot ONE QUARTER of the distance *BELOW* YOUR HORIZONTAL line, along the VERTICAL bisect (6-26). For the follow through, LIGHTLY connect your 3 dots with 2 lines (6-27).

6-24 Place a dot ON your base line a QUARTER distance between the VERTICAL bisect & LEFT corner.

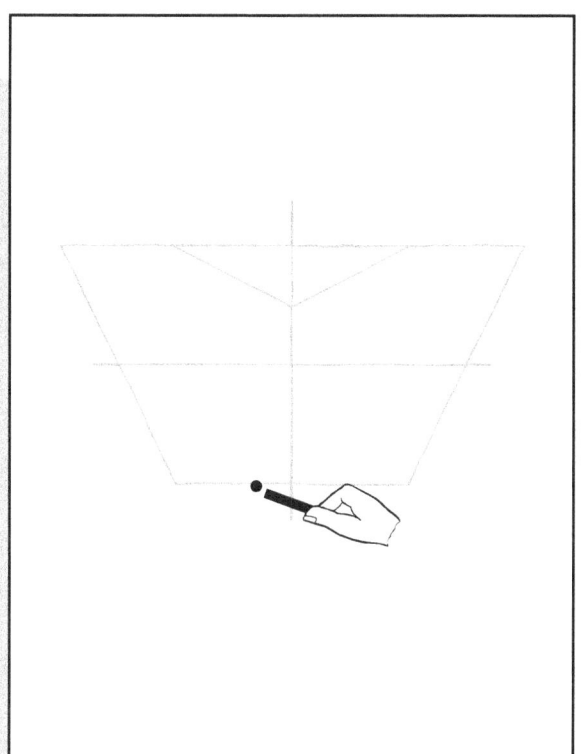

6-25 Place a dot ON your base line a QUARTER distance between the VERTICAL bisect & RIGHT corner.

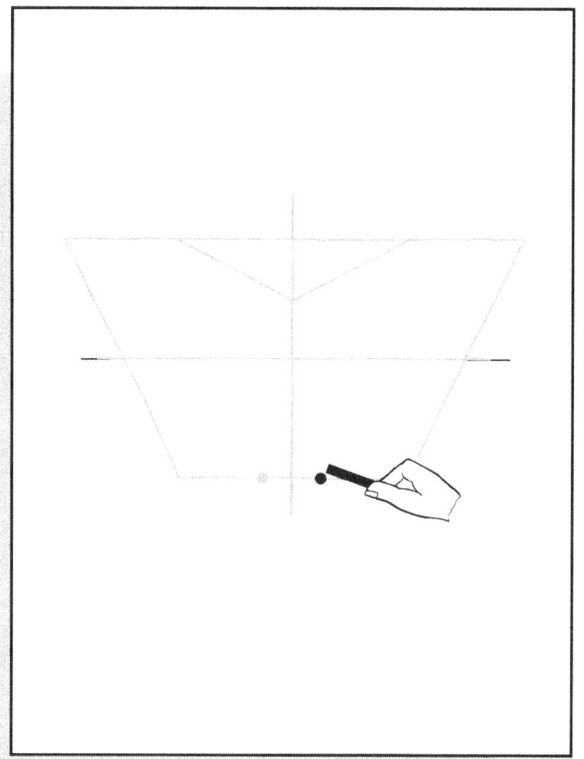

6-26 PLACE a dot ON your VERTICAL bisect a 1/4 span DOWN from the HORIZONTAL bisect.

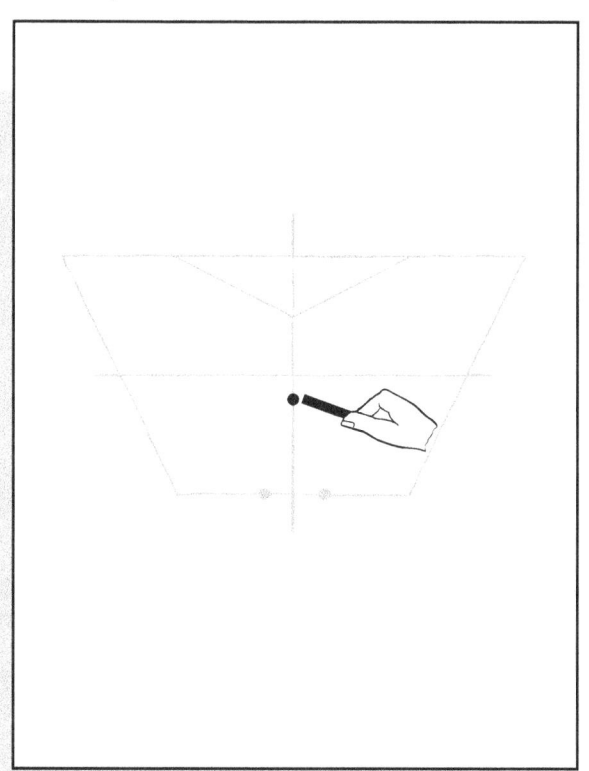

6-27 LIGHTLY connect your 3 dots with 2 lines.

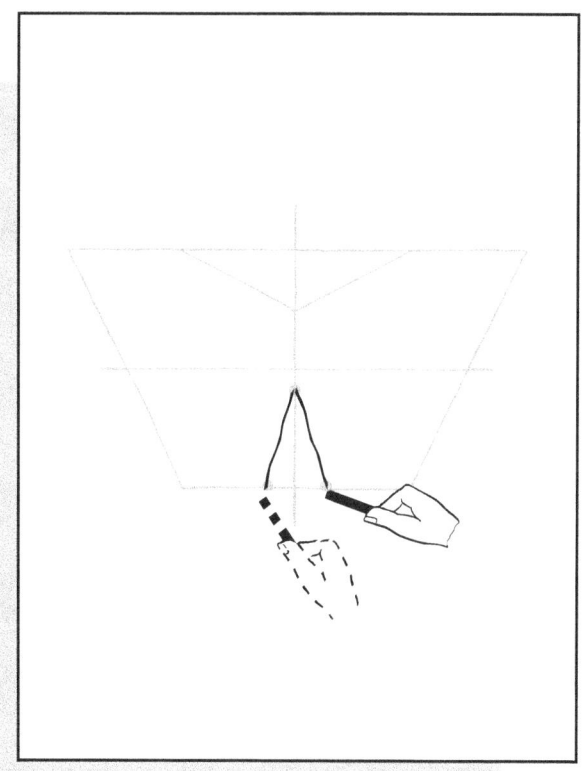

Illustration 6-28 below reveals that TWO horizontal points align level, midway between the **horizontal** dividing line and the *tip* of the *lower taper*. The reference point on the right is plumb with the bottom left corner of the figure, whereas the lower middle point, and the left reference point, locate on the *side*.

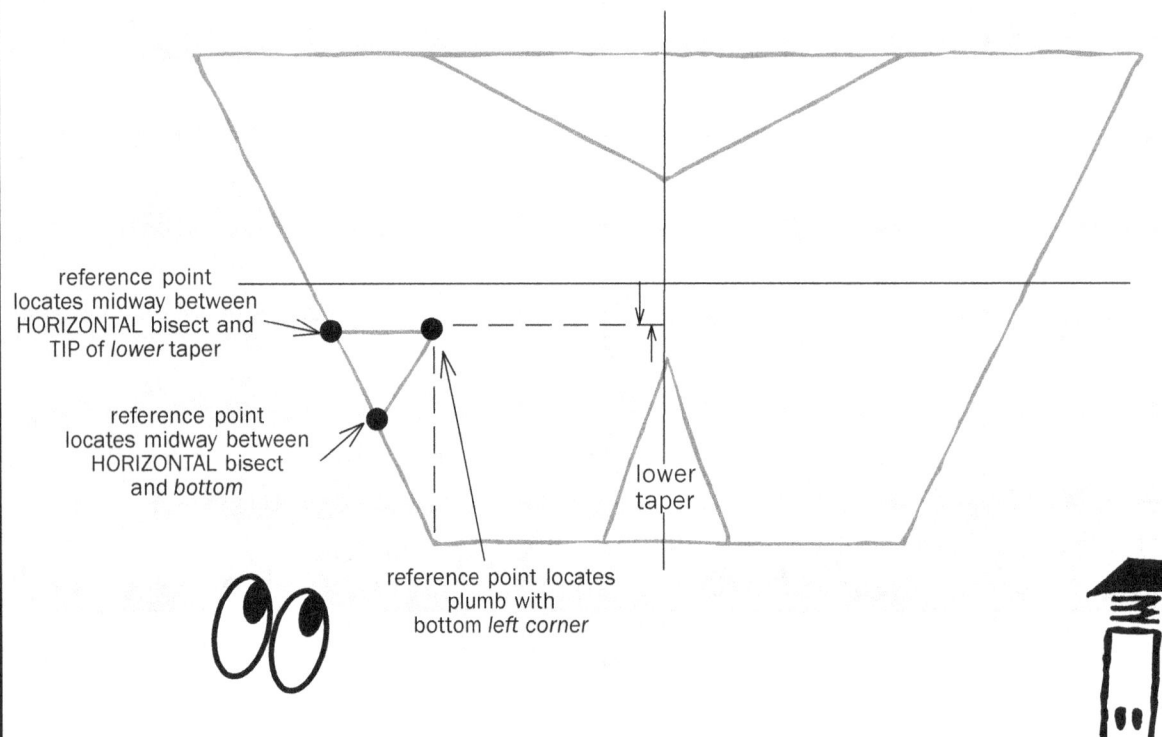

6-28   Left taper survey shows 2 reference points locate on the SIDE.
One of those points, plus another, align level MIDWAY between
the *horizont* bisect and the top of the lower taper. The point on
the right is plumb with the bottom left corner.

reference point
locates midway between
HORIZONTAL bisect and
TIP of *lower* taper

reference point
locates midway between
HORIZONTAL bisect
and *bottom*

reference point locates
plumb with
bottom *left corner*

lower
taper

By now, as I'm sure you've gathered, the
special feature of the crisscross method
is that you only need to look for the
NEAREST horizontal and/or vertical
bisect, in order to locate reference points.

To position YOUR left taper, illustration 6-28 (above) can be your guide. Or if you prefer, you can follow the procedures shown on the next page. Begin by aligning one reference point horizontally between the HORIZONTAL bisect line and the TIP of the LOWER taper (6-29). After that, position a dot LEVEL with the previous one, and PLUMB with the bottom left corner (6-30). Then, mark the third dot HALF WAY between your HORIZONTAL bisect line and the base of your figure (6-31). Finish the triangle by LIGHTLY connecting your dots with lines (6-32).

6-29 Place a dot on the left side, horizontally aligned midway between the TIP of your lower taper and horizontal bisect.

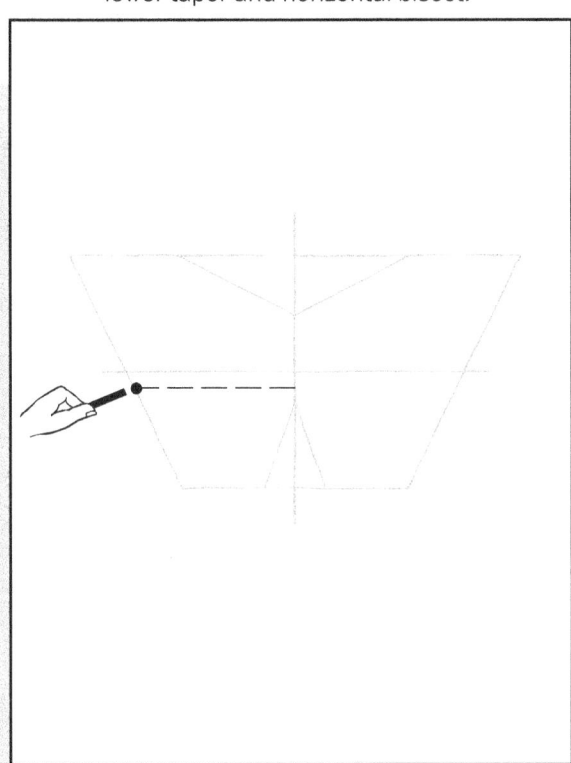

6-30 Locate a dot VERTICALLY aligned with your BOTTOM, left corner and EVEN with your SIDE dot.

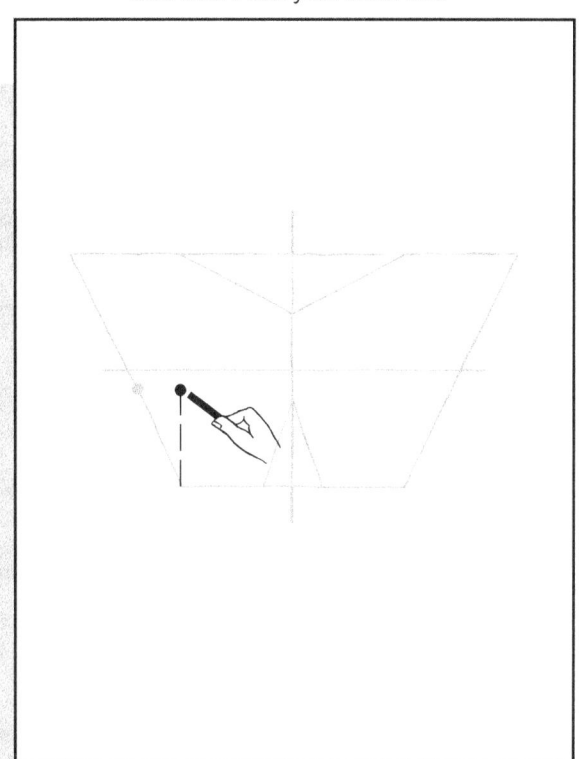

6-31 Place a dot on the LEFT **SIDE** midway between your HORIZONTAL bisect and the LEFT corner.

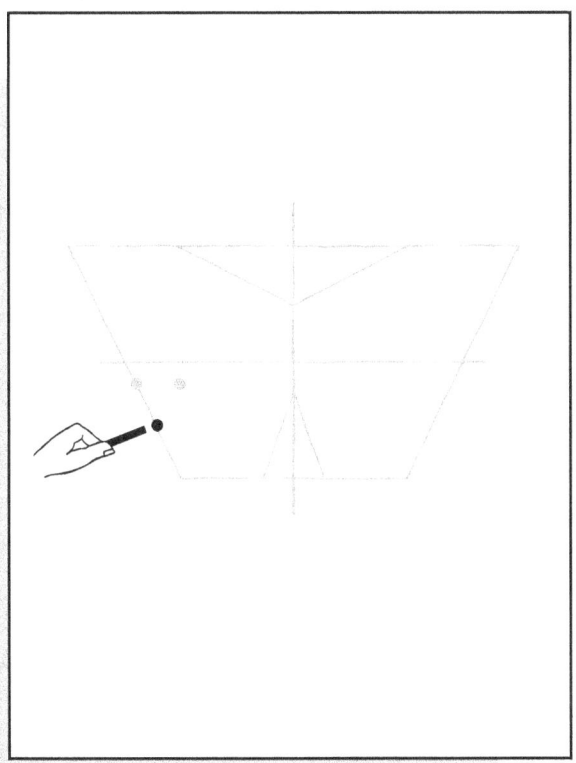

6-32 LIGHTLY connect your 3 dots with 2 lines to establish the LEFT taper.

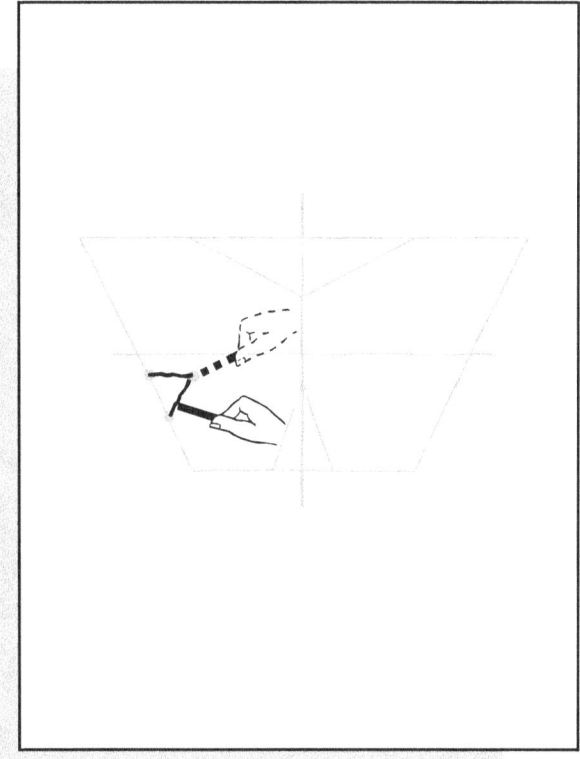

STEP 4 STUDY, THEN ESTABLISH THE *RIGHT* TAPER

Illustration 6-33 shows us that TWO of the right taper reference points fall conveniently on the HORIZONTAL bisect. In fact, one of them aligns with the bottom right corner, and the other intersects at the right SIDE of the figure. As for the 3rd reference point, it locates along the SIDE, about halfway BETWEEN the middle HORIZONTAL bisect line and the bottom.

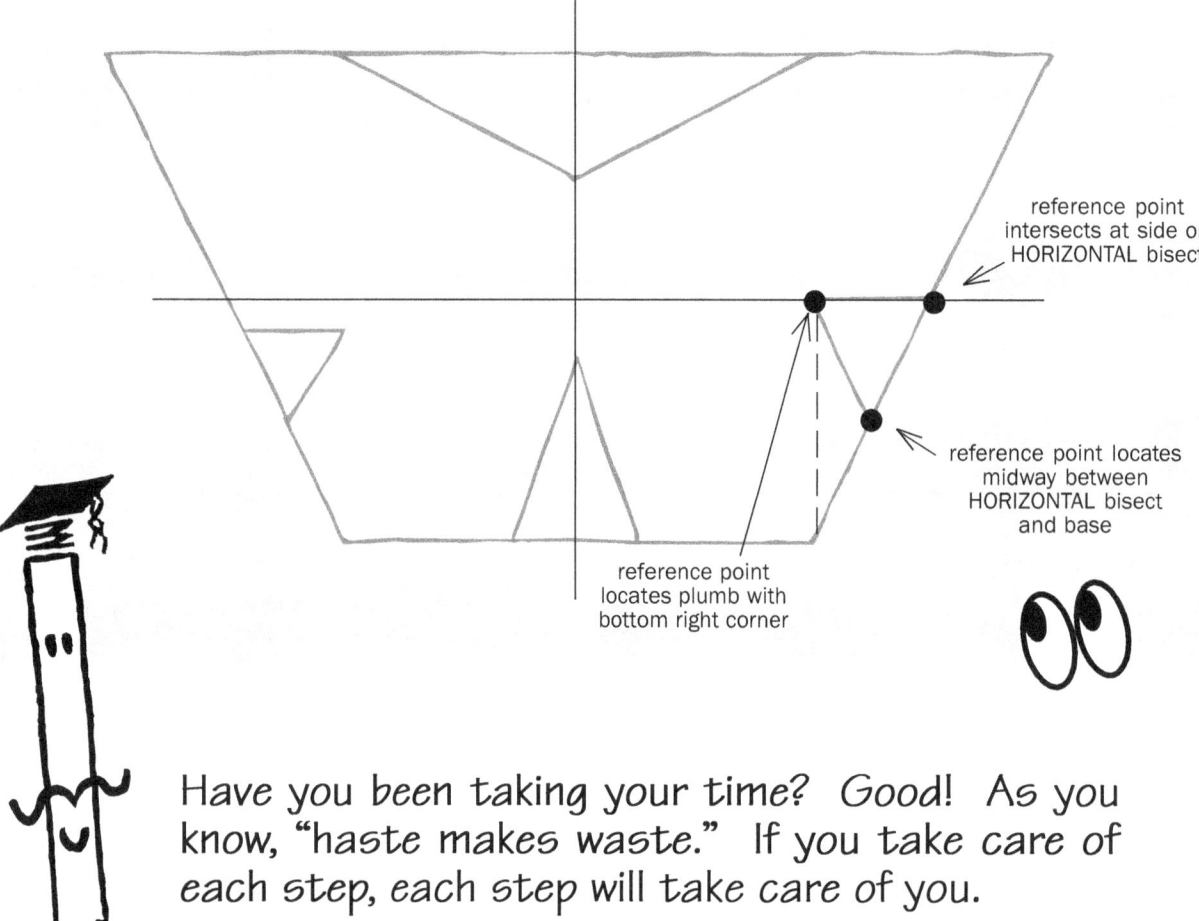

6-33 Right taper survey shows two reference points are on the horizontal bisect. One is EVEN with the bottom corner. The other is on the SIDE. The third is also on the side but MIDWAY between the horizontal bisect and the bottom.

reference point intersects at side on HORIZONTAL bisect

reference point locates midway between HORIZONTAL bisect and base

reference point locates plumb with bottom right corner

Have you been taking your time? Good! As you know, "haste makes waste." If you take care of each step, each step will take care of you.

To help you find the "coordinates" (or positions) PROPORTIONALLY on *your* drawing, use illustration 6-33 (above) and/or follow the step by step instructions shown on the next page. Begin by marking a dot on *YOUR* HORIZONTAL bisect. Make sure it's PLUMB with the right bottom corner (6-34). Once that's done, place another dot. This one should be positioned DIRECTLY on your figure's RIGHT **SIDE, half way** between your horizontal bisect and the bottom (6-35). In order to establish the taper, you just need to LIGHTLY connect your two reference points with a line (6-36). The rest of the sides are already there (along your horizontal line and streamline edge).

6-34 Place a dot on the HORIZONTAL bisect PLUMB with bottom right corner.

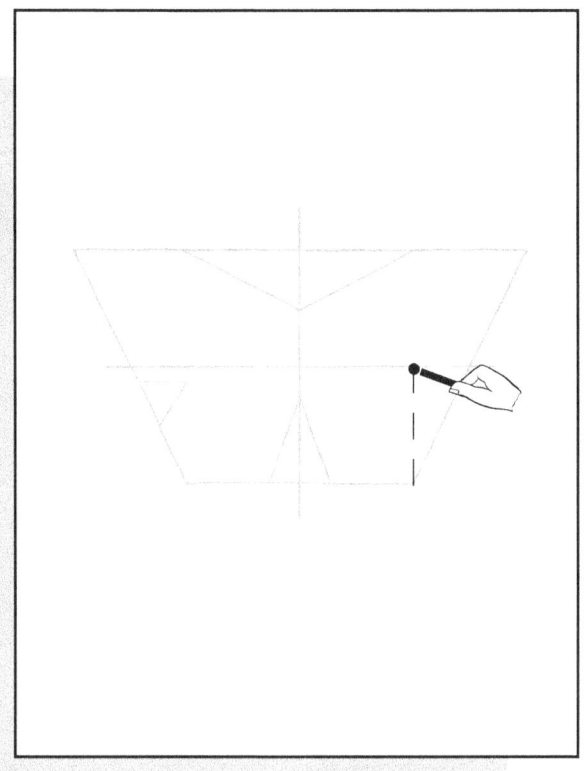

6-35 Place a dot on bottom half of RIGHT side midway between horizontal bisect & corner.

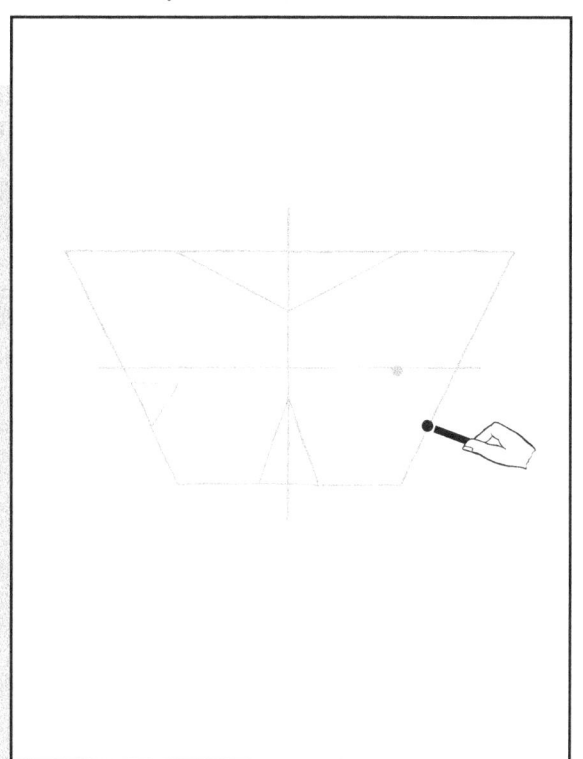

6-36 LIGHTLY connect 2 dots with a line.

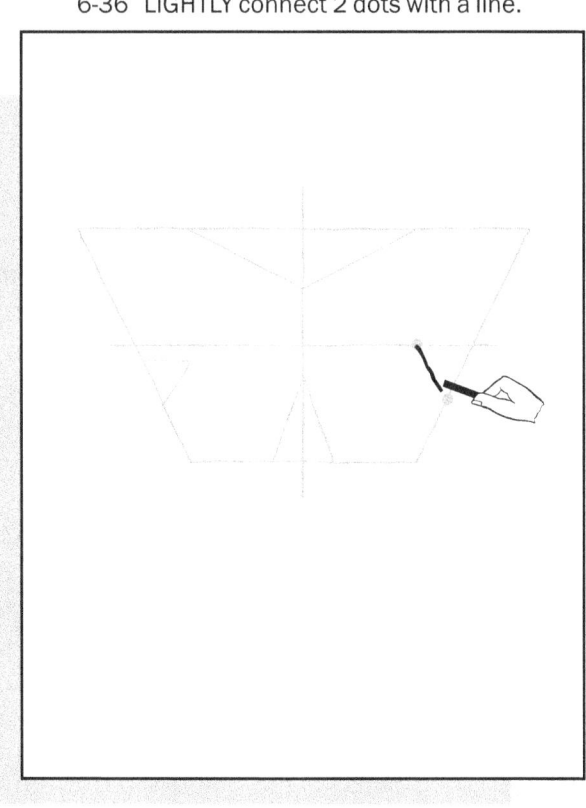

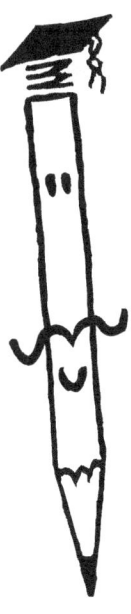

See? Like I told you in Chapter 5, just about any shape can be STREAMLINED. We're making fabulous headway!

Put three major structural components of the TRUSTY SEVEN to work, the way you learned in the previous chapter. The ones I'm referring to are: ALIGNMENT, REVERSE SPACE and PROPORTION. These usually interact and often affect all, or some of the other remaining four, namely *reference points, straight lines, curves, and angles*. To see what I mean, compare *accurate* streamline 6-37 as it SHOULD appear, to *inaccurate* sample drawing 6-38. Notice that the **reverse space** verification reveals the LEFT SIDE of the flawed example has much less **angle** than it should have. In turn, this automatically elongates the base, and alters both **proportion** and **alignment**. *The culprit is the LEFT BOTTOM CORNER.* It needs to be moved slightly to the right. Because of that, the left taper and upper taper's *left corner* have to also be moved to the right. How much? Until they become aligned plumb with the bottom left corner's *new* location. No sweat though; while the figure is still in "simplified" format, the modifications are easy to handle. The dotted lines and dark field show the adjustment.

6-37 Reverse space (gray areas) confirm side angles are correct.

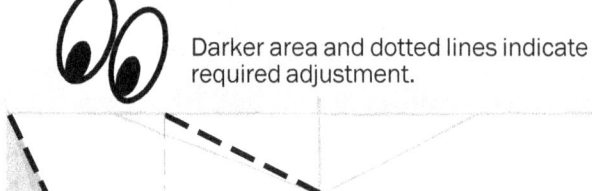

6-38 Reverse space (gray areas) indicates left side needs modification.

Darker area and dotted lines indicate required adjustment.

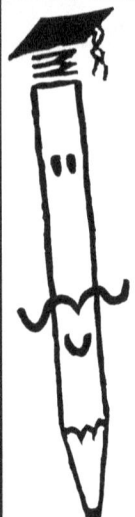

Now compare YOUR streamline to illustration 6-37. Modify yours only if really needed. Look for the OBVIOUS and keep your attention on BOTH your work and the model. Otherwise, your drawing can quickly get out of hand. After you're done refining, advance to STAGE 3.

DIRECTIONS: Using illustration 6-39 below as your guide, draw one arc at a time, *proportionally* on *YOUR* streamline. Follow a clockwise direction, or your own preferred sequence.

TIP Please do not place your drawing sideways because some curves may seem "easier" for you to duplicate in another position. This kind of practice can form a habit, and become an undesirable crutch. As you complete each curve, check for accuracy by comparing not only your arcs, but also the *reverse shape* they create, with respect to the same corresponding portions on the model. The upper left corner, shown in gray, exemplifies.

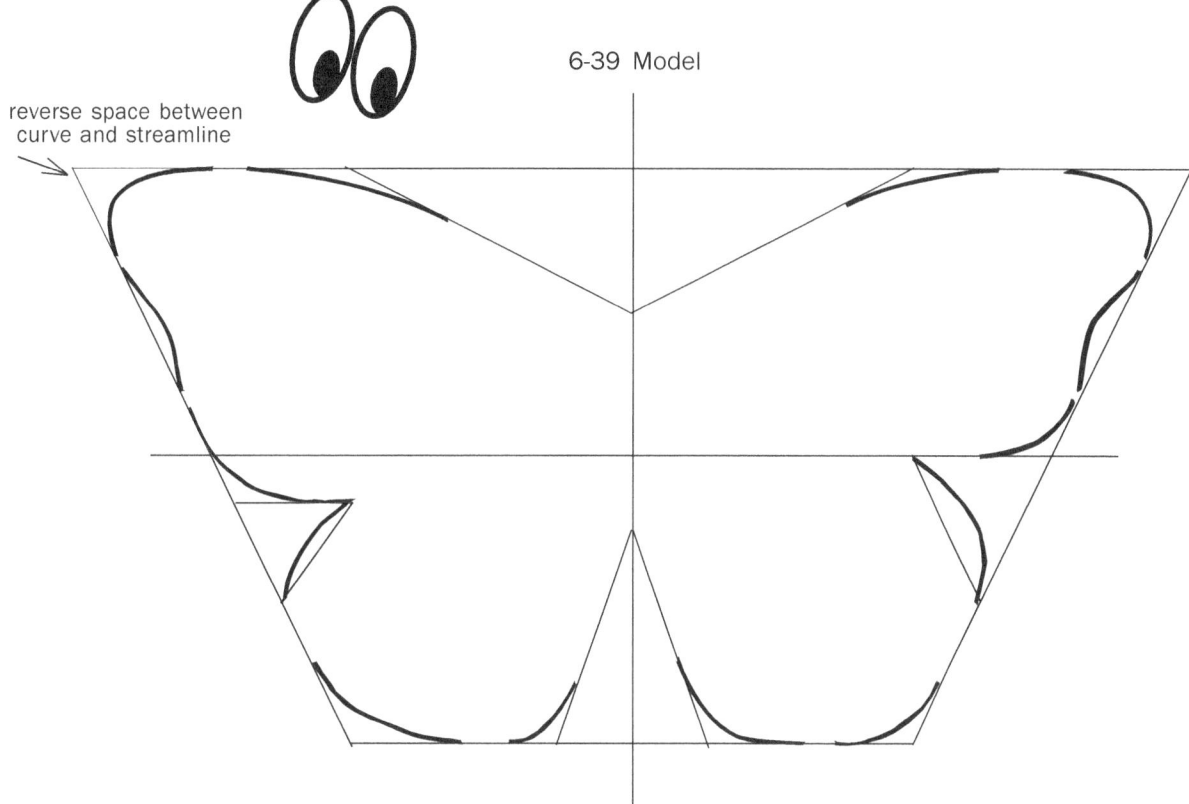

6-39 Model

reverse space between
curve and streamline

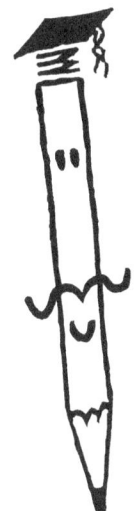

Having made certain your figure "reasonably"matches model 6-39 above, erase your streamline and the crisscross. Then, marvel at your results, and those of others, displayed on the next page.

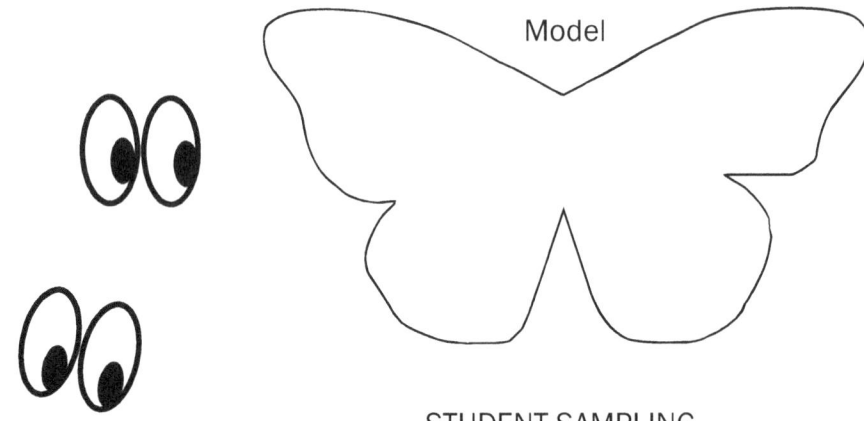

Model

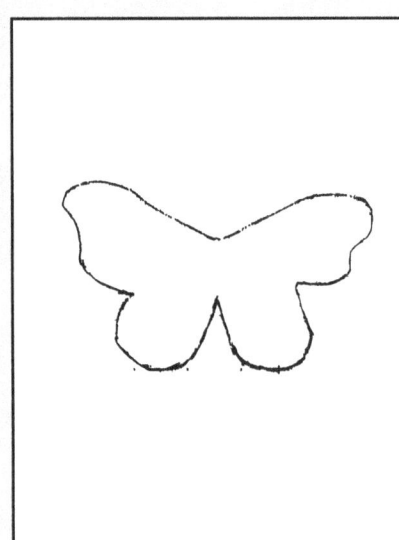

STUDENT SAMPLING

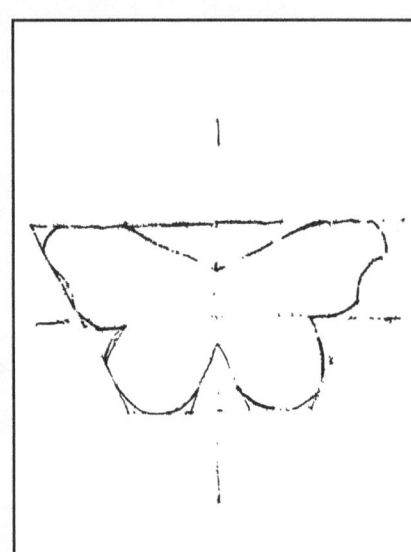
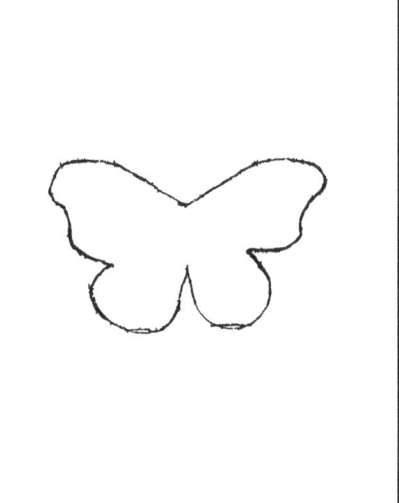

From my view point, these examples are not an exact match compared to the book illustration, but they are all pretty good. Be content with your drawing too! Prize what you learned as much if not more than what you drew. After you've rested, and had a chance to reflect on your experience, put what you've absorbed to good use.

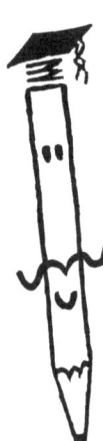

Do the supplemental exercise.

CHAPTER 6
SUPPLEMENTAL EXERCISE

Objective: Replicate the Clover Leaf
(in PROPORTION and LARGER than shown)

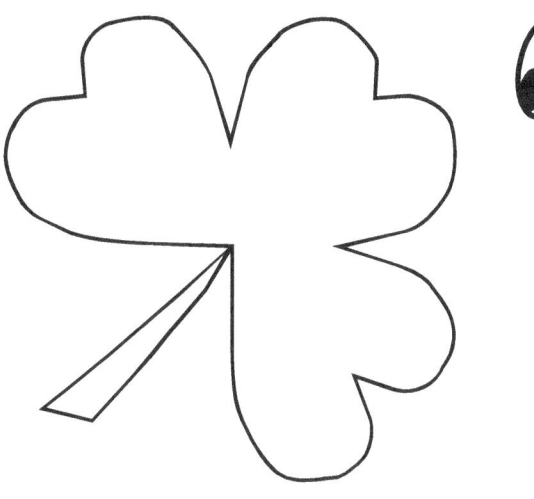

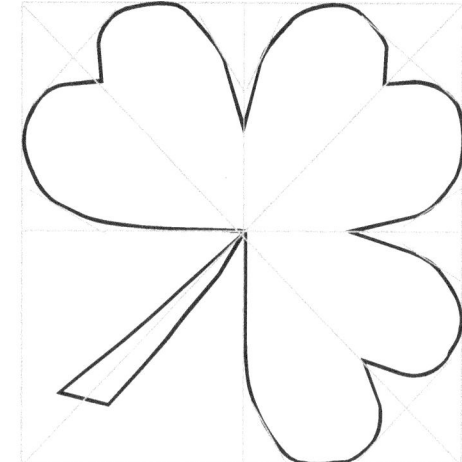

RECOMMENDATIONS

1. Visualize the figure streamlined, bisected vertically and horizontally as well as *diagonally* (6-40).
2. Use illustration 6-40 to make your observations.

NOTICE THE SYMMETRY & DISTINCTIVE TRAITS

- The overall length and width are the same.
- The mid-point, where the stem and leaf connect, is smack dab in the center.
- The bottoms of the middle petal and left petal are *level* with the center.
- The left side of *middle* petal and *left* side of *bottom* petal are *plumb* with the center.
- The bottom *right* taper and upper *left* taper align, corner to corner.
- The top right taper and stem also align corner to corner.
- Each leaf taper point locates about a *third* of the distance from corner to center.
- The two taper points, *between* leaves, locate about *midway* from edge to center.

3. On a new sheet of paper, proceed to draw. Initiate with a square, along with not only a standard crisscross (or plus symbol), but also an "X" shaped bisect. Together, they will help you form the clover leaf in two main stages: first, the streamline, then the curves.

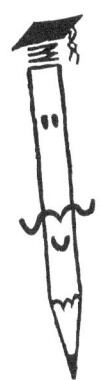

If you'd like to see the illustrated steps, please turn the page.

6 Easy Steps to Replicate the Clover Leaf

1 On a blank piece of paper, lightly form a square. Make it bigger than shown (6-41).
2. Divide your square into quarters with a plumb and level line (6-42).
3. Divide your square with 2 *diagonal* lines by connecting opposite corners (6-43).
4. Draw the figure STREAMLINED in your square by locating taper angles and reference points (6-44).
5. Add curves to your streamline, making sure to guide by the model, and reverse spaces. Also, remember what you learned in Chapter 5. Specifically, you should pay special attention to distinguishing features in order to catch a better likeness of THIS *particular* clover leaf (6-45).
6. Erase the excess, as indicated by broken lines, to reveal your finished rendition (6-46).

6-41   **Step 1**   6-42   **Step 2** 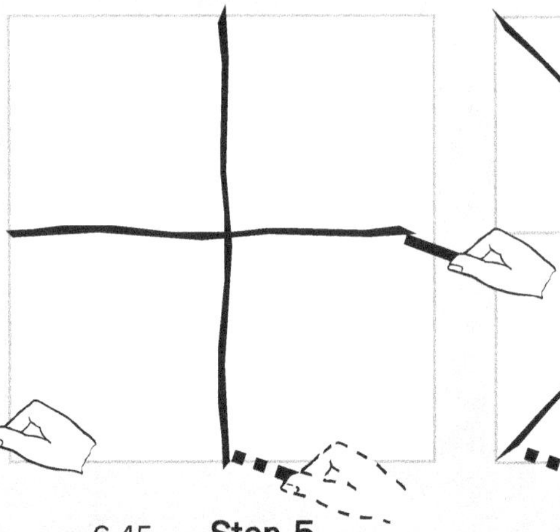   6-43   **Step 3**

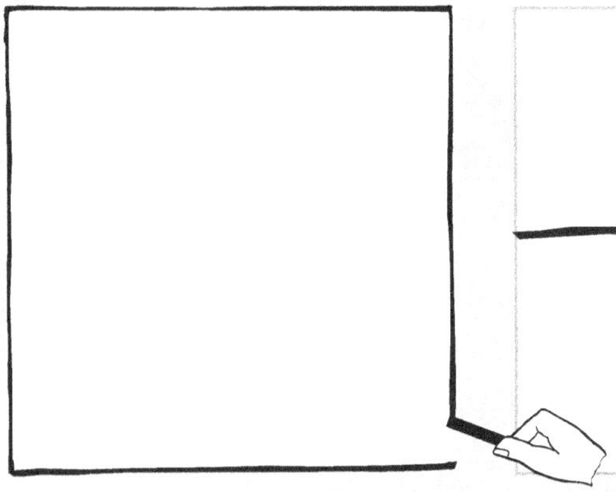

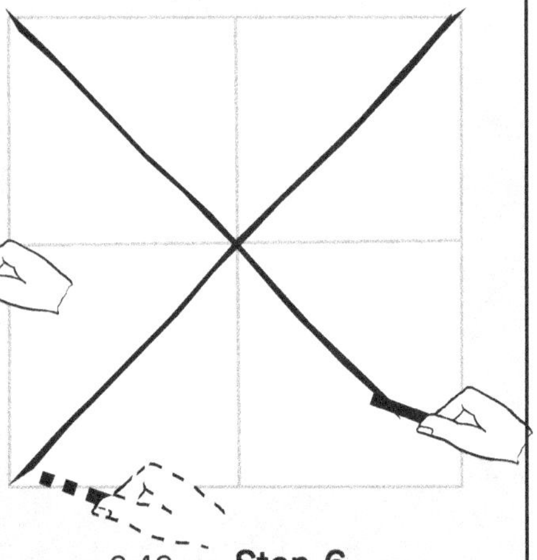

6-44   **Step 4** 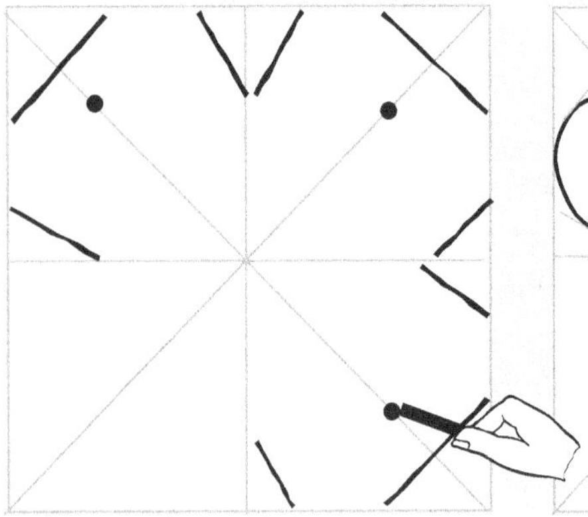   6-45   **Step 5** 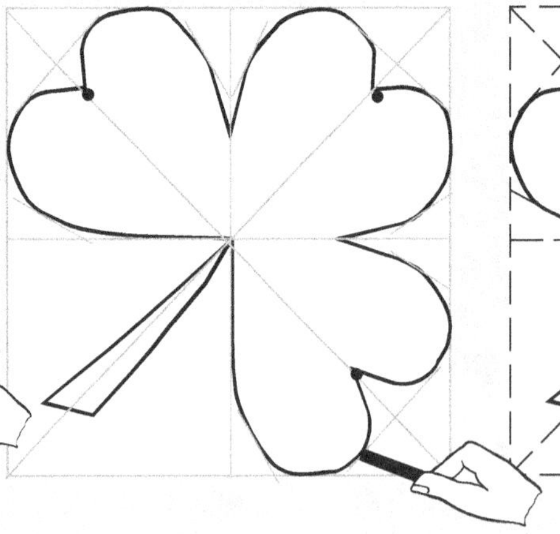   6-46   **Step 6**

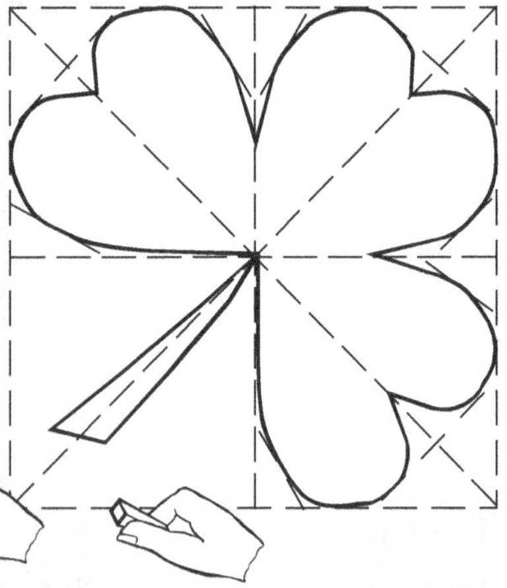

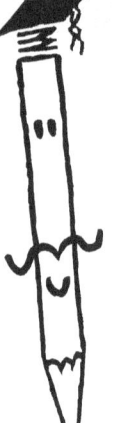

Are you wondering how well others completed their supplemental exercise? Assuming you've finished yours, feel free to take a peek at theirs on the next page.

CHAPTER 6
SUPPLEMENTAL EXERCISE
WITH STUDENT EXAMPLES

Model

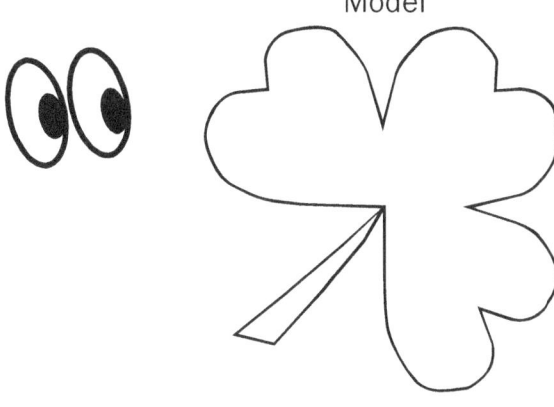

STUDENT SAMPLING

6-47	6-48	6-49

 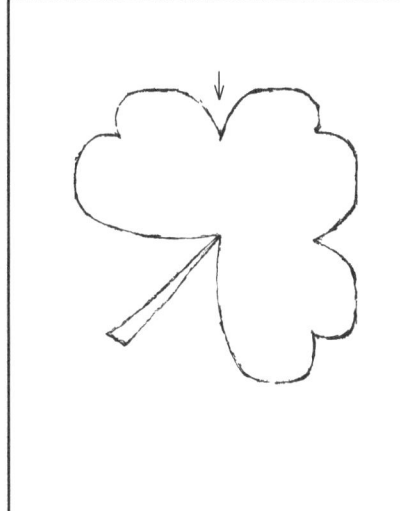 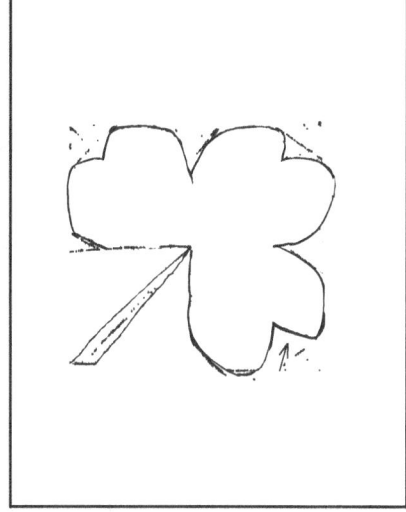

These student works are all fine. But this is not to suggest that yours should match or surpass them. The name of the game isn't to see which is the best. Compare yours to the *model* in order to spot differences and to learn from your observations. For instance, see if any of your *tapers* are short, like those on 6-47 and 6-48. Or maybe some of your curves are a little irregular, as exemplified by drawing 6-49. To help you notice subtle details like these, reverse space checks will come in handy, along with the rest of the TRUSTY SEVEN. It's a process of elimination. Make it a game of hide and seek. Pretend the culprits are trying to remain concealed and your role is to uncover them.

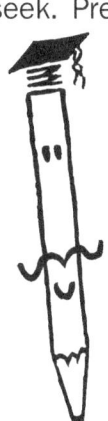

Having examined YOUR clover leaf a little more closely, (and perhaps having refined it a bit more), now be sure to read the follow-up. You have much to celebrate.

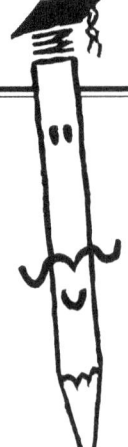

Chapter 6
FOLLOW-UP

Pat yourself on the back!
You've reached new heights!

During the entire chapter you performed brilliantly. Think about it. You completed both the streamline and the final shapes of not one, but two subjects. The first came with detailed instructions but the second was somewhat vague. This was intentional, to encourage you to prioritize (organize the sequence of stages). And guess what? You came through with flying colors.

Whether you followed the suggested steps entirely or partially, you had to depend a lot on your own devices. Beginning with the overall format, including vertical and horizontal bisects, you eased your task. Equally commendable, you estimated most of the reference point locations by eye. On top of that, during the supplemental exercise, you discovered there's another type of crisscross, specifically the DIAGONAL.

Without a doubt, this is another breakthrough for you, especially since we both know, most shapes and their subsections rarely divide at EVEN increments (or parts). That's why the CRISSCROSS method exists. Serving as extra sets of guide lines, the bisects help locate reference points more easily This is done by spotting which positions strike directly and which ones do not. Those that stray are found by simply estimating how far they appear to be from the nearest division. A nifty approach, wouldn't you agree?

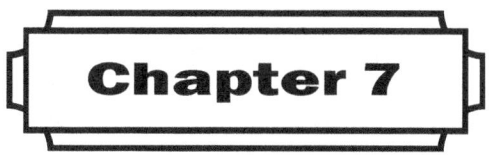

THE AD-LIB METHOD

QUESTION: What if a shape is already fairly simple and the crisscross method doesn't seem to apply?

Take the drawing of this vase.

The height is taller than twice the width, and not a single reference point falls directly on any of the medians.

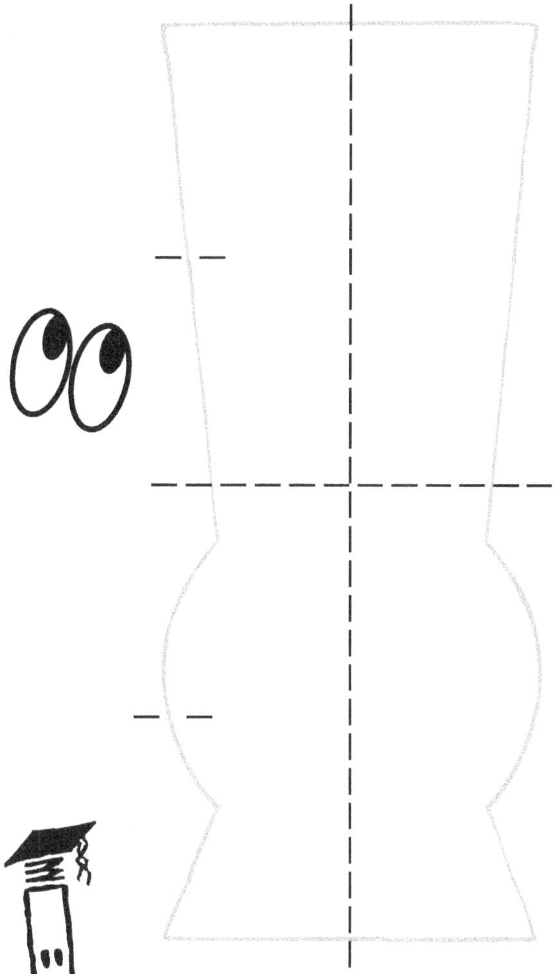

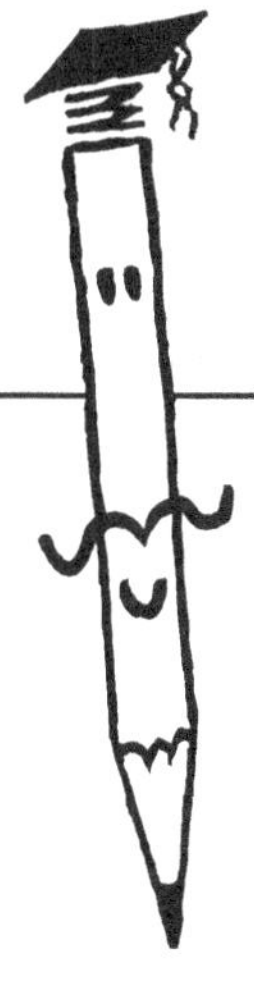

What *do* we do, now?
Read on to find out.

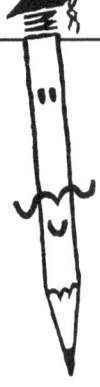

OBSERVATION 1

It's often said, "Seek and ye shall find."
There's much truth to that. Look closely
and useful clues are likely to appear.

A vertical alignment check immediately shows that the figure's top and bottom corners, along with the respective side curves are ALL aligned PLUMB (7-1). Next, we see that the converging points (where the straight lines and arcs meet) are also aligned plumb (7-2). Let's call those areas the "upper" and "lower" TAPERS. Interestingly, when we check them *horizontally*, we discover yet another distinctive feature. They are LEVEL (7-3).

7-1 Side curves, plus top & bottom
CORNERS align PLUMB.

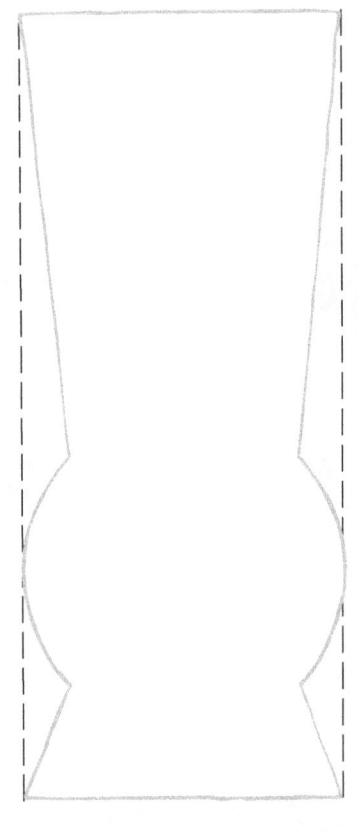

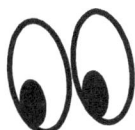

7-2 Upper & lower tapers
align PLUMB.

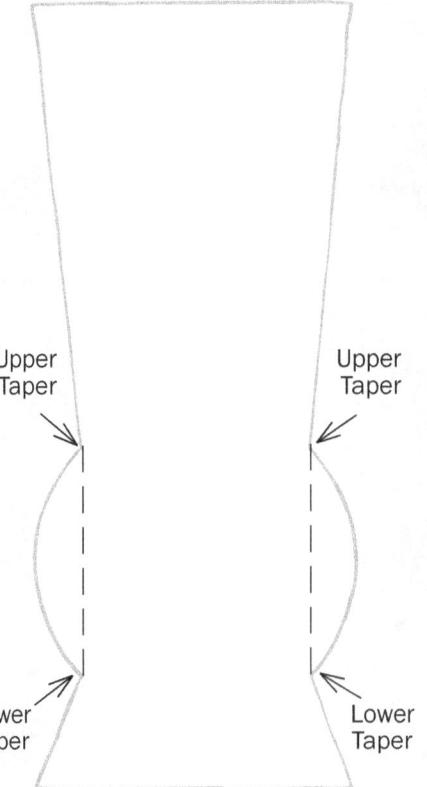

Upper
Taper

Upper
Taper

Lower
Taper

Lower
Taper

7-3 Upper & lower tapers
align LEVEL.

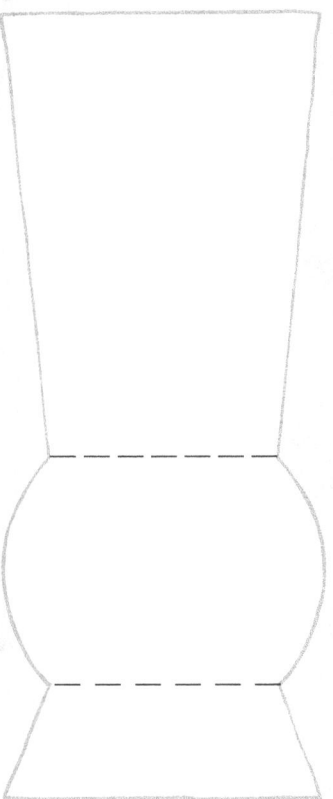

A *vertical* proportion check, indicated by illustration 7-4, reveals another important point: the distance from the **BOTTOM** of the figure to the **LOWER taper** is the same as **HALF** the distance from the **LOWER taper to the UPPER taper**. Next, by taking a reading **between** the **upper** and **lower tapers,** and comparing that **HORIZONTALLY,** we see one more helpful characteristic. Lo and behold, the spans are identical (7-5). That means they form a **SQUARE** (7-6).

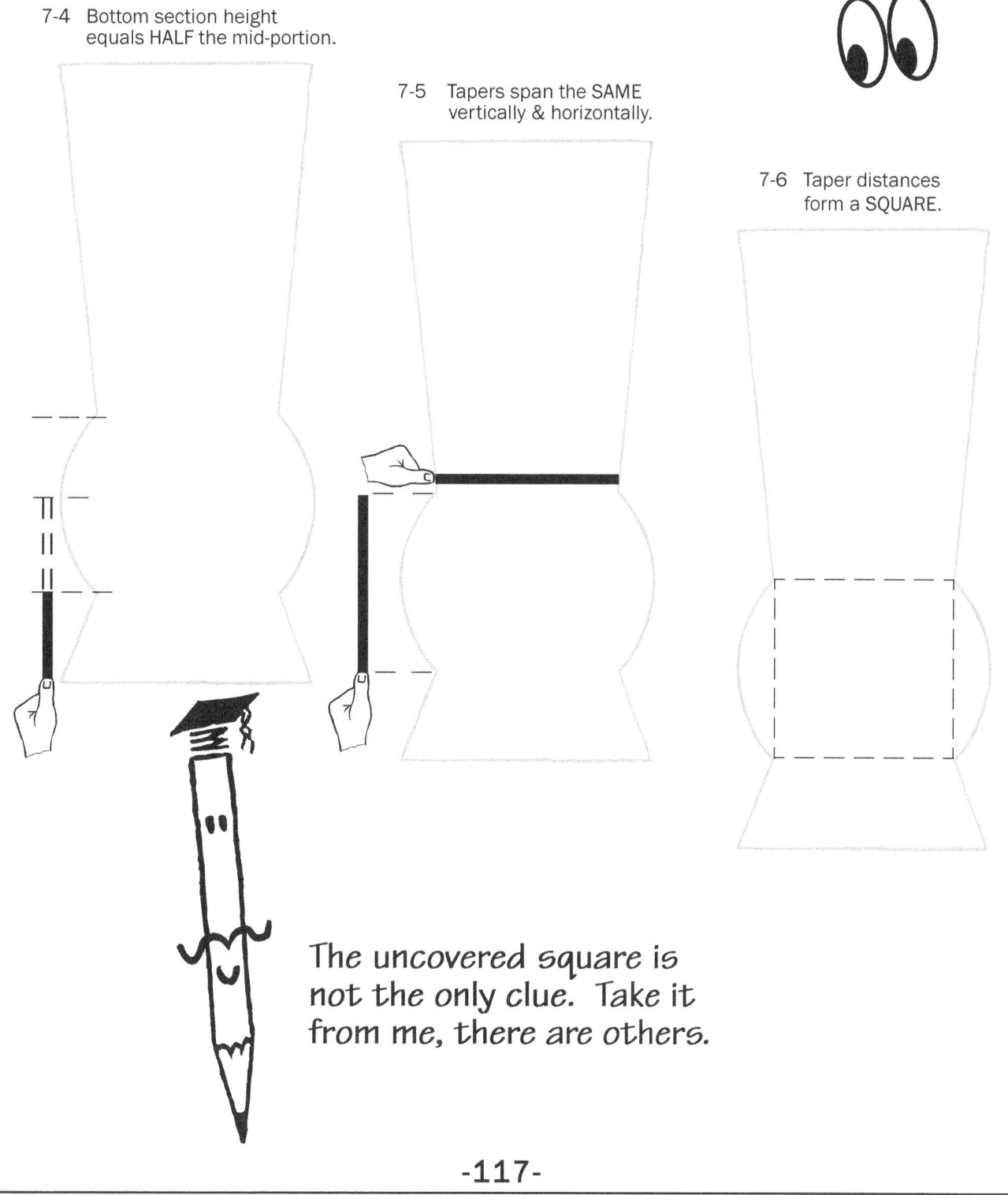

7-4 Bottom section height equals HALF the mid-portion.

7-5 Tapers span the SAME vertically & horizontally.

7-6 Taper distances form a SQUARE.

The uncovered square is not the only clue. Take it from me, there are others.

Continuing with our survey, please look at illustration 7-7. When we take a pencil reading *from the base of the figure to the UPPER taper* and go one identical span up, we notice there is *remaining space*. The question is: how much? So, let's put our *thinking* cap to work. *If we pretend the side curves continue from the upper tapers and connect,* we can anticipate that another arc will form (7-8). Next, by taking a reading from the *bottom of the figure* to the *highest point of the IMAGINARY arc,* and by comparing that distance from the *crest to the TOP of the figure,* we uncover an amazing coincidence. Clearly, the two distances are about the SAME (7-9). Suddenly the upper section's height is not a mystery anymore, is it?

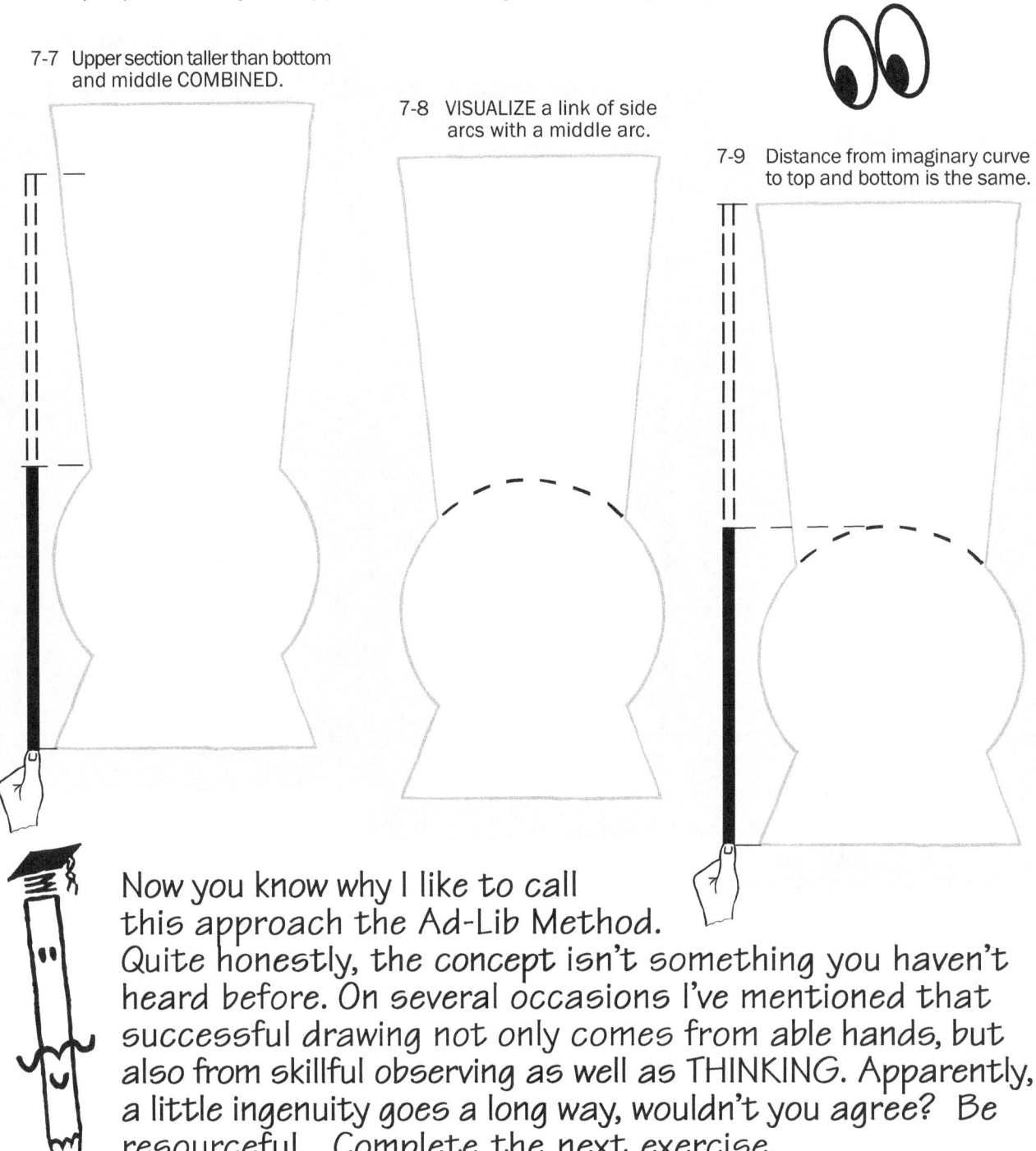

7-7 Upper section taller than bottom and middle COMBINED.

7-8 VISUALIZE a link of side arcs with a middle arc.

7-9 Distance from imaginary curve to top and bottom is the same.

Now you know why I like to call this approach the Ad-Lib Method. Quite honestly, the concept isn't something you haven't heard before. On several occasions I've mentioned that successful drawing not only comes from able hands, but also from skillful observing as well as THINKING. Apparently, a little ingenuity goes a long way, wouldn't you agree? Be resourceful. Complete the next exercise.

EXERCISE 7

OBJECTIVE: Draw a likeness of the vase (larger than shown).

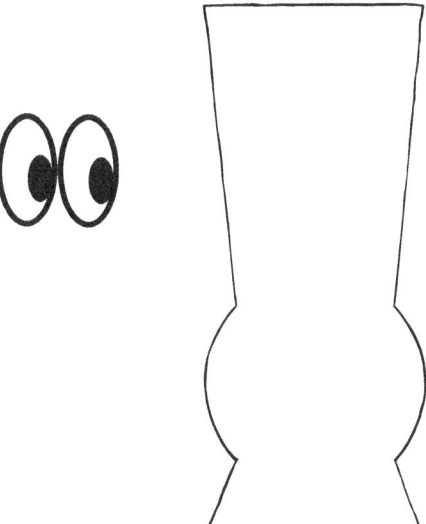

STEP 1 ESTABLISH THE FOUNDATION

Since we found an imaginary square within the figure, let's take advantage of it. Starting near the *lower* portion on a fresh sheet of paper, *LIGHTLY* center a square. It will provide the footing on which to draw your vase (7-10).

7-10 A square starts the framework.

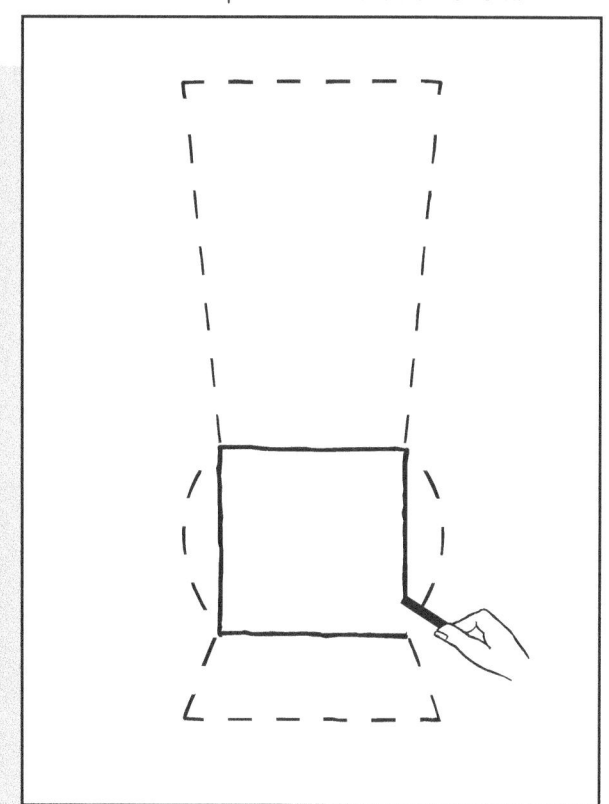

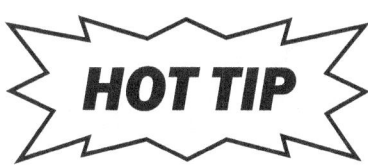

PLAN AHEAD! The size of your square should NOT be longer than about a *FOURTH* of the SHORT span on your paper. Also, it should start *less* than that distance *from the BOTTOM*. Otherwise, there will be inadequate space for the upper section.

Since two arcs are needed for the sides and one will be used later (for upper portion height), we might as well form all three arcs (7-11). Start by dividing the left side of *your* square in half with a dot, and bisect the halves again (7-12). Using one division (or quarter increment), place a dot above your square at that span and draw a horizontal guide line even with the top corners (7-13). Then form an arc between your guide line and the top of your square, from corner to corner (7-14). Follow the same procedure for the left and right sides of your square (7-15). *After that, you can erase your guide lines.*

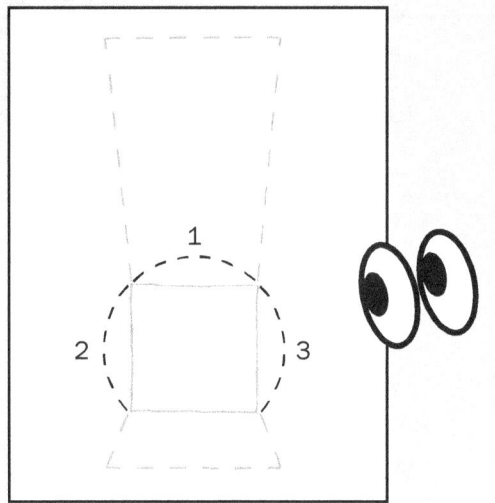

7-11   Three arcs are needed.

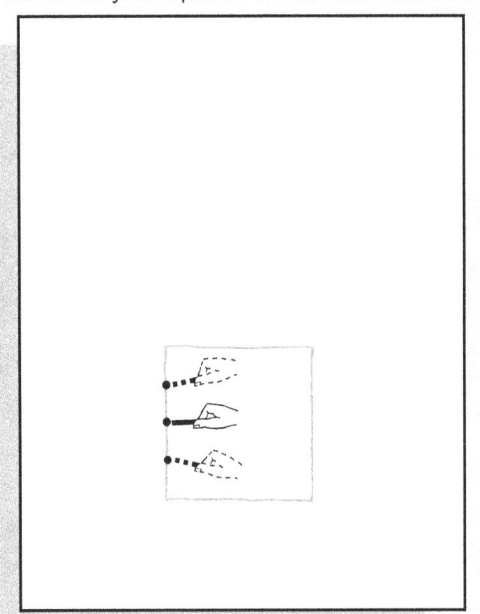

7-12   Bisect your square's left side into FOURTHS.

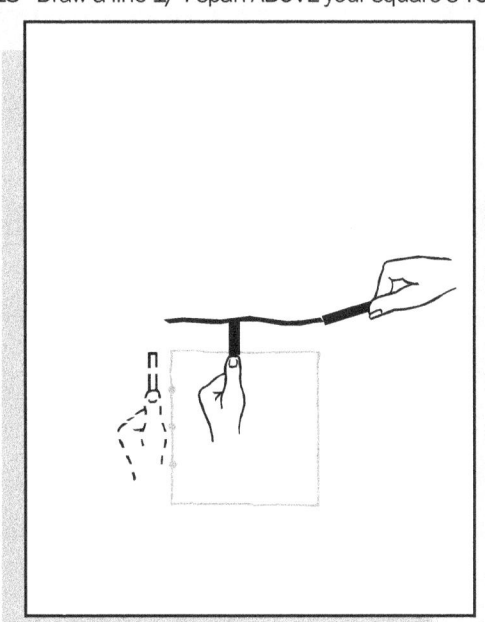

7-13   Draw a line 1/4 span ABOVE your square's TOP.

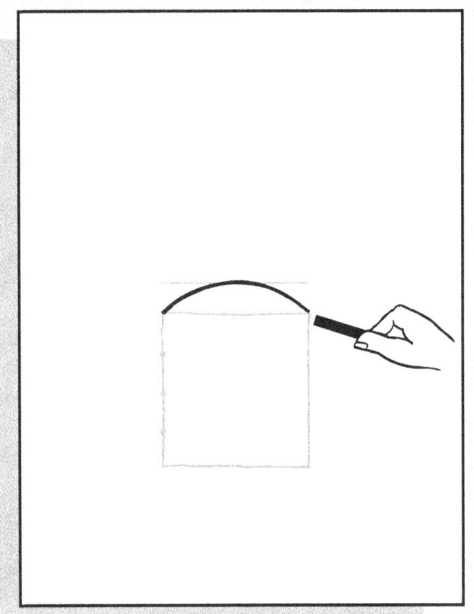

7-14   Form arc between top of your square & line.

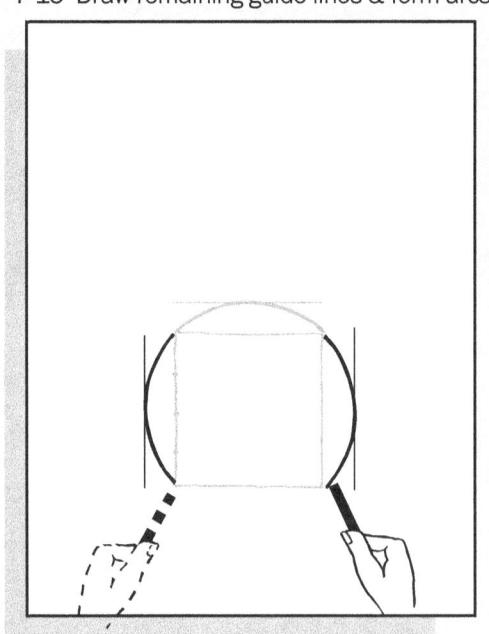

7-15   Draw remaining guide lines & form arcs.

STEP 3   LOCATE THE BOTTOM

Illustration 7-16, here on the right, reminds us that the base corners are PLUMB with the side arcs. As for the *HEIGHT* of that lower section, it's equal to about **HALF** the **mid** section. With this in mind, take a vertical pencil reading of YOUR square to midway, and transfer that interval below by centering your pencil tip at the bottom. Next, mark a dot beside your thumb (7-17). Then, gently follow up with a *level line, even with your SIDE curves* (7-18).

TIP	**DON'T rely *ONLY* on your pencil reading**. If the height of your base appears proportionally too tall or too short, be sure to adjust it by *EYE*.

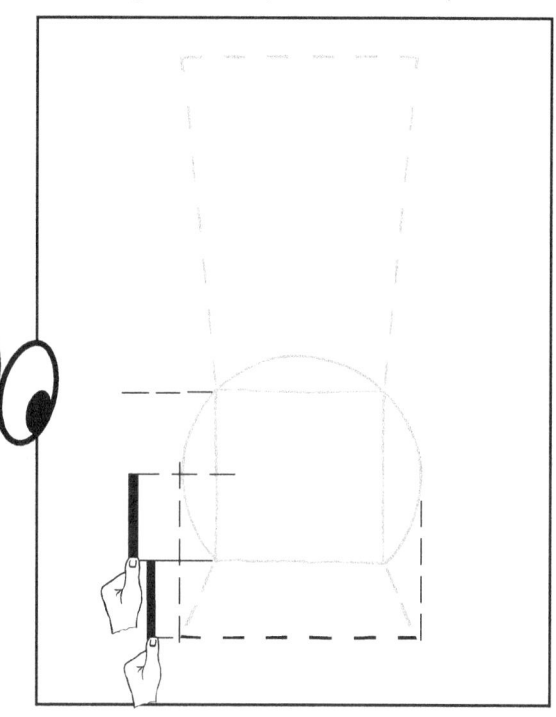

7-16   Bottom corners are EVEN with side curves. Height of base spans HALF the square.

7-17   Transfer HALF of curve height to the bottom and erase excess *guide lines*.

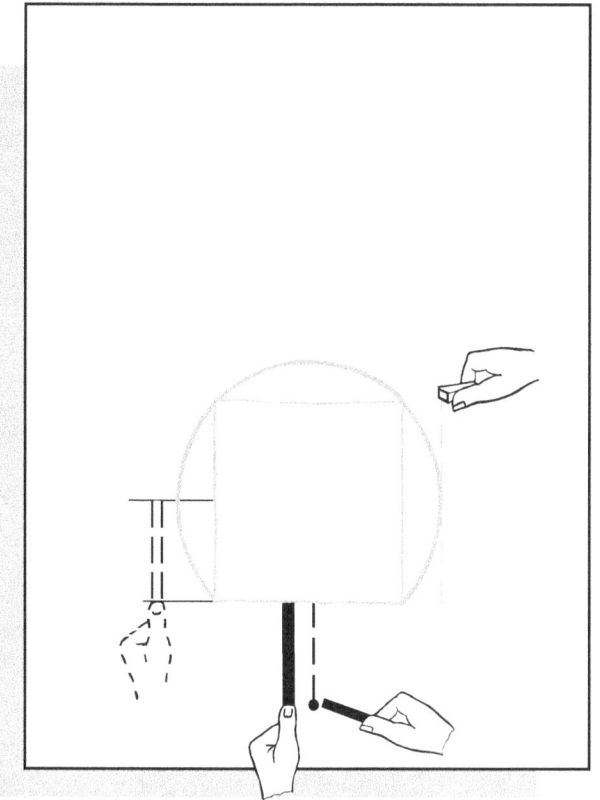

7-18   Draw a HORIZONTAL line through your dot, FLUSH with side curves.

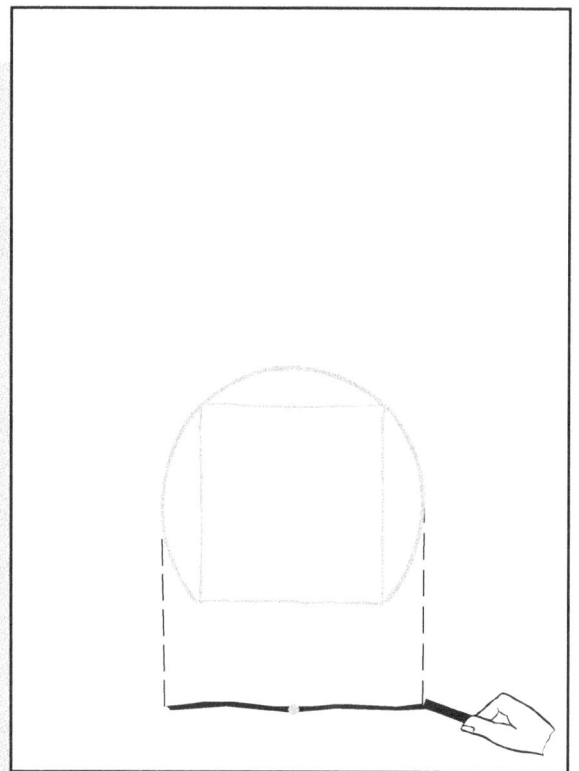

STEP 4   POSITION THE TOP

Illustration 7-19, here on the right, reconfirms that the figure's top corners are even with the side arcs and base. Plus, the span from the *imaginary* curve crest to the **top,** compared to the **bottom,** is the SAME distance. To apply this observation, take a *VERTICAL* pencil reading from the **base of YOUR figure** to the **CREST of your arc.** Second, **transfer** that interval by placing your thumb at the **crest,** and mark a dot beside your **pencil tip** (7-20). Then, lightly follow through with a level line. Make sure it's *EVEN* with your base and side arcs (7-21.)

| TIP | Please keep in mind, pencil checks only get you so far. **Your eyes must be the ultimate judge.** I can't emphasize this enough. While verifying your present status, be sure your figure's top and bottom are even with each other and parallel with your paper. Otherwise, your vase will appear to tilt. Also, should your figure seem to be too tall, or short *proportionally*, it probably is. This is a good time to make needed adjustments.

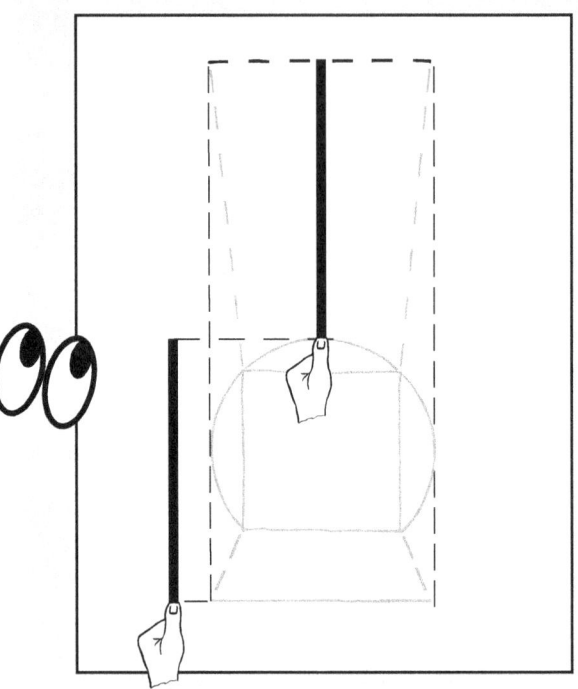

7-19   Distance from middle curve to top & bottom is the same. Top corners are even with the side arcs & base.

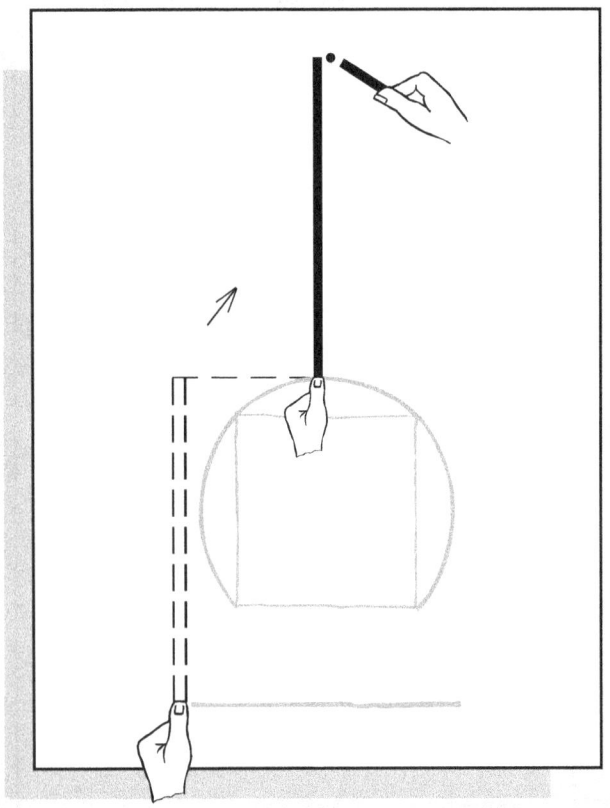

7-20   Distance from base to curve crest moved one span up, and marked with a dot.

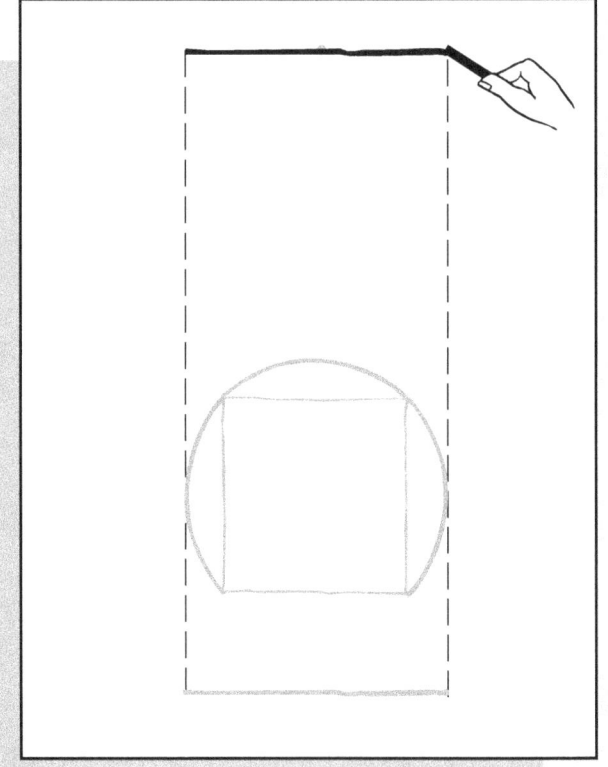

7-21   Draw a LEVEL line through your dot EVEN with the side curves and base.

STEP 5   LINK REMAINING SIDES

7-22   Upper & lower sides link from square to respective top and bottom corners.

Illustration 7-22, to the right, reminds us that the sides of the *upper and lower sections* connect at the respective corners of the imaginary square. To establish the rest of the sides, you will need four lines. One will extend from the UPPER **left** corner of your square to the **left** end of your **top** line. The other line will go from the UPPER **right** corner to the **right** end of your **top** line. Then, a pair of lines need to connect from the LOWER corners of your square to the corresponding ends, at the bottom of your base. You can follow the sequence as shown by illustrations 7-23 & 7-24, or your own preferred order.

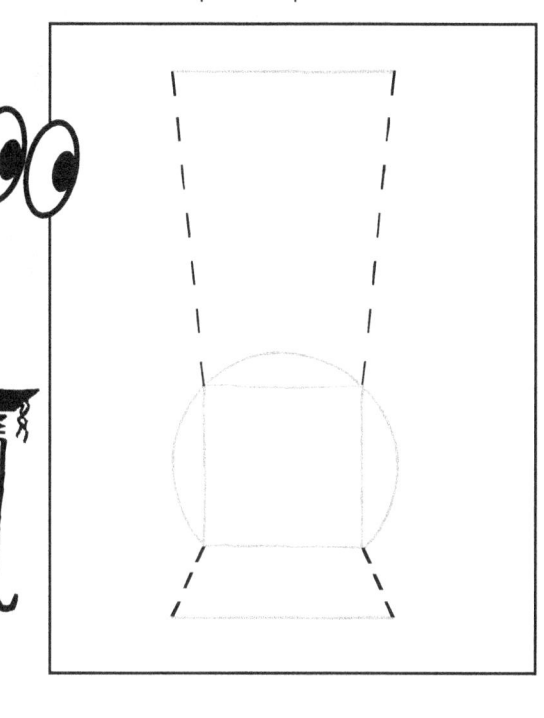

You're not rushing, are you? Have you stopped to double check your status? If not, don't you think you should?

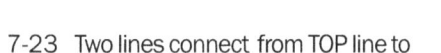

7-23   Two lines connect from TOP line to UPPER respective corners on square.

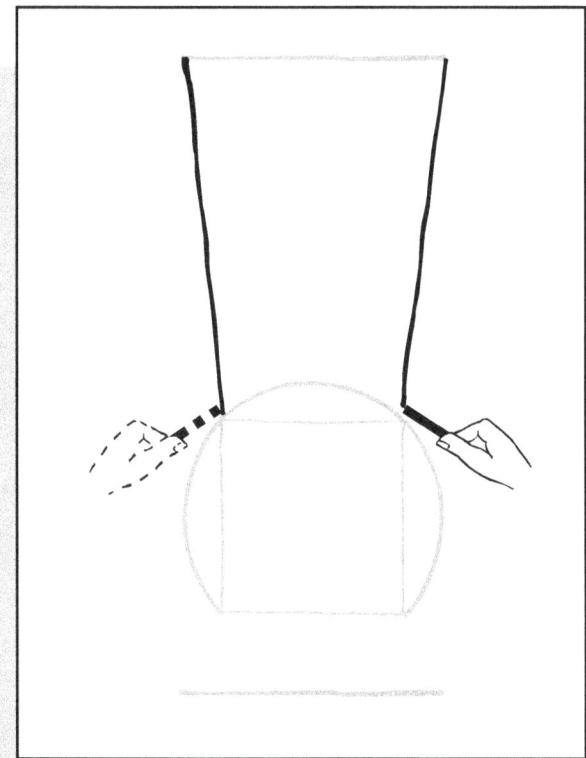

7-24   Two lines connect from LOWER square corners to BOTTOM line.

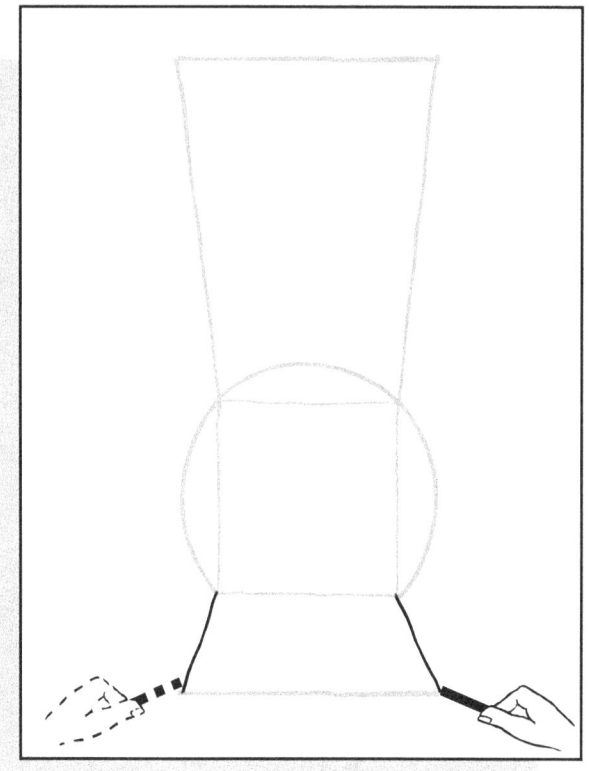

Your square and the middle arc, which served as guide lines, can now be erased (7-25). If you accidentally remove too much, you will need to reconnect the lines. After you've applied the finishing touches, your vase should resemble illustration 7-26.

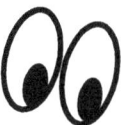

7-25 Delete guide lines.

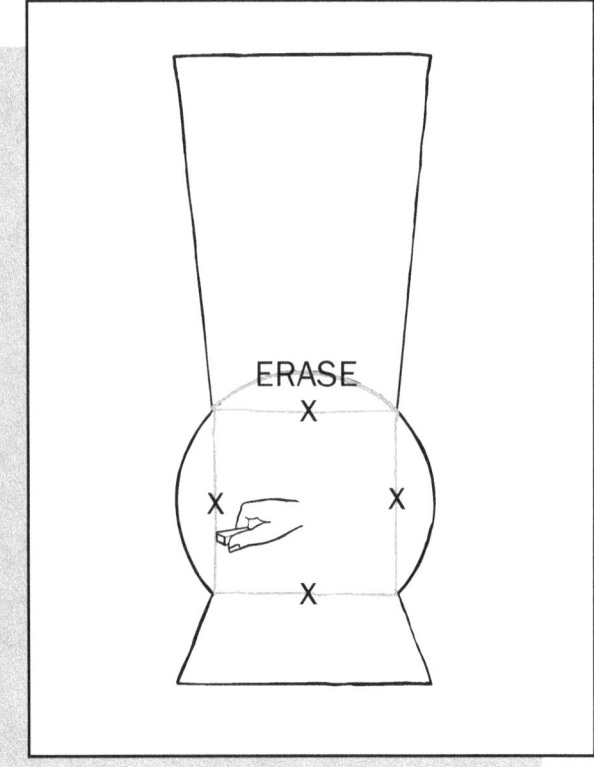

ERASE

7-26 Example of finished replica.

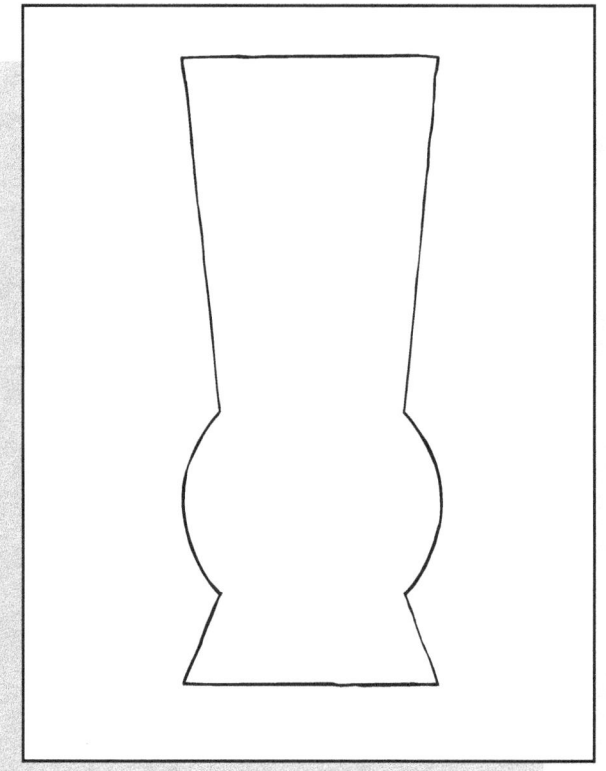

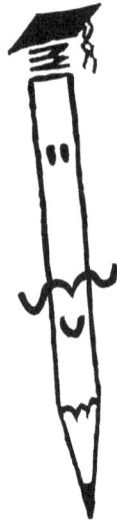

Don't forget...
there's still another important step.

Compare your drawing to illustration 7-26 (previous page) to see whether there is a fair likeness. If your version doesn't appear quite right, don't fret. Apply the "trusty seven" to help you determine the reason(s) for the dissimilarity. For instance, start by checking for **proportions**. Then, in no particular order, scan for the others. These are: *alignments, reference points, angles, straight lines, curves, and reverse space.* Some typical situations are shown below in examples 7-27, 7-28, and 7-29.

HOT TIP The natural urge is to tally everything and attend to them together. The trouble is, this can be extremely overwhelminng and things may get out of hand. To avoid such predicaments, it's better to compare ONE aspect, and one part of your figure to the model, at a time. Not only that, it's recommended that you focus on the OBVIOUS first, and when you find an adjustment is needed, attend to it right away. Then start the cycle again. Above all, please don't go overboard. Remember, your drawing should be a *reasonable* facsimile, not an exact match.

7-27 Top left corner not aligned with middle & bottom.   7-28 The base is not level.

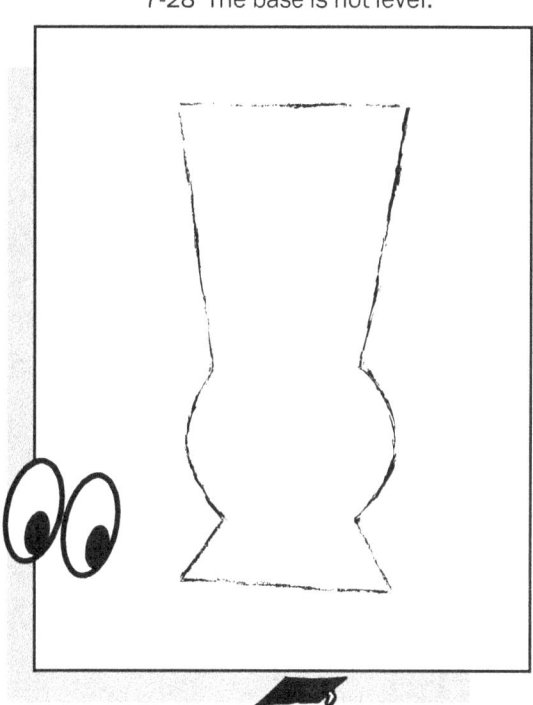

7-29 Proportion is too wide.

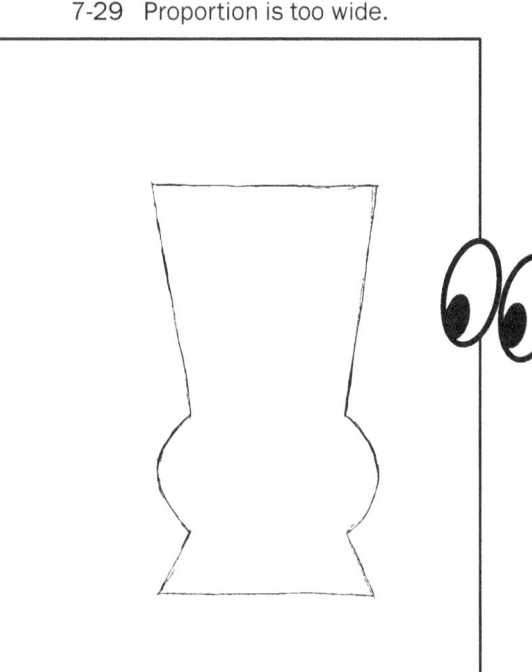

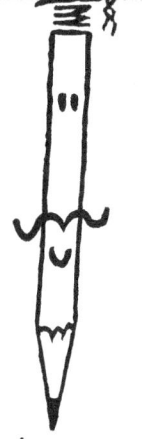

These examples are fine, despite the slight set-backs, don't you think? I'm sure you've done an excellent job, too. Next, read the follow-up and savor your well deserved accomplishment.

Chapter 7
FOLLOW-UP

Like the well known saying goes, *"sometimes good things come in small packages,"* and guess what? This is one of those times. Granted, although you may feel that the *style* of the vase you drew is not too terribly exciting, the lesson you learned while drawing it is worth a bunch. From here on, you can be forever secure in the knowledge that even when a shape and its subsections appear elaborate, and probably disproportionate (meaning they seem to have many parts and a variety of odd sizes), you don't need to feel uneasy anymore. You've got plenty of options, including a valuable asset you may have taken for granted: your remarkable ability to IMPROVISE. All that's needed is a willingness to look a little closer and apply some extra thinking. When you do, you're bound to find your way.

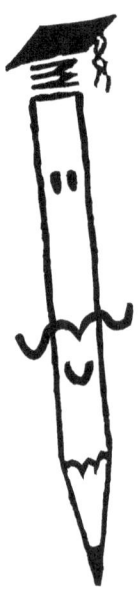

Now rest awhile and get ready
for another exciting adventure.

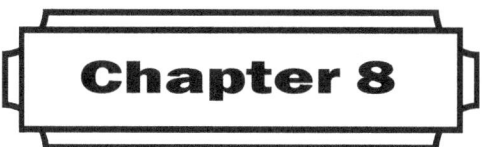

Chapter 8

THE ACTUAL SUBJECT APPROACH

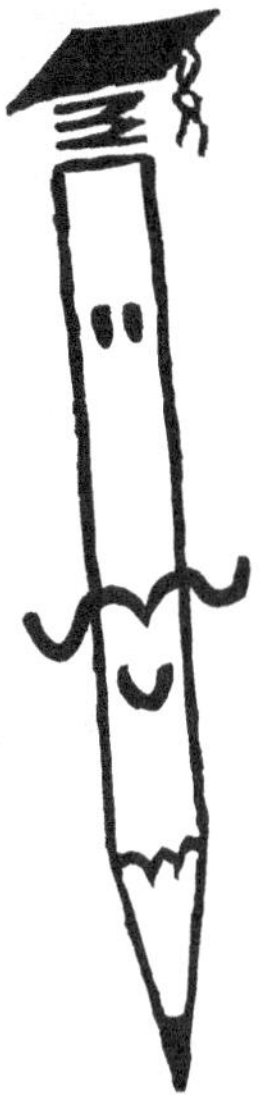

For this exercise, you will need a common 32 ounce mayonnaise jar, as shown.

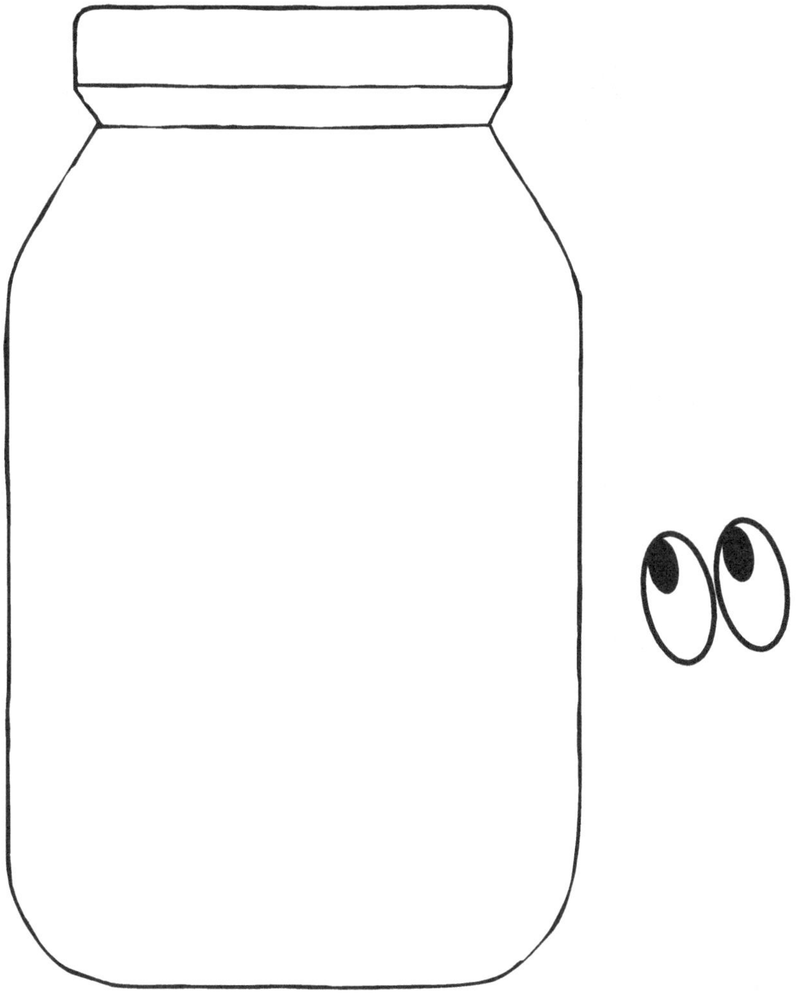

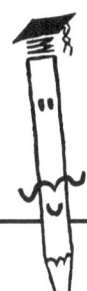

Since your subject is REAL, before you proceed to draw
its likeness, you should do 3 important things.

1. POSITION YOUR JAR AND YOURSELF

For example, you can place your jar atop your kitchen counter and take a seat a couple of
paces away (8-1). If you see the FRONT, and *also* the TOP of the cap (like drawing 8-2), please
elevate your jar. Use books, a box, or some other solid material, **until your line of sight,**
from your chair, **matches the FRONTAL view,** as shown by illustration 8-3.

8-1 Set your jar at eye level, to be viewed from your seat.

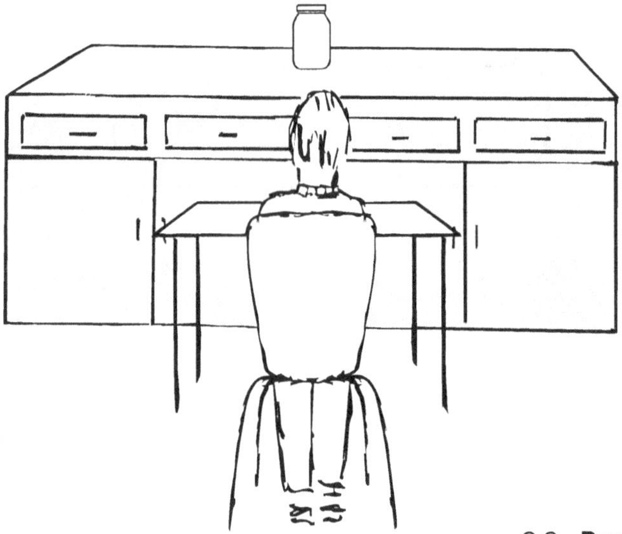

8-2 **Undesired View**
TOP portion of cap (shown in gray) should NOT be visible..

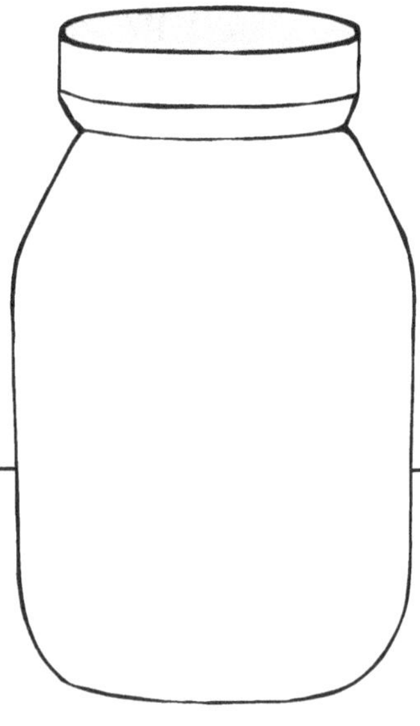

8-3 **Desired View**
after jar elevated.

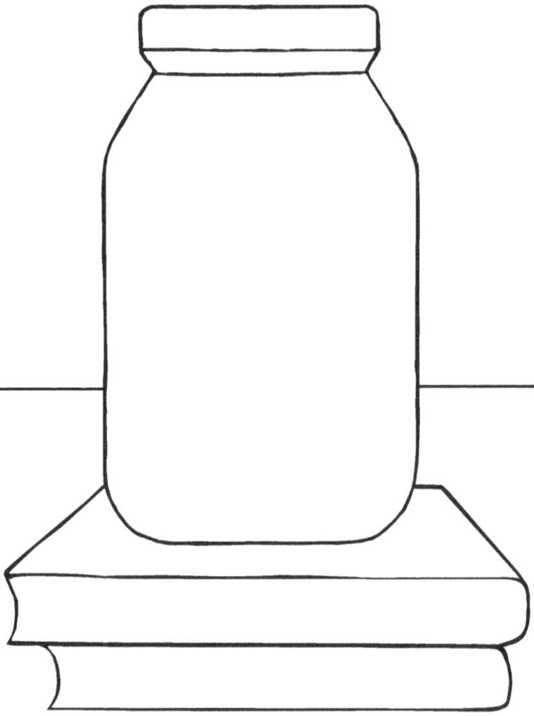

2. SIMPLIFY YOUR JAR IN YOUR MIND

Disregard both the label and the small details as you study your subject. Squint: you will find that with your eyes partly open, this helps you observe the figure as an *overall* shape. Next, picture it as straight lines and curves (8-4). Then, *imagine* your jar STREAMLINED (8-5). In this fashion, it can be divided into five parts: the cap, neck, shoulder, body and base.

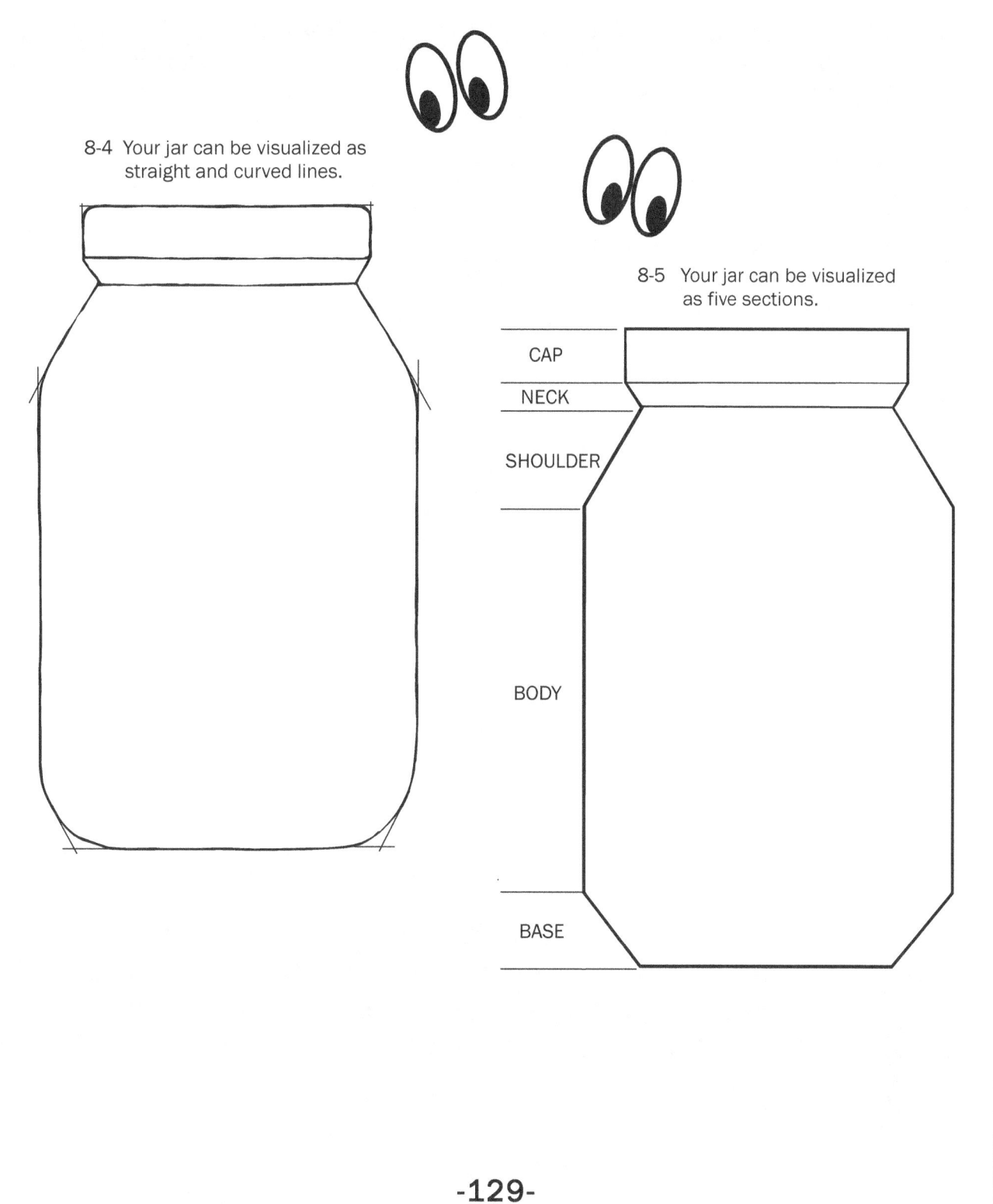

8-4 Your jar can be visualized as straight and curved lines.

8-5 Your jar can be visualized as five sections.

CAP

NECK

SHOULDER

BODY

BASE

3. LEARN HOW TO TAKE PENCIL READINGS FROM A DISTANCE

Wait a minute! Until now, pencil checks were taken from the *surface* of pictures in the book. This time, the subject is REAL, and too far away to reach. Should one go up to the object and measure it, up close? The answer is NO. "Measuring" is not what drawing is about. Besides, in most situations, the notion would be impractical. For instance, try taking a direct pencil reading right up next to a tree you intend to draw. Pretty silly idea, don't you think? **The proper way is from a sensible distance, with your pencil held at full arm's length in front of you, and one eye closed.** Generally, this is how it's done. But there's another wrinkle. From just a few feet away, sizes can appear TINY on your pencil (8-6).

8-6 Sample check of the jar cap from just a few paces reads very small on your pencil.

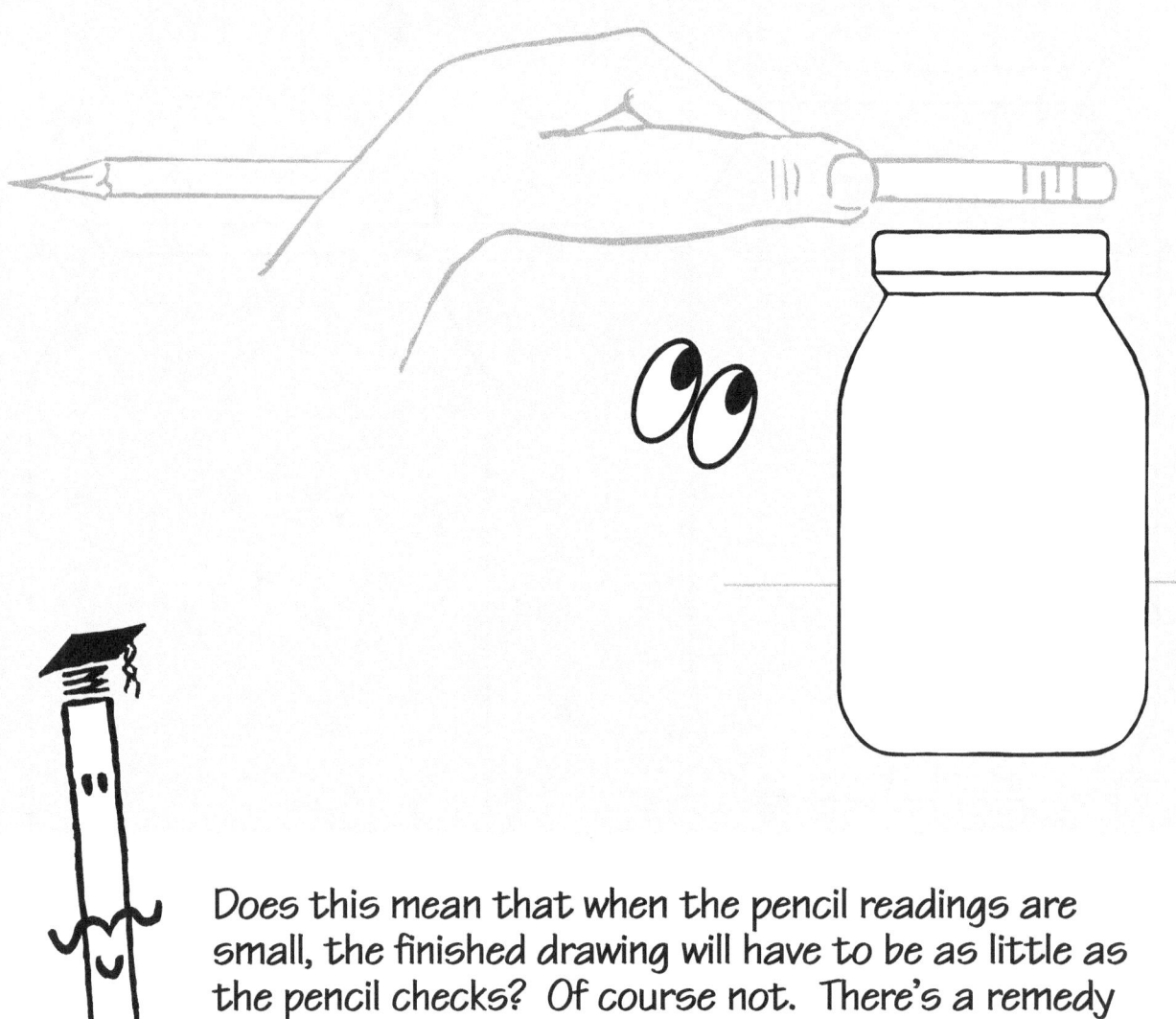

Does this mean that when the pencil readings are small, the finished drawing will have to be as little as the pencil checks? Of course not. There's a remedy for that too. Read on to discover the secret.

Whether your model is a PICTURE or REAL, if you're close or far away, *your drawing should reflect its PROPORTION.*

All along, you've been replicating pictures from the book, at a *different size, proportionally.* Well, guess what? You can do the same thing when your subject is *real.* Take a look at simulation 8-7. Notice that from just a few paces the actual jar seems dwarfed, even though the shape in the drawing is a close likeness. How was this feat accomplished? As usual, just *one dimension* and *one section* started the action. To understand what I mean, let's turn back the clock and assume my drawing of the JAR began with the TOP. From the moment I drew a line to represent its LENGTH, that span dictated the *overall* drawing size of the figure. Why? Because the rest of the parts had to fit according to *relative proportion* (Chapter 3, page 50). If I had initiated with a *shorter* cap length, a smaller *finished* replica would have been the outcome, like example 8-8. Conversely, a longer cap size would have led to a larger completed drawing (8-9). So you see, it doesn't matter how big or little the subject appears in your view, nor which segment you decide to start with. In this case, it could have just as easily been the *base* and its *length,* or perhaps the cap's *height.* The point is, once the decision is made, the name of the game is proportion, whether you draw from a picture, or from a real subject.

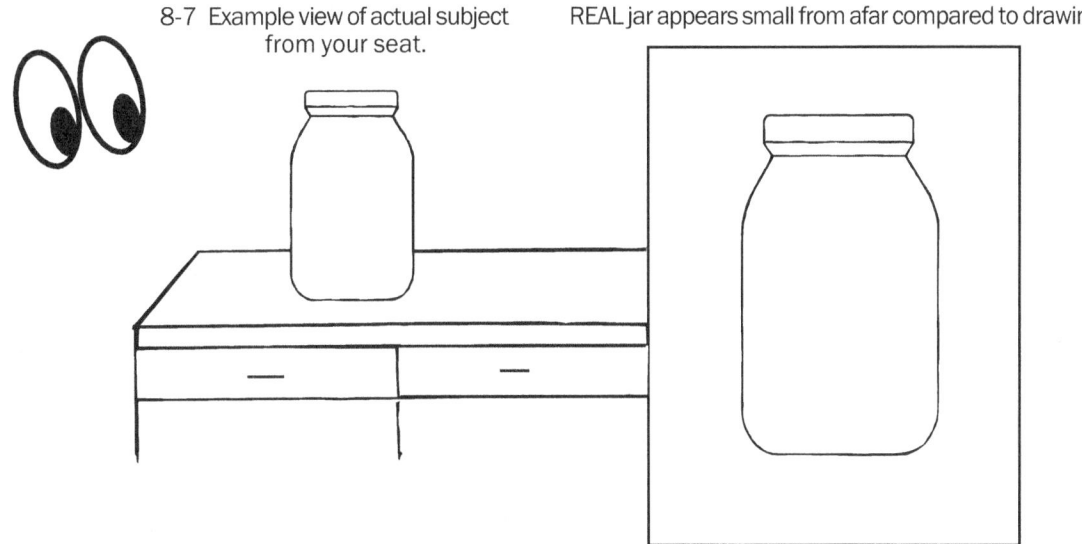

8-7 Example view of actual subject from your seat.

REAL jar appears small from afar compared to drawing.

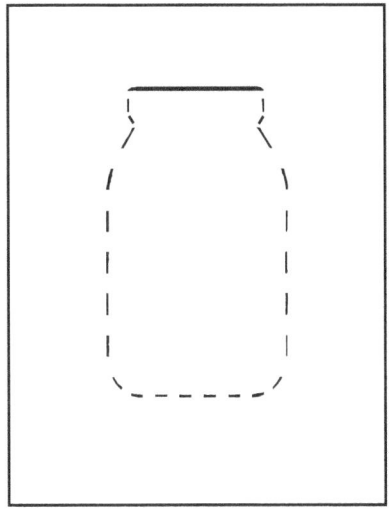

8-8 A smaller starting cap length leads to *proportionally* SMALLER drawing of jar.

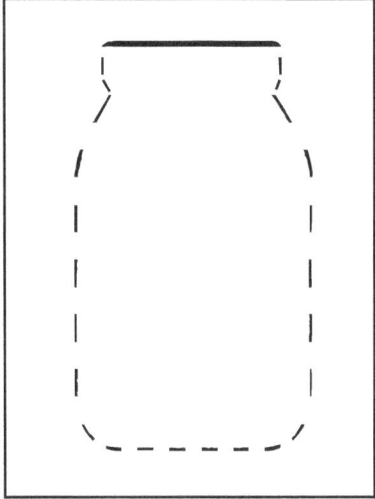

8-9 A larger cap length leads to LARGER scale drawing of jar.

PENCIL READINGS FROM *ACTUAL* OBJECTS
are EASY but a little tricky.

TRY THIS! Resume (or maintain) your frontal view by taking your seat a few feet away from your jar. CLOSE ONE EYE, EXTEND YOUR ARM TO FULL LENGTH, and hold your pencil *vertically*. Then, take a reading of your jar's NECK. Next, while continuing to keep your eye closed, and your arm outstretched, compare the neck height reading to the CAP height. Your span comparison should indicate that the cap is about TWICE as tall as the neck (8-10).

STRAIGHT ARM reading of neck compared to cap.

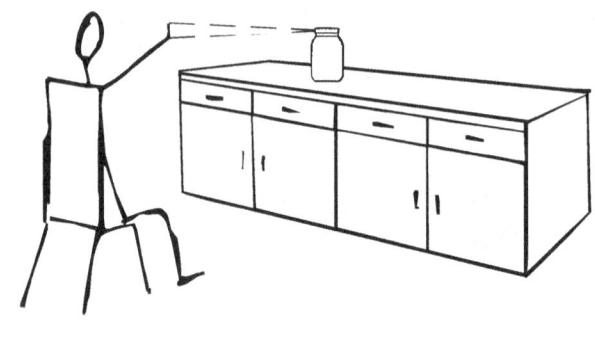

8-10   Pencil reading of neck reveals it's about HALF the height of the cap.

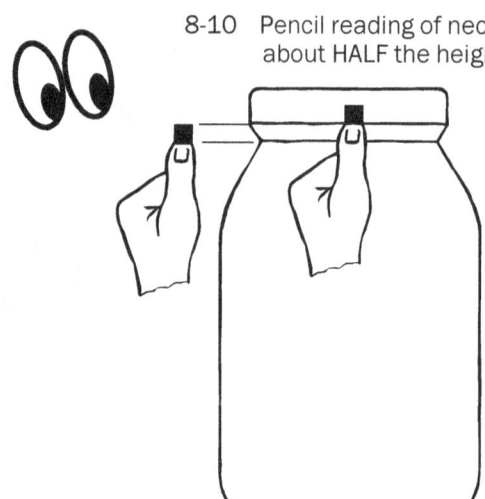

NOW, TRY THIS! With your arm ***fully extended*** and one eye shut, take another vertical pencil check of the neck height. Next, while ***HOLDING the reading, BEND your elbow*** *so your forearm is nearly UPRIGHT.* Then, with one eye closed, compare the reading to the cap again. This time, your pencil check comparison surprisingly indicates that the neck is about the SAME height as the cap (8-11).

STRAIGHT ARM reading of neck is taken. Then, ELBOW is BENT. As pencil comes closer to eye, reading seems to enlarge.

8-11   When NECK reading with arm STRAIGHT is compared to CAP with arm BENT, reading grows making neck & cap height appear *identical*.

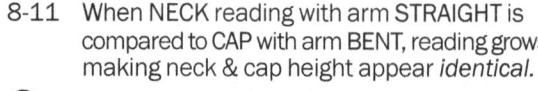

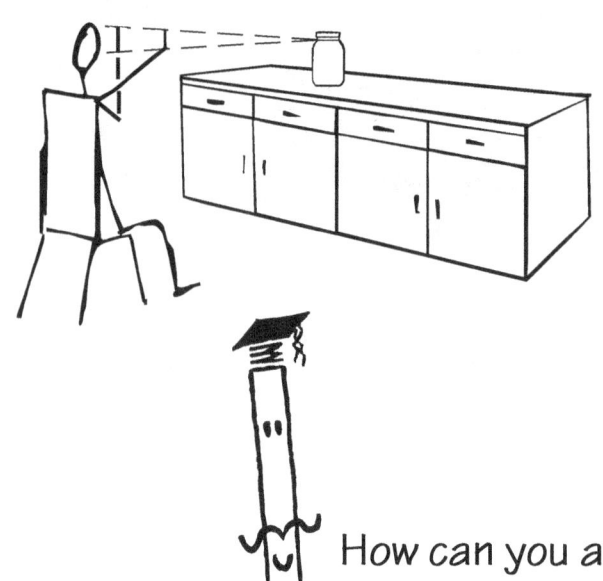

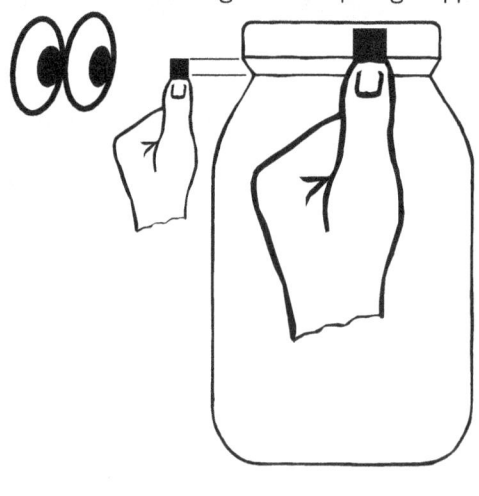

How can you avoid CONFLICTING
READINGS? Keep going to find out.

You can compare pencil checks with your arm straight or bent, but NOT both. The question is, WHICH WAY IS BETTER?

We know objects seem to shrink when we are further away from them, and they appear to enlarge when we approach. This principle also holds true when we hold our pencil at full arm's length, then bring it near to us (by bending our elbow). As soon as we do, both our hand and our pencil reading seem to *enlarge*. That means, when you take one check with your arm *STRAIGHT* and *COMPARE THAT READING to another part of your figure* with your *arm BENT,* you will receive an *inaccurate* assessment, like the one shown on illustration 8-11 (previous page).

The act of flexing the elbow is not the problem, however. If you took your pencil check with your arm bent and *held* it in that position while making your comparison, the reading would be OK. The trouble is that it's difficult to keep your elbow consistently bent at the same rate and to keep it steady. As a result, you are apt to receive *VARIABLE* readings. Maintain your arm fully extended though, and the effectiveness of the procedure is maximized. And that's your answer. ***THE STRAIGHT ARM METHOD IS GENERALLY MORE RELIABLE.*** But there's a catch. As you can tell, pencil checks taken from actual subjects, at a distance, present a little more challenge, so here are a few tips to remember:

1. Aside from keeping your arm outstretched, be sure to lock your wrist as well as your elbow. In addition, it's best to stay still and don't slouch or lean while comparing a pencil reading of one section to another.

2. Close one eye. The image will appear sharper.

3. The more space there is between you and your subject, the smaller it will appear on your pencil. In light of this, and the tendency to fidget no matter how hard you try not to move, it's best to rely even LESS on pencil readings whenever taking them from actual subjects.

4. Since pencil checks *from a distance* are slightly tricky, be sure to refine VISUALLY, as usual.

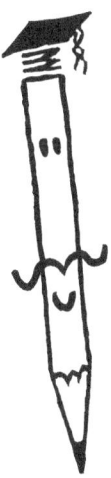

OK. Now that you know the limitations of DISTANCE pencil readings, give them a whirl. Get ready to draw your jar by LOOKING at IT as much, if not more, than the diagrams in the book.

EXERCISE 8

OBJECTIVE: Draw a likeness of YOUR actual jar.

STEP 1 INITIATE A PROPORTION CHECK AND SELECT YOUR START
Do this FROM YOUR SEAT. Begin by keeping one eye closed, your arm outstretched, and your hand steady. Then, take a HORIZONTAL pencil check of YOUR jar at its widest expanse. Next, with your arm still fully extended and one eye shut, tilt your reading UPRIGHT, and compare it to the jar's *main body* HEIGHT (between shoulder and base). You will see that your pencil readings are about the *same* (8-12). That means you found a *square, and your ideal foundation.* Why? Because the square automatically establishes *BOTH* the WIDTH *and* the HEIGHT of the mid-section. From there, you can "construct" the rest of your jar (the same way you used a square, along with the AD-LIB and ATTACH METHODS in Chapter 7 to "build" your vase).

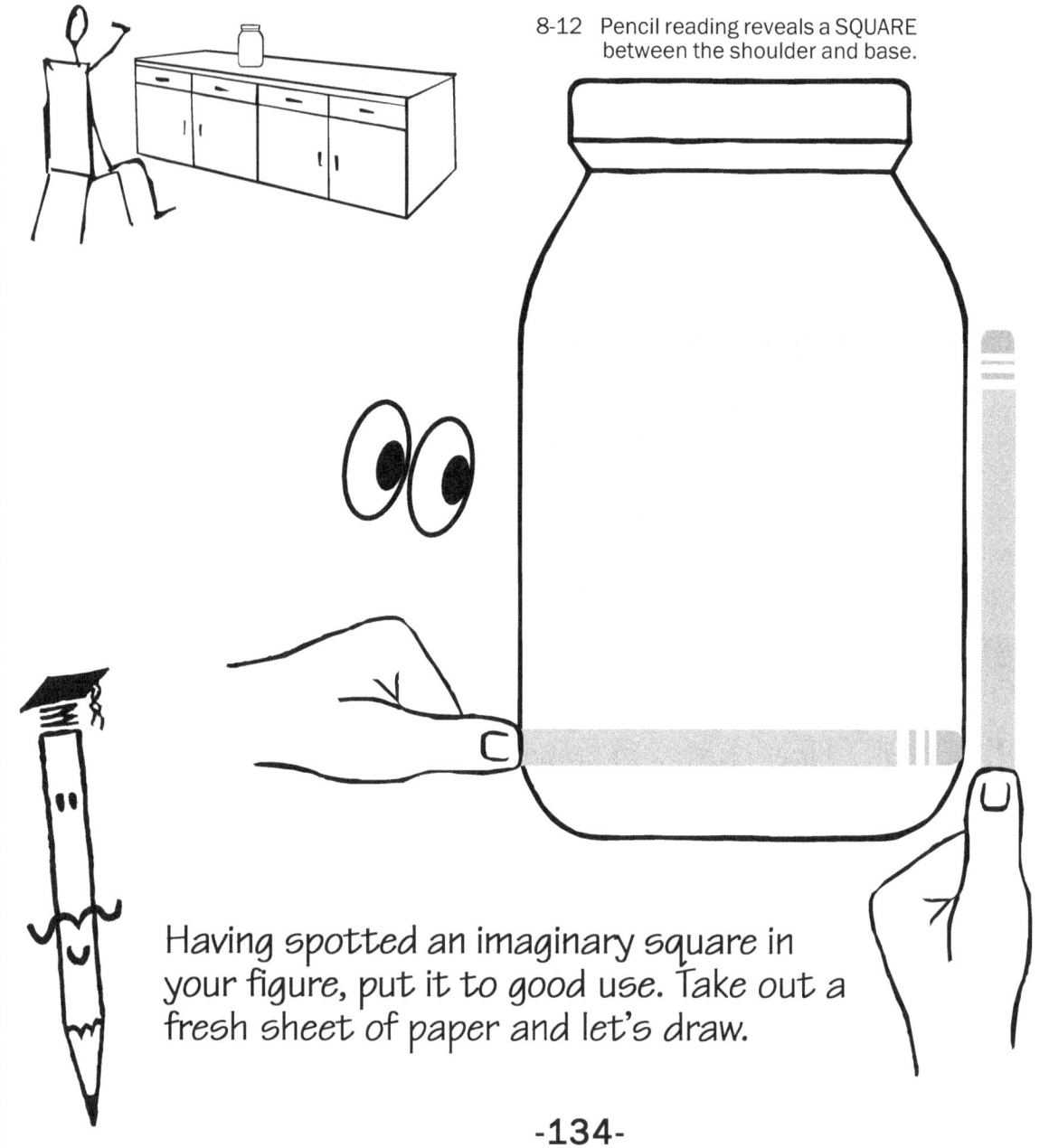

8-12 Pencil reading reveals a SQUARE
between the shoulder and base.

Having spotted an imaginary square in
your figure, put it to good use. Take out a
fresh sheet of paper and let's draw.

STEP 2 | CHOOSE SIZE AND POSITION FOR YOUR SQUARE AND DRAW IT

Remember that the starting size you choose, and its placement on your paper, will affect the final outcome (see page 131). If you fashion a small square in the lower portion, for instance, you can be fairly certain that a small finished picture of the jar will end up near the bottom (8-13). On the other hand, should you decide to begin with a large square, closer to center, that's where the completed version of your jar will probably appear, except slightly bigger and closer to the upper portion of your paper (8-14). Of course, that's not to say you can't change your mind along the way, but if you do, some alteration and proportional adaptation will be required. Get the hint? *Forethought is definitely recommended.*

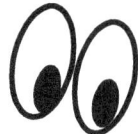

8-13 A small square near the bottom leads to a small *finished* drawing in lower area.

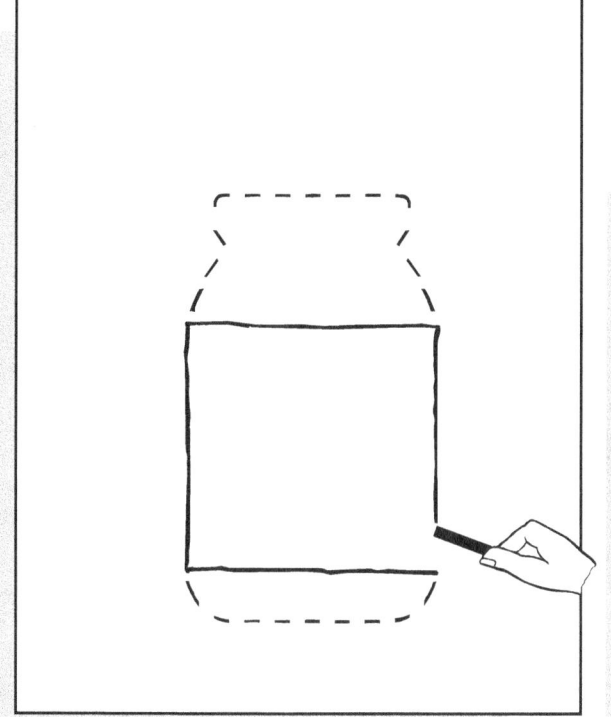

8-14 A large centered square leads to a large *finished* drawing above middle.

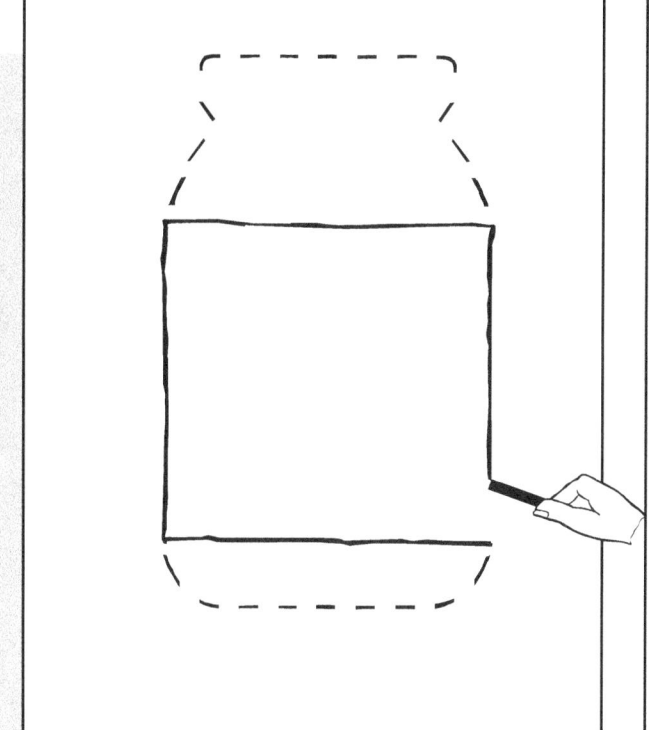

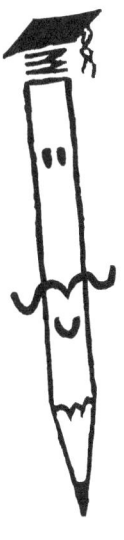

Whether you prefer to work large or small, in the middle of you paper or not, it's a good idea to think about these things BEFORE-HAND. In other words, try to PLAN AHEAD.

STEP 3 — DETERMINE THE *PROPORTIONAL* HEIGHT OF YOUR JAR'S SHOULDER

Take a VERTICAL pencil reading of your jar's shoulder and compare that distance to the main body (8-15). The distance fits about FOUR times, doesn't it? That means the shoulder height for your drawing will have to be one fourth of YOUR square.

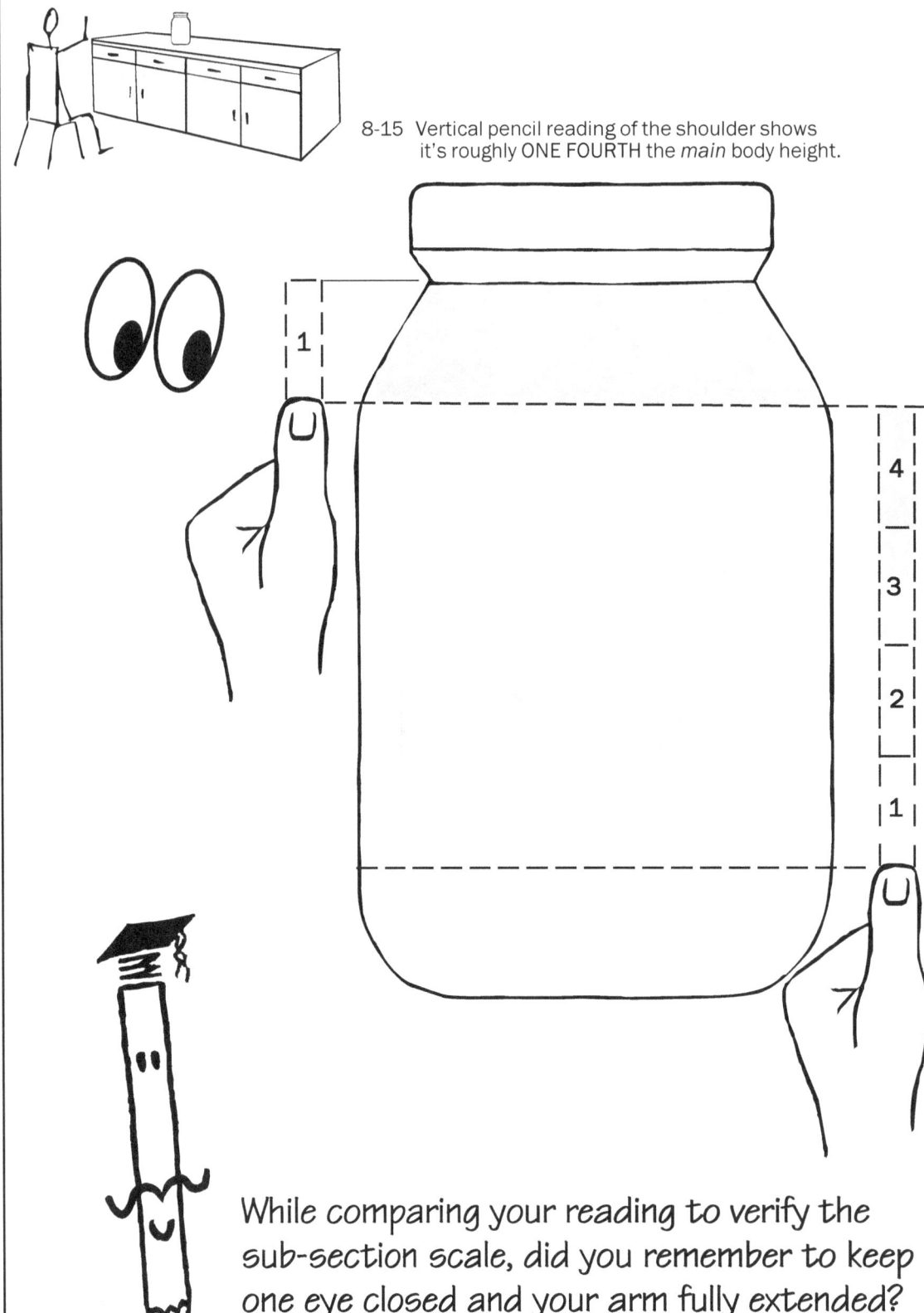

8-15 Vertical pencil reading of the shoulder shows it's roughly ONE FOURTH the *main* body height.

While comparing your reading to verify the sub-section scale, did you remember to keep one eye closed and your arm fully extended?

Divide the side of your square in half (8-16). Subdivide the halves into quarters (8-17). Next, take a pencil reading of a quarter span, and place a dot *ABOVE* the LEFT corner of your square (8-18). Then draw a HORIZONTAL line from the dot until it's EVEN with your square's RIGHT corner (8-19).

8-16   Divide your square in HALF on left side.

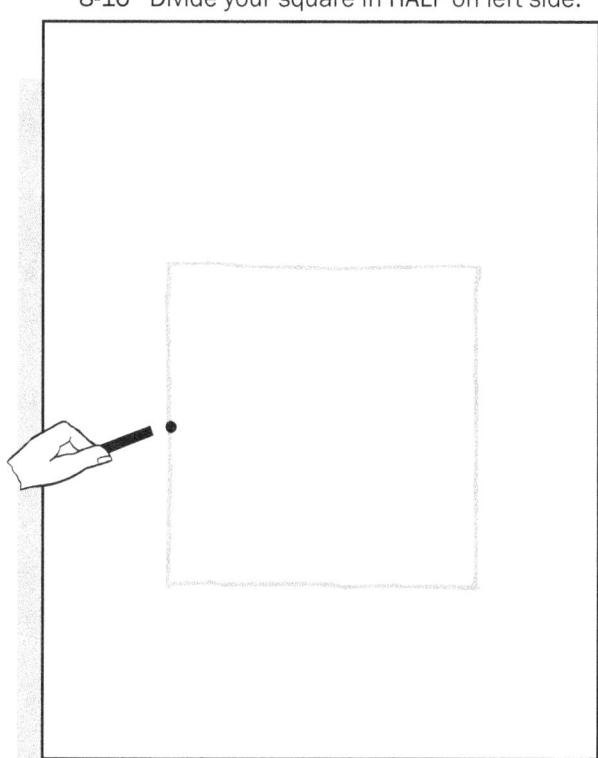

8-17   Bisect both your HALVES into FOURTHS.

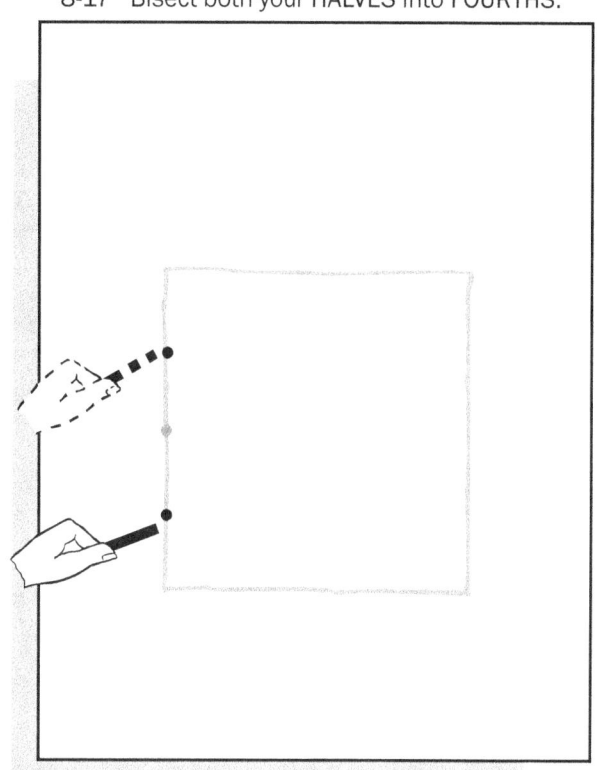

8-18   1/4 height reading of *your* square marked above with a dot locates shoulder height.

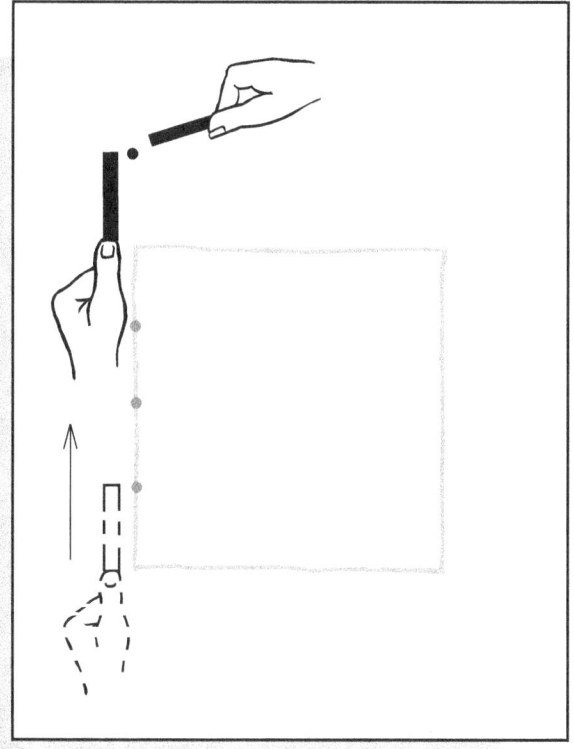

8-19   Line from your dot, even with your square's *right* corner establishes shoulder height.

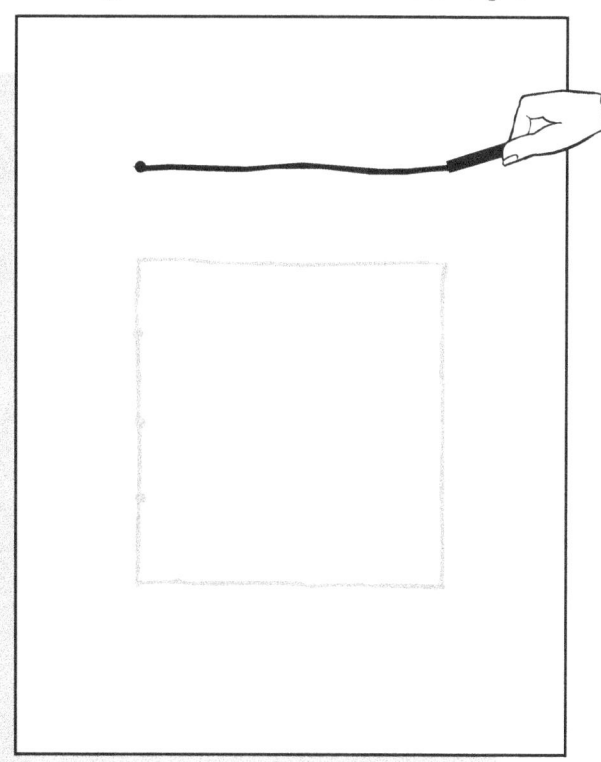

Initiate by taking a VERTICAL pencil reading of YOUR jar's base. Then, compare that span to the shoulder. Notice that the base height is about ONE FOURTH *LESS* than the shoulder (8-20).

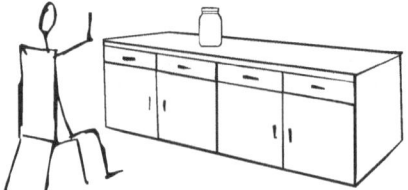

8-20 Pencil reading of jar shoulder compared to base
shows the BASE is about ONE FOURTH *SHORTER*.

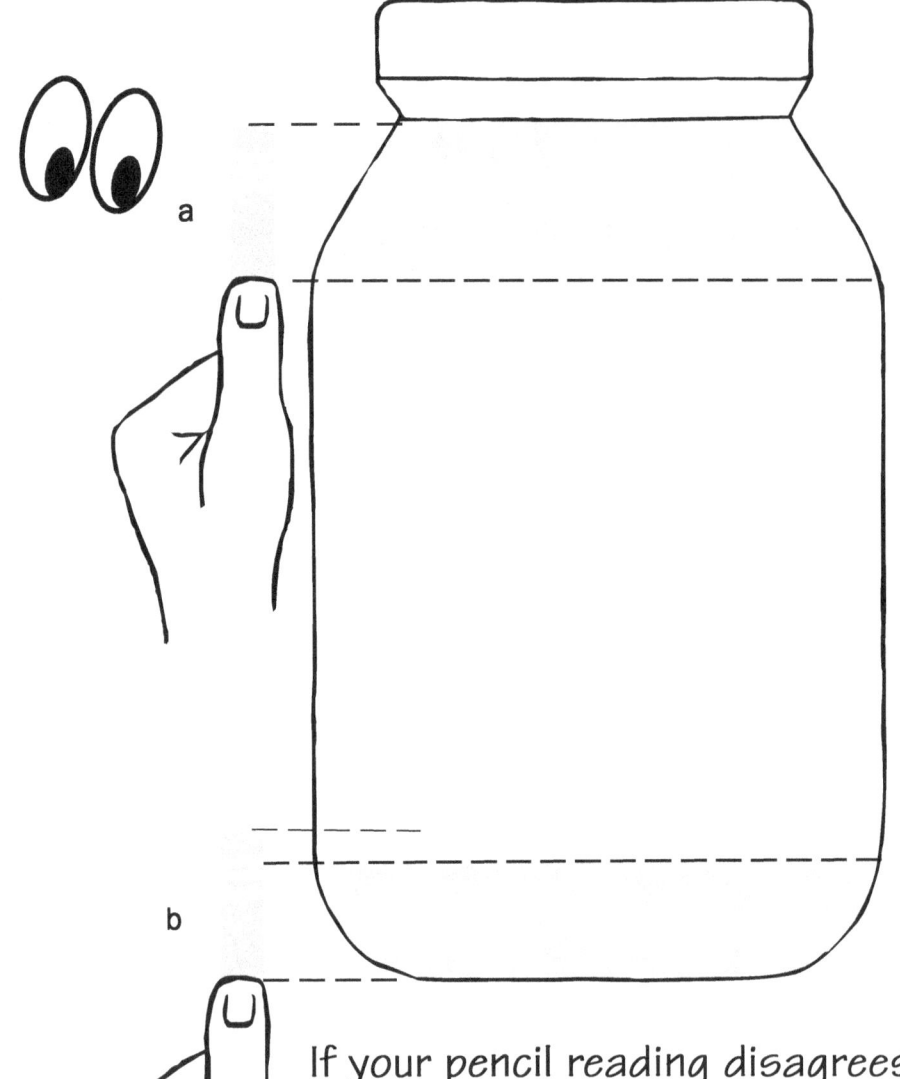

a

b

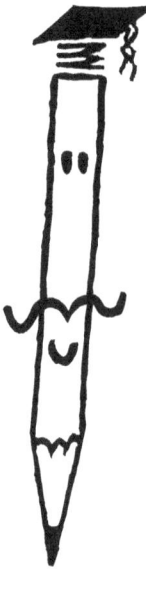

If your pencil reading disagrees with mine, chances are your jar is a different style, or maybe you bent your elbow while making your subsection scale comparison.

CONVERT THE BASE HEIGHT *PROPORTIONALLY*

Assuming your vertical reading agrees that your jar's BASE *height* is about **ONE FOURTH** *shorter* than the SHOULDER, you need to adapt this dimension to fit YOUR drawing. In order to do that, simply *estimate* **three fourths** of the VERTICAL span between *your* square and the line above it, or take a pencil reading. Next, place a dot equal to that distance BELOW the left corner of *your* square (8-21). Then check visually to make sure your dots are properly placed. Adjust if needed and lightly draw a horizontal line from your dot until it's even with your square's *right* corner (8-22).

8-21 **3/4** span between your top line to square moved down to left lower corner locates jar's bottom.

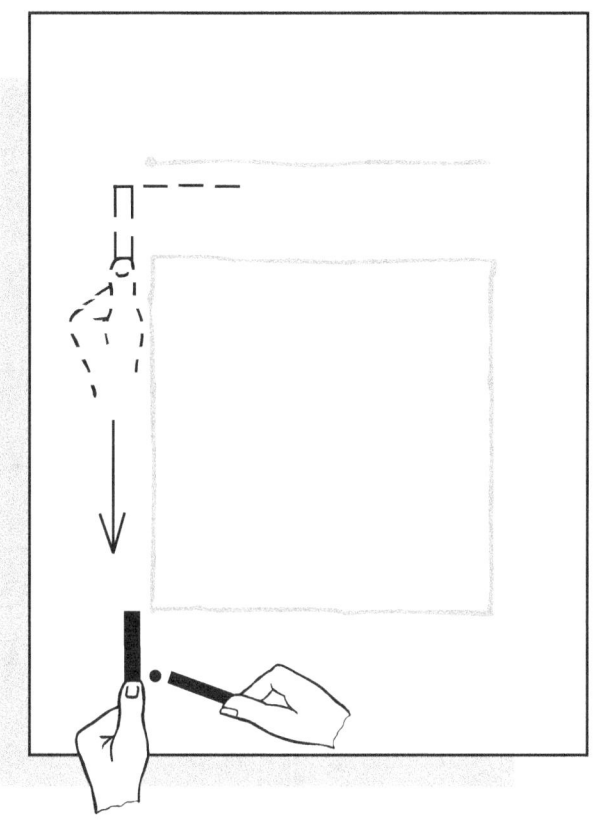

8-22 Line from your dot until even with the RIGHT corner of your square establishes jar bottom.

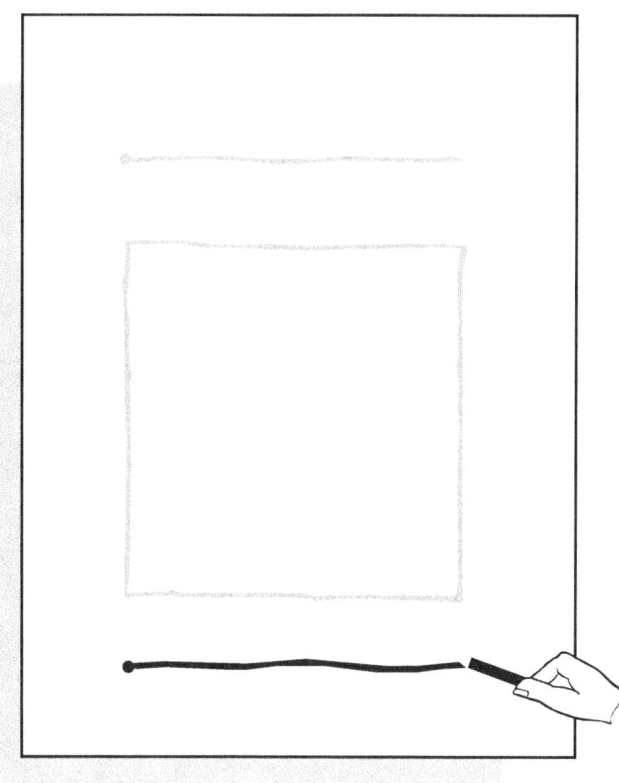

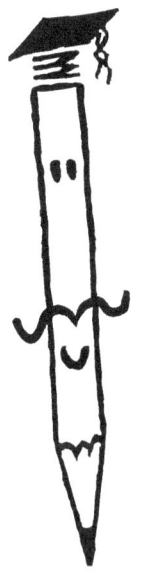

Is your favorite soothing music on?
Good. Proceed slowly and have fun!

Take a VERTICAL pencil reading of YOUR jar's *cap and neck*, COMBINED AS ONE UNIT. Then compare that span to the *height of the base*. You'll discover they are about the *same* distance (8-23).

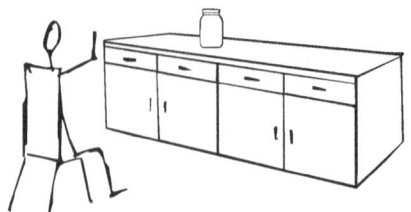

8-23 Vertical pencil reading of your jar's neck and cap TOGETHER
should appear fairly equal to the *height* of the BASE.

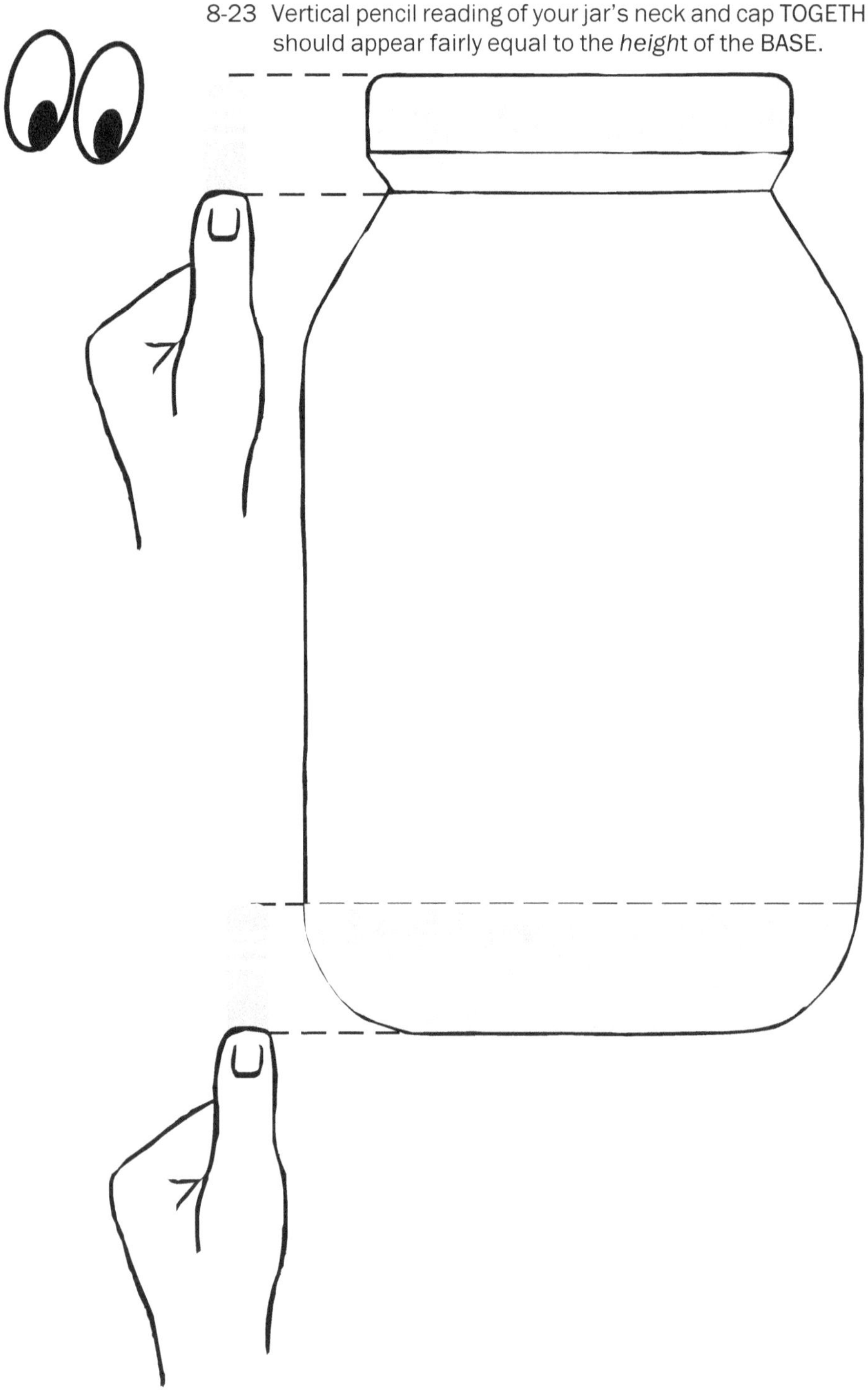

Since the *combined* HEIGHT of the cap and neck proved to be *equal to the base HEIGHT,* take a VERTICAL reading of YOUR drawing's bottom portion. Next, place your thumb one interval up, (by the shoulder *line)* and mark the span with a dot by your pencil tip (8-24). Then draw a parallel horizontal line from your dot until it's even with the line below. This will establish the jar's top (8-25).

8-24 Reading of YOUR base height marked above shoulder line locates jar's top.

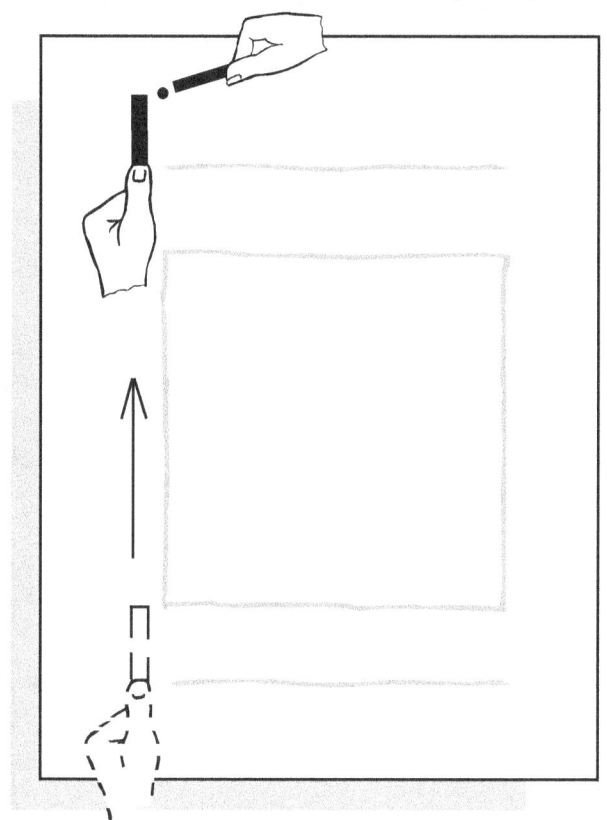

8-25 Horizontal line from your dot establishes jar's top.

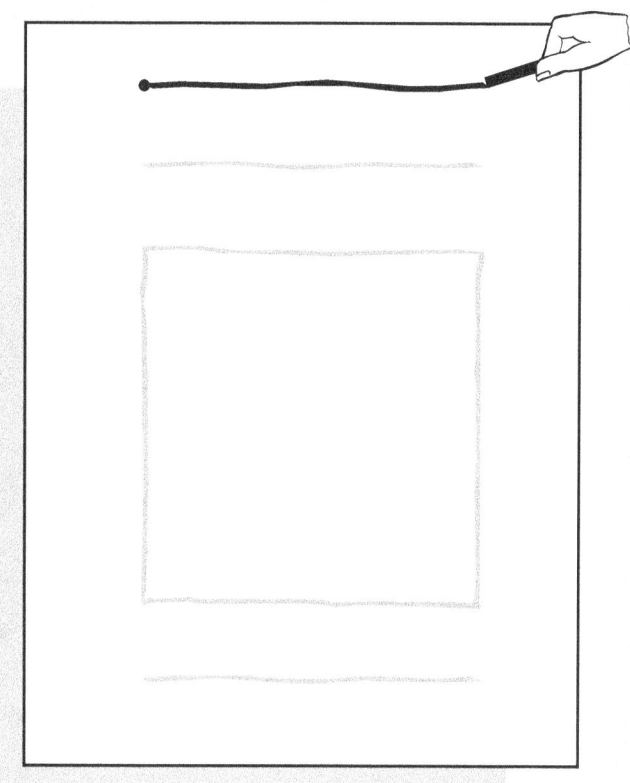

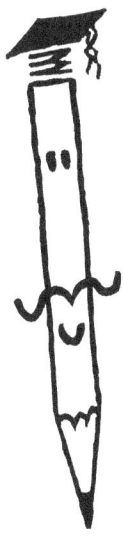

You're taking pencil checks of YOUR jar, instead of just accepting the book's findings as you draw, aren't you? Plus, you're double checking visually, right? If you've been lax, be sure to confirm your accuracy up to the present, adjust if needed, and verify from here on.

STEP 9	DETERMINE THE NECK HEIGHT AND ADAPT DISTANCE TO SCALE

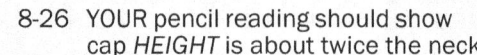

8-26 YOUR pencil reading should show cap HEIGHT is about twice the neck.

A **visual** check of YOUR jar, as shown here on the right, should verify that the neck is about half the height of the cap (8-26). In order to CONVERT that observation to YOUR drawing, place a dot TWO THIRDS of the way DOWN between your top line and the line below it (8-27). This will pinpoint the *HEIGHT* of the neck. Then, by drawing a *HORIZONTAL* line from your dot to the opposite end of your figure, you will form the boundary between your jar's neck and cap (8-28).

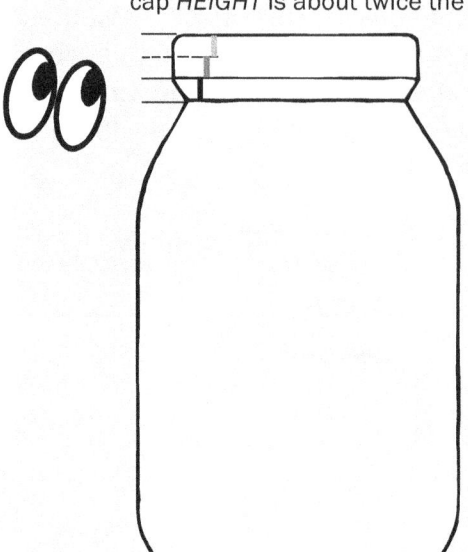

8-27   Dot locates cap & neck boundary.

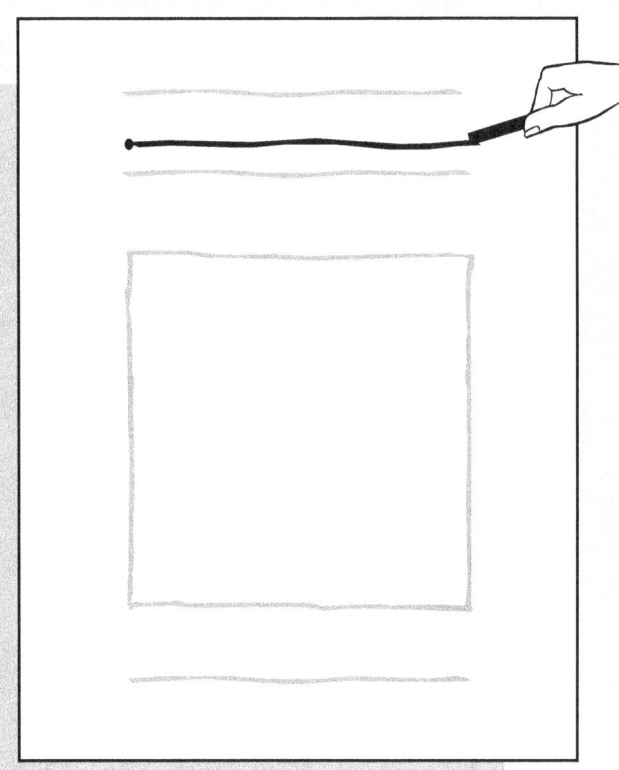

8-28 Line establishes the edge between cap and neck.

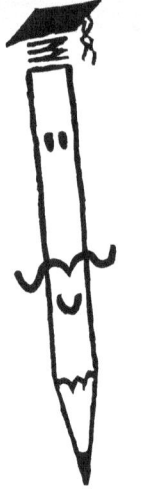

Excellent! You've adapted the HEIGHT of the cap, neck, shoulder and base to fit your drawing, proportionally. Next, prepare to do the same for the HORIZONTAL distances.

STEP 10 — DETERMINE THE CAP *LENGTH* AND ADAPT DISTANCE TO SCALE

Take a *LATERAL* (sideways) pencil check of your jar's cap, and compare it to the body (8-29). You should find that it reaches about three fourths of the way. Since the horizontal span of your square also stands for the body width, next take a pencil check three quarters of the way across. Then, CENTER that span on the top line of your drawing and mark 2 dots. One should be by your thumb and the other at your pencil tip (8-30). Follow through with a line DOWN from each dot to the HORIZONTAL line below. This will "BOX IN" the rectangle, which represents the cap (8-31).

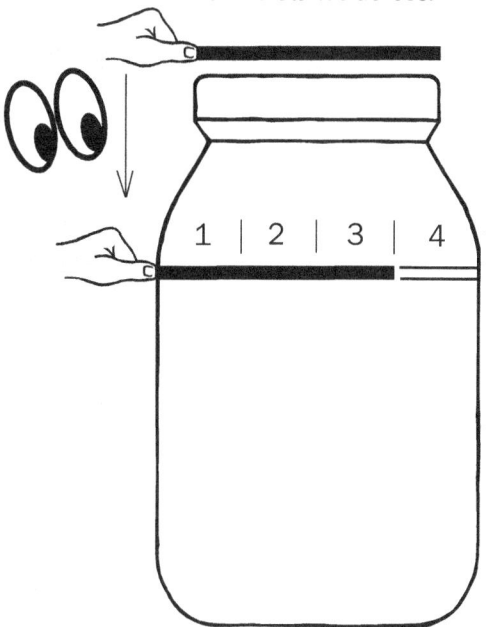

8-29 Cap about THREE FOURTHS BODY distance *across*.

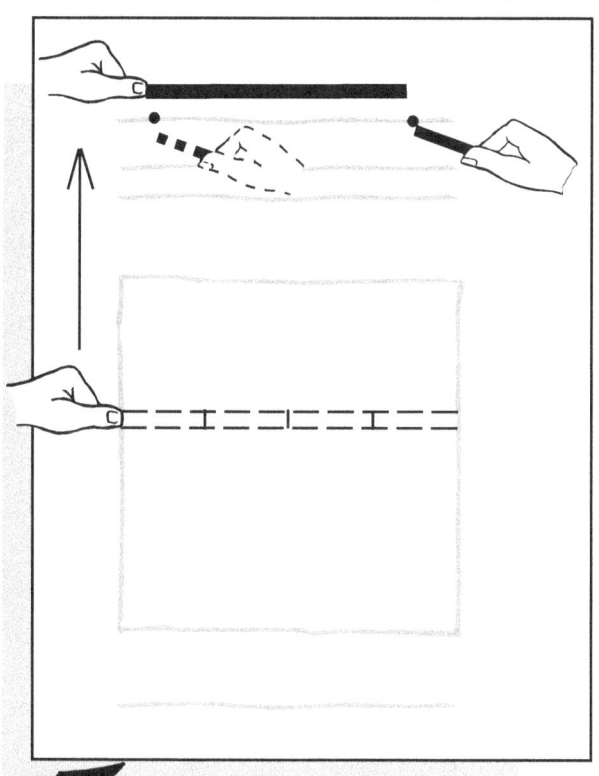

8-30 Three fourths of YOUR square gives cap length. *Center* that span with 2 dots on your top line.

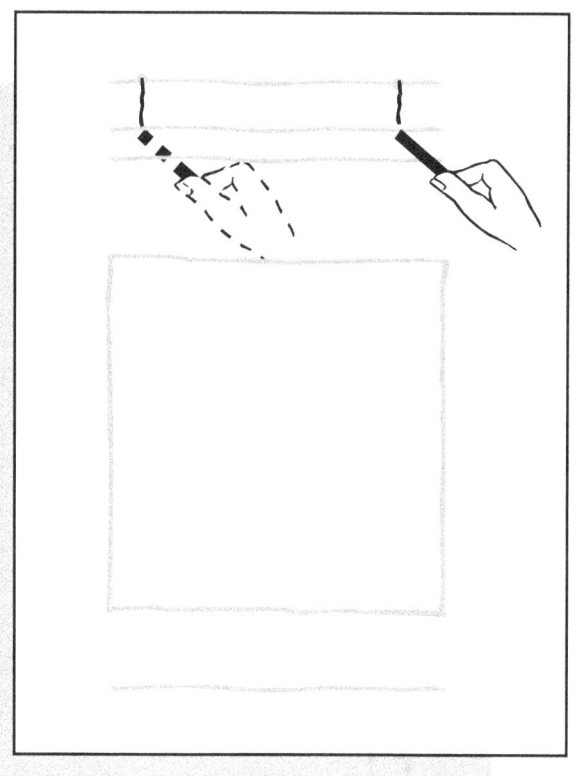

8-31 Vertical lines from dots establish cap sides.

Again, just as a reminder, look at YOUR jar along with the book illustrations in order to check the position of your reference points BEFORE you draw your lines.

STEP 11 — ESTABLISH NECK ANGLE AND CONVERT TO SCALE

Concentrate on the neck TAPERS of YOUR jar. You will notice they slope IN from both sides, a distance approximately the SAME LENGTH as the neck HEIGHT(8-32). This span is on YOUR drawing between the 2nd and 3rd line from the top. Estimate that distance visually or take a pencil check. Next, use the dimension to place two dots on your THIRD *line from the TOP*. One dot should be IN from the LEFT of your short vertical line (left end of cap) and the other dot should be IN from the RIGHT (8-33). To establish the neck ANGLES, draw a line DIAGONALLY from the LEFT *DOT* to the LEFT *CORNER* of your "cap." Then, repeat with a diagonal line from the RIGHT *DOT* to the RIGHT *CORNER* (8-34).

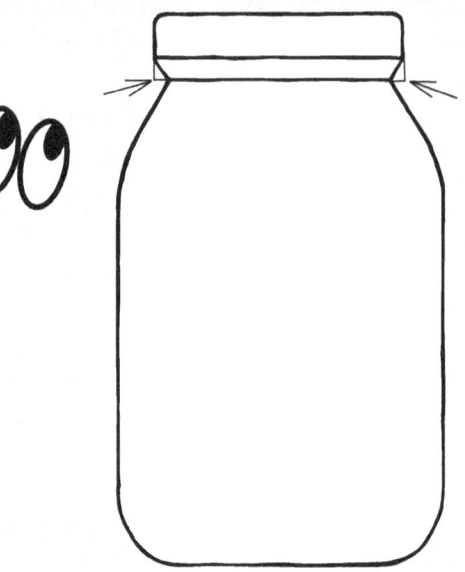

8-32 Focus on YOUR jar's NECK. The angles extend inward about same span as height.

8-33 Two dots locate the neck angle extension.

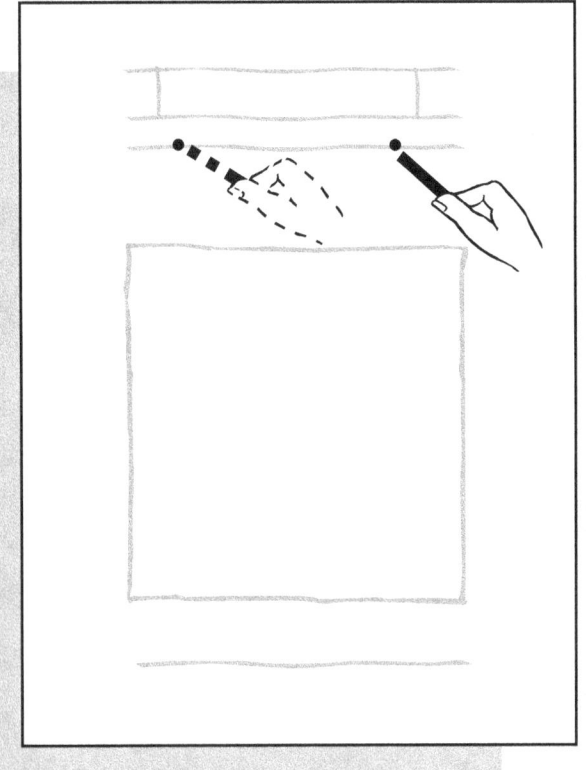

8-34 Two lines establish the neck angles.

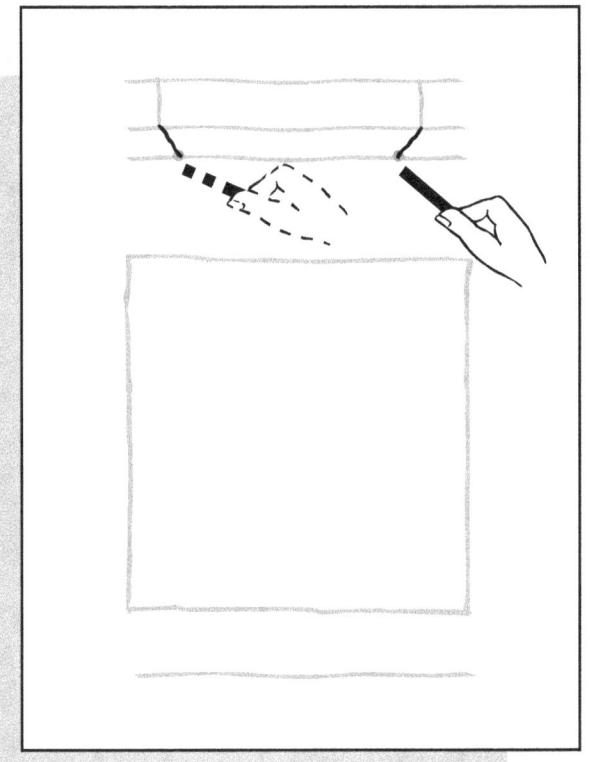

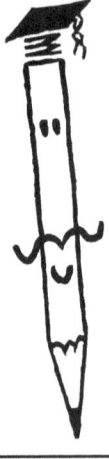

If you're growing impatient, it's time for a breather. You and your drawing should be allowed to take as long as needed.

STEP 12 | ESTABLISH THE BASE AND SHOULDER ANGLES

A visual check of YOUR jar's base will verify that its angle is aligned PLUMB with the point where the neck and shoulder meet (8-35). In order to locate those positions on *your* drawing, imagine a plumb line from both sides of the neck to the bottom line. If you like, you can also lightly draw a couple of guide lines. Where they intersect, place TWO dots (8-36). Next, fashion the BASE angles with a couple of lines by connecting them from each dot to the corresponding LOWER corners of your square (8-37). Then, establish the SHOULDERS with a pair of diagonal lines from the neck tapers to the respective TOP corners of your square.

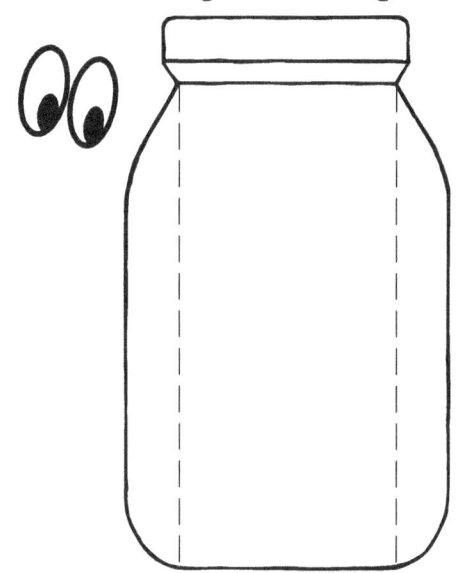
8-35 Shoulder angles and base angles are PLUMB.

8-36 Two dots plumb with neck locate base angle.

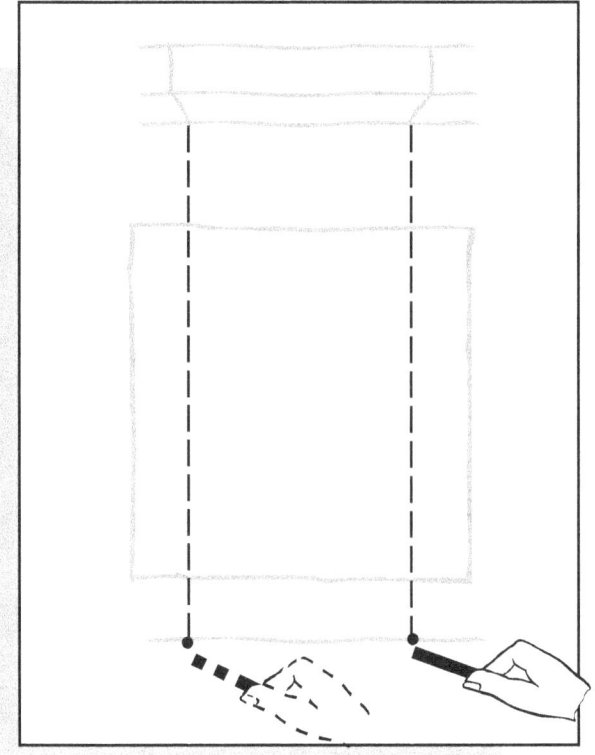

8-37 Two lines establish the BASE angles.
Two lines establish the shoulders.

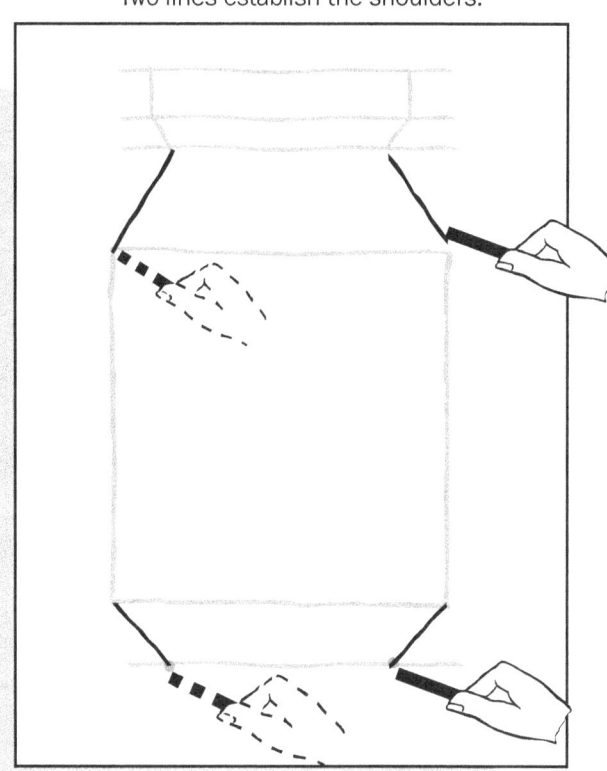

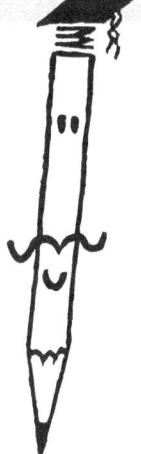

Congratulations! You've completed the streamline. Next, check it overall. The following page reveals a nifty method.

COMPARE SIDE-BY-SIDE, *FROM A DISTANCE*

Early on, you discovered it's helpful to STOP drawing occasionally in order to study your work in progress. That way *all* your energy can be channeled for spotting differences between your rendition and the model. As illustration 8-38 indicates, we're about to add a new dimension to the process. We are going to make a side-by-side comparison to *check status* from a DISTANCE.

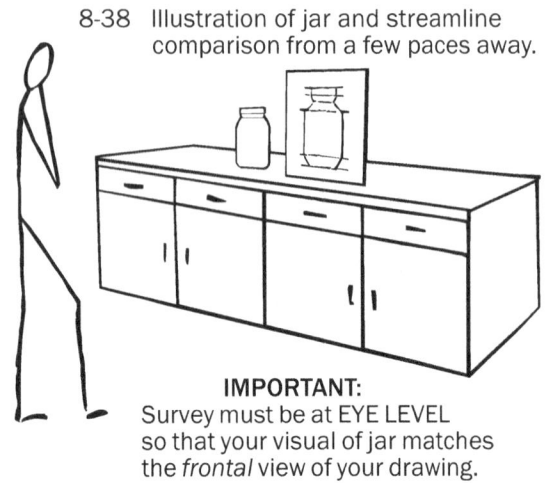

8-38 Illustration of jar and streamline comparison from a few paces away.

IMPORTANT:
Survey must be at EYE LEVEL so that your visual of jar matches the *frontal* view of your drawing.

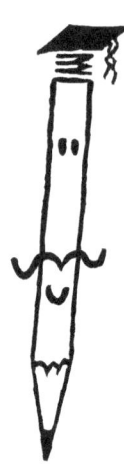

I know what you're thinking. Side-by-side comparisons at a distance can't make much DIFFERENCE, *especially* at the STREAMLINE stage. Trust me! They CAN and they DO!

Take a look at following side-by-side comparison 8-39. Notice that the *streamline* drawing of the jar appears too tall, *proportionally*. Chances are, the reason is that the original square (serving as the foundation) didn't start out a square, but rather as a rectangle (longer in height). Fear not, however. All is not lost. Recall what you learned in Chapter 5, specifically that it's much easier to modify a streamline before curves are added. In this case, the base just needs to be raised a little. This is indicated by the broken lines. Then the *former* base (indicated by light gray) can be erased.

8-39 Example *comparison* reveals the base needs to be raised.

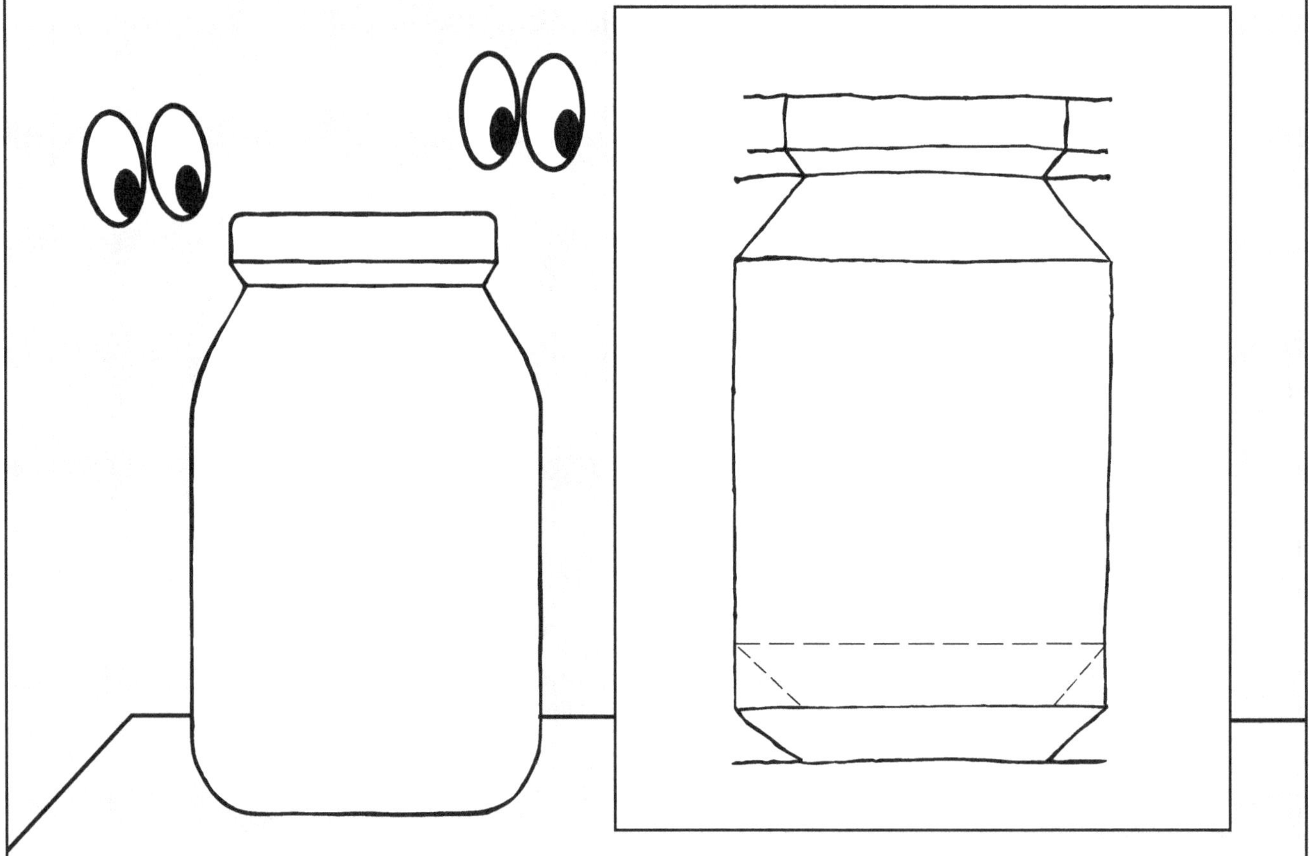

Consider a side-by-side comparison, from a distance, like a **picture in a picture**. In this manner, you can see both your drawing and your model TOGETHER, virtually at the SAME TIME. How is this useful? With less chance for you to lose memory between glances from the real object to your drawing, differences just seem to STAND OUT! This includes situations where it's impractical to place your drawing next to your subject. For instance, when it's too big, like a tree or a mountain, take a few paces back anyway. You'll be amazed how much sharper your ability to compare will be when you have your drawing and your model *simultaneously* in sight.

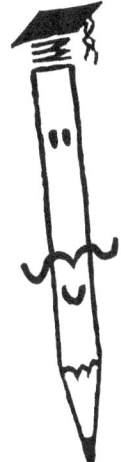

There's no need to be bashful. Proudly prop up your drawing beside your jar. Position yourself at EYE LEVEL so that your frontal view of your jar appears like your drawing. Then read the following carefully.

HOT TIP Finding "flaws" in your drawing is a lot like noticing a fresh stain on the carpet. You feel compelled to scrub like mad to remove the unwanted spot as soon as possible. The rub (no pun intended) is that this usually causes more harm than good. The same can happen when adjusting your work. Although you will have a natural urge to tally ALL, then "fix" EVERYTHING AT ONCE in order to make the "problem" vanish *FAST*, I implore you NOT to try to do that. Counter the tendency to act in haste and/or cram (overload). Instead, *calmly* take your picture apart with your eyes, like you do when drawing. *Compare whole to whole, as well as parts to parts, in search of ONE glitch at a TIME.* Scan for the OBVIOUS first, the way you learned. Start with proportion, followed by alignments, then reverse space. As you know, these usually affect the other four of the "TRUSTY SEVEN," namely angles, curves, straight lines, and reference points. Handle each needed change INDIVIDUALLY and in stride. Then VERIFY your result IMMEDIATELY. All the while, keep in mind *you are NOT searching for mistakes*. You are seeking to make improvements. Leave well enough alone and you lose your chance to do better. Go overboard and things can get out of hand. Either way, you could easily end up with POT LUCK! Remember you're human and you're learning. Don't demand perfection of yourself, or be content with less than what you feel you're capable of. Find a satisfactory medium. If any of this sounds new to you, please reread the follow-up in Chapters 3 and 5, along with pages 108 and 125. After you've made your refinements, advance to the next step.

You need not concern yourself with minor details like the ridges at the sides of your jar's cap, for instance. Just concentrate on the main arcs. Make sure you notice not only WHERE they are, but also HOW much they "bow." In addition, try to imagine your streamline wrapped around your jar as shown by illustration (8-40). This will help you form your arcs, similar to the way you drew the curves for the ivy leaf in Chapter 5, as well as the the butterfly wings and the cloverleaf in Chapter 6.

8-40 Pictured in your mind, the curves may appear something like this.

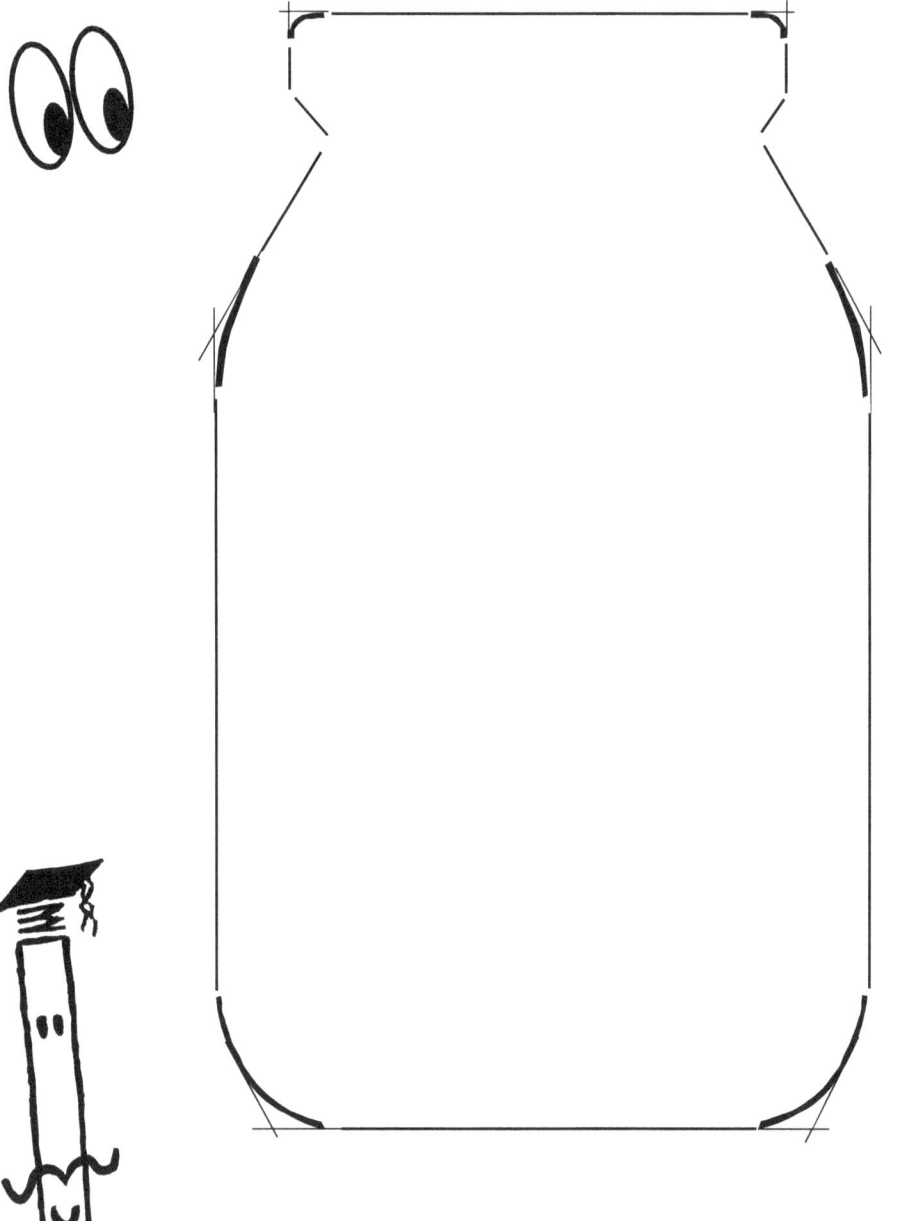

Did you study YOUR jar's curves? If not, please get acquainted with them, one by one, now.

STEP 15 | PREPARE TO ADD THE CURVES

You can start anywhere or follow a clockwise direction. Either way, before you begin, read the following:

1. Your jar could have slightly different features. For instance, yours could have ridges on the cap. If not, maybe the neck is a little more angular or possibly less. Whatever the variations are, you can ignore them or adapt your drawing accordingly.

2. Look at your jar again. Pick a curve and study it very carefully. Trace it in the air several times to get a better sense for its specific shape. Next, locate its corresponding position on your drawing. Then duplicate the curve you observed, in proportion to your drawing.

3. Please, don't rely on just your memory. Glance back and forth between your drawing and the real jar while forming each curve.

4. Compare your result after every curve and adjust as needed before advancing.

5. Erase the unnecessary lines and do a little clean up.

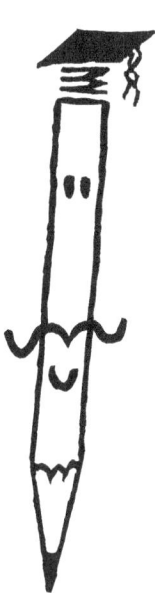

After having applied the curves, compare your jar, SIDE-BY-SIDE, with your drawing again. Why? Because POST evaluations are also very helpful. Turn the page and learn more secrets.

A THOROUGH ONCE OVER CAN DO WONDERS

It's normal to feel uneasy when your picture is about done. That fearful moment of truth is near. It's time to see what turned out.

Wow! What a scary thought. To discover something may not be right on your work means you goofed, isn't that so?

Not at all! Let's face it. Nobody is perfect and when it comes to drawing, as you know, virtually everything is a visual ESTIMATE, not an exact measure. So be fair to yourself. The only way you can improve on what you've done is to be willing to work on it some more. Read between the lines and you will understand the message. Specifically, you should NOT expect your pencil strokes to be *precise*. *Adjustment* is part of the program. There is a snag, however. You can overdo or underdo it.

If you settle for second best because you might spoil what you already have (although you notice there are areas that still need attention), you end up cheating your potential. Then there's the opposite extreme. This is where you're never content and overindulge by making too many changes. Ultimately you lose either way.

One sure sign you're fussing occurs when you only see ever so slight variations between your picture and your model but not enough to make any real difference, yet you continue to revise.

In order to help find a balance, I suggest you apply the following rule. When your drawing looks *reasonably* accurate to you (beside the model and alone), that's the ideal place to stop. After all, just as Mt. Everest can not be conquered in a day, you shouldn't expect to be a master over night. Besides, look how far you've already come.

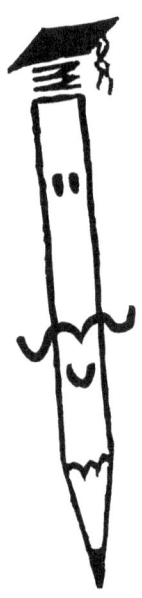

Be brave. Take the plunge. Double check your drawing. Then examine the student examples shown on the next page.

EXERCISE 8
MODEL & STUDENT EXAMPLES

Model

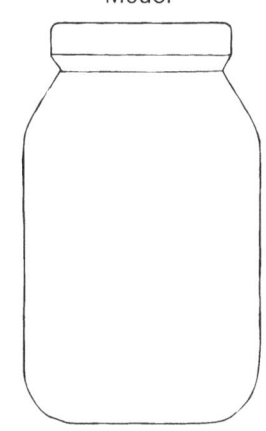

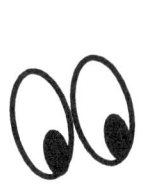

STUDENT SAMPLING

| 8-41 | 8-42 | 8-43 |

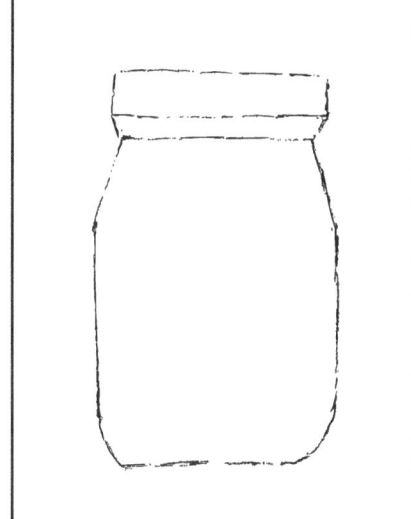 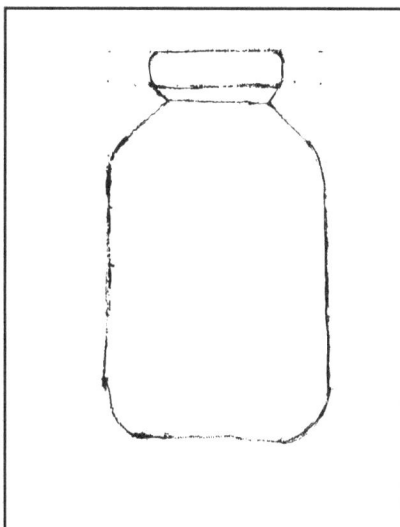 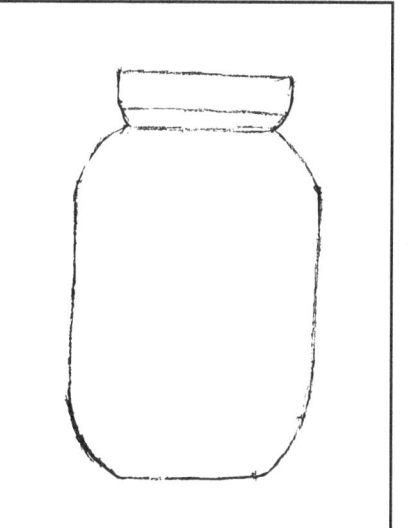

These drawings are quite good, aren't they?
You can learn much from them. Following are my suggestions for improvement.

On figure 8-41, the cap and neck could use a little *shortening* horizontally, with respect to scale.
On figure 8-42, the cap and neck need to be *extended* horizontally.
On figure 8-43, the shoulder curves should not be so exaggerated, and the sides are tilted.

Did you *observe* some of the same things I did? Hopefully, you're gaining a great deal of valuable insight by assessing not only your work but others as well. Remember, it's not a contest to see whose work is best. The goal is to sharpen your vision. As you know, there's a lot more to seeing than just looking. The follow-up helps put things in focus.

Chapter 8
FOLLOW-UP

For the most part, whether you draw from a picture, or from an actual subject, the process is about the same, isn't it? All that's essentially required is to keep a few important things in mind. They are listed as follows:

1. The principles of scale, which you utilize when using a picture as your reference, can also be applied to *real* things.

2. Squinting your eyes makes it easier to see the overall shape. The small details seem to vanish. In turn, this helps you visualize your streamline.

3. While comparing pencil checks for proportions from a distance, close one eye, keep your arm fully extended, and remain still.

4. Pencil readings from afar tend to be much smaller and therefore less reliable. As always, you need to refine *visually*.

5. The practice of standing back and making side-by-side comparisons between your drawing and the subject you're working from (whether real, or a picture), is not only vital *during* the drawing stages, but *afterward* as well.

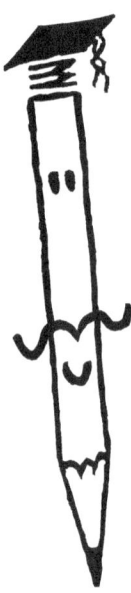

Look at your subject as much as, if not more than, your drawing. That's where the answers are. And since you've performed such a terrific job with your mayonnaise jar, go ahead and make yourself a sandwich.

THE RANDOM MODE
Drawing "randomly" means you can proceed as you please.
Take a look at the illustration.

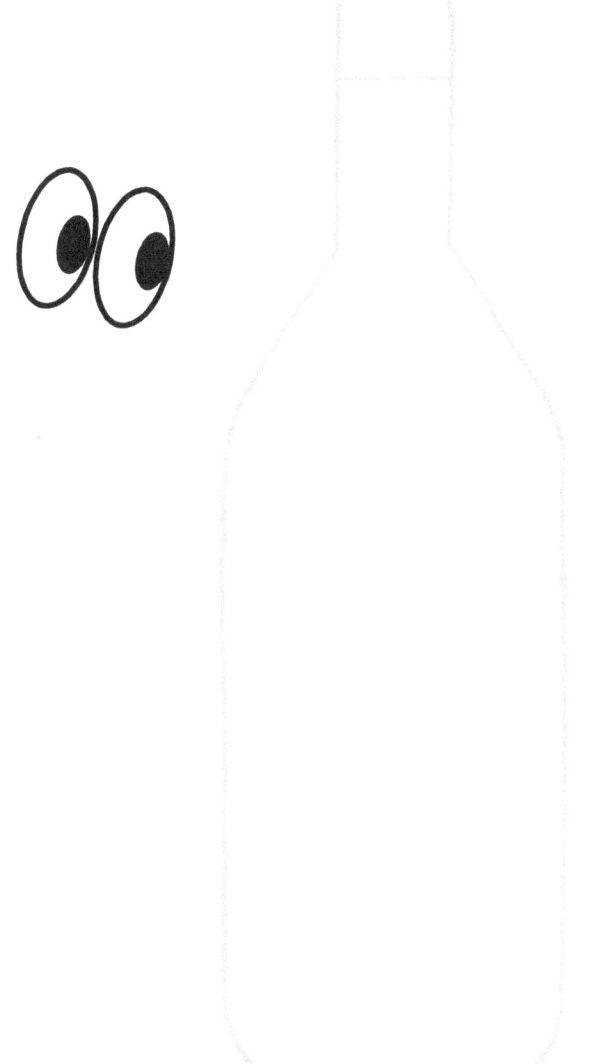

Yep! This is a CONTINUOUS LINE drawing of a bottle. But that's not all. There's a lot more going on.

Here we have a SKETCH version of the bottle. Which style do you prefer, the one shown on the previous page, or this one?

The beauty is that while you scanned, just as your eyes were able to roam, such freedom can also be adapted to drawing. You can begin at the top and work your way down, or vice versa. You can also start in the middle and proceed in either direction. You can even skip around. It's nice to have options, don't you think? So let's put the random method to work.

OBJECTIVE: Draw a likeness of the bottle.
Choose *EITHER* the CONTINUOUS line, or SKETCH line technique.

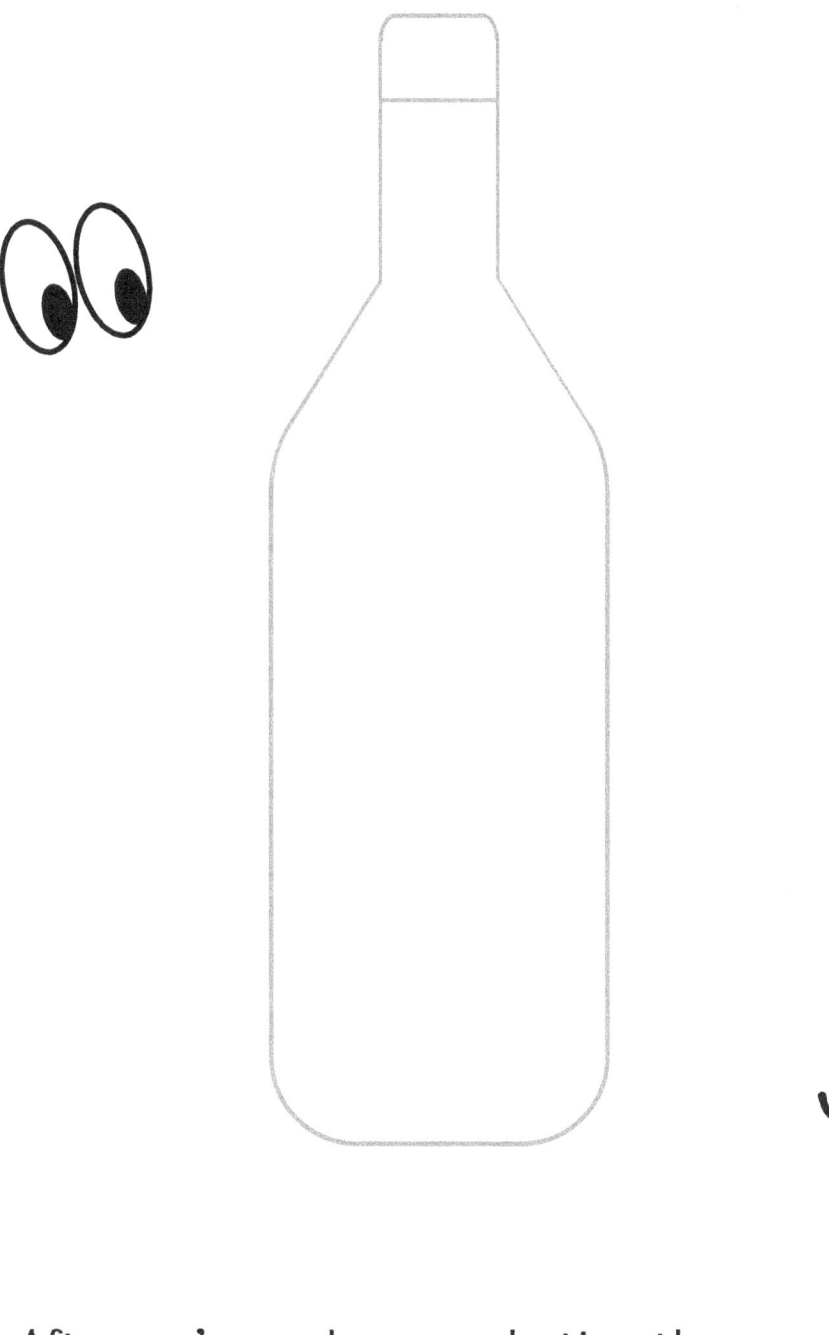

After you've made your selection, there are
suggested steps which begin on the next page.

As illustration 9-1 shows, if we imagine the figure as if it were wrapped with straight lines, our streamline emerges. Next, with a simple visual or pencil check, we quickly see that three times the width reaches the bottom of the cap (9-2).

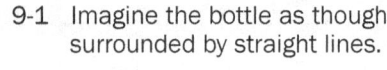

9-1 Imagine the bottle as though surrounded by straight lines.

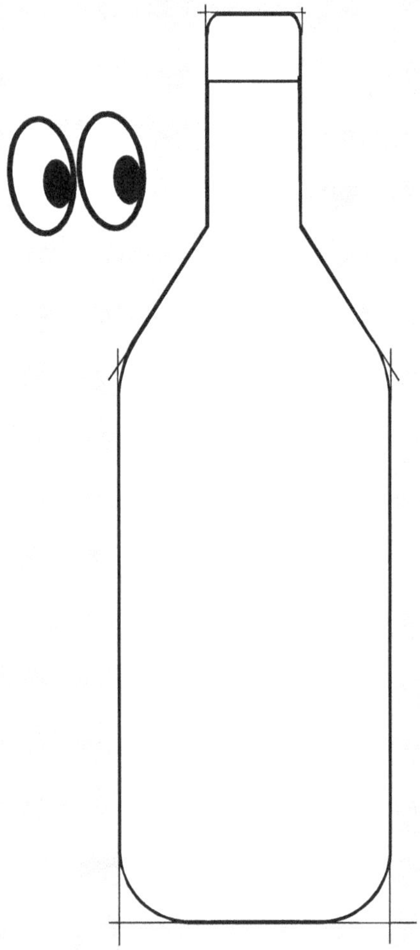

9-2 Check overall proportion to find that bottle *width* fits 3 times in *height* up to *base of cap.*

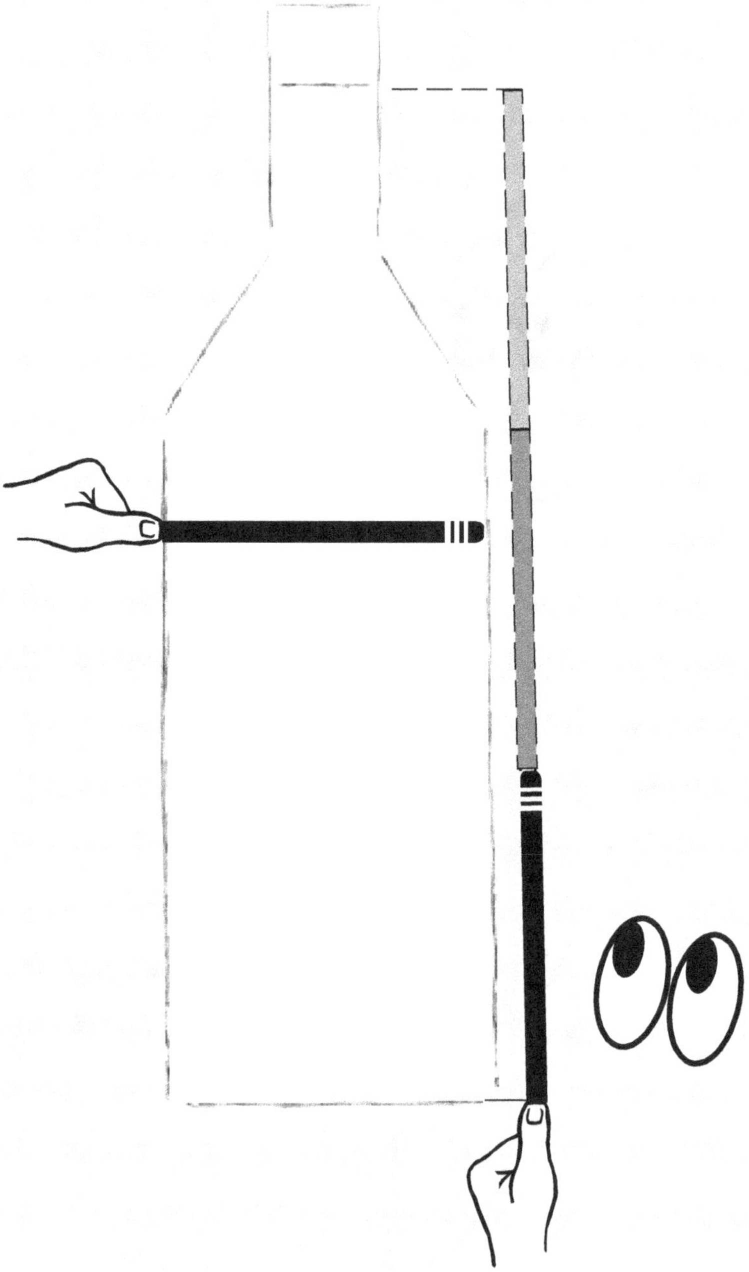

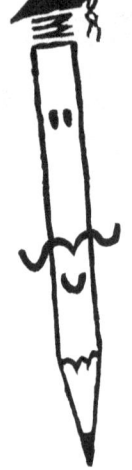

Do we have enough information to start drawing already? You bet! How is this possible, without more observations? Because we are proceeding "randomly." That means we can LOOK, THINK, and DRAW, AS WE GO.

STEP 2   CHOOSE A STARTING PLACE AND SIZE

We can begin anywhere, and elect a size that suits our fancy.   But since this might be your first experience with the random method, I suggest you take out a fresh sheet of paper, then follow my lead. We already know the subject's *height* is *over* THREE times its WIDTH, so whatever dimension we elect to represent the maximum *HORIZONTAL* distance (for OUR bottle drawing), the span will have to to fit at least FOUR times VERTICALLY. If not, we will run out of room. With this in mind, I recommend beginning with a size *no more than* HALF the *horizontal* extent of your palm. Mark that distance with 2 dots, slightly above the center of your sheet (9-3). They will represent the shoulder expanse and the bottle width, at the same time.

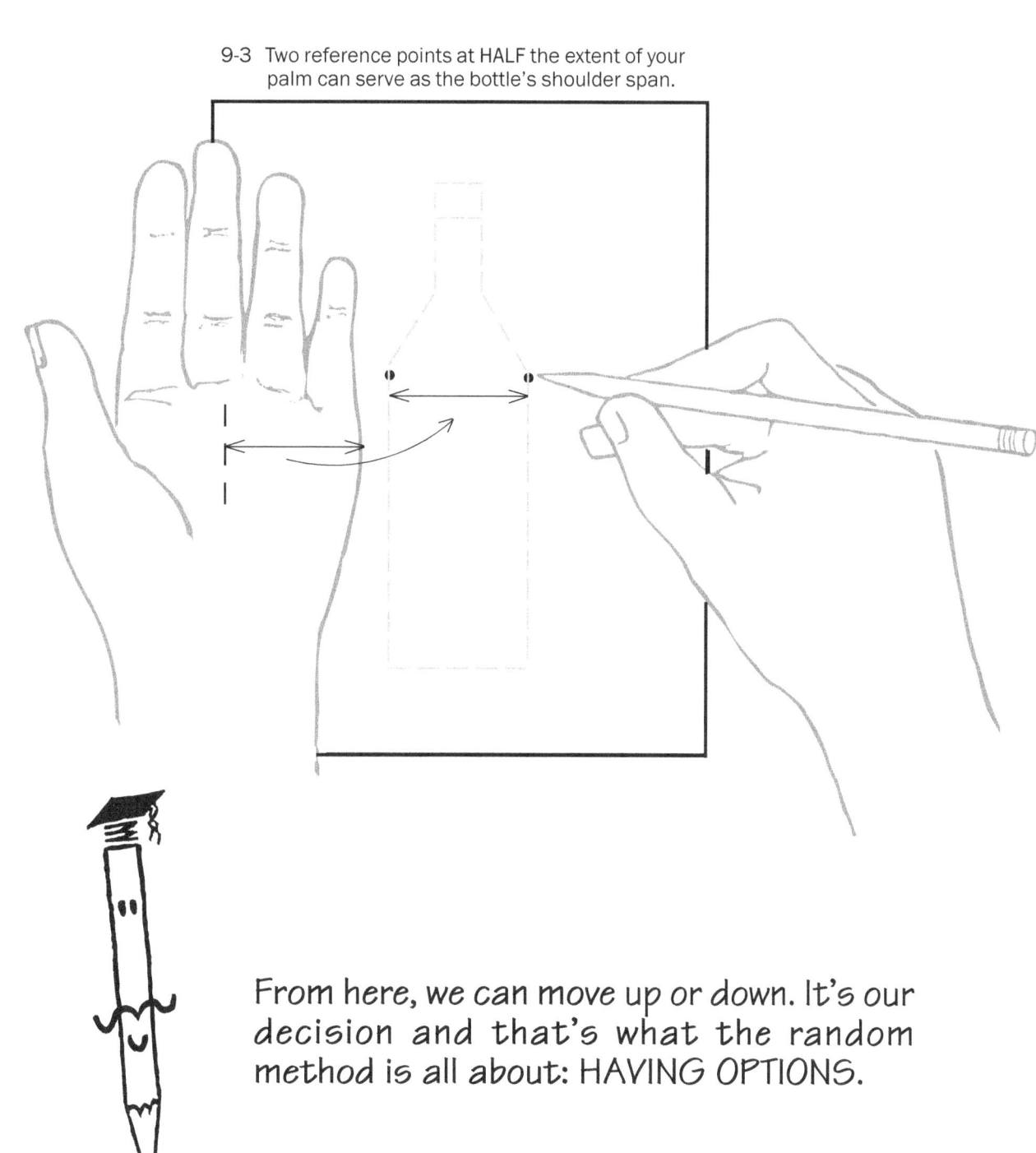

9-3 Two reference points at HALF the extent of your
      palm can serve as the bottle's shoulder span.

From here, we can move up or down. It's our decision and that's what the random method is all about: HAVING OPTIONS.

STEP 3   TAKE A LOOK AT THE LEFT SHOULDER

Notice when we take a visual or pencil reading HORIZONTALLY from ONE shoulder to the neck, and check that across, we uncover an interesting feature about our subject. Its width is equally divided into three parts (9-4). The shoulders each take one third of the total span, and the neck is also a third.

9-4   The neck and both shoulders EACH extend
about ONE THIRD of the entire way across.

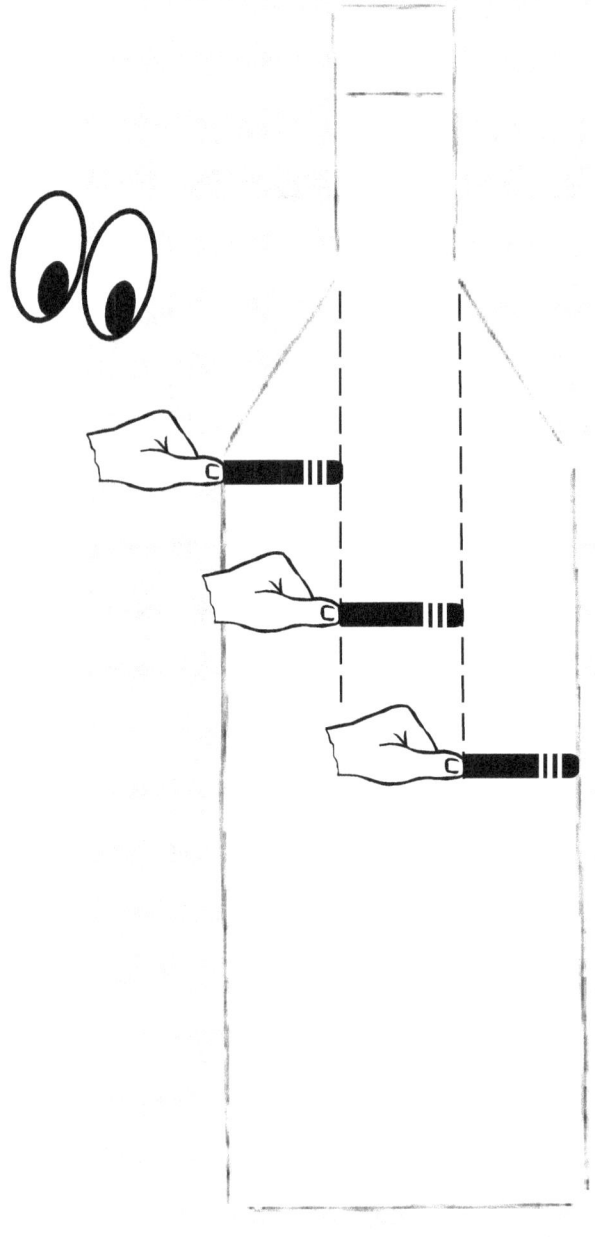

STEP 4 | ESTABLISH BOTH SHOULDER *WIDTHS* ON *YOUR* DRAWING

Initiate by taking a visual or pencil check, a **THIRD** of the way *IN* from YOUR left dot, and mark the distance with another dot (9-5). Next, do the same from the RIGHT dot. The two "inner" dots will not only locate the **WIDTH** of each shoulder but also the neck between them (9-6).

9-5 One third in from your LEFT dot locates the LEFT shoulder span.

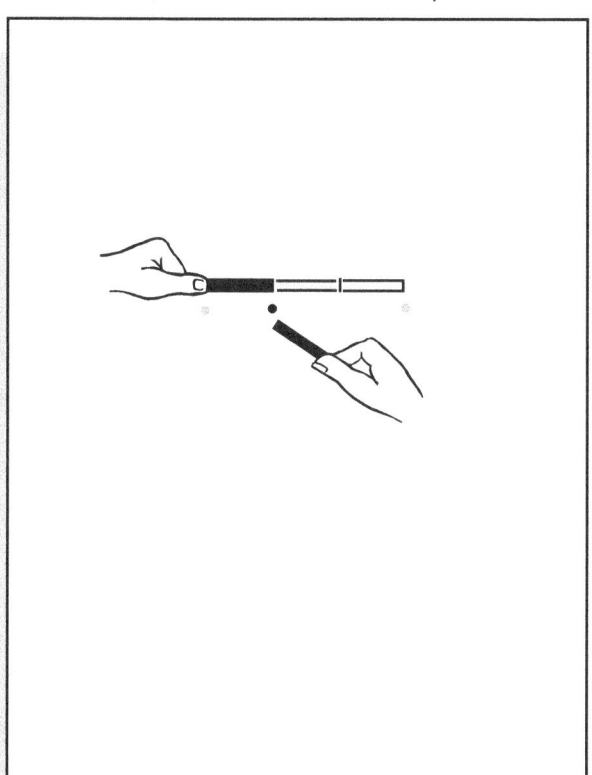

9-6 One third IN from your RIGHT dot locates the RIGHT shoulder span.

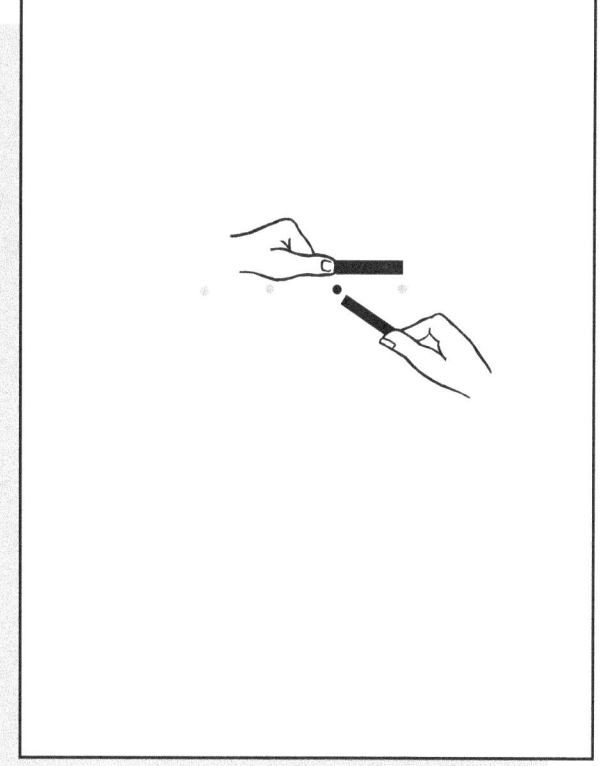

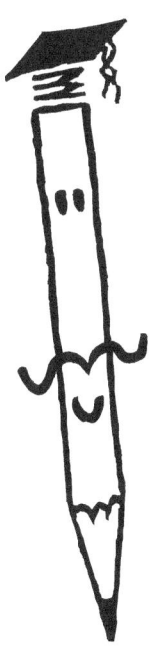

I trust you're enjoying the process more, and thinking about the outcome less. Draw for the fun of it.

Take a visual or VERTICAL pencil reading of the left shoulder's *height*, and compare that to the bottle's *width*. As you can tell, the span reaches about HALF WAY (9-7).

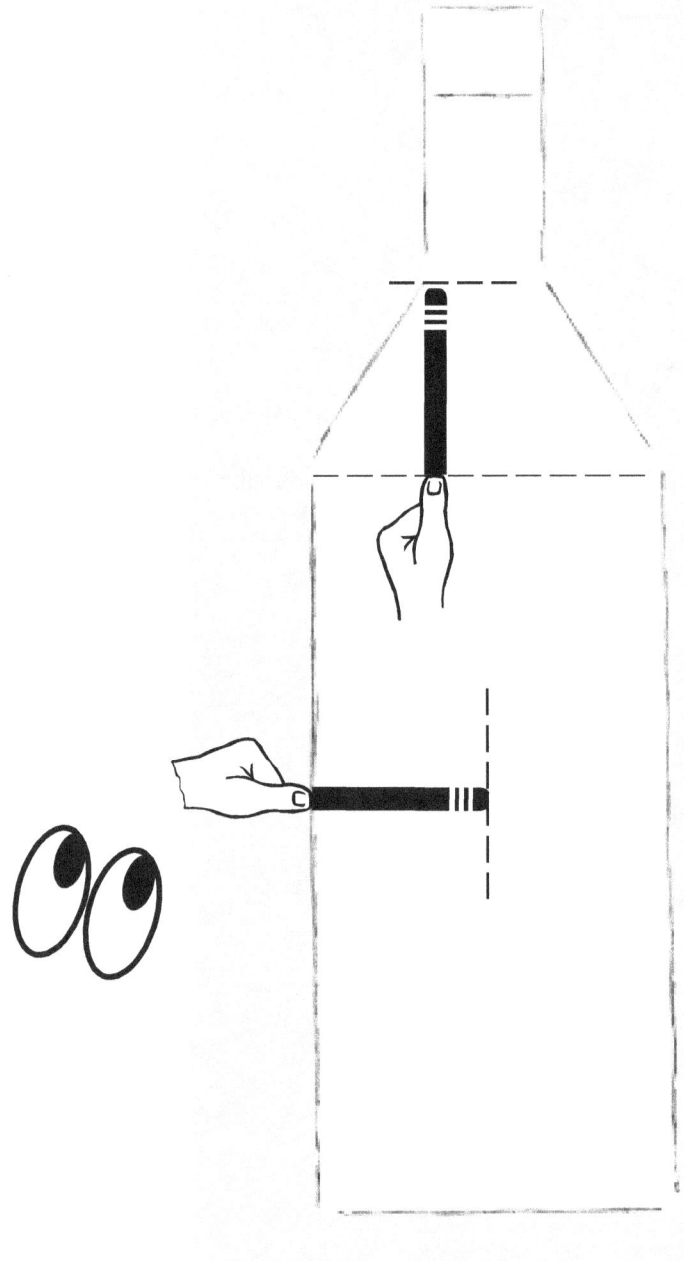

9-7 Shoulder *HEIGHT* appears to be about HALF the bottle WIDTH.

After this very useful find, we are prepared to draw some more.

Since the shoulder *height* proved to be **HALF** the bottle *width*, and that distance is represented by ***YOUR 4 dots,*** take a pencil check **HALF** way across (9-8). Next, *rotate* the distance above both of your TWO "inner" dots and mark the span with 2 more dots, one at a time (9-9). At this point, your 2 *lower* "inner" dots have done their job, and are no longer needed, so erase them (9-10). Once that's done, link your remaining 2 sets of respective dots with a couple of lines to form the shoulder angles (9-11).

9-8 Find 1/2 span between your 4 dots.

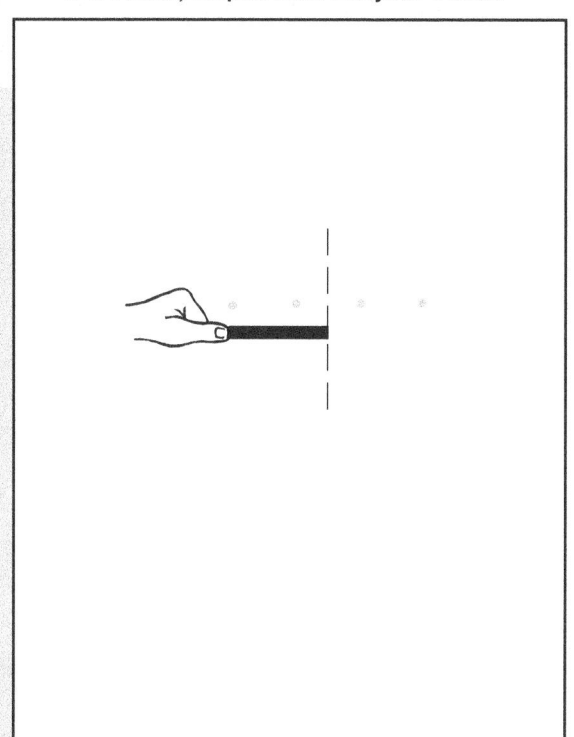

9-9 1/2 span marked with 2 dots above your 2 *inner* dots.

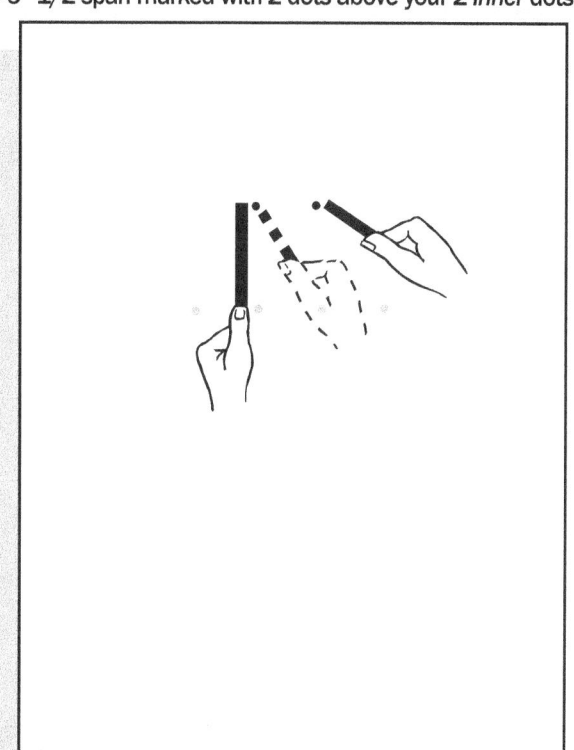

9-10 Erase *your LOWER "inner"* 2 dots.

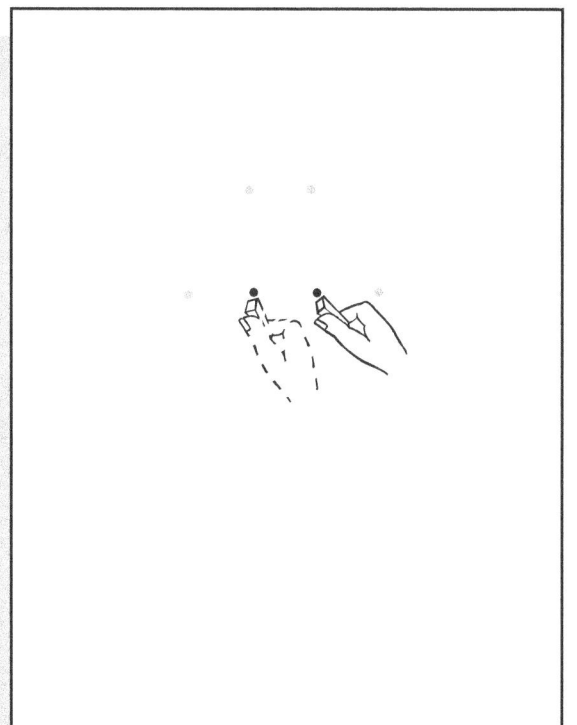

9-11 Lightly draw shoulders with 2 lines.

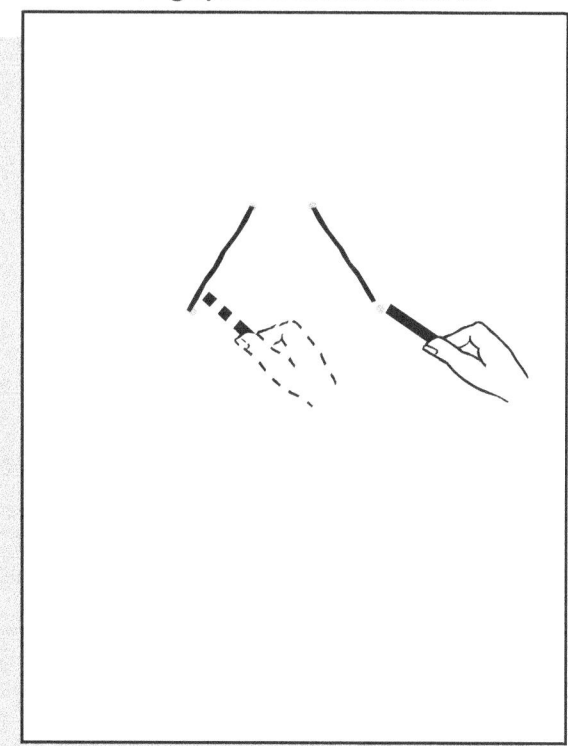

STEP 7 | DECIDE WHICH DIRECTION TO GO NEXT

At this stage, we have two options. We can "attach" the body or the neck. I vote for the latter, because we've already located the width when we drew the angle of the shoulders. Where they converged (pointed inward), the distance in between created the base of the neck. That means, all we need to do is find the HEIGHT. As illustration 9-12 indicates, by making a visual or pencil check comparison between the neck and the shoulder, we learn their *vertical* dimension is about the same.

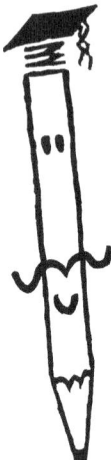

Now you know why I like to refer to our latest approach as the RANDOM METHOD. Whenever we have options, we have the freedom to make choices & roam at will.

9-12 Shoulder & neck *height* appear to be identical.

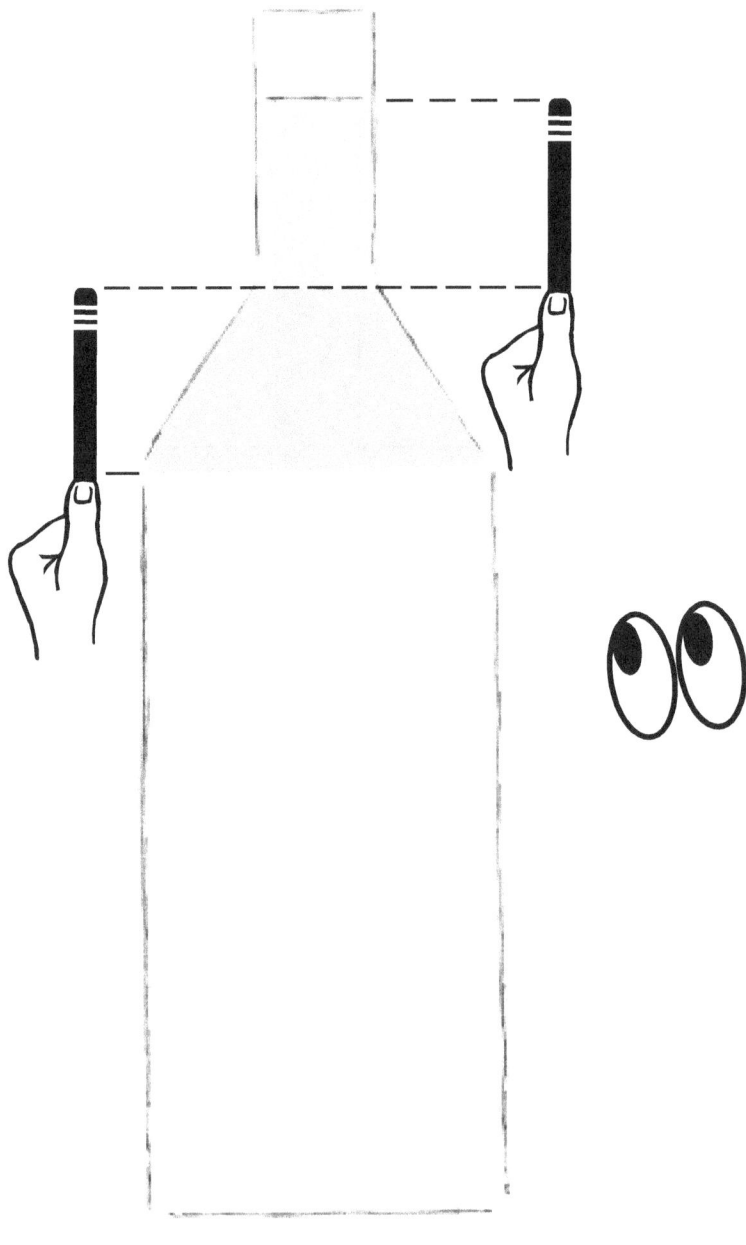

ESTABLISH THE NECK TO SCALE ON *YOUR* DRAWING

Take a vertical reading of YOUR drawing's left shoulder and move that span up by positioning your thumb beside the TOP of the left shoulder. Next, mark the distance with a dot by your pencil tip (9-13). Do the same above the right shoulder, making sure it's plumb (9-14). The result will be 2 dots which locate the *height* of the NECK. To establish it, draw a lines from your dots to the respective shoulders below (9-15). Then close the neck by lightly drawing a HORIZONTAL line between your 2 dots (9-16).

9-13 Apply *shoulder* height to locate *neck* height on the LEFT side.

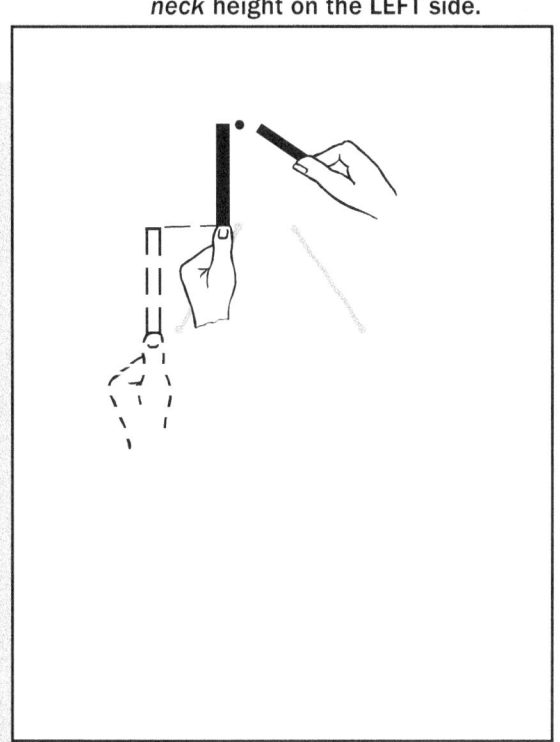

9-14 Place a 2nd dot for the neck height on the RIGHT side.

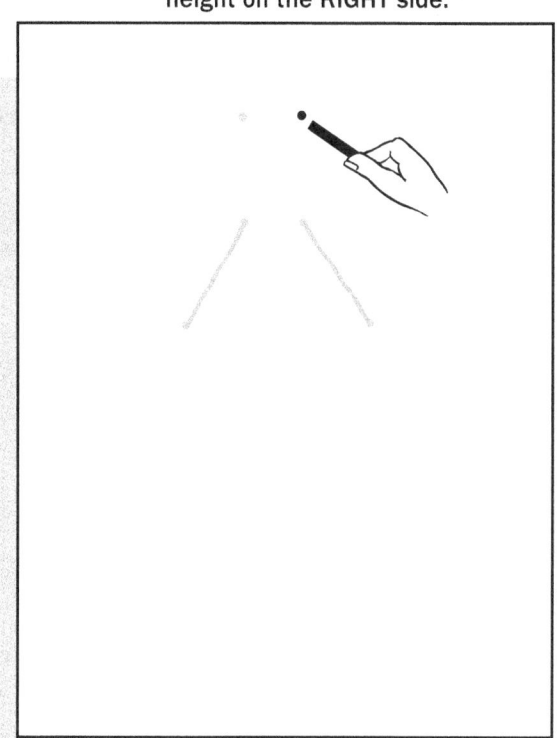

9-15 Draw *VERTICAL* lines to establish neck *sides*.

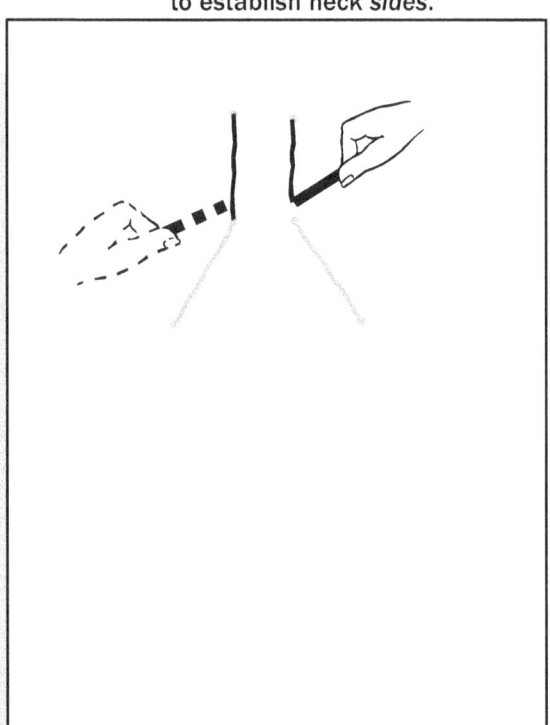

9-16 Draw a *HORIZONTAL* line to border the *top* of the neck.

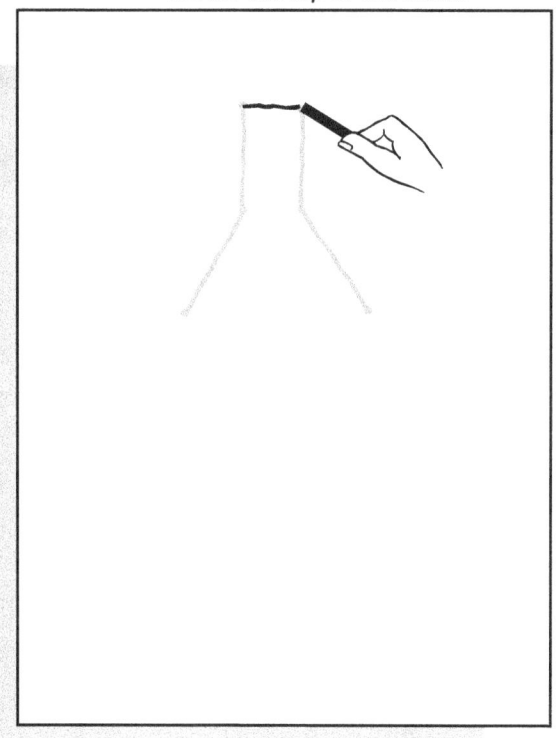

STEP 9 · DECISIONS, DECISIONS, AND MORE CHOICES

We can draw either the bottle cap or the body. Which do you prefer? I favor the body. Why? Because we've already located the bottle's width when we established the span for the shoulders. The **remaining** dimension to determine is the **BODY height** (excluding shoulder, neck and cap). As you can tell, whether we estimate visually, or with a pencil reading, the *body height* appears to be about DOUBLE the width (9-17).

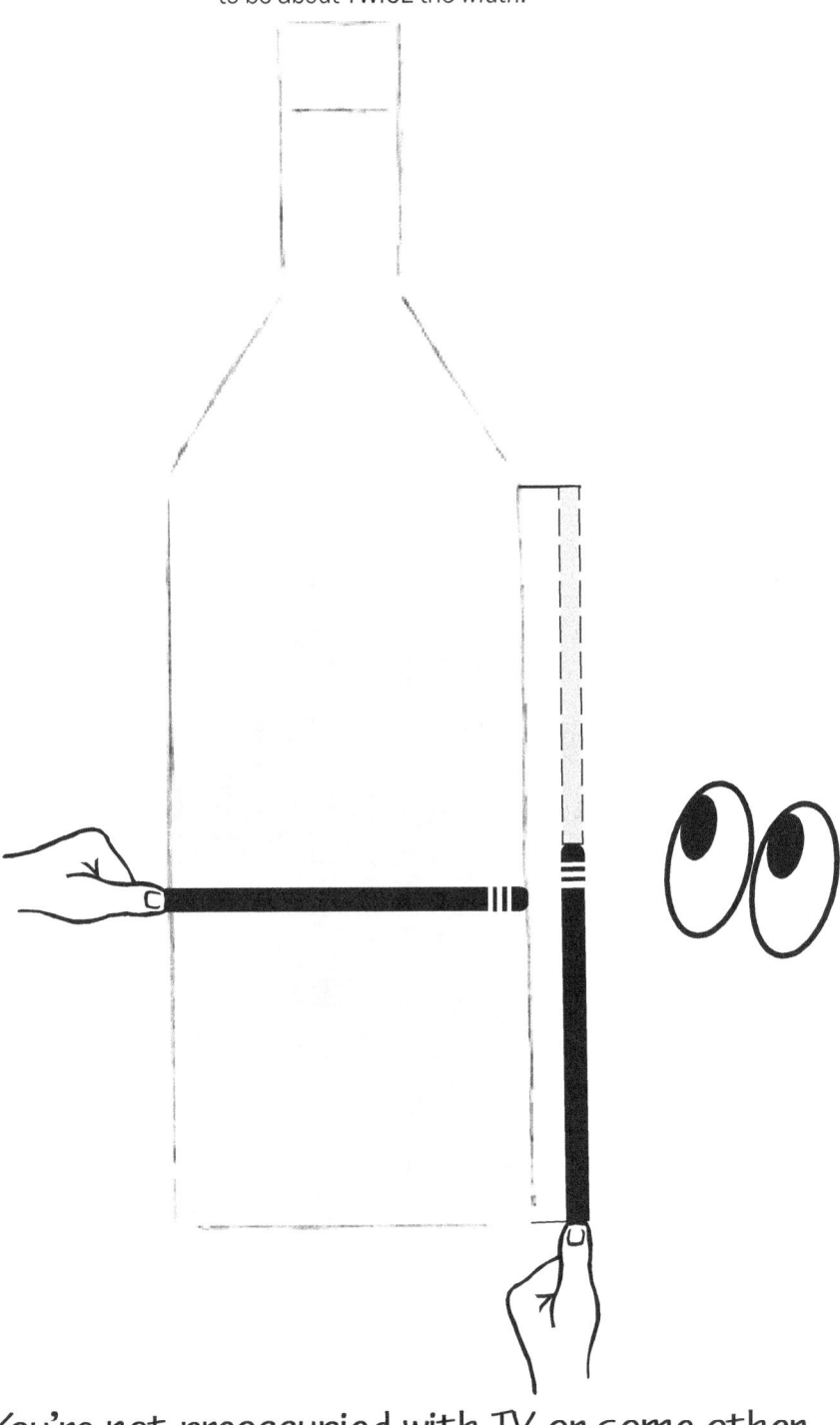

9-17 MAIN BODY *height* appears
to be about TWICE the *width*.

You're not preoccupied with TV or some other
distraction while you're drawing, are you? All
your attention should be channeled.

ESTABLISH THE SIDES AND BASE ON *YOUR* DRAWING

Since the bottle's height from the shoulder to the base is about TWICE the width, find that scale to fit *your* drawing. Start by simply estimating visually, or taking a lateral (sideways) pencil check of YOUR bottle's shoulder width (9-18). Next, rotate the span PLUMB. Then, from the bottom of the LEFT shoulder, DOUBLE the distance with 2 dots. Do the same from the bottom of the RIGHT shoulder (9-19). After that, draw a pair of VERTICAL lines from the shoulders to the lower dots to form the SIDES (9-20). Lastly, include a HORIZONTAL line between them, at the bottom, for the base (9-21). You need not connect all the way because curves will be added at the corners later.

9-18 Determine span of YOUR bottle's shoulders.

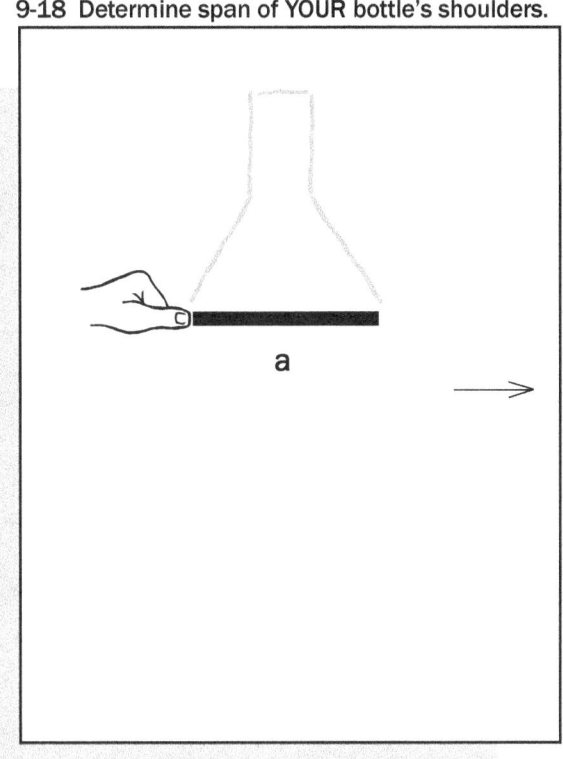

9-19 Rotate span & double from shoulders.

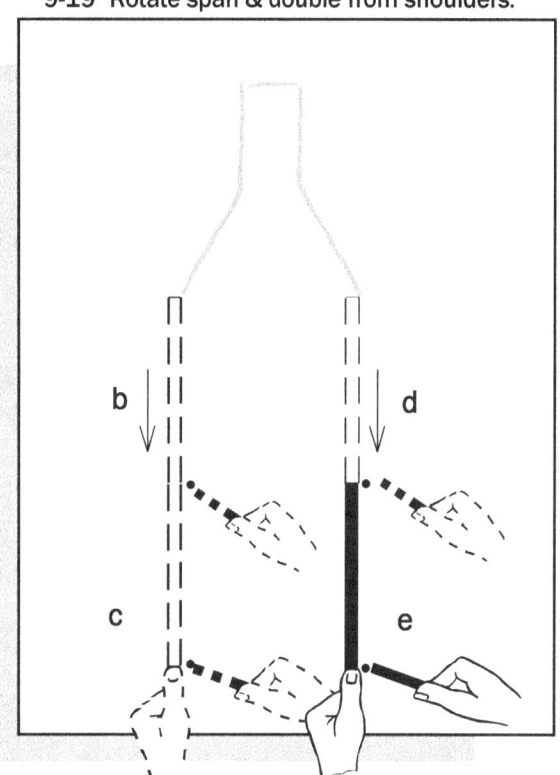

9-20 Draw PLUMB lines through your dots for sides.

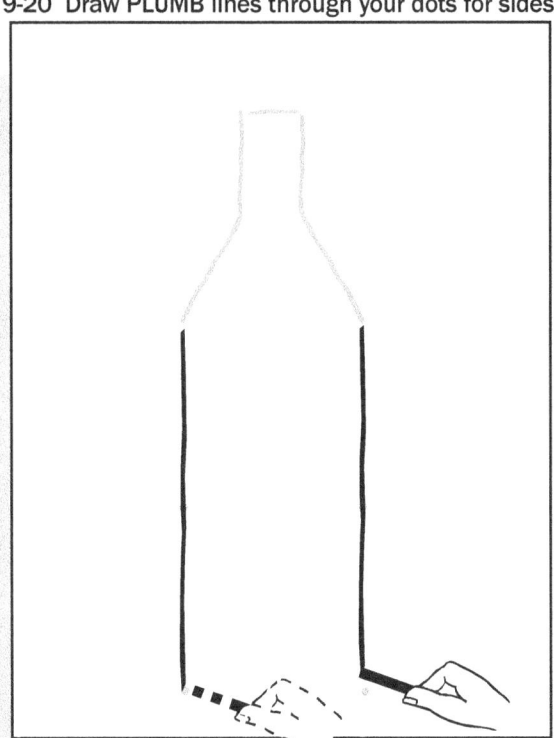

9-21 Draw a LEVEL line between your lower dots for base.

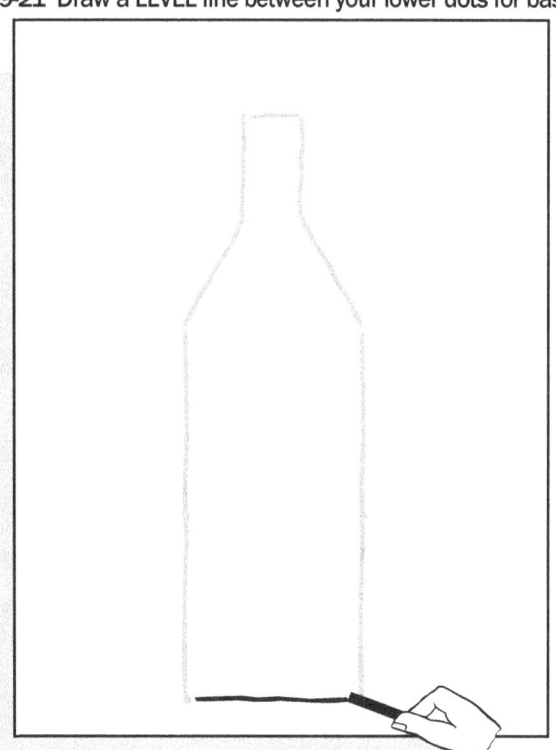

The cap's distance *sideways* is pretty straightforward. Clearly, it's the same as the neck. In order to determine the proportional HEIGHT, just take an upright visual, or pencil check. When you do this, you will see that the distance is about HALF the *vertical* span of the neck (9-22).

9-22 Cap height is about HALF the neck height.

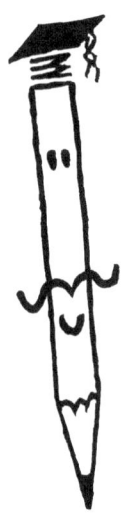

Have you been taking your time?
There's no need to rush, you know.

STEP 12 CONVERT THE SCALE OF THE CAP TO FIT *YOUR* DRAWING

Take a VERTICAL pencil reading, or a visual, to determine HALF the height of YOUR bottle's neck as shown by illustration 9-23. Next, transfer the distance above both corners of your bottle's neck with a couple of dots (9-24). Then, draw a *horizontal* line between your two dots (9-25). Lastly, form the cap *sides* with a pair of *vertical* lines (9-26).

9-23   Check HALF your bottle's neck height.

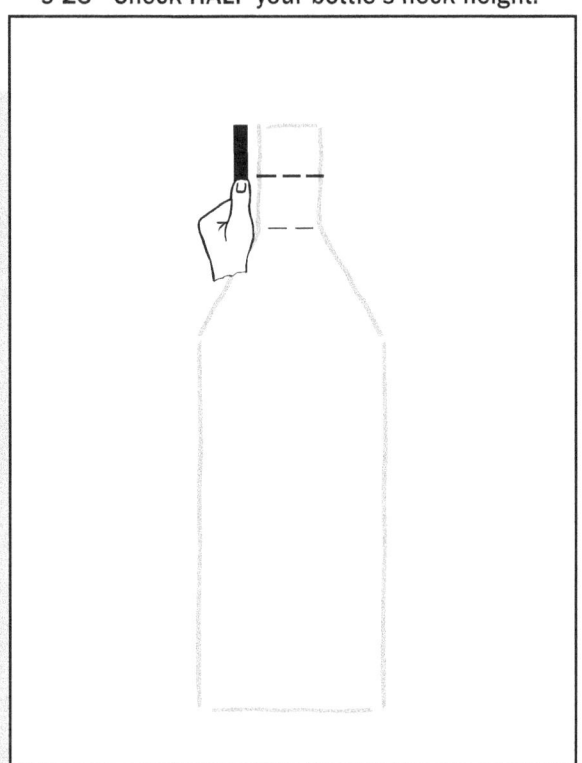

9-24   Mark 1/2 neck HEIGHT above neck SIDES with dots.

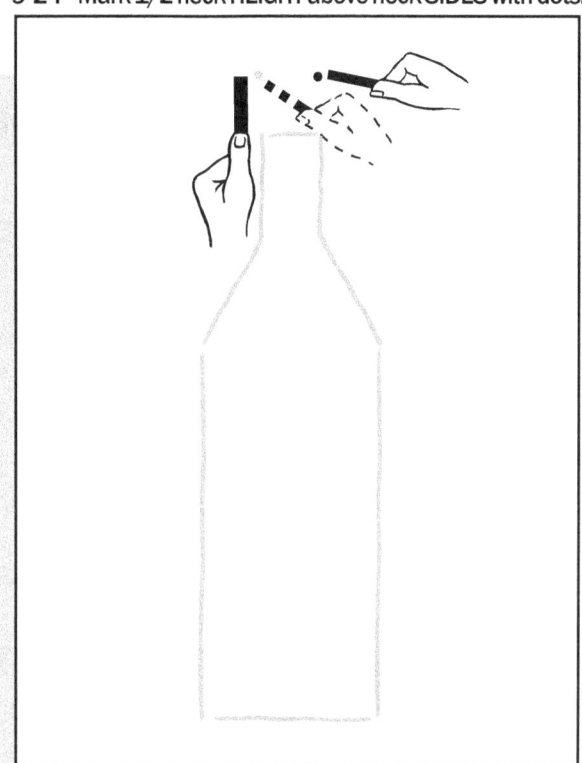

9-25   Connect your 2 dots with a *horizontal* line.

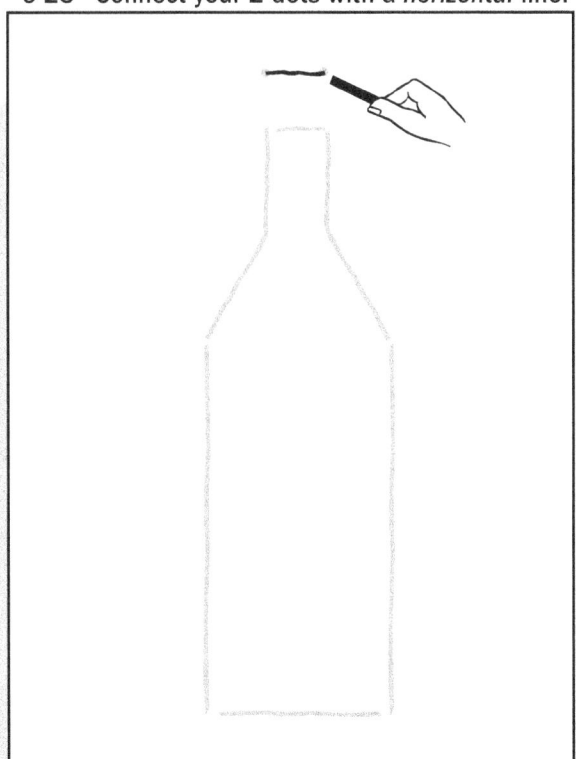

9-26   Establish your cap SIDES with 2 *vertical* lines.

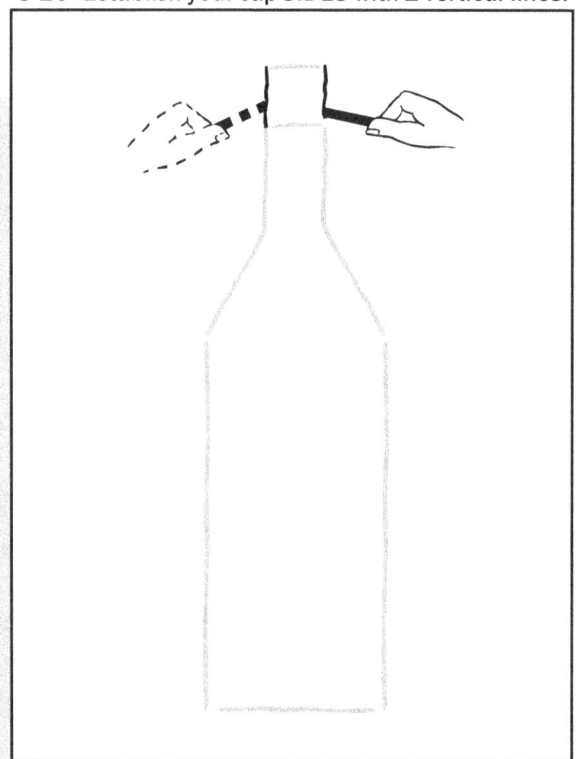

STEP 13 CHECK YOUR STREAMLINE FOR ACCURACY

As you know, it's important to *often* verify your status (condition of your drawing as it progresses). One very good way to do that, if you will recall, is to stop briefly and study your drawing in progress, *beside* your model, not only up close but also at a *distance*. That way you can see them *simultaneously*. Take a look at the following example, as seen from a few paces (9-27). Using the book's streamline on page 166 for comparsion, we can see that the RIGHT SHOULDER on the sample "drawing" is out of place. If we hadn't compared, we might have *accidentally* changed the *left* shoulder to go with the right shoulder, instead of vice versa. The dotted lines indicate the recommended change.

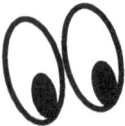

9-27 SAMPLE SIDE-BY-SIDE COMPARISON

Page 166 in Miniature.

Miniature streamline drawing example.
Broken lines show where adjustment is needed.

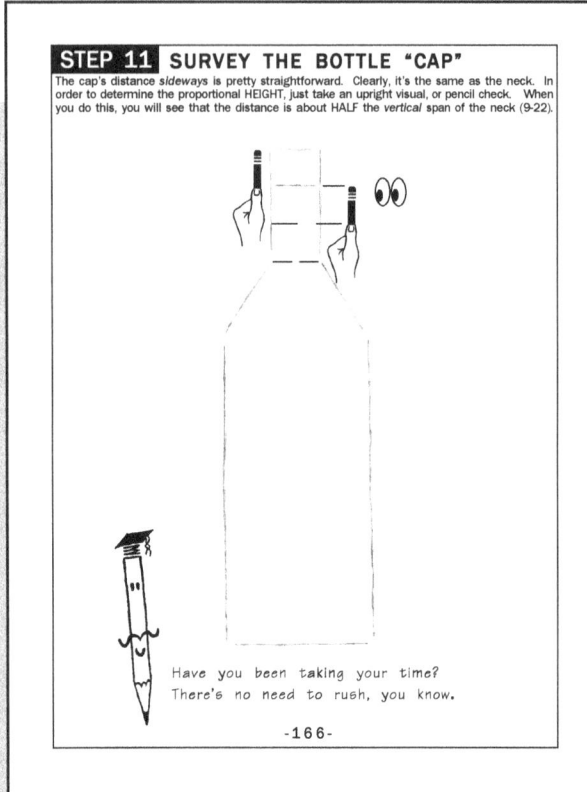

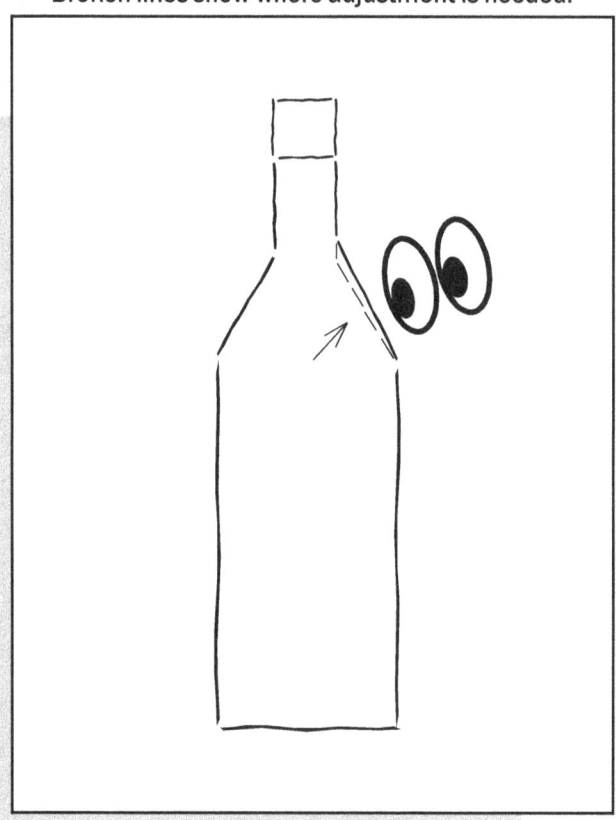

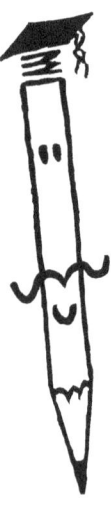

Now, it's your turn. Please stand your streamline side-by-side with the book illustration on page 166. Then survey them from a few paces. Don't worry about the small stuff. Begin by looking for signs of proportional abnormalities and possible tilting due to mis-alignments. Next, follow up by comparing reverse spaces. Should this sound new, you're well advised to review Chapter 5 and re-read pages 146 and 147 in Chapter 8. Then make your refinements on your bottle rendition as needed, BEFORE moving on.

Observe the curves in streamline 9-28, below. Be sure to form them separately, to fit YOUR drawing. Afterward you may erase the excess lines.

TIP Trace EACH curve in the air before you draw it. Then fashion your curves, ONE BY ONE. *Don't just take a quick glance, draw an arc, assume it's accurate, and simulate its mirror image on the opposite side.* This may seem as though it would save time, but actually it takes longer, should you have to rework. Also, while we're on the subject of shortcuts, please avoid placing your drawing sideways because certain curves may seem "easier" for you to duplicate in a different position. Such practices can form a habit and become an undesirable crutch. If you feel you *must* rotate your page, do it for a fresh view and turn your book sideways, too. That way, the illustration can continue to serve as a dependable source of reference. In turn, your curves are more likely appear like the model.

9-28   Guide the rate of *your* curves *proportionally* by this model.

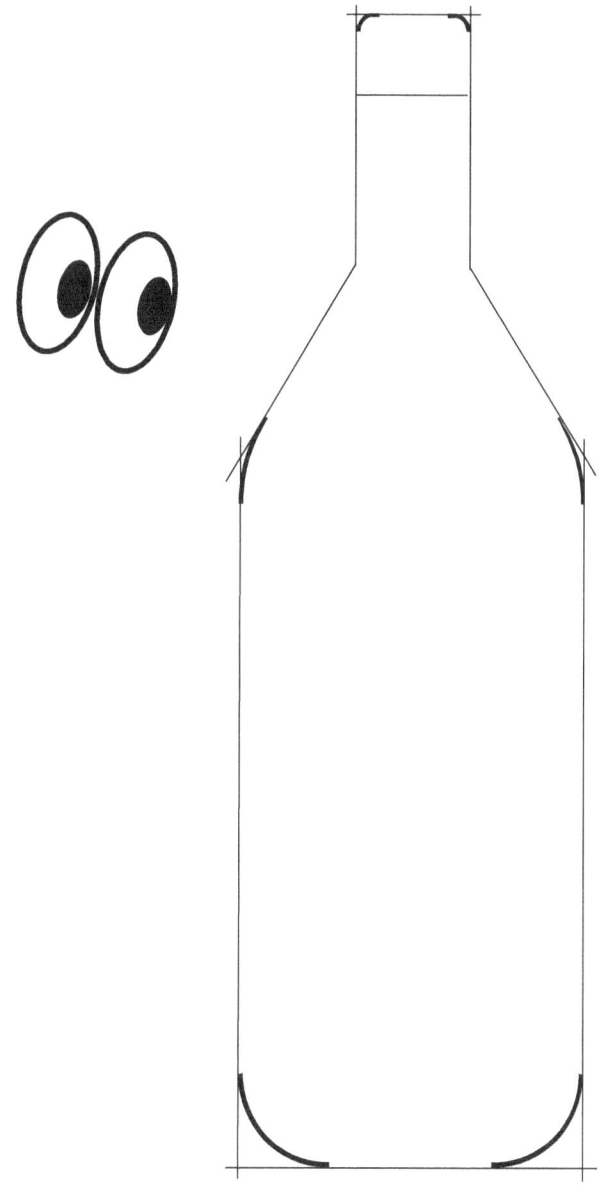

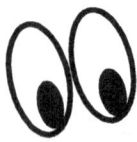

STEP 15 CHECK YOUR RESULTS ONCE MORE

After you have finished your arcs, and eliminated unwanted lines, go ahead and prop your drawing beside the book illustration again. This time, use page 155 and, as usual, observe from a distance. You may find something unexpected. For instance, look at sample comparison 9-29. As you can tell, the bottom curves differ. By comparing them to the model, we can see it's the bottom **LEFT** curve which needs revision. If we hadn't compared both curves to the model, we might have matched the right curve to the left, rather than the other way around, and that wouldn't have been any help. The dotted lines show where adjustment is advisable.

9-29 SAMPLE SIDE-BY-SIDE COMPARISON

Page 155 in Miniature.

Miniature drawing example. Broken lines show suggested adjustment.

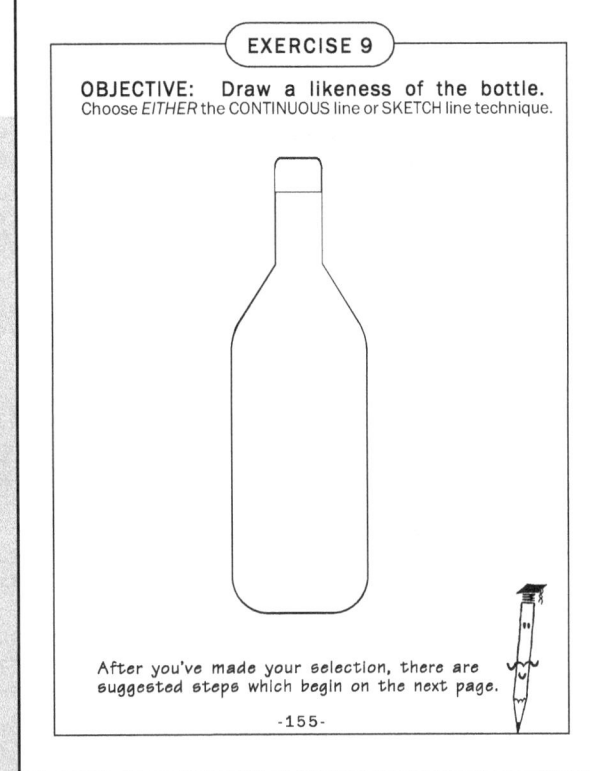

EXERCISE 9

OBJECTIVE: Draw a likeness of the bottle.
Choose *EITHER* the CONTINUOUS line or SKETCH line technique.

After you've made your selection, there are suggested steps which begin on the next page.

-155-

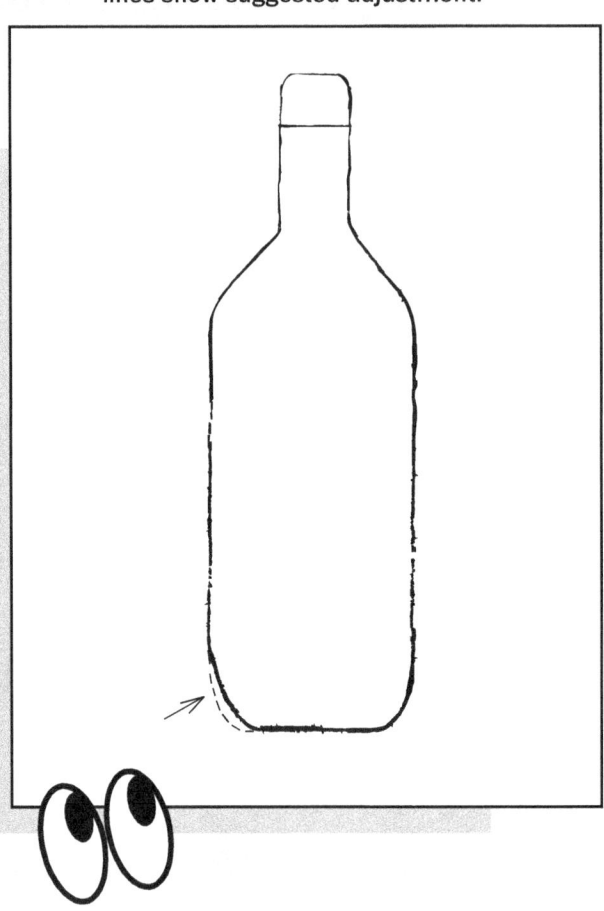

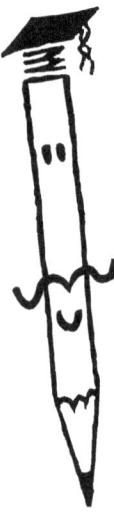

Sound the trumpets! You can draw RANDOMLY! This ability requires some special consideration, though. To understand what I mean, treat yourself to a peek at the way other student works turned out. They are proudly displayed on the next page.

EXERCISE 9
MODEL & STUDENT EXAMPLES

Model

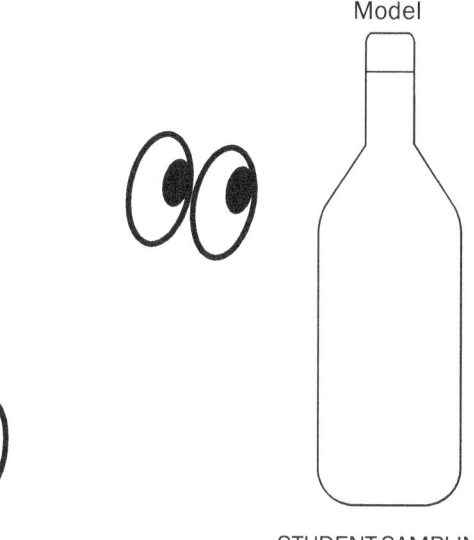

STUDENT SAMPLING

| 9-30 | 9-31 | 9-32 |

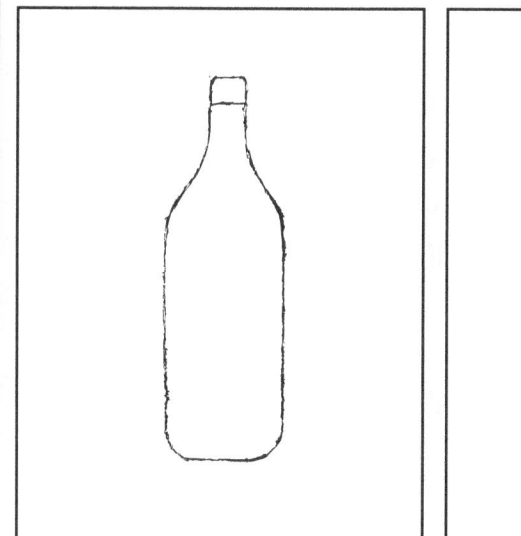 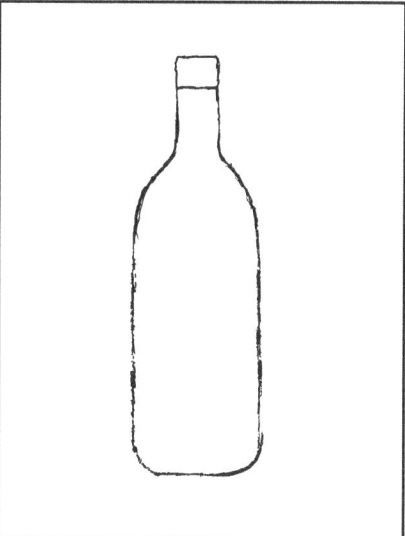 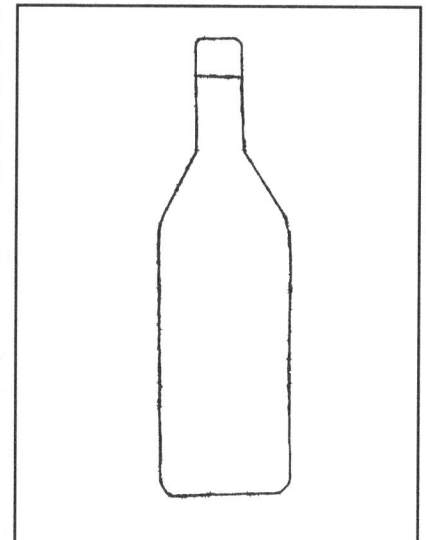

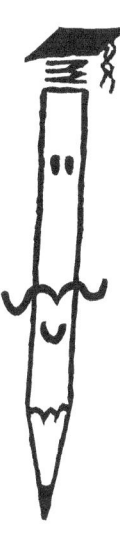

The three bottle renditions above are pretty good, aren't they? Each has specific traits that were achieved by exercising what is often referred to as *"creative freedom."* For instance, drawing sample 9-30 shows the bottle with a *neck* which tapers outward to meet the shoulder angle. Yet, the *model's* neck is plumb. Version 9-31 represents the bottle with overly rounded shoulders. Example 9-32 depicts the figure with small *base* curves. Are these alterations OK? Absolutely, as long as the changes were made by *choice,* not by accident. As you know, there is a natural tendency to satisfy one's preferences. And with the leeway that comes with the random method, the urge is likely to be even stronger. To keep it in check, my advice is that you should compare your drawing and your subject all the more. When you do, you're apt to remain in charge.

Please mull over what you've learned.
and don't forget to read the follow-up.

-171-

Chapter 9
FOLLOW-UP

Admit it, having replicated the bottle may not have seemed like much challenge, but finding out that you have options and the freedom to make choices is exciting news, isn't it? And that's the idea. I'm happy to say, you're now ready to take initiatives. That's right. At this stage of your development, it's not just all right to be selective, it's *encouraged*! You see, drawing isn't supposed to be restrictive. In fact, the next chapter introduces ways that offer even more flexibility.

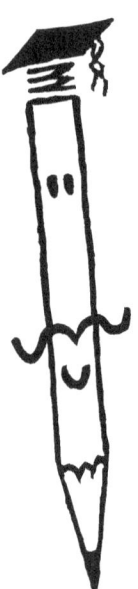

Rest comfortably, then prepare
yourself for another thrilling route
to pictorial expression.

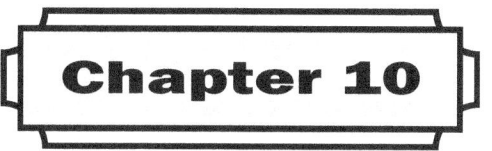

Chapter 10

THE SQUIGGLE METHOD

Remember the bottle you drew in Chapter 9?
Here it is again, except in DOODLE form.

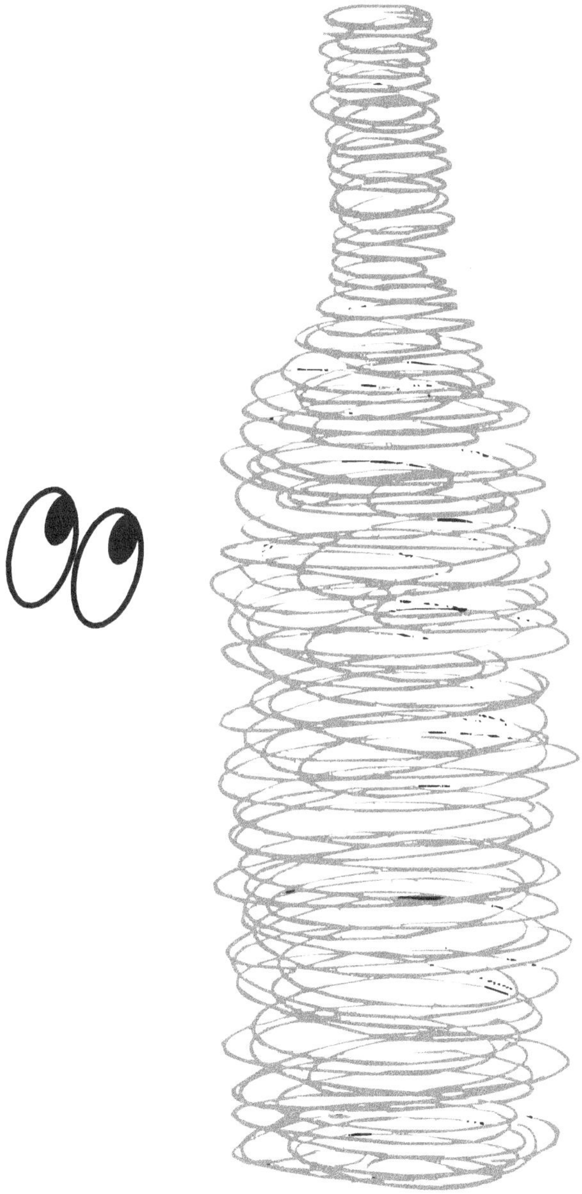

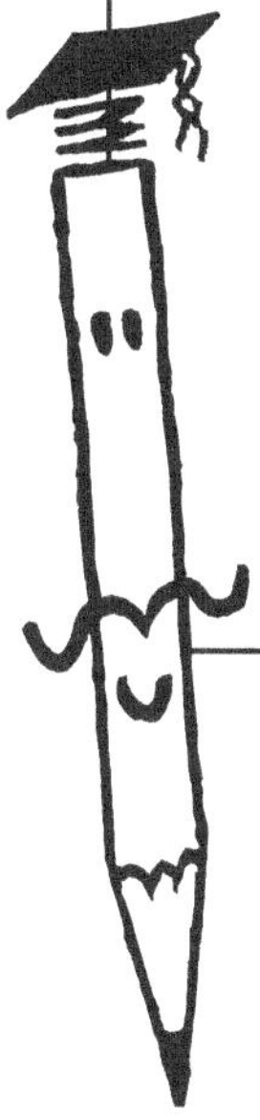

Before you chuckle, maybe you should look
a little closer. Doodles, or Squiggles as
I also like to call them, have much to offer.

In order to answer this, please indulge me a little. When bored, while listening to a one-sided phone conversation, or a long-winded speech, do you doodle? If you don't, you're really missing out.

It's not your fault though. At some point, a teacher probably told you it's wrong to DOODLE and that's unfortunate. Your instructor should have been more specific. What he or she might have clarified is that you shouldn't doodle in CLASS.

I think doodles (or squiggles) are a link to your personality, much like your individual signature. When "drawing" however, it's your quality of line that mainly expresses you, rather than your unique letter style.

How is this accomplished? Imagine that your brain takes a back seat, and your eyes assume charge. As soon as your hand receives messages, it guides the pencil without hesitation. In turn, your *intuitive, carefree* movements are recorded by lines, similar to the way a seismograph records the rumblings of the earth.

For example, let's turn back the clock and try to recall that moment when you spotted the bottle illustration on page 153, in Chapter 9. First, you might have noticed the cap. That is, until your eyes probably began to descend, in search of more details. If your pencil captured the movements, your lines could very well have turned out like the swirling doodle, shown on the previous page of *this* chapter.

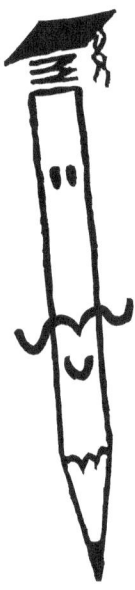

But, WHY *doodle*, you're probably wondering?
There are many, many reasons for DOODLING.

DOODLES HELP YOU LIMBER UP

EXPERIMENT A Take your pencil in your hand, the way you normally write. Hold it close to the point, as illustration 10-1 indicates. Then, make a **CONTINUOUS** figure 8, as BIG as you can, beside mine. *The catch is, you may move your wrist, but NOT your elbow.*

10-1 Standard pencil grip with fingers NEAR point made this continuous figure 8.

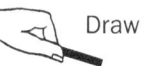 Draw YOUR *continuous* figure 8 here.

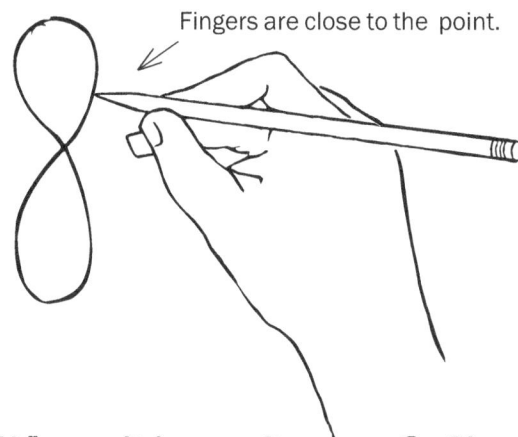

Fingers are close to the point.

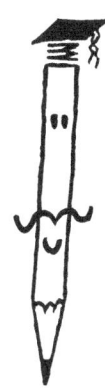

What did you discover? Chances are your figure 8 isn't much bigger than mine, would you agree? Now, try another technique.

EXPERIMENT B Once again, use the space provided to form the biggest continuous figure 8 you can make. This time, relax your grip and hold the pencil GENTLY with the *pencil point further away from your hand* (10-2). How much distance? About the span of your index finger. And, there's one more thing to remember. *You may still move ONLY your wrist.*

10-2 Loose grip, with fingers further from point made this continuous figure 8.

 Draw YOUR *continuous* figure 8 here.

fingers are further from the point

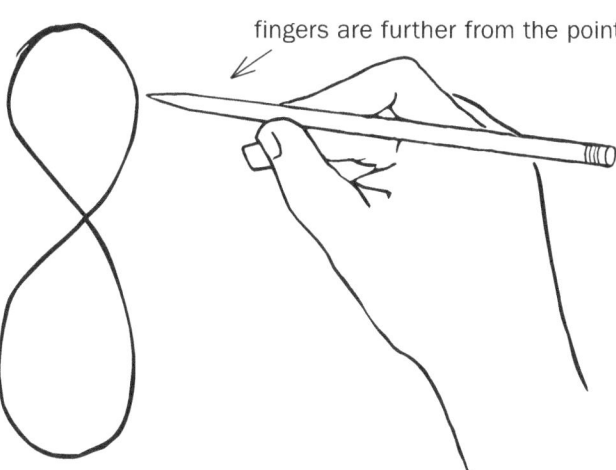

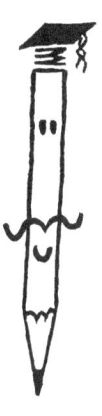

Your figure 8 grew slightly, but remained restricted, didn't it? Want to learn the secret to making LARGER continuous figure 8's? Terrific! Read ON!

TRY THIS FOR SIZE

EXPERIMENT C On a separate sheet, draw another *continuous* figure 8 with EITHER the writing grip (close to your pencil point), or distance grip (further back from the point). However, on this round, no matter which way you choose, you **must allow your ELBOW to move INSTEAD of your WRIST.** When you do, you will see that your movement will be able to actually exceed far beyond the limits of your paper.

So why didn't I just introduce this alternative right off? Because I wanted to impress upon you that there is more than one way to hold a pencil and more than one method by which to steer it. Bear in mind, there is nothing wrong with the traditional mode. For delicate work, it's especially useful. But there are advantages for both the conservative grip and the liberal grip (loose or tight). In Chapter 1 you already learned the benefits for varying your line techniques. During the previous chapter, you discovered how the variation can add *style* to your drawing. And now that you are also aware that a greater range of motion is possible (by drawing from the elbow and/or holding the pencil further from the point), I highly recommend that you make a bunch more continuous figure 8's this way. Try them at different tilts and sizes, made with NUMEROUS passes. Also, do several in both directions. In other words, start left, and after a few passes, stop and switch to the right, on the *same* figure 8.

For instance, note the following examples shown in illustration 10-3. There are narrow figure 8's, and wide ones, in various positions. Each was made with rapid, continuous lines, using soft, even strokes. In order to do likewise, you shouldn't press hard by clutching your pencil tightly near the point. Instead, hold it *slightly back,* between your thumb, index, and middle finger. Then, *TENDERLY* GLIDE the lead, at an angle. With this way, you enable only the weight of the pencil to caress your paper as well as allow your fingers to be more nimble.

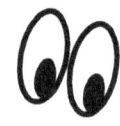

10-3   Sampling of continuous figure 8's completed with numerous passes.

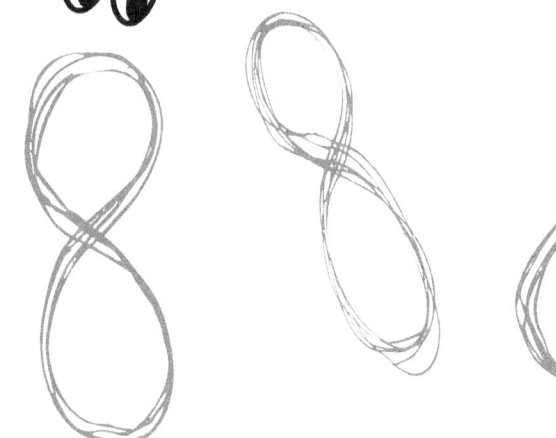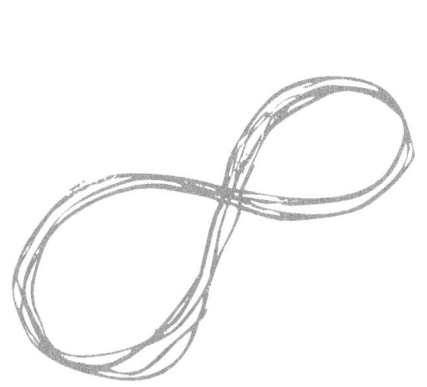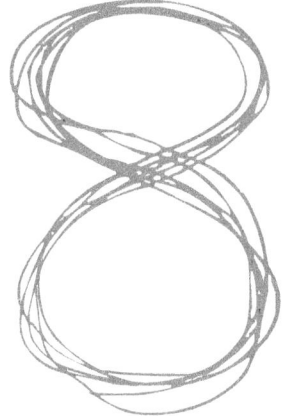

TIP As you begin to make your laps, move at a steady pace in order to keep your lines reasonably uniform and fluid. An exact tracing of your previous line is not the goal. *The objective is to guide your pencil gently, and at a comfortable speed, while maintaining control.* If you can count to 5 before a cycle is completed, you're going too SLOWLY.

After you've practiced, check out the next page, to learn more about the benefits of SQUIGGLES.

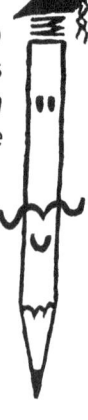

What is SYNCHRONIZATION?
It's your willingness to cooperate with yourself.
(This is not as crazy as it sounds).

As you know, drawing is essentially achieved by three main factors. These are your eyes, head and hand. When they are *synchronized*, they work *together.* The trouble is, usually they would rather battle for supremacy. While your hand is busy finishing a task, typically your eyes tend to wander. If they do, concentration is split. On top of that, should your mind begin drifting to worries about how good your picture will turn out, or to some irrelevant topic like lunch, forget about teamwork entirely. Your attention becomes hopelessly divided.

What is the remedy? Pretend your eyes and your pencil are connected by an invisible rod. When your eyes scan the figure you are drawing, your hand (holding the pencil) moves at the same rate. In the event your eyes accelerate (or slow down), so does your hand. All the while, your brain acts as referee to ensure that everyone travels in unison.

Now, let's imagine the outcome if you were to squiggle the bottle shown on page 155, WITHOUT synchronization. Starting from the top, your eyes would probably advance quickly right (since we read in that direction). All the while your pencil in hand would struggle to keep up. Soon your peepers might get impatient. Should they suddenly switch to high gear, or worse, they skip around, they could leave your hand behind. Connection would be lost and your brain would have to blow the whistle. In order to reunite, your eyes would need to back track and find your hand before the journey could continue.

The moral of the story is that you need to learn to channel your attention and energy while drawing. Does this seem difficult? It's not.

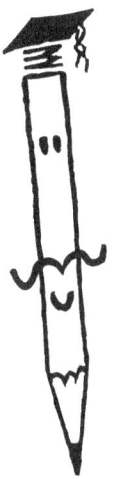

Prove to yourself that you, too, can synchronize. Turn the page and complete the next experiment.

DIRECTIONS: Observe the bottle drawing in illustration 10-4, and especially note the picture of the "ant" on top. Next, place your pencil point on the "x," to the right. Then look to the ant again and pretend it's beginning to travel SLOWLY along the bottle edge: in **ONE** direction (left or right). *You decide which way.* During the trip around, your eyes must follow and your pencil must trace the action, as you glance back and forth between your advancing line and the ant. "Lefties" may invert the page and work upside down. That way, your hand doesn't block your view.

| TIP | On this occasion, it's both necessary and wise to combine straight and curved lines. The reason is, once you start, *you're not permitted to lift your pencil until you're done*. That is, unless you've lost contact with the ant because your eyes jumped ahead, your thoughts wandered, or you were distracted. If so, make a mental note of how it felt to lose your concentration. Then, begin again on another sheet. *Do not erase.* Your picture is not expected to be a masterpiece. Illustration 10-5 is an example. BUT DON'T COPY. DO YOUR OWN. Your continuous line squiggle is primarily meant to teach you how to improve your sense of distance, direction and synchronization.

10-4 The ant is your guide.

Place your pencil point on the "x." It marks the spot where you start.

x

10-5 Finished Sample.

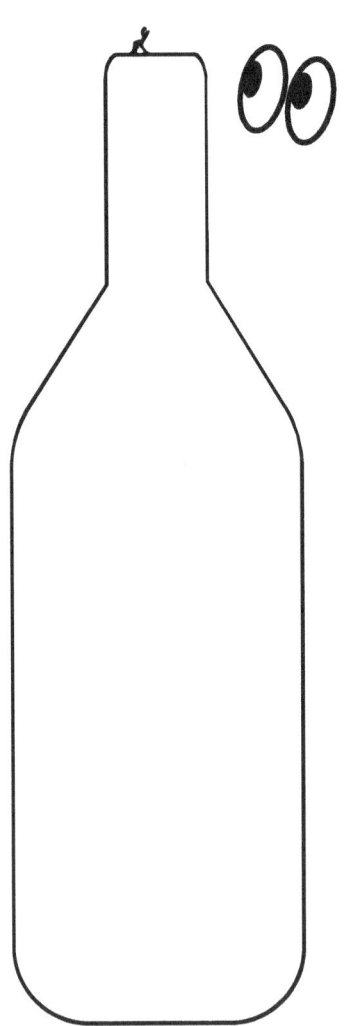

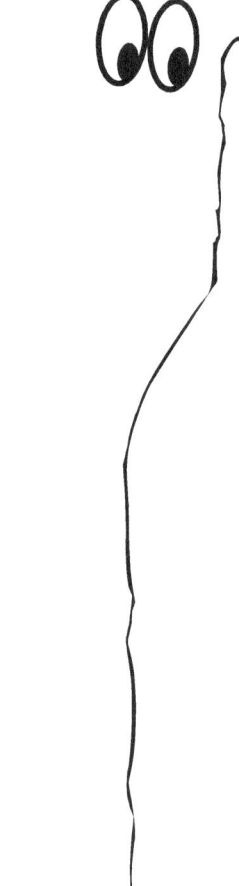

REMEMBER: How accurate your squiggle turns out is not the goal. Its main purpose is to help you GET IN SYNCH. Besides, there's room for modification. Check out the next page.

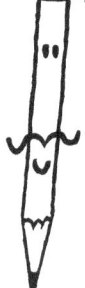

Consider this: in one respect, a drawing is like a chronicle (or record) of your journey, as you explore your subject. In such fashion, even your simple doodles can be accepted as finished pieces. But for those of you who want more, you can alter your squiggles. You see, just as you learned to develop drawings from other types of formats, including overall foundations and streamlines, you also have that option with doodles. For instance, notice example 10-6, below. It's the same as illustration 10-5, from the previous page, with a slight distinction. The dotted lines indicate where an alteration could be useful. Essentially, what I am saying is that by applying the principles of the *"TRUSTY SEVEN"* (alignments, proportions, reference points, straight lines, angles, curves, and reverse space) you can change your squiggle too (just as you can modify any drawing). If your squiggle seems too tall, shorten it. If a curve is too narrow, or wide, adjust it. If a line needs to be straightened, straighten it. It's that simple.

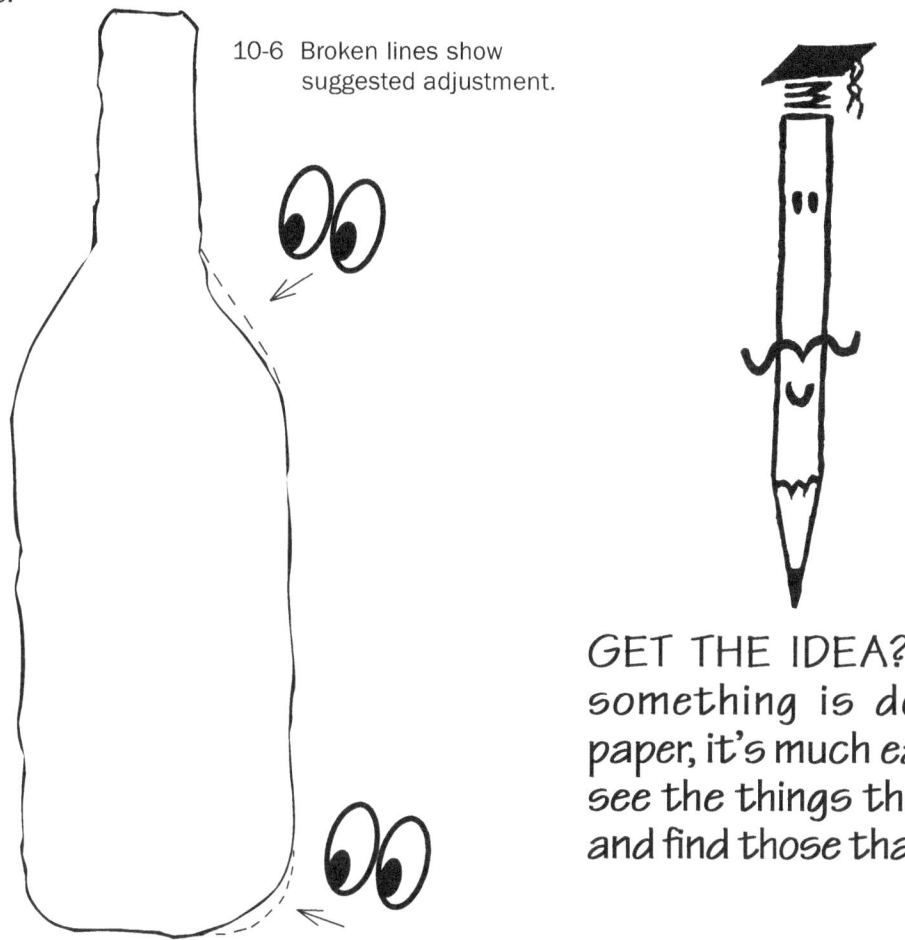

10-6 Broken lines show suggested adjustment.

GET THE IDEA? Once something is down on paper, it's much easier to see the things that work and find those that don't.

Why not just map out your drawing from the get-go, and bypass doodling entirely, you ask?

Good question. There is no reason you shouldn't play it safe. In fact, when your subject seems elaborate, you may find it pays to organize a layout. However, unlike most "construction" methods, the squiggle approach doesn't require a "blue print," so to speak. For example, the squiggle you drew on the previous page didn't need much forethought, did it? Apart from that, certain rewards often come only from taking risks. These I like to call *pleasant surprises*. Put another way, they are results that are usually achieved intuitively and turn out differently than you may have wanted or expected. Yet, they are perhaps, more desirable or preferred. So what have you got to lose? Since you've already experienced drawing structurally, as well as randomly, plus learned the value of a SLOW squiggle, you might as well get acquainted with another kind.

THE SPEEDY SQUIGGLE

No doubt, you gathered that SQUIGGLES can be formed with one CONTINUOUS line. You already did one by following the make-believe ant as it traveled around. What may not have occurred to you, however, is that you can also go FAST. And like the figure 8's you practiced, you can make *numerous* passes, in any direction you prefer. Following are two examples of QUICK squiggles.

10-7 Example of surrounding continuous sweeps.

10-8 Example of meandering continuous sweeps.

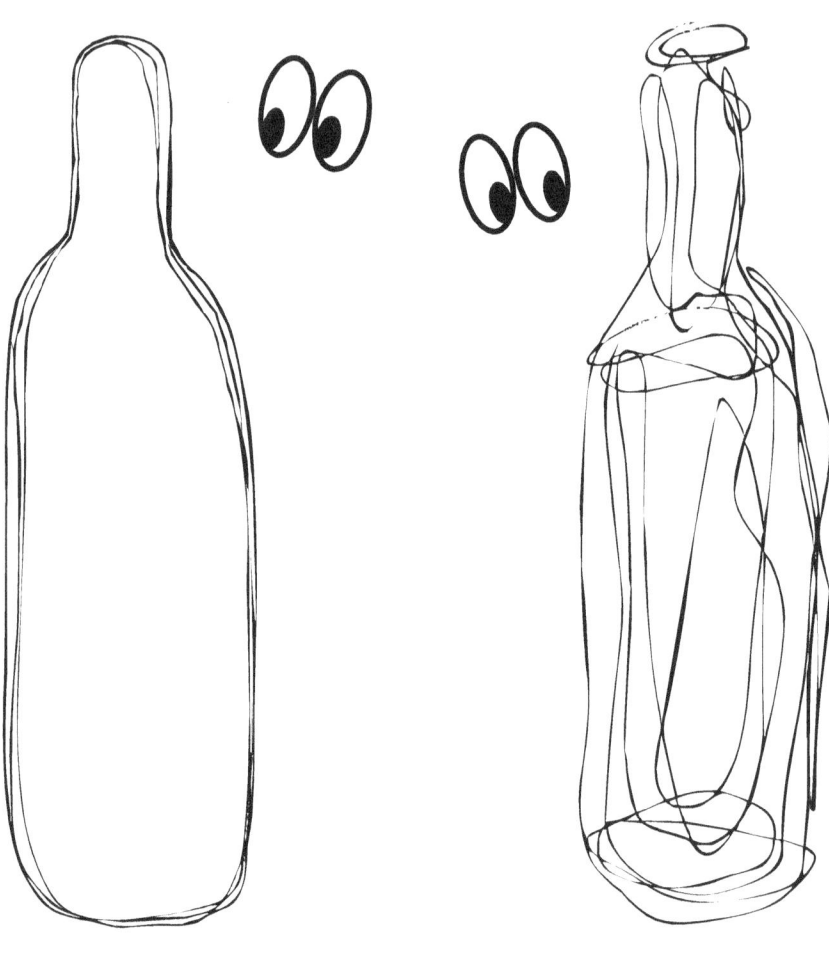

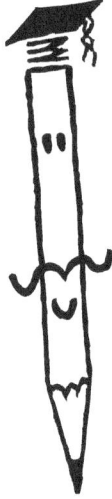

Evidently, doodle 10-7 suggests that a pair of human scanners revolved AROUND the figure several times. In contrast, squiggle 10-8 reveals that the eyes jumped hither and yon. In both cases, what came about are two more, distinctly different, squiggles that remind one of wire sculptures, except they are formed with lines, similar to the way a ski run leaves telltale signs etched in the snow. The long and the short of it is that squiggles can have amazing charm and meaning, *when you give them, and yourself, a chance.*

Drawing is a voyage of discovery.
Go the distance! Do exercise 10.

EXERCISE 10

OBJECTIVE: Explore the *Spontaneous* Squiggle

DIRECTIONS: Using the illustration below as your model, and the space beside it for drawing, do a doodle *INSTINCTIVELY.* In other words follow your whims. Start with any part of the bottle shape, but whichever portion you choose, place your pencil in that corresponding area of the space. Otherwise you could run out of room. "Lefties" can invert the page and work upside down. That way, your hand doesn't block your view. Once you start, the action should come from the elbow. As your eyes begin their sweep, record the movements with FAST *continuous* lines. You only have about 30 seconds: not enough time to think, only to react, so keep your eyes more on the model than your drawing. This is not as scary as it might seem. Trust your intuition (feelings and impulses) to guide your hand. Proceed clockwise, counter clockwise, or both. You can also cross over. *Erasing is not permitted, however.* Stop only when you feel you're done. Whatever happens, happens.

| TIP | *I know, all along I've advised that you should THINK, before you act, but here I'm asking you to do the opposite. Don't plan what you're going to do! Just do it! Let your SPIRIT move you!* |

10-9   Your model.

Use this space to squiggle.

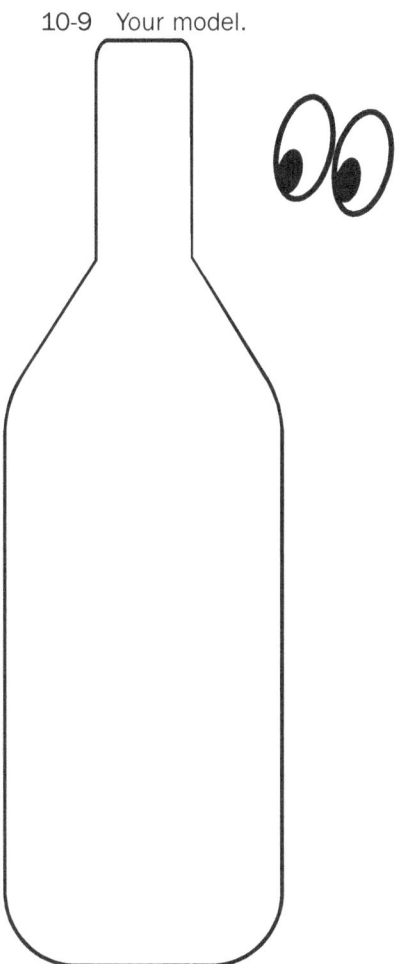

Your first effort may appear rigid and seem awkward. If this happens, you're probably distracted, wondering how your picture can possibly work without a plan. Squiggling is like dancing. Soon you'll feel the beat. On a fresh sheet of paper, experiment by doodling objects around you. Allow only a minute or two for each squiggle. Those who are "lefties" try doodling with your right hand, and "right handers" do vice versa. Why? Because this gives your untrained, subordinate hand an excuse to be less than precise, and gives YOU the opportunity to relax. *With the pressure off, you can enjoy the ride.* So loosen up. IT'S FUN TO LET YOURSELF GO! DOODLE OFTEN!

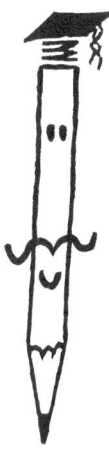

Whether you prefer to draw at a snail's pace, fast, or
in between, orderly, or on the spur of the moment,
strive to remain FOCUSED, in SYNC, and above all, have
a BLAST with your squiggles! Then read the FOLLOW-UP.

Chapter 10
FOLLOW-UP

I bet you were shocked to learn that what you thought were useless, trivial doodles, or perhaps even silly scribbles, are actually spectacular drawings, worthy of respect and recognition. Not only are they thought provoking and brimming with character in their own right, from my professional view, they are also extremely beneficial drawing tools. Aside from helping you UNWIND and STAY TUNED, doodles PROVIDE A BASE. Plus, they tend to ENHANCE YOUR CREATIVITY.

Not meant to be detailed, doodles operate best when unplanned and unrestrained. Like your signature, they reflect YOU. Tap into your individual rhythm and you'll be amazed by your accomplishments.

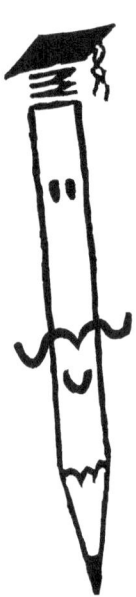

*Many other thrilling adventures
are yet to come.*

THE FREESTYLE APPROACH

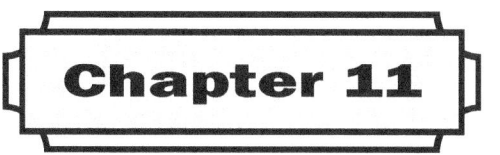

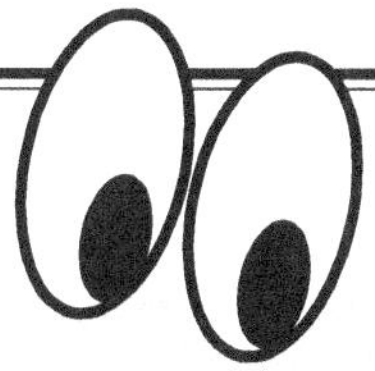

SUBJECT: The Gladiator
But, don't grab your pencil.

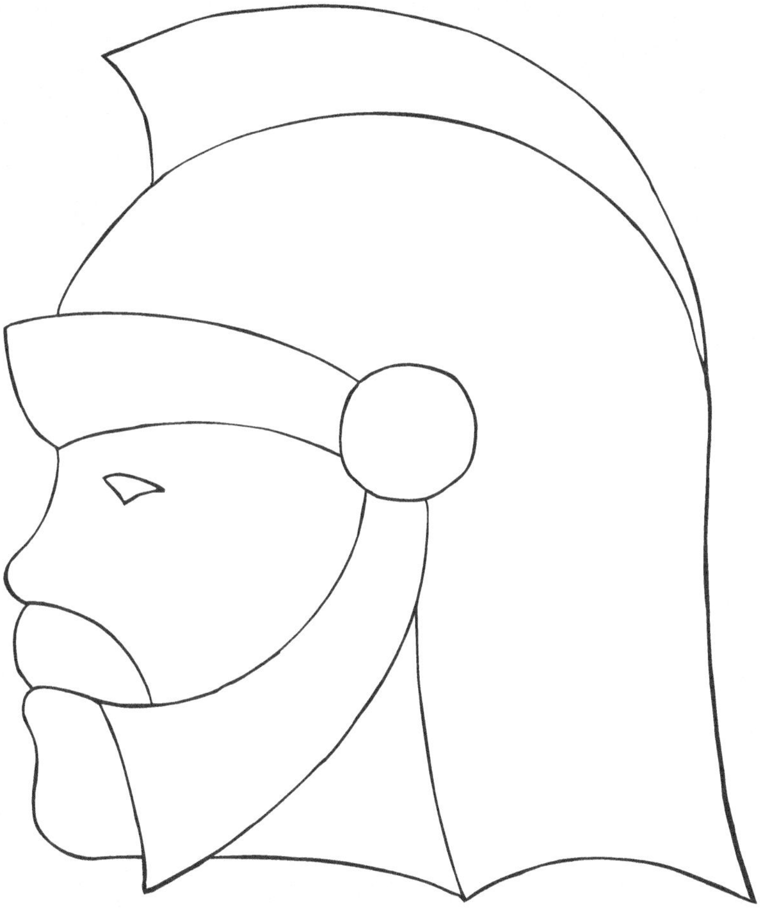

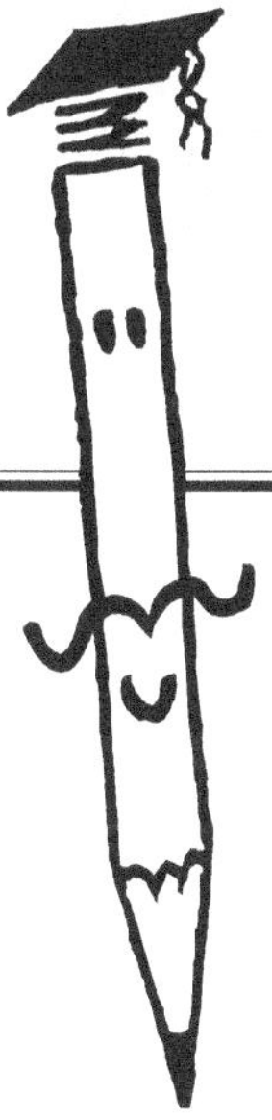

It's not time to draw, just yet. And in *case* you've got the notion that people are more difficult to draw, perish the thought. The process for all subjects is basically the SAME, including the fellow above. You'll see.

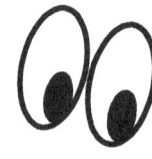

WHICH METHOD
STRIKES YOUR FANCY?

METHOD 1

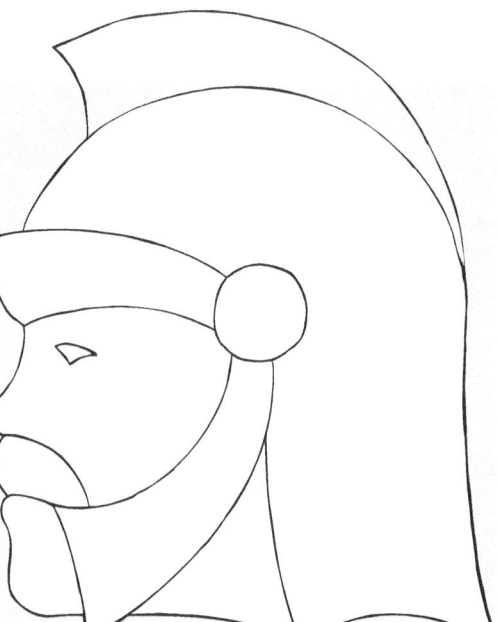

METHOD 2

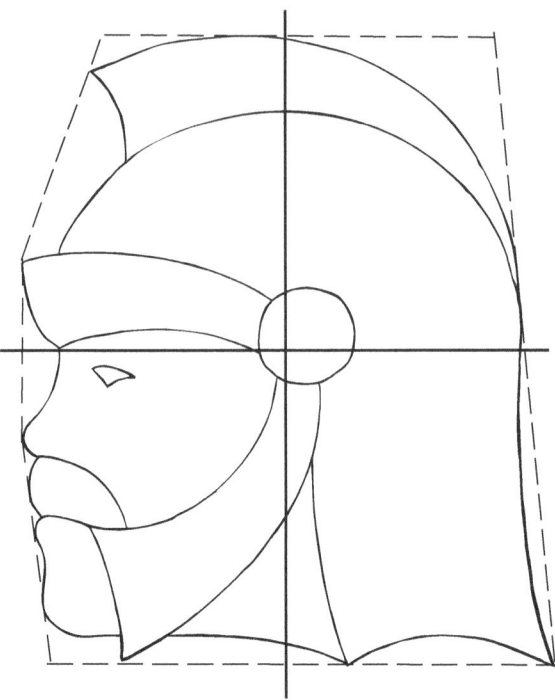

METHOD 3

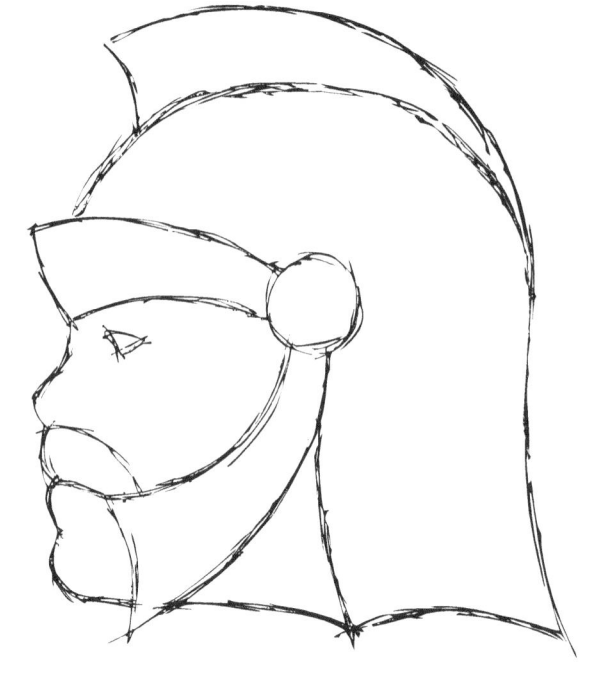

THERE ARE LOTS OF WAYS TO APPROACH YOUR SUBJECT

For instance...

METHOD 1

Initiate with a square, and the rest of the helmet ornament can be added. In this fashion, the *adlib, reverse, random,* and *attach principles are implemented.*

METHOD 2

The *streamline and crisscross* procedure is also effective. It starts with a simplified overall format and proceeds with four divisions.

METHOD 3

The gladiator can be doodled, or sketched, and remain as such. Or, if desired, it can then be sharpened to your heart's content.

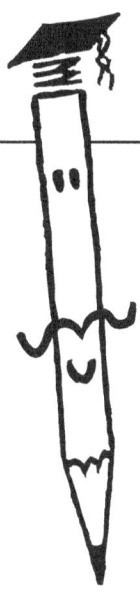

And these are just some of the many possibilites. Let's apply yet another combination. The first step begins on the next page.

EXERCISE11

OBJECTIVE: REPLICATE THE GLADIATOR
(Curve by Curve & Piece by Piece)

STEP 1 TAKE THE FIGURE APART WITH YOUR EYES

Permit me to call your attention to illustration 11-1. Notice that although we're going to be replicating the profile of a person, the features can be separated into individual lines and shapes just as easily as it can be done with any subject. When we disassemble visually, then put sections back together by drawing them, the gladiator will magically appear, much like a jigsaw puzzle.

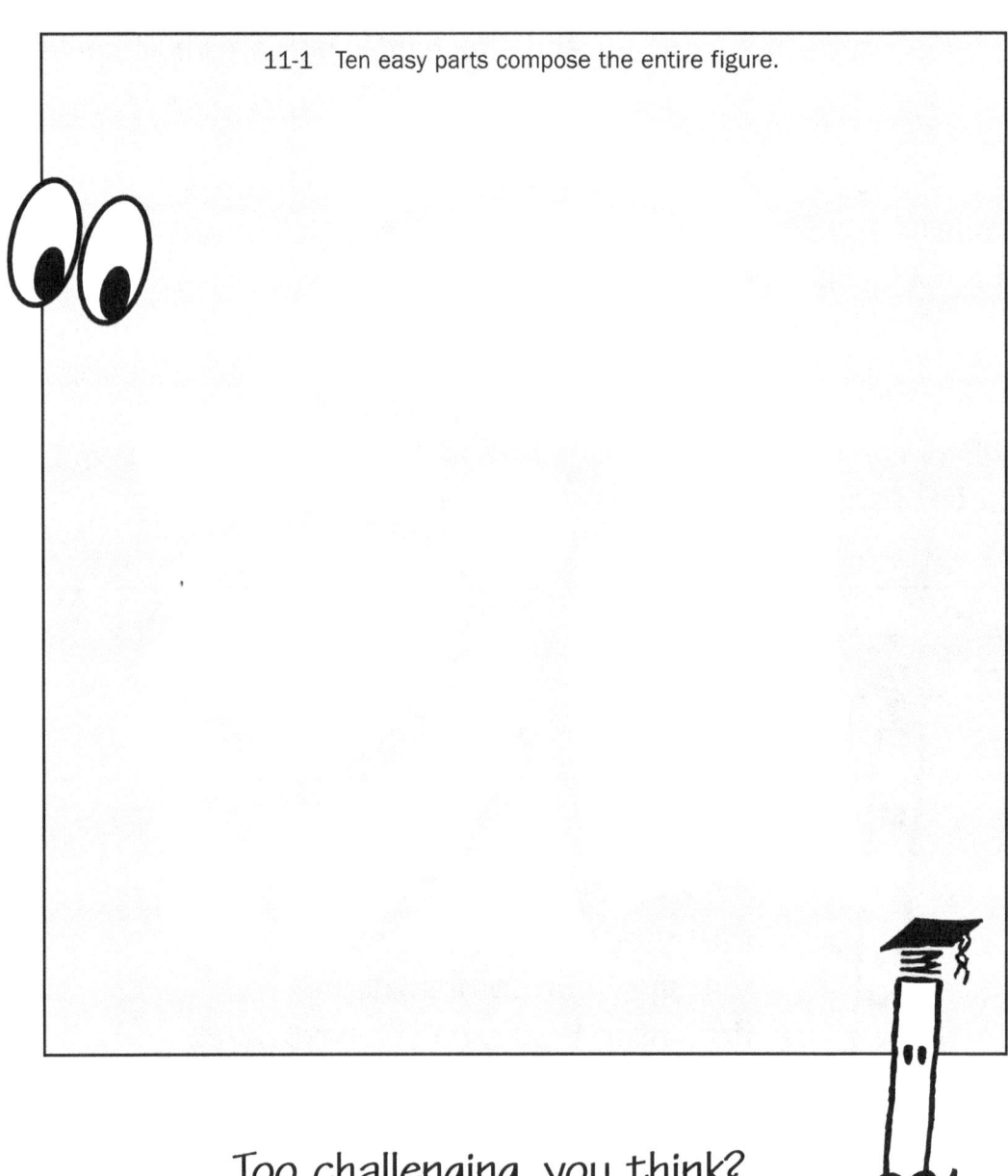

11-1 Ten easy parts compose the entire figure.

Too challenging, you think?
Not at all. Take it from me.

On a new sheet of paper, initiate with the circle which will represent the"helmet hinge." Place it above center; not much larger than shown, in order to reserve space for the rest of the parts (11-2).

HOT TIP Since we're going to be adding one section to the next with the *random* and *attach* methods, be sure to always consider THREE things: the whole, the specific piece to be replicated, and the adjacent parts. This will help ensure that all the sections will fit to scale.

11-2 Form a circle to replicate the "helmet hinge." Be sure your size and position will fit on the page with respect to the other parts yet to come.

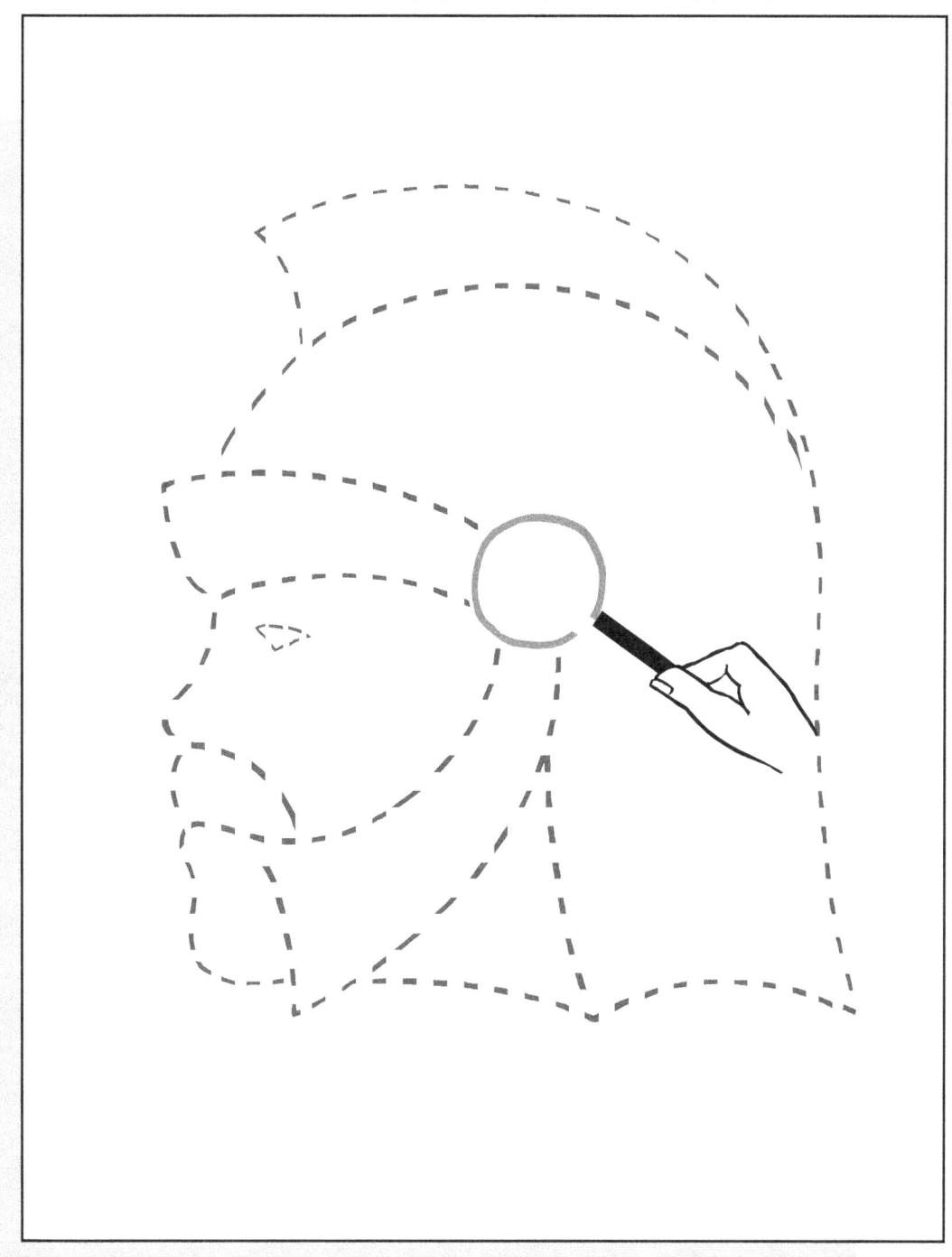

Observe that THREE angular arcs make up the shape which attaches to the circle "hinge" (11-3). Note too, that the LONGEST arc originates about a fourth of the way *IN* from the RIGHT of the circle, and slants downward to the left. Its *height* appears to be about THREE times the circle, whereas its *width* seems to equal about two times the circle (11-4). Next look at the MEDIUM size *upper* arc (11-5). It connects from the circle too but the starting point indents from the *LEFT of the starting circle at one fourth span.* Another interesting feature is that the amount of BOW levels out at roughly *half* the *HEIGHT* of the LARGE arc. However, it goes PAST the large arc, laterally, about 1/2 the diameter of the original circle. This distance helps locate the SMALL front curve and its angle (11-6).

11-3   "Cheek Guard" is made with 3 simple curves.

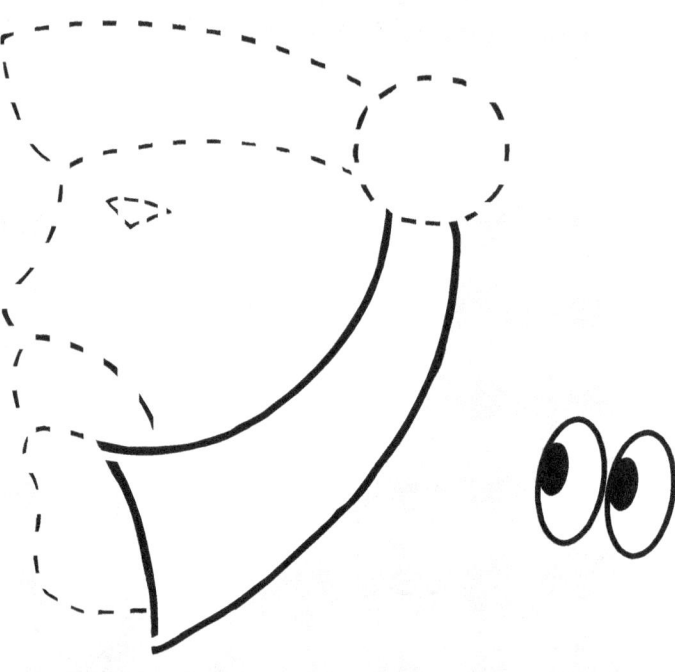

11-4   LOWER curve is 3 circles tall and 2 circles wide.

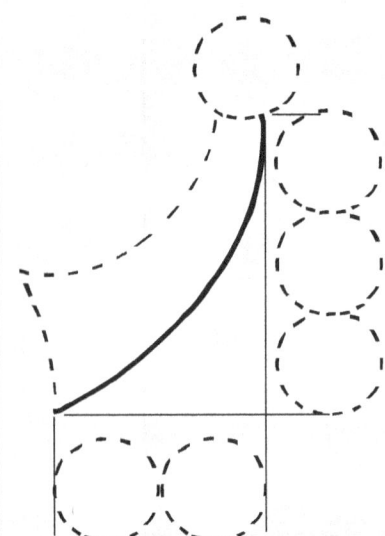

11-5   UPPER curve reaches MIDWAY DOWN and a 1/2 circle past LOWER curve.

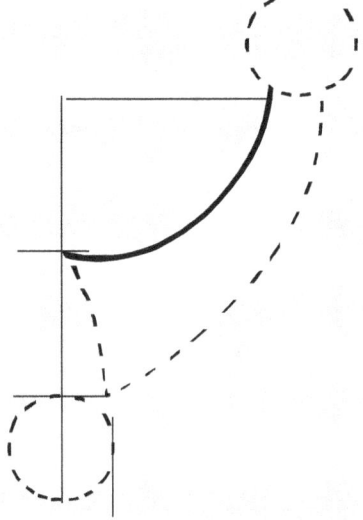

11-6   FRONT curve links the other 2 curves at an angle.

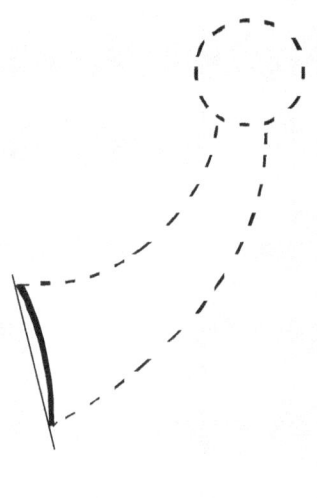

Focus on illustration 11-3 (previous page) and the shape accented by bolder lines. Next, picture the intended segment already *attached* to your *circle.* Use reference points and YOUR circle for scale. Then, draw ONE curve at a time, in proportion with *CONTINUOUS OR SKETCH LINES.* Illustrations 11-7, 8, 9 & 10 show the sequence. You can also follow your own *random* order.

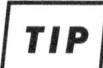 **TIP** It helps to trace each arc in the air, several times before you draw them. This procedure can give you a better sense for the amount of bow. Use illustration 11-3 (previous page) during your dry run and as you form your actual curves.

11-7 Use YOUR circle's SIZE to locate Ref.Pts.

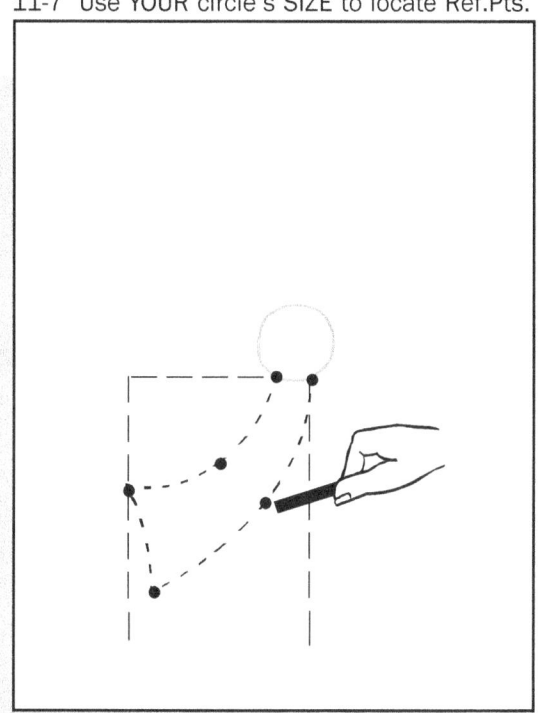

11-8 Draw your *LARGE* LOWER arc.

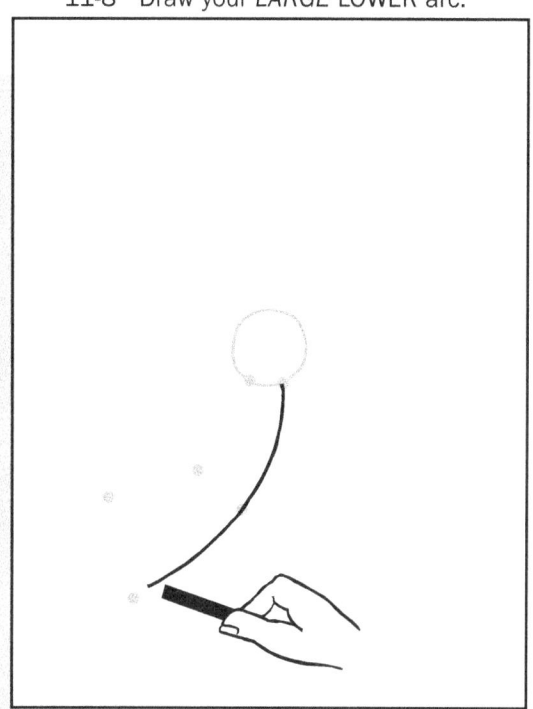

11-9 Draw your MEDIUM *UPPER* arc.

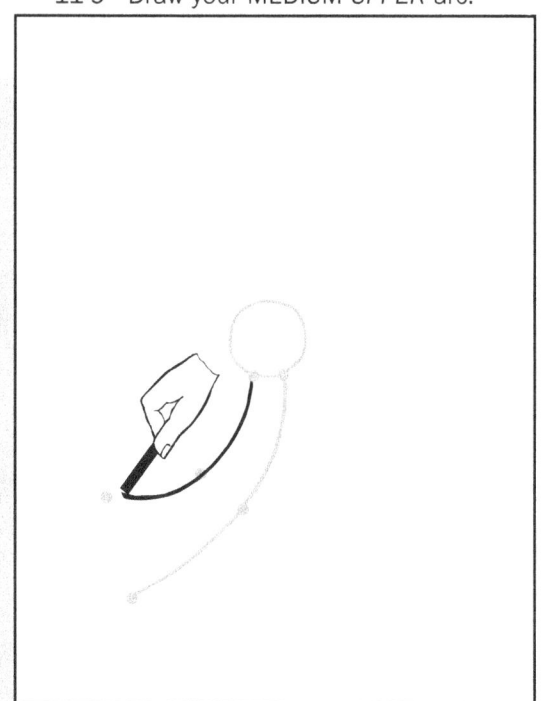

11-10 Draw your SMALL *FRONT* arc.

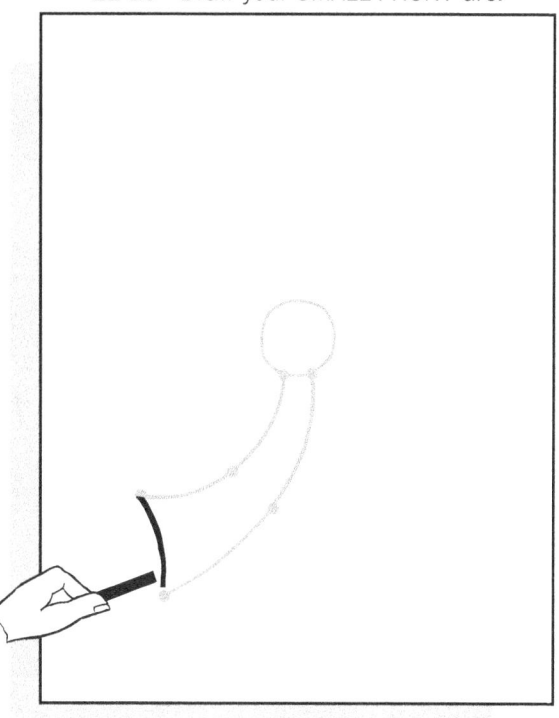

CHECK YOUR STATUS

Be sure to compare your two pieces *individually* with the model, and also as a *pair*. Why? Because, as you know, they have to be in proportion to one another and resemble the model. Although this sounds difficult, it's really easy. Simply place your drawing next to the LARGE illustration of the gladiator (page 183). Then glance back and forth between your rendition of the "circle hinge" and "cheek guard" to see if their shapes resemble the book version. For instance, look at the way those sections appear on the sample side-by-side assessment below. When we compare example drawing 11-11 with the corresponding parts on the *model* (accented with gray), we see that the shapes *differ*. The BOW of the upper *medium* size curve of the *replicated* "cheek guard" is too thin near the middle, and sports an *upward* tilt, not featured on the original, agreed? Also, the circle (or "hinge") is too small, *proportionally*. Both adjustments are shown by broken lines & light gray.

SAMPLE SIDE-BY-SIDE COMPARISON

Page 183, copied here in miniature shows the model accented with gray to help focus on the "cheek guard."

11-11 Drawing example shows "cheek guard" is a poor match to the model. The dotted lines indicate needed adjustment.

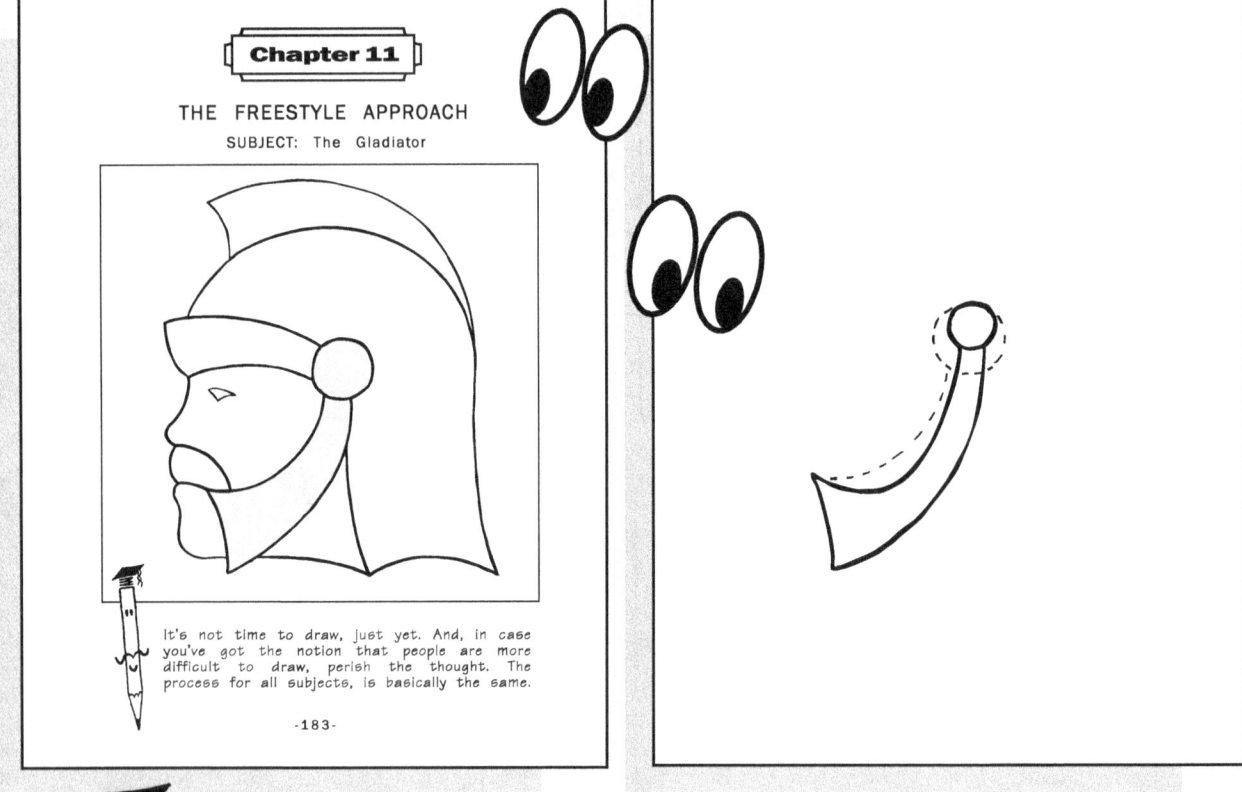

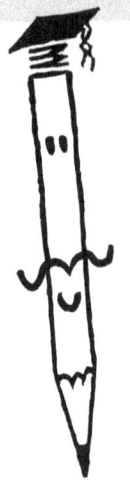 HINT, HINT. After EACH shape is formed, it's smart to VERIFY your results.

Granted, it may seem bothersome to be concerned about accuracy at such an early stage. But, believe me, the few extra moments are well worth it. Since we're applying the random and attach methods, and since *parts build from one to the next, each should be on a "fairly" secure footing.* Take a look at example drawing 11-12, below. Notice that the "cheek guard" (serving as the foundation) is too narrow. Ultimately, this could lead to distortion, like the skinny figure shown, for instance. Next, study sample drawing 11-13. In this case, the "cheek guard" is formed too wide, and could cause a rotund (plump) gladiator, or some other type of deformity (inaccurate shape).

11-12 A narrow "cheek guard" can lead to a very slim profile.

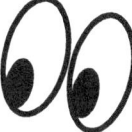

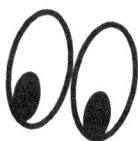

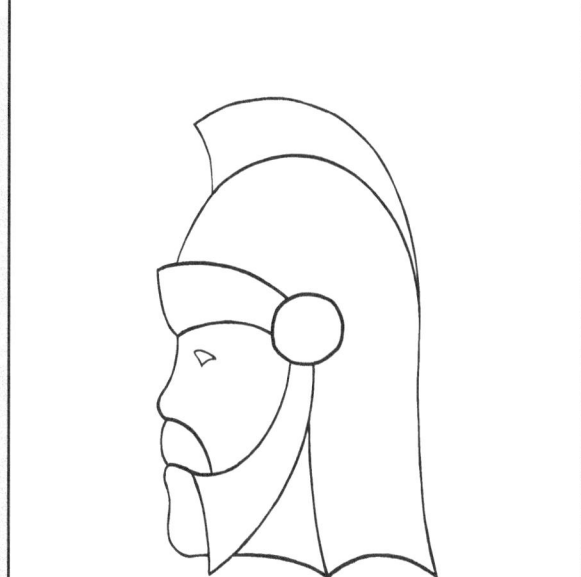

11-13 A wide "cheek guard" can lead to a profile that's too stocky.

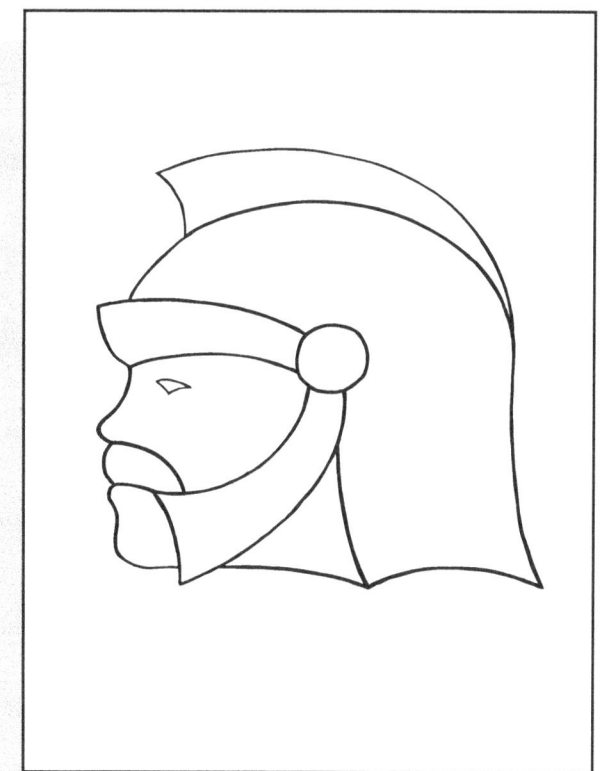

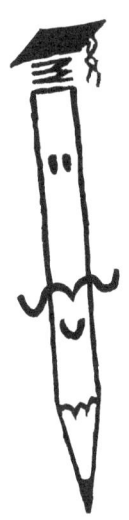

Now, please verify YOUR current status, if you haven't already.

TIP When you make your comparison, don't be too fussy. If your rendition of the "cheek guard" *is clearly* off, make adjustments. Otherwise, leave things be for now. As you know, your initial lines are not expected to be right on. While making headway, further revision will likely follow. This, too, is normal and routine.

By now I'm sure you've noticed that I keep referring to shapes which stand for something. There's a definite reason for this. To understand what I mean, I call your attention to Chapter 3, specifically the *Follow-Up*. There, if you will recall, I explained that it's important to focus on shapes and how they actually appear as parts that contribute to the whole. This concept certainly applies here. For instance, the area that signifies the gladiator's "neck" is really just a tilted TRIANGLE made by TWO additional arcs, isn't it? These attach to the "cheek guard" (11-14). Next, illustration 11-15 shows us that the *VERTICAL* curve, on the right, seems to connect about one third of the way down along the lower edge of the "cheek guard." Then it turns outward to align PLUMB with the right side of the circle. That causes a tilting to the right, before the curve ends nearly LEVEL with the bottom of the "cheek guard." As for the *HORIZONTAL* curve (11-16), it also connects to the "cheek guard," except that the link is a little above the bottom corner, as it slopes downward to meet the end of the VERTICAL curve. Are you beginning to get the picture? Essentially, what I am saying is that when subjects are reduced to basics, and observed as shapes, they can be much easier to draw.

11-14　"Neck" area is composed of 2 curves. With the "cheek guard" edge, a TRIANGLE is formed.

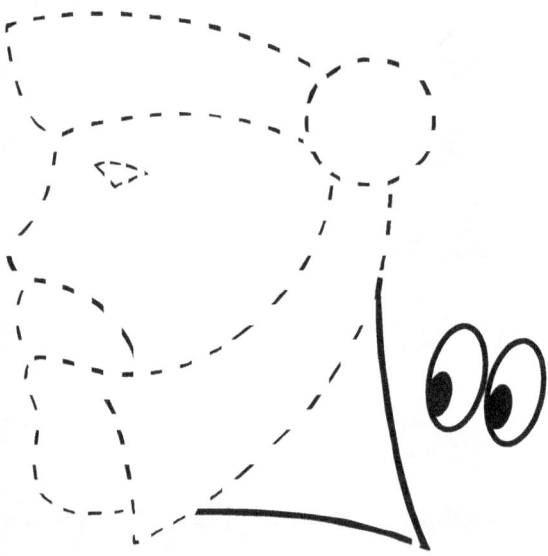

11-15　Right edge of triangle ends PLUMB with circle.

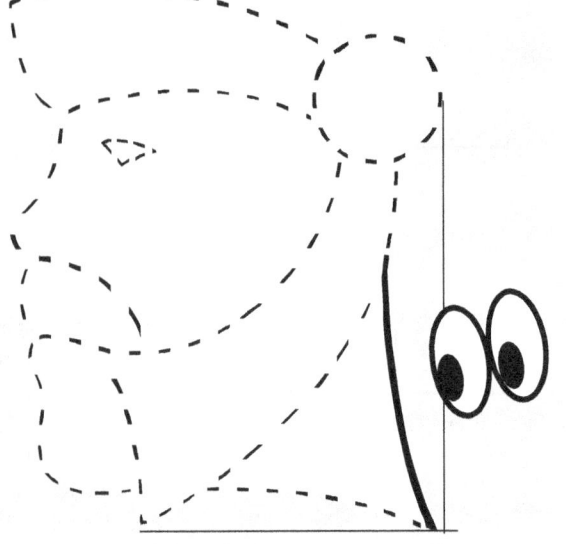

11-16　Bottom edge of triangle slopes down to meet right corner.

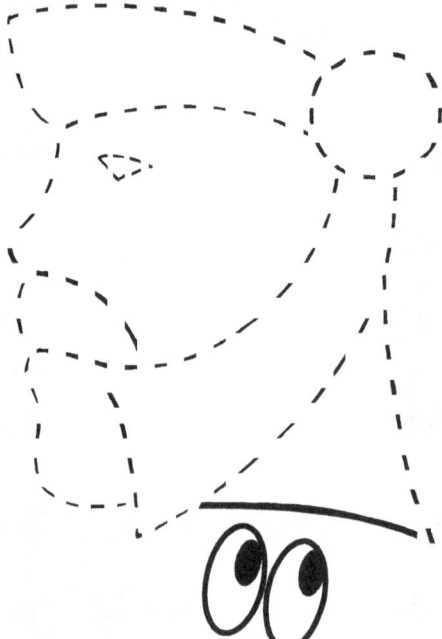

Locate reference points or visualize them (11-17). Use illustration 11-14 (previous page) as your guide. Refer to it as you fashion your arcs with either *sketch or continuous lines* (11-18 and 11-19). Then check your results and modify as needed.

11-17 Locate reference points.

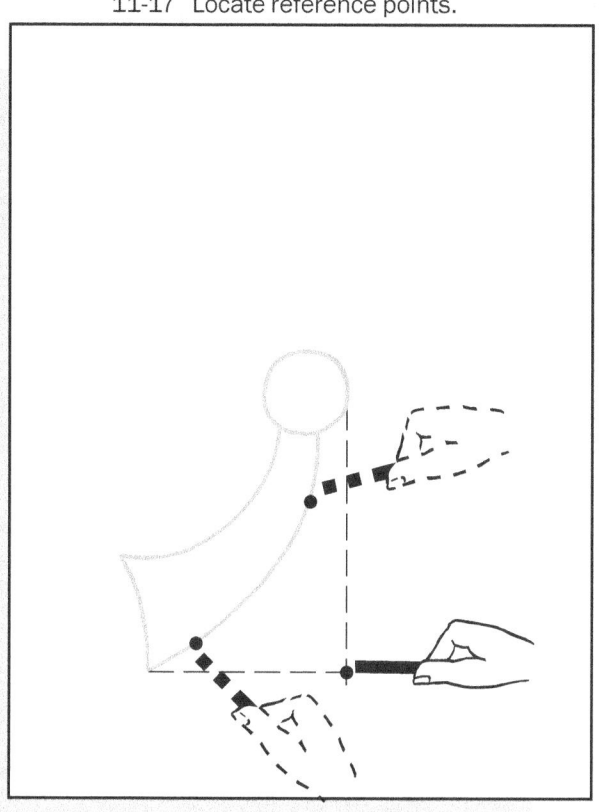

11-18 Draw your VERTICAL curve.

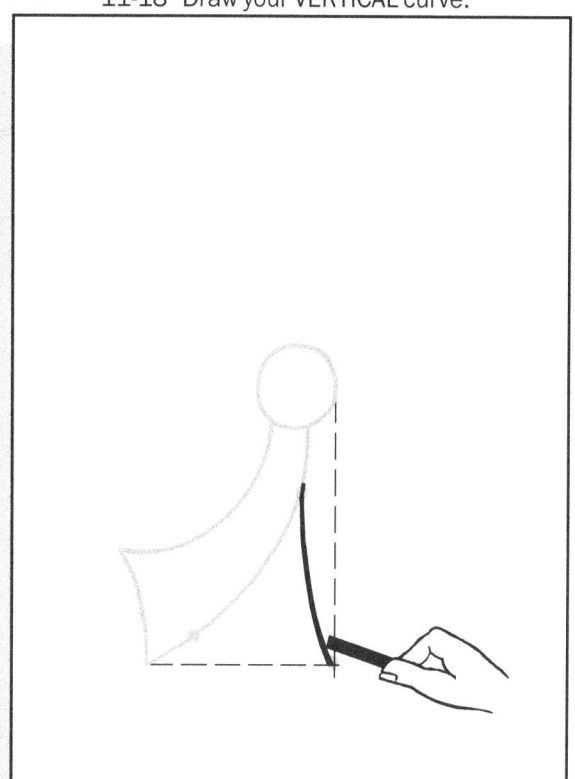

11-19 Draw your HORIZONTAL curve.

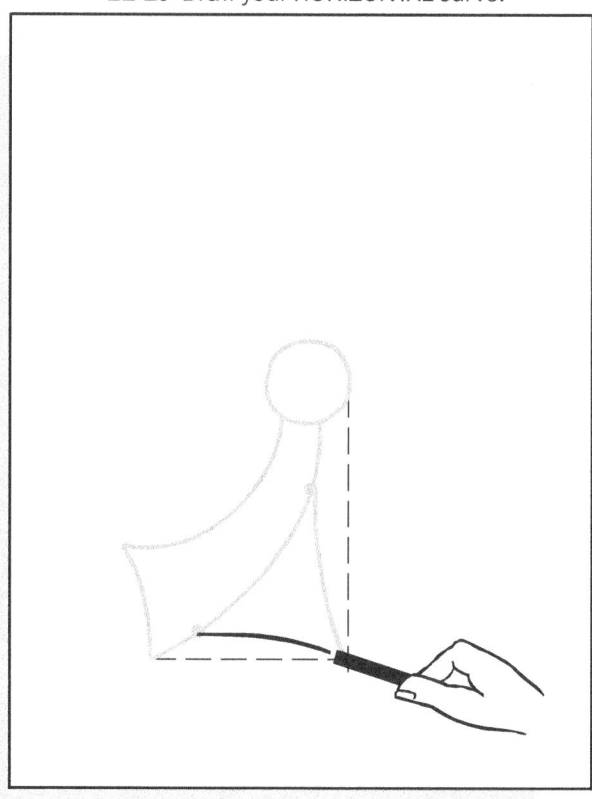

Check your status again. At this point, there are three parts to compare as separate pieces and as a whole.

TIP The further you advance without verifying your progress, the more likely things will get out of hand. In order to help prevent that, keep drawing lightly, don't hurry, and provide equal care to all parts. Whenever possible, check your accuracy after *each* new section is added by comparing your pieces, not only to each other, but also to the model. If something seems amiss, be willing to adjust.

Notice that the "chin" consists of 3 curves, including the "dip." Also observe that the bottom curve is even with the base of the "neck." When we proceed to estimate the "chin" WIDTH and HEIGHT, we see they are just a little smaller than the circle "hinge" (11-20). The "mouth," on the other hand, seems to be made with 2 curves (11-21). The front vertical curve's height appears to be only about a third of the circle. Next, take note that the horizontal curve slopes down to meet the upper corner of the "cheek guard." Also, please note that the "tip" of the "mouth" juts out a little past the "chin."

11-20 "CHIN" lines up with base of "neck" and is slightly smaller than circle.

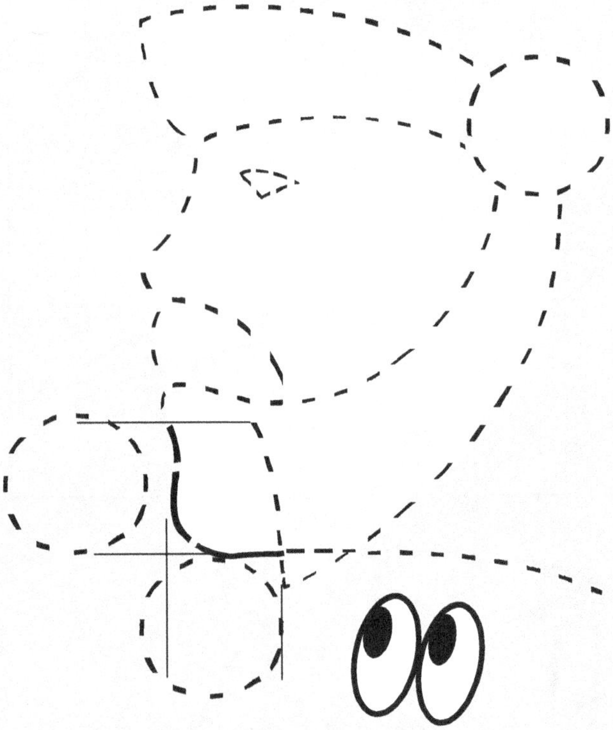

11-21 "MOUTH" juts out slightly past "chin." Its height is about 1/3 of circle and meets top corner of "cheek guard."

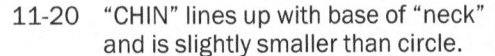

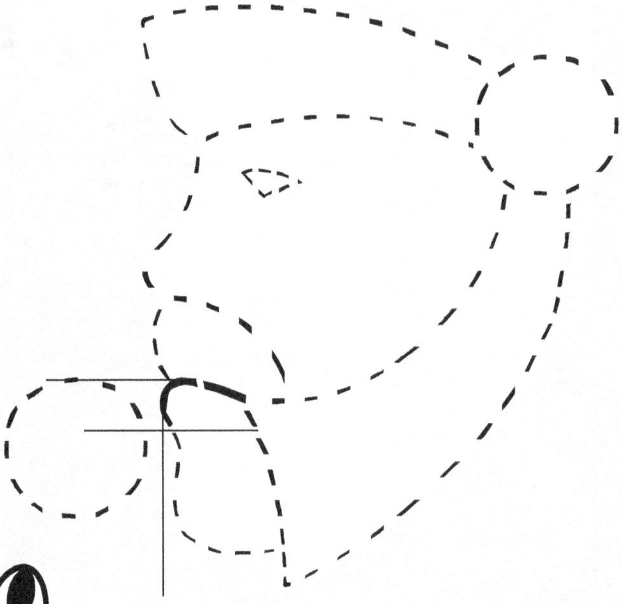

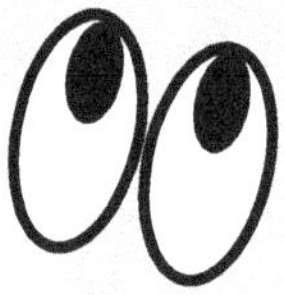

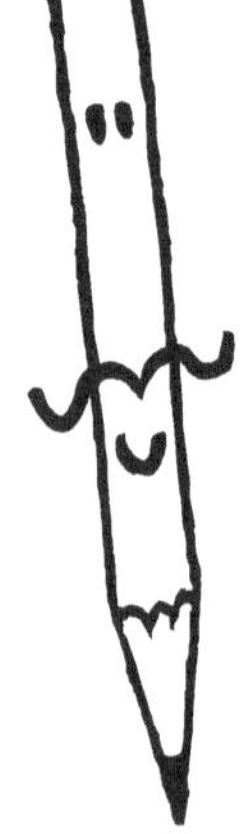

Remember when you learned to compare parts and pieces in Chapter 3? There you determined relative proportions for your champagne glass and goblet, didn't you? Well, guess what? The concept is also very handy for drawing people, isn't it?

STEP 9 | *DRAW "CHIN" & "MOUTH"*

For preliminaries, it may help to find where the "chin" aligns with the visible part of the "neck." To do that, simply "AD-LIB" by pretending you have *X-RAY VISION*. This will enable you to see *through* the "cheek guard." Next, you can place reference points prior to forming the curves (11-22). Then be sure you use the model (previous page) as you form your curves (11-23 & 24).

| TIP | Artists visualize and/or apply reference points. The more intricate the shape, the more dots are required. Envisioned, or actualized, they are an asset. With practice, you will be able to picture them in your mind while drawing. But don't be in a rush. Place as many dots as YOU need.

11-22   Locate reference points.

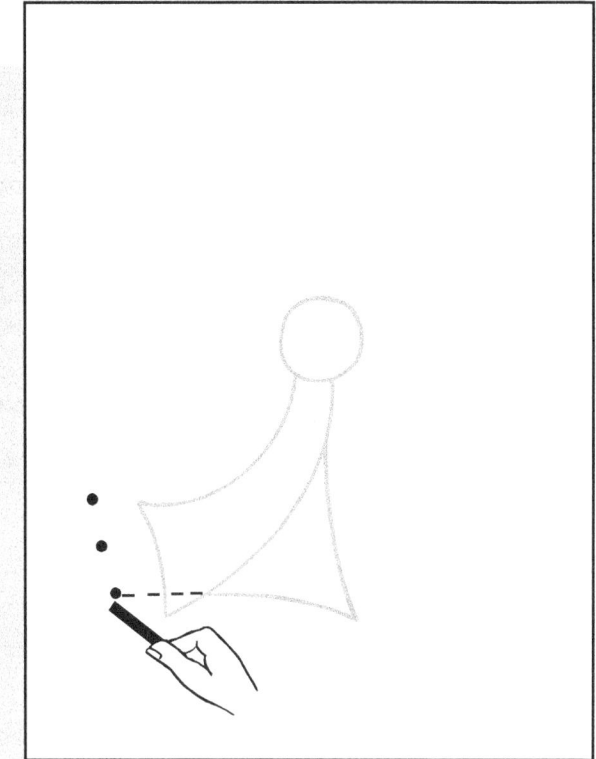

11-23   Sketch the "chin" curve(s).

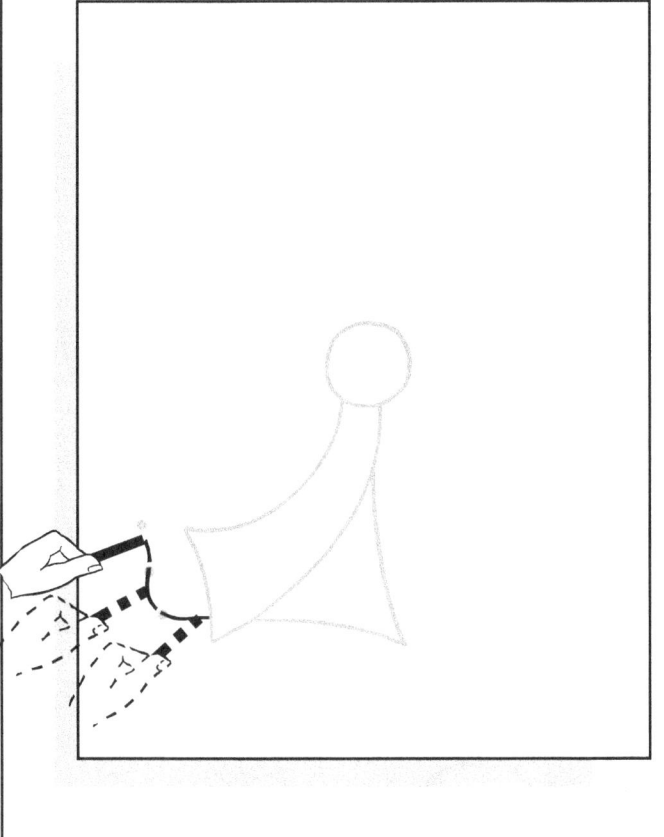

11-24   Form the "mouth" curve(s).

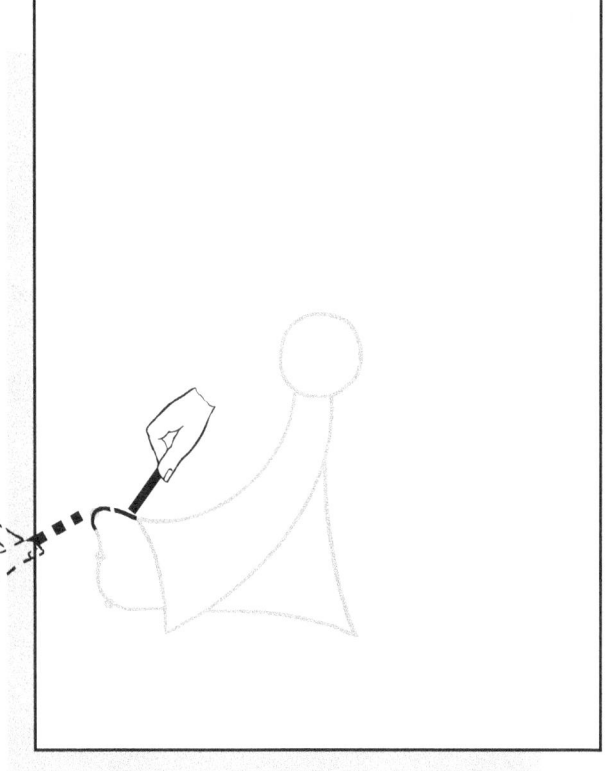

Observe that TWO curves essentially make up the section which stands for the "mustache." The front curve, forming the HEIGHT, spans about HALF the distance of the "chin" and "mouth" **combined** (11-25). Plus, there is another feature about the front curve. Its crest lines up at an ANGLE with the "chin" and "mouth" (11-26). The LARGE curve, on the other hand, starts from the top of the front curve and slants downward to connect with the **upper part** of the "cheek guard," directly plumb with its bottom corner (11-27).

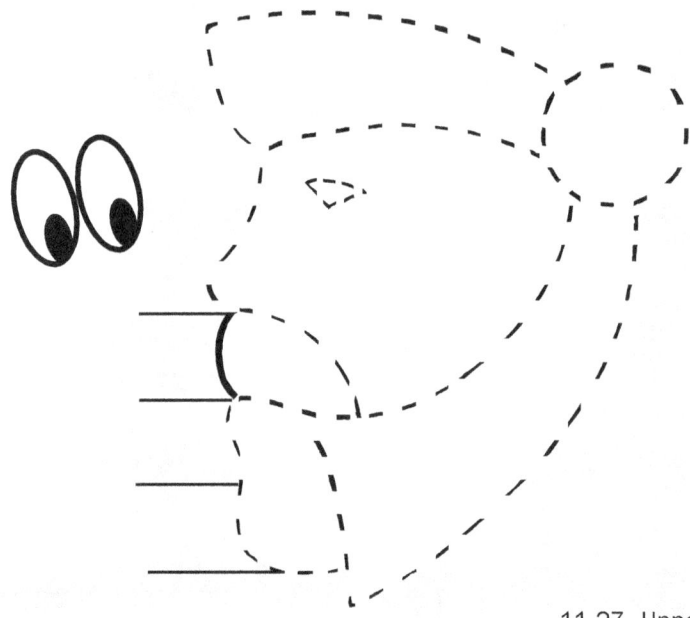

11-25 "Mustache" height is roughly half the "chin" and "mouth," together. The width aligns with the bottom corner of the "cheek guard."

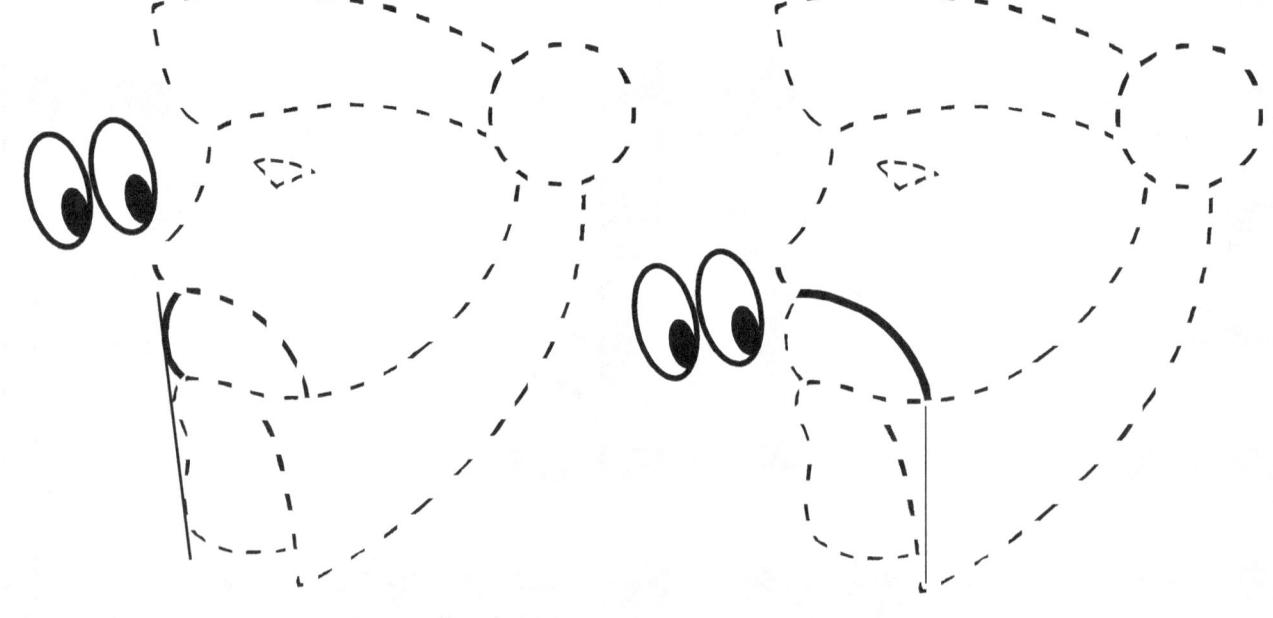

11-26 Front curve meets "mouth" and aligns at a slant with the "chin."

11-27 Upper curve descends at an angle to meet the "cheek guard" PLUMB with the bottom corner.

FASHION THE ARCS THAT DEPICT THE "MUSTACHE"

Start by forming the front arc which connects to the "mouth" on your drawing (11-28). Bear in mind that the height should be roughly half the height of your figure's "chin" and "mouth" TOGETHER, and that the curve aligns at an ANGLE with them. Don't depend solely on your memory. Glance back and forth between your work, and the model(s) shown on the previous page. See CURVES, not a "mustache." After your front curve is formed, continue from there by fashioning the top curve (11-29).

11-28 Connect a curve from the "mouth" at an ANGLE with the "chin." The height is about HALF the "mouth" and "chin" COMBINED.

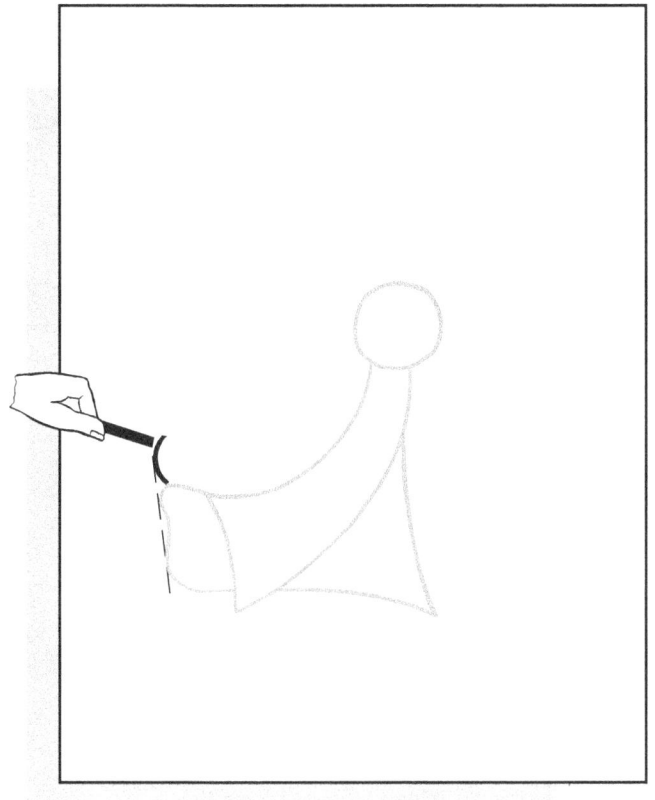

11-29 Continue from top of front curve and slant down to meet top of "cheek guard," plumb with bottom corner.

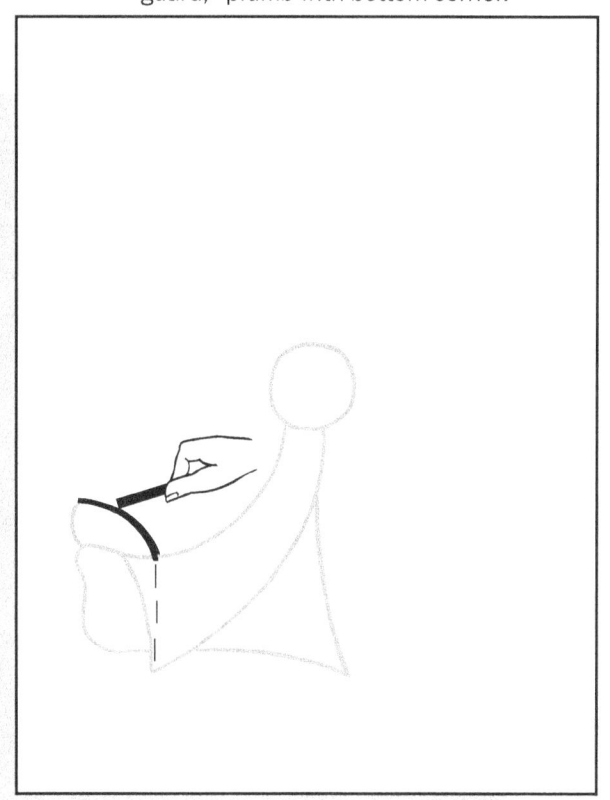

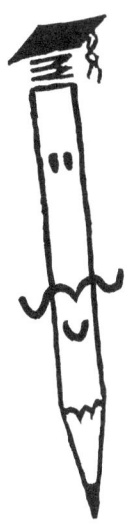

Does your drawing appear more or less like mine? Did you compare the SHAPE of the piece you just drew with the model? Are you checking to see how all the parts are interacting? You will save a lot of backtracking if you do. Take your time. Verify EACH phase and make adjustments along the way, as needed. Remember: ACCURACY means VISIBLY close.

ASSESS THE ARCS THAT FORM THE "NOSE"

Only 2 curves are required for the "nose." A *convex* arc extends upward from the "mustache" until the crest lines up *diagonally* with the "chin" (11-30). Then, a *concave* arc continues from there and ends *LEVEL* with the *middle* of the "cheek guard hinge" (or circle). Plus, it *VERTICALLY* aligns roughly a half way between the "dip" of the "chin" and "cheek guard" (11-31).

Hoo wee! This sounds like a lot of fuss for such a simple portion, doesn't it? But please keep in mind, all parts contribute to the whole. So pay close attention no matter how minor a section, or its lines, may seem.

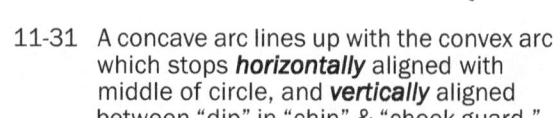

11-30   A convex arc for "nose" *TIP* aligns with "chin," "mouth," and "mustache" at an ANGLE.

11-31   A concave arc lines up with the convex arc which stops *horizontally* aligned with middle of circle, and *vertically* aligned between "dip" in "chin" & "cheek guard."

You can locate reference points or visualize them. Either way, **see arcs, NOT a "nose." This will tend to help you observe the shape more easily.** Be sure to look for the amount of bow and the alignments, along with stopping and starting locations, by using the models (previous page) as your guide. Form one curve at a time (11-32 and 11-33). Then check your result.

TIP Enjoy each stroke. Just as separate pieces build the total figure, it's the individual lines that create the sections. So before you make any changes, finish the entire portion you set out to draw. The exception is when a line you formed is obviously way off course. In most cases, though, it's easier to see where change is needed *AFTER* you have completed a segment.

11-32 Align a CONVEX arc *diagonally* with lower portions.

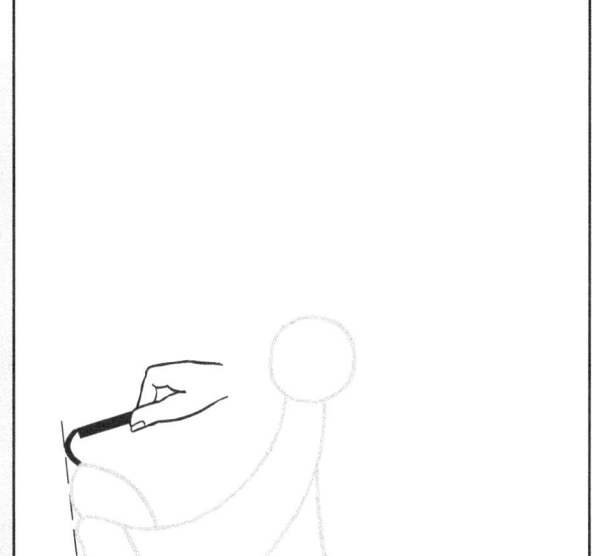

11-33 Align a CONCAVE arc level with circle center and PLUMB midway from "chin" to "guard."

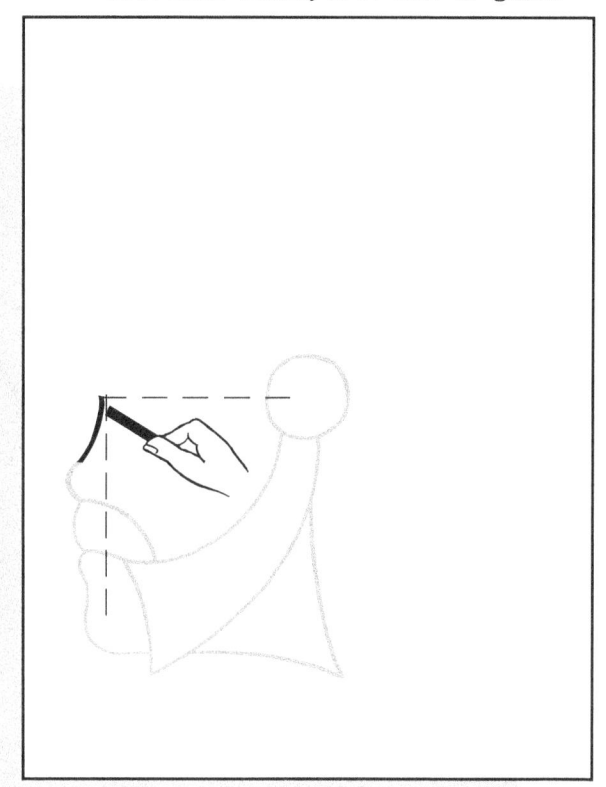

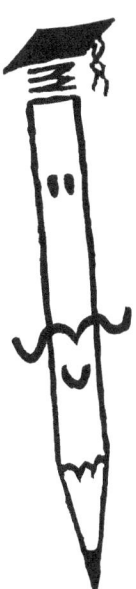

OK. The moment has arrived. If you haven't stepped out of your chair yet, don't wait any longer. Do it now. Place your drawing side-by-side with page 183, move back a few paces, and compare your drawing with its existing parts to those on the model. Then, one by one, make any necessary adjustments. You've already learned the many benefits of doing this procedure in chapters 8 and 9. After making sure your present status is okay, proceed to the next phase.

Observe that the "visor" shape is made by THREE curves. The LOWER arc's base line is located just under the **center** of the circle "hinge," and rises a little above its center. Next, take note that the FRONT arc climbs at an angle to a height that's about the same as the diameter of the circle "hinge." Plus, it aligns PLUMB with the **tip** of the "nose" (11-34). Then, the UPPER arc ascends slightly before gently descending toward the **middle** of the circle "hinge" (11-35).

11-34 The base line of the LOWER arc lies just below the center of the circle "hinge." The FRONT arc aligns with the "nose." The "visor" height is about the same as the circle "hinge."

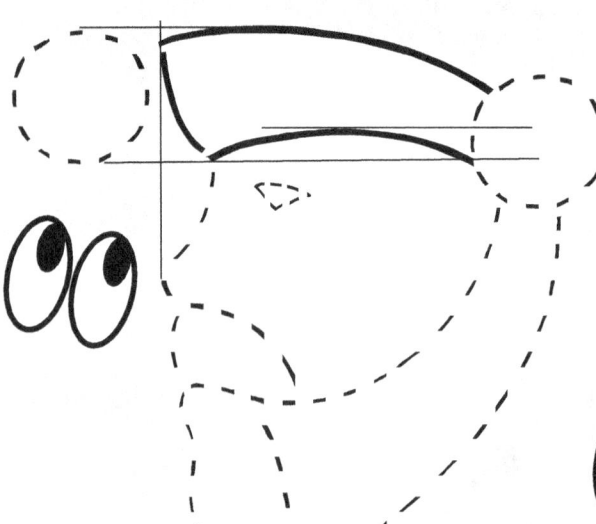

11-35 UPPER curve connects from front arc, rises slightly, then bends downward toward the center of the circle "hinge."

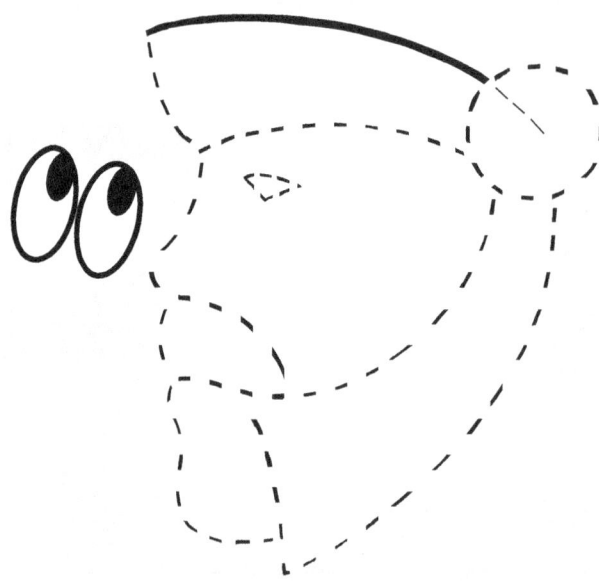

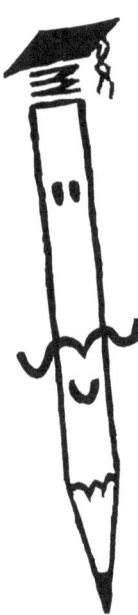

At this stage your figure will increasingly begin to appear like the model. Because of this, you will likely feel a stronger urge to speed up, so you can see how things turn out. But please resist the temptation. Instead of hurrying, concentrate on the steps that assure your success. The gladiator has about twice the number of shapes you've been accustomed to drawing. Expect to devote extra time. Besides, your picture should be allowed to take as long as it takes.

Having acquainted yourself with the scale coordinates for the "visor," next place some reference points. This will enable you to visualize how the shape will appear before you draw it (11-36). Then link 3 arcs, one at a time, as shown by illustrations 11-37, 38 & 39, or follow your own sequence.

11-36 Position reference points.

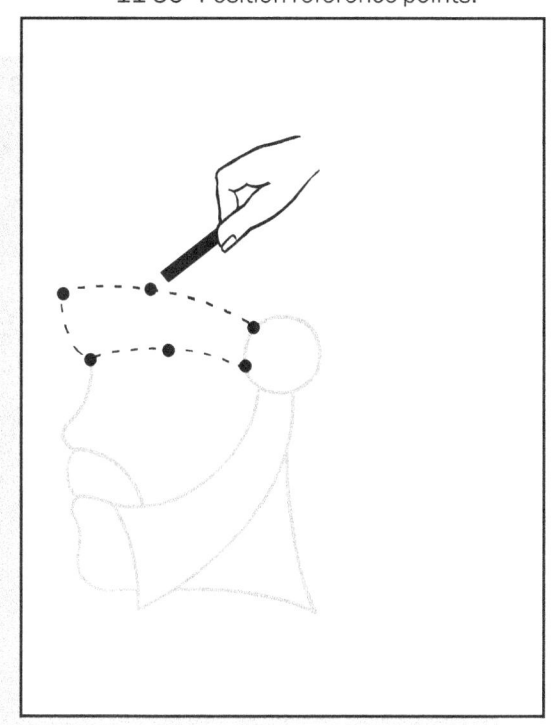

11-37 Draw "visor" BOTTOM.

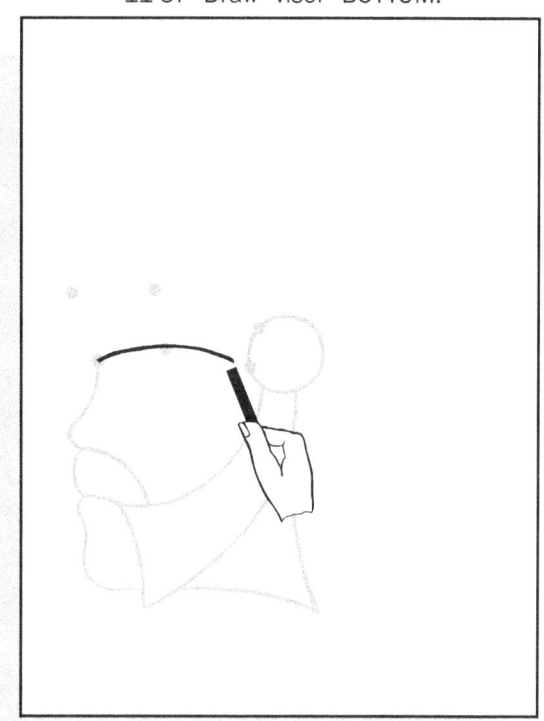

11-38 Draw "visor" FRONT.

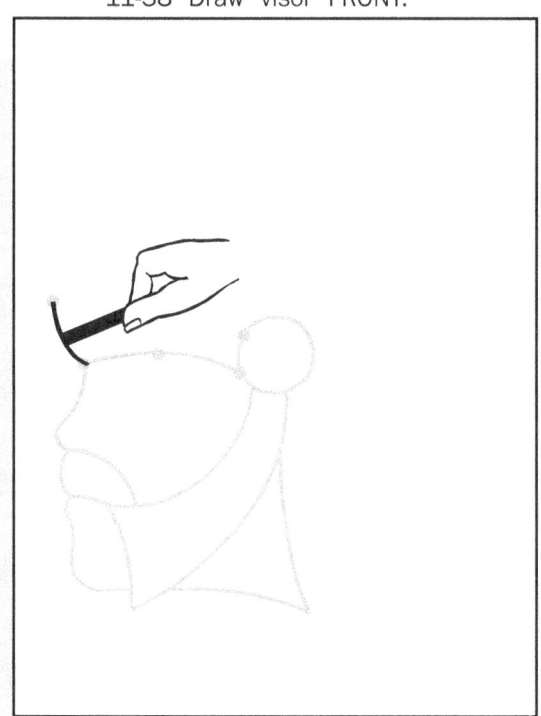

11-39 Draw "visor" TOP.

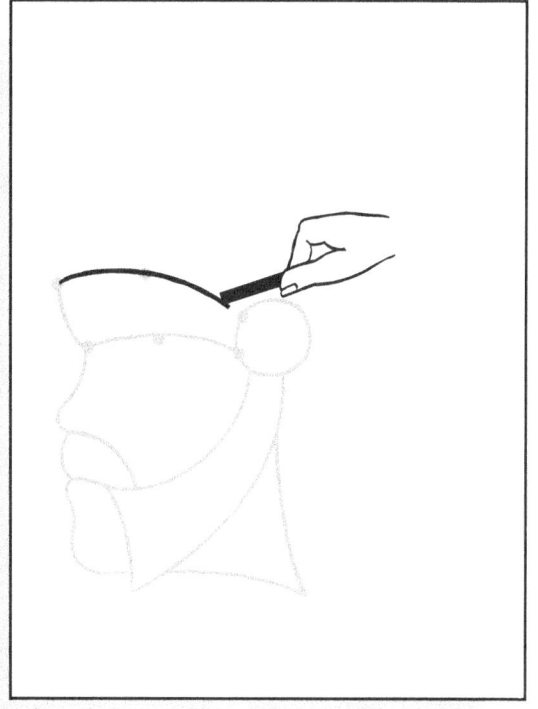

HOT TIP As segments continue to be added, remember to STOP drawing after each new portion is completed, in order to give yourself a chance to compare results. Do this side-by-side with the LARGE illustration of the model on page 183, not only up close, but also at a DISTANCE. You will likely spot variations between your version and the orginal more easily. If you're wondering why, please refer to pages 190 and 191. Then re-read page 36, as well as page 146 and 147.

Take a look at illustration 11-40 below. Notice that the shape of the "helmet" (*excluding the "crown ornament"*) entails 3 ARCS. A LARGE, *horizontal* arc forms the **upper portion**. Then, a *narrow* VERTICAL arc follows downward on the right. A *SHORT, horizontal* arc turns left at the bottom. Next, study illustration 11-41. Observe that the bow of the BIG arc is about the same HEIGHT as the VERTICAL distance from the "mouth" to the bridge of the "nose." Interestingly, it starts aligned with the bride of the "nose" but, on the opposite end, the arc extends *lower*, until it's LEVEL with the TOP of the circle "hinge." How long is the curve? Good question. The LEFT edge of the circle seems to be the mid-point. Moving on, let's focus on illustration 11-42. As you can tell, the concave VERTICAL arc connects from the right side of the LARGE curve, runs parallel with the "neck" arc, and ends even with it at the bottom. Last but not least, study illustration 11-43. There we can see that the adjoining small HORIZONTAL arc is on the same base line as the "neck" and rises to a height LEVEL with the lowest portion of the gladiator's "chin."

11-40 Three arcs form the "helmet" (without the "ornament").

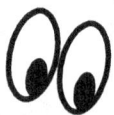

11-41 Large arc HEIGHT equals distance of "mouth" to bridge of "nose," and aligns PLUMB with it. The RIGHT end of large arc is level with top of circle.

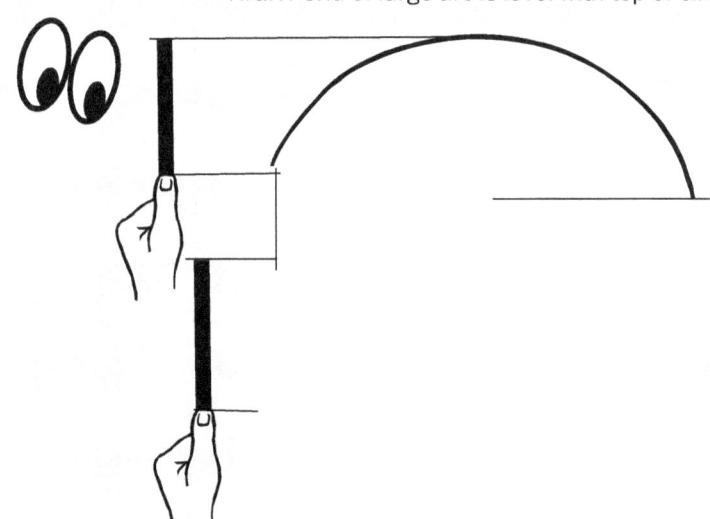

11-42 Right VERTICAL curve slants parallel with "neck" arc, and ends even with it at the bottom.

11-43 Small curve is on same base line as "neck" and rises to the same height as the "chin."

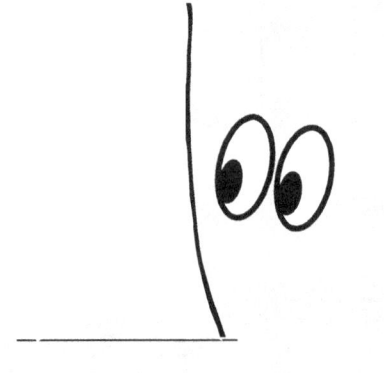

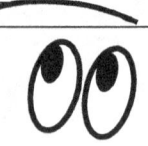

Similar to the way you formed the "chin" and "mouth," for this fairly elaborate segment, it might pay to trace each intended curve in the air, while referring to the model (previous page). Also, you may find it useful to locate preliminary dots, especially the starting, middle and ending points (11-44). Then lightly draw your arcs, in sections, via the continuous line or sketch line method (11-45, 46 & 47).

11-44 Place reference points. They will help visualize, and sketch your curves.

11-45 Sketch your LARGE top ARC with two, or more smaller curves.

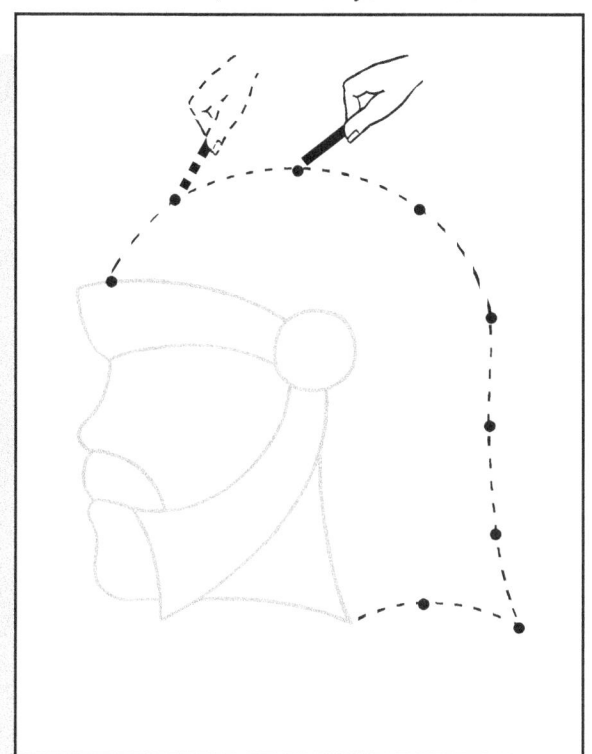

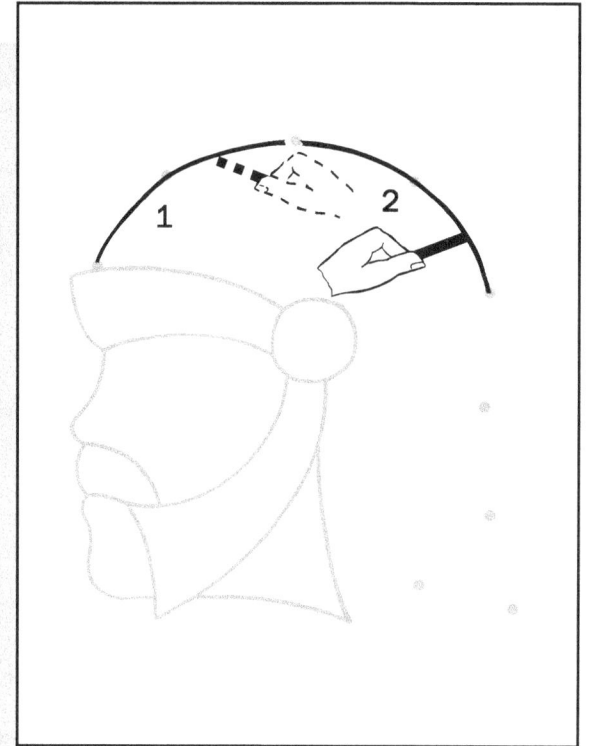

11-46 Connect your VERTICAL arc.

11-47 Connect your BOTTOM arc.

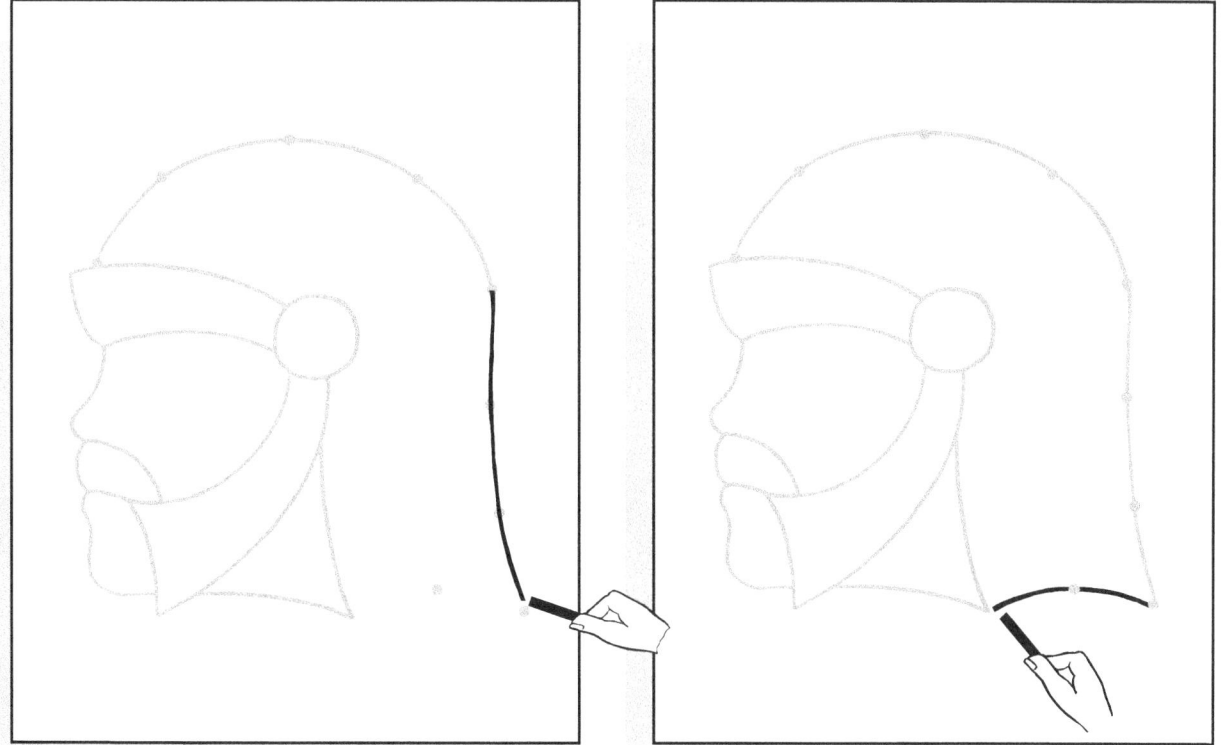

Observe that the "helmet ornament" (or "crown") is composed of one long, *horizontal* arc, plus one short *vertical* arc, and both are at a slant. The extensions and sizes can be easily estimated to scale by comparing them to other parts of the figure. For instance, the base of the SMALL arc appears to be even with the *LOWER front corner* of the "cheek guard," whereas the top part of the curve looks to be even with the *UPPER front corner* of the "cheek guard." The height is easy to estimate, too. Notice that it's about the same vertical span as the "visor's" front (11-48). As for the LONG curve, it continues from the upper portion of the small arc. First it climbs a little, before gradually descending and narrowing to end at the back of the "helmet." The stopping point, as you can tell, is fairly LEVEL with the top of the circle "hinge" (11-49).

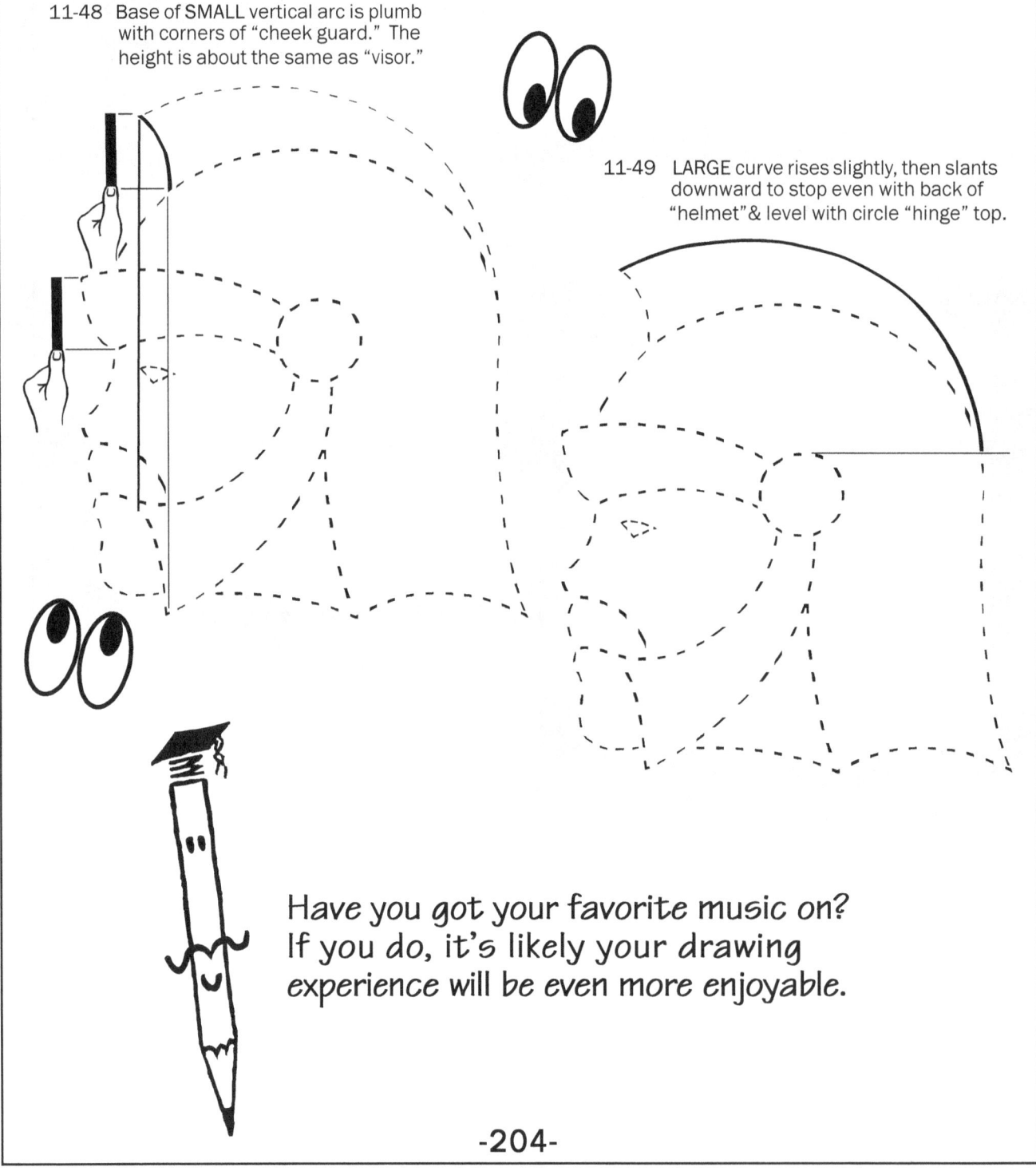

11-48 Base of SMALL vertical arc is plumb with corners of "cheek guard." The height is about the same as "visor."

11-49 LARGE curve rises slightly, then slants downward to stop even with back of "helmet" & level with circle "hinge" top.

Have you got your favorite music on? If you *do*, it's likely your drawing experience will be even more enjoyable.

ATTACH THE CURVES TO *FORM* THE "HELMET ORNAMENT"

Before you draw the "helmet ornament," you may want to plot reference points as shown in illustration 11-50. Also, please be sure you refer to the models on the previous page to help guide your hand while you fashion your arcs (11-51 & 11-52). Use the continuous line or sketch method.

TIP After forming your curves, compare them to the larger figure on the previous page.

11-50 Place reference points.

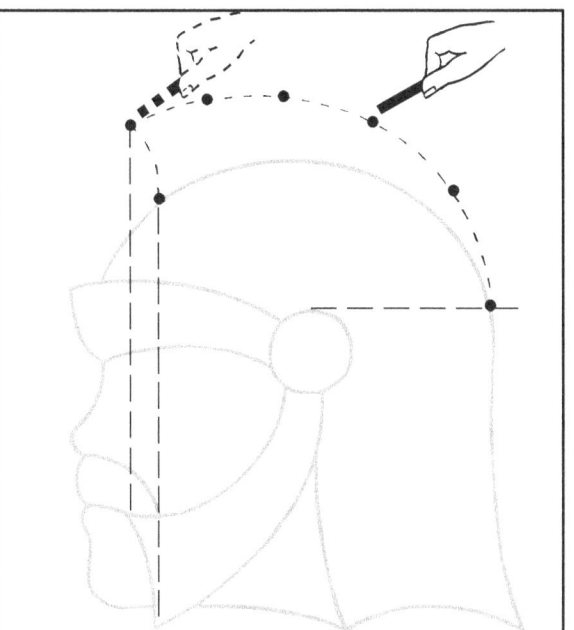

11-51 Draw your small "crown" arc.

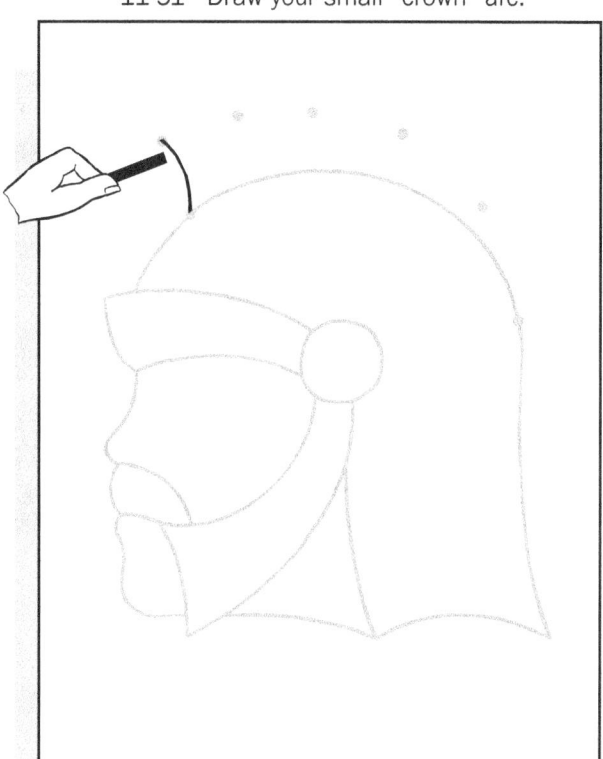

11-52 Draw large "crown" arc with 2, or more arcs.

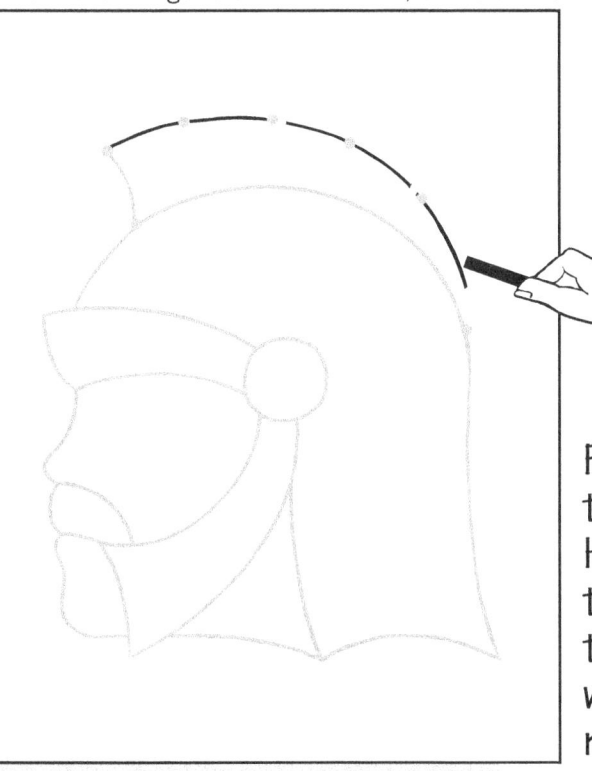

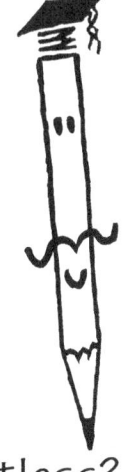

Feeling restless? Are you eager to finish and see the end result? Hang in there. It's time again to compare the large version of the model on page 183 to your work. Modify as needed, then move on to the next phase.

EXAMINE THE SHAPE WHICH STANDS FOR THE "EYE"

Don't look for "pupils." There aren't any, at least not showing. Actually, like the "neck area" (which you drew earlier), just three simple arcs form the "eye" (in the shape of a TRIANGLE. Notice it's situated nearly parallel between the two front corners of the "helmet ornament," or "crown," and level with the circle "hinge" (11-53). As for the *height*, it's about HALF the length, and drops down about that same interval of distance from the "visor" (11-54).

11-53 Triangular "eye" aligns almost parallel
with front curve ornament." Its lowest
point is level with the bottom of circle
and nearly *centered* between front curve.

11-54 Length roughly double the height.
Space between bridge of "nose,"
and height of "eye" about equal.

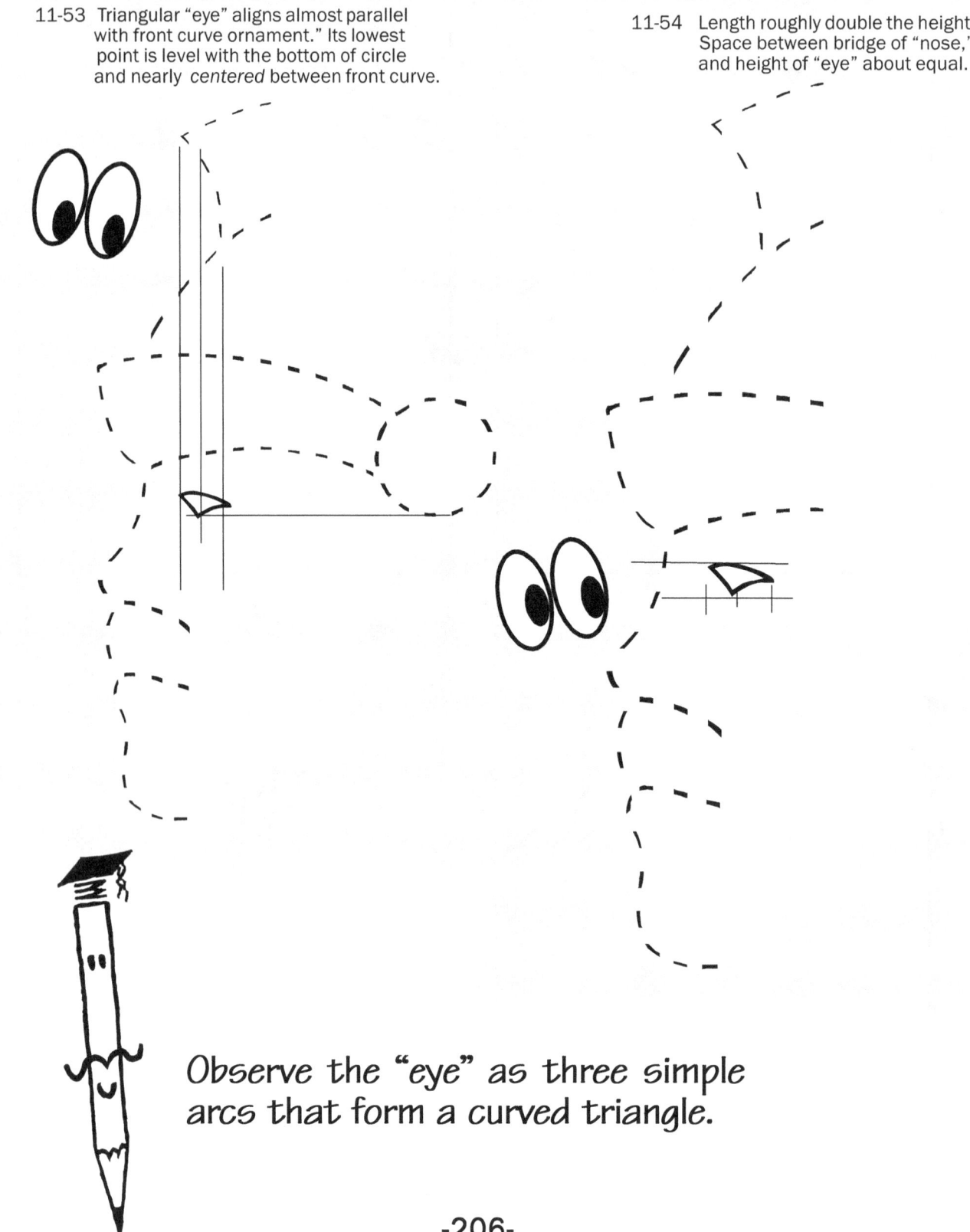

Observe the "eye" as three simple arcs that form a curved triangle.

STEP 21 — *DRAW* THE 3 CURVES TO REPLICATE THE "EYE"

Place a dot, LEVEL with the bottom of your circle "hinge," and PLUMB between the two front corners of the "helmet ornament" (11-55). As you refer to the model, form a slanted letter "V" with 2 arcs. When combined, they should be twice as wide as their height (11-56). Next, look to the model once again to form the triangle by closing up your "V" with a "convex" arc that gradually slopes downward (11-57).

11-55 Position a dot centered between front curve of "crown" & LEVEL with bottom of circle "hinge."

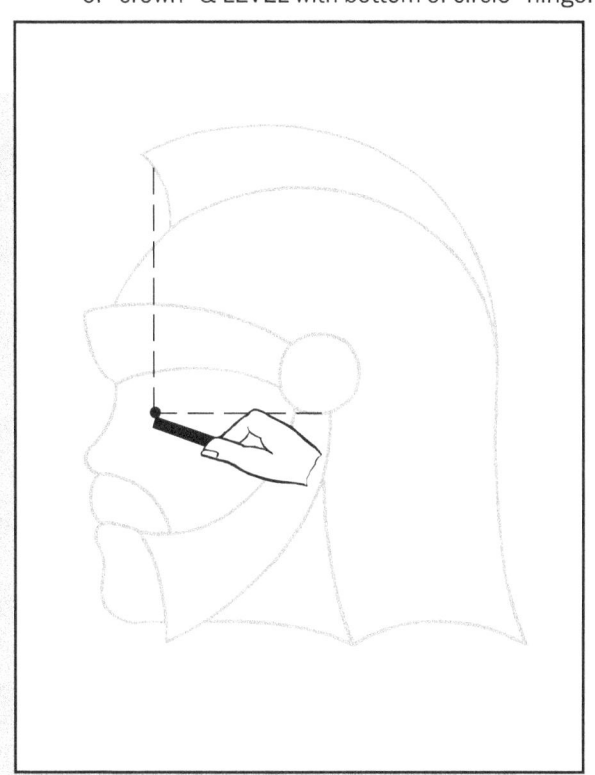

11-56 Form a letter "V" twice the width compared to height.

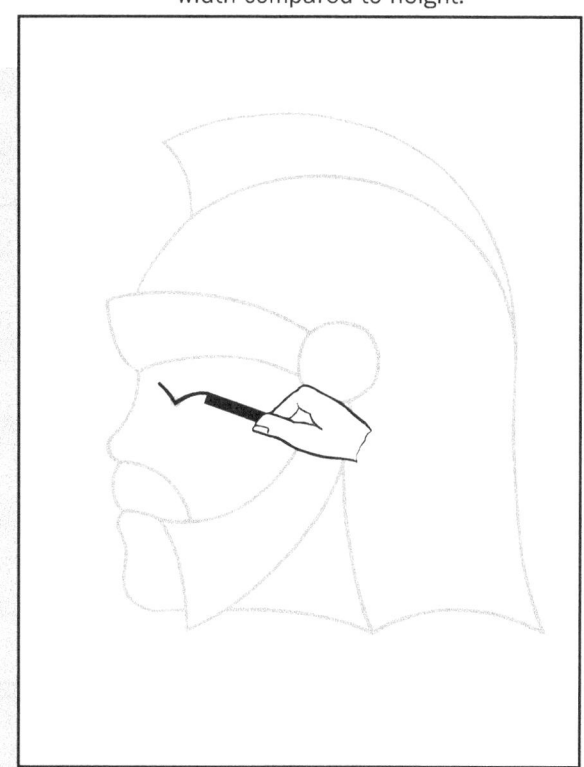

11-57 Close up your "V" to form triangle.

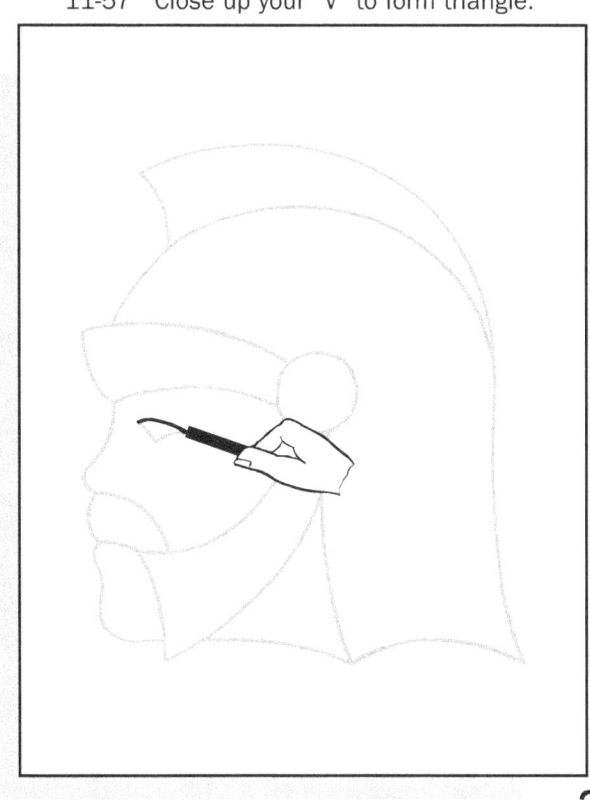

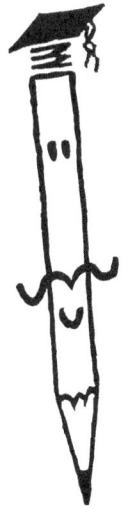

I know you're eager to call your work "DONE." But stay with me. A thorough "once over" is next. As you know, without it, your efforts will not be fully realized.

Yes, I'm absolutely serious. You already learned how important side-by-side comparisons are, especially from a distance. Now treat yourself to *another kind.* Prop the book illustration on page 183 next to your drawing once more. This time place them SIDEWAYS and observe. You may find some unexpected things. For instance, look at sample drawing 11-58, below. The miniature copy of the model indicates the tips of the"nose,""mustache," "mouth," and "chin," align at an ANGLE. But, on the finished drawing example, you can see they do NOT line up at an angle.

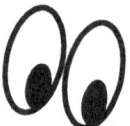

SIDEWAYS SIDE-BY-SIDE SAMPLE COMPARISON OF
PAGE 183 WITH A DRAWING EXAMPLE

Model indicates"chin,""mouth"
and "mustache," line up at a SLANT.

11-58 Drawing example indicates "chin," "mouth"
and "mustache" are NOT at a SLANT.

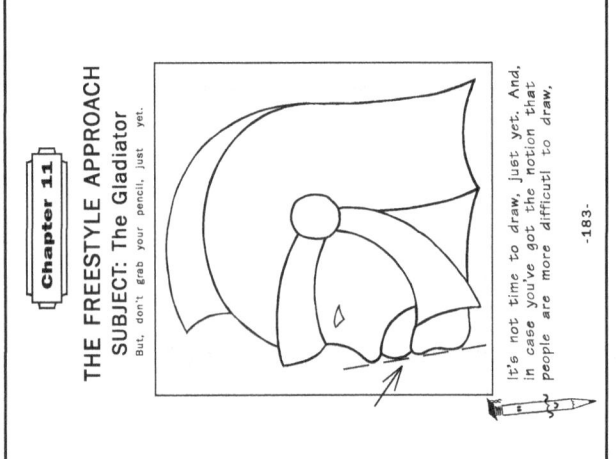

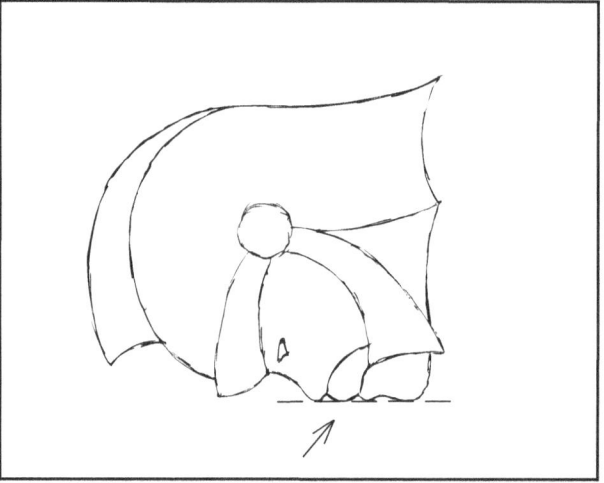

BUT WHY COMPARE *SIDEWAYS*, YOU MAY BE WONDERING?

The reason is simple. While drawing the gladiator, you've studied both YOUR rendition and the book illustrations *a lot.* Naturally, you may be tired of looking at them, and probably convinced you're totally familiar with all aspects. Well, you know what? This kind of thinking will usually cause a false sense of security. A *FRESH sideways view,* on the other hand, or even inverted, with BOTH your drawing and your model upside down, offers a "NEW PERSPECTIVE." For instance, if you will recall, near the outset of this chapter, the ten shapes which composed the gladiator were shown on page 186. In like fashion, you can study YOUR gladiator's shapes by comparing them with the model, ONE SHAPE AT A TIME. In other words, consider the parts as INDEPENDENT sections which MAKE THE WHOLE. To do this effectively, allow your eyes to perform like a close-up camera lens. "ZOOM" in and focus on individual lines, and the *separate* shapes they create. Next, zoom out a little to see how each shape relates to other adjacent shapes. Then, zoom out further to observe their effect on your ENTIRE figure. You need not even make any further changes. It's sufficient that you see the differences between the book version and yours. "Seeing" is not just looking. The more you truly observe, the more enjoyable and meaningful your drawing experience can become.

*After you've studied YOUR drawing, take
a gander at the student examples.*

EXERCISE 11
MODEL & STUDENT EXAMPLES

Model

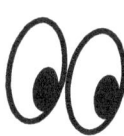

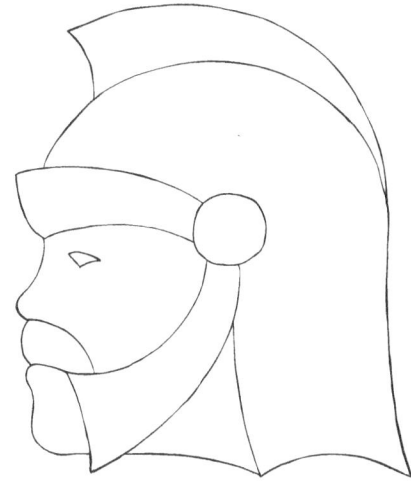

STUDENT SAMPLING

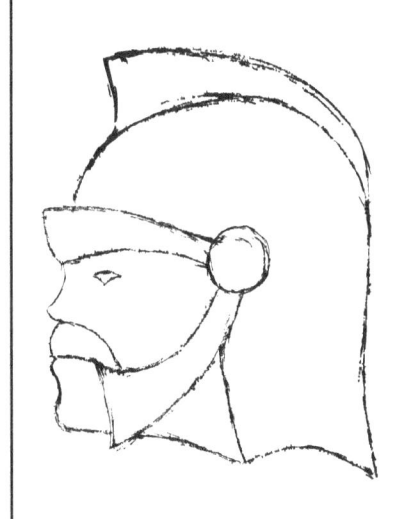 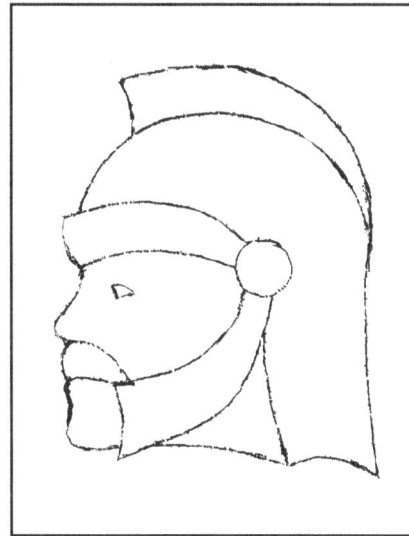 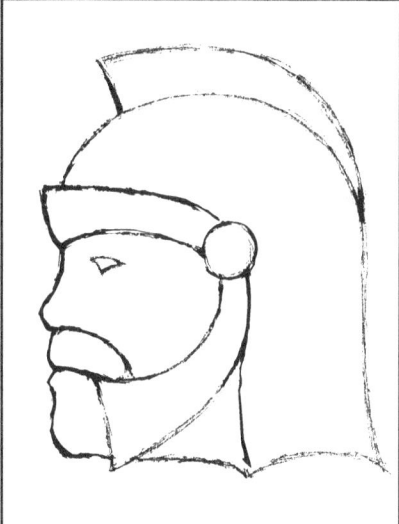

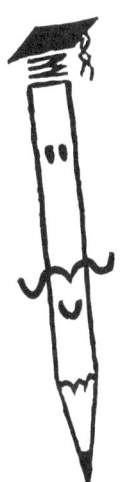

Wow! All three drawings resemble the model, yet they are different, aren't they? Individual styles are shining through, and yours, I'm sure, does too. On another day, put your know-how to work. The supplemental exercise awaits on the next page.

DO IT YOUR WAY!

CHAPTER 11
SUPPLEMENTAL EXERCISE

OBJECTIVE: Replicate The Warrior
(at a different size)

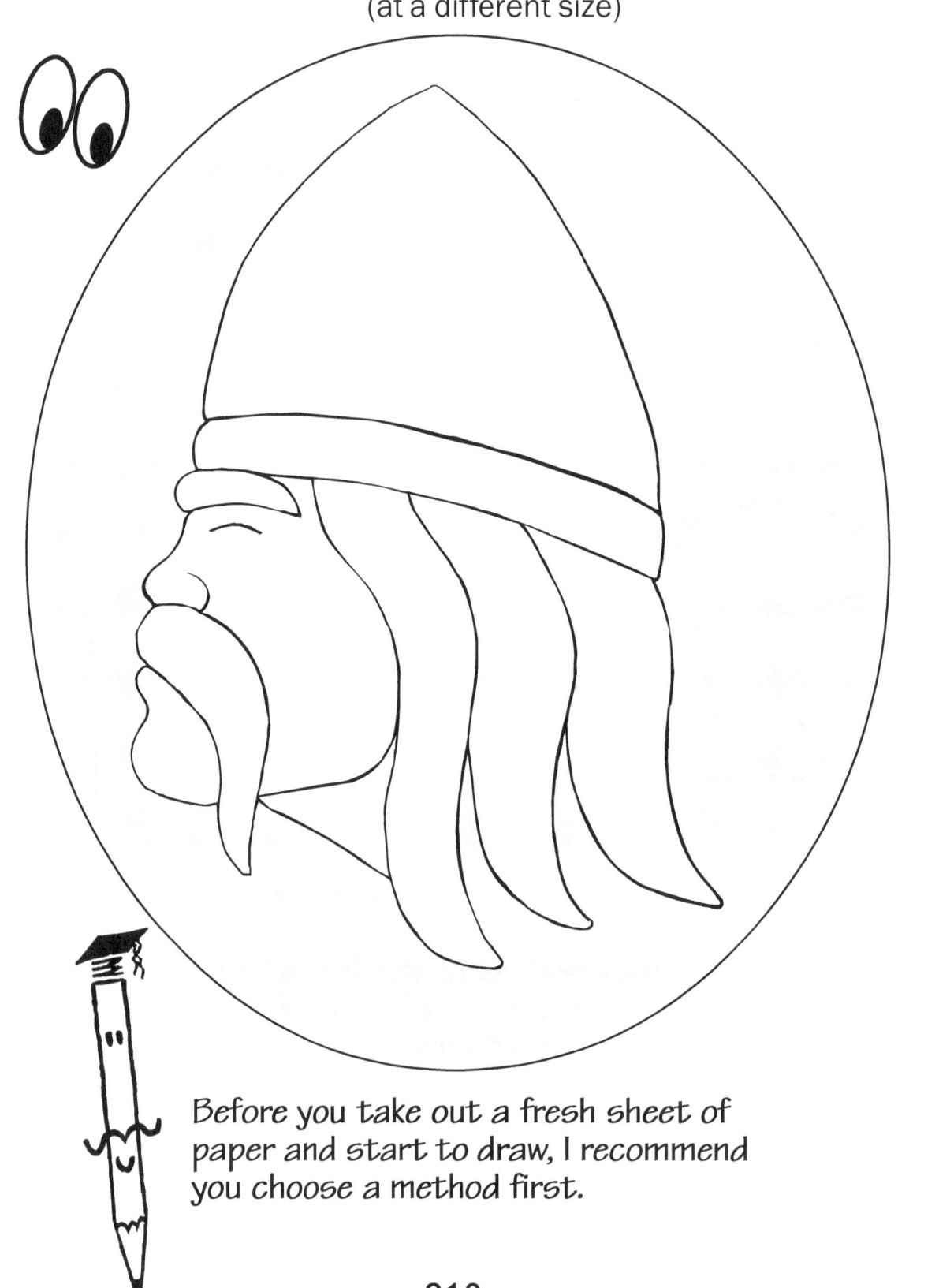

Before you take out a fresh sheet of paper and start to draw, I recommend you choose a method first.

TAKE YOUR PICK

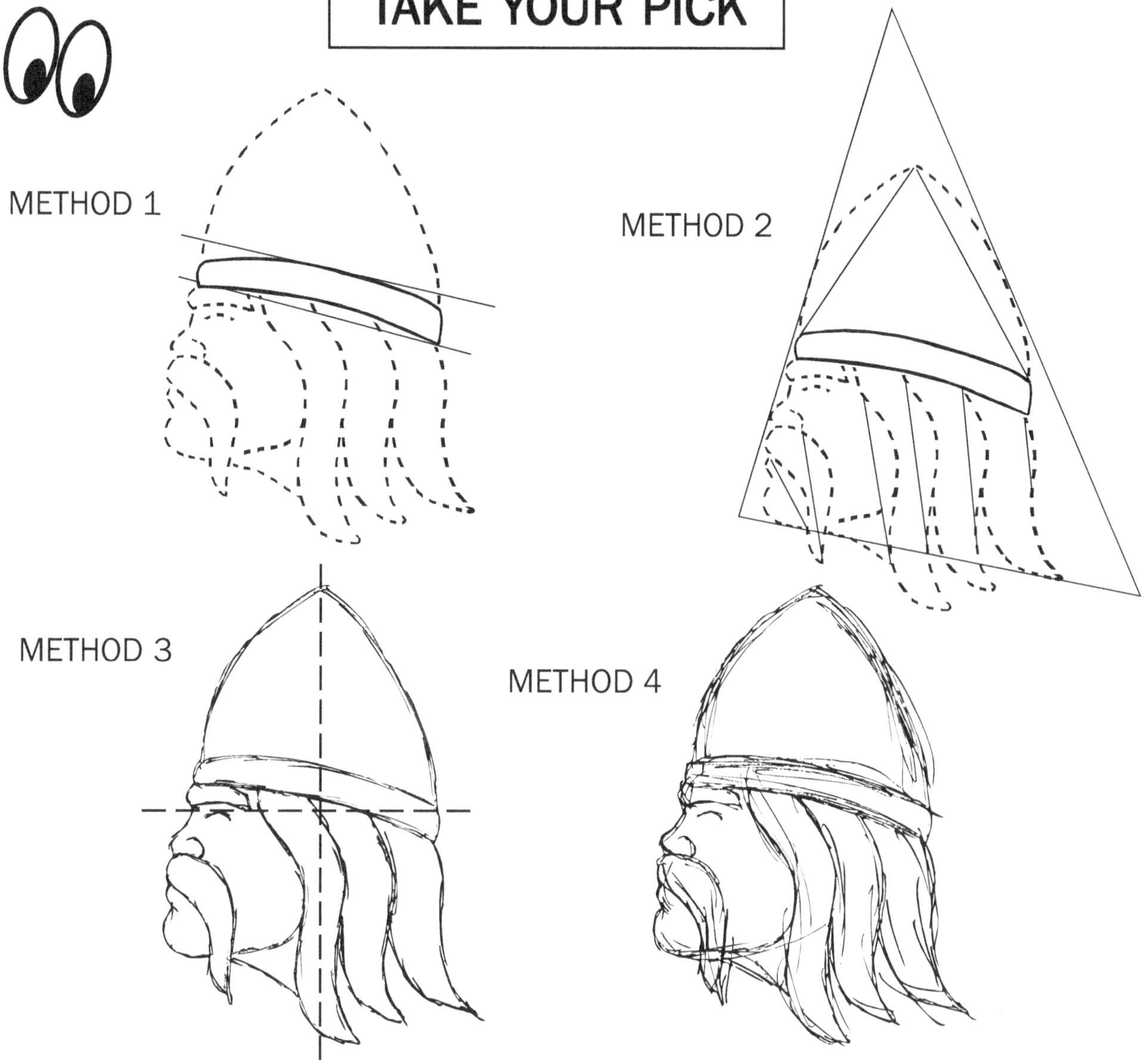

METHOD 1

METHOD 2

METHOD 3

METHOD 4

METHOD 1 Using guide lines and reference points, find the angle for the "helmet base." Draw it and attach the other parts randomly, with the help of the "trusty seven."

METHOD 2 *Ad-libbed and streamlined*, the figure fits into a TRIANGLE. Fashion one to scale. Next, apply straight lines to simplify the *reverse space* and main curves. Then, starting with any piece you prefer, attach the sections individually.

METHOD 3 Visualize the figure crisscrossed as you SKETCH the subject, randomly.

METHOD 4 DOODLE the warrior. Refine if desired.

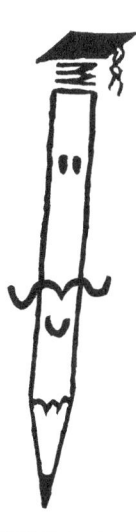

OR, you can COMBINE methods. Whichever way you prefer, keep in mind that a reasonably close (not a perfect) match is the goal. Enjoy your creative freedom. Experiment with several ways, then be sure to read the follow-up.

Chapter 11
FOLLOW-UP

Did it sink in yet? You actually drew a likeness of not one, but *two* different people! To be sure, what began as seemingly unrelated sections became recognizable figures, and herein lies another gigantic SECRET! As lines appeared and joined with others, faces eventually emerged, didn't they? So you see, whether destined to be a vase, a leaf, a human profile, ANYTHING - they are all made of *shapes*. You proved this on every occasion.

And look how well you did it! This time you drew FREESTYLE - a technique that's really a harmonious blend of many methods you've practiced, through a series of collective observing, thinking, and drawing procedures. For instance, in order to form all those individual curves (which made the various shapes, and in turn, produced the profiles), you had to apply many of the principles and components you learned in Chapters 1, 2 and 3. Then your evaluations, both during and after your drawings were completed, built upon the knowledge you gained from Chapters 4 and 5. Equally commendable, the way you kept pace with the agility of the random mode (Chapter 9) and the flair of the squiggle (Chapter 10) shows your growing versatility.

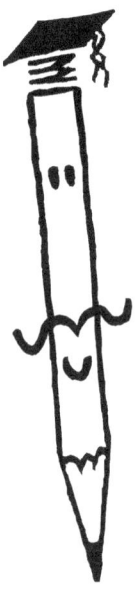

Without a doubt, you've made tremendous strides, haven't you? Now rest easy. Soon you'll be off on another grand adventure.

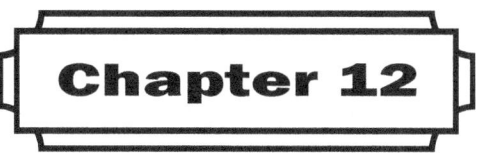

THE CHIAROSCURO METHOD

From hollow and flat...

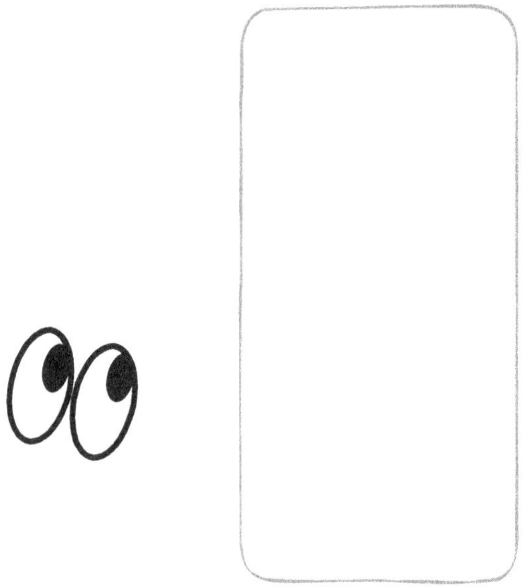

...to solid and curved.

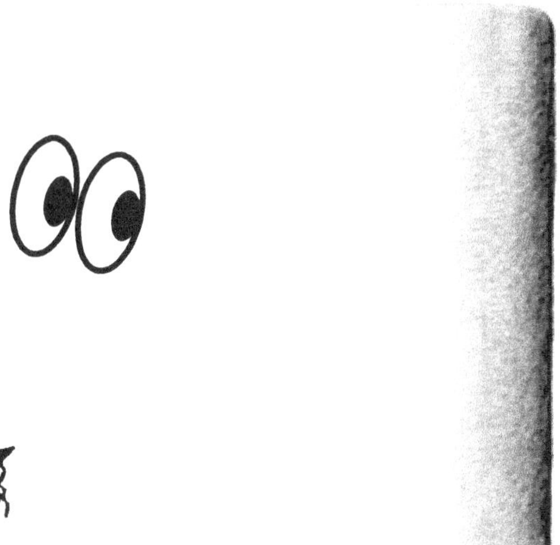

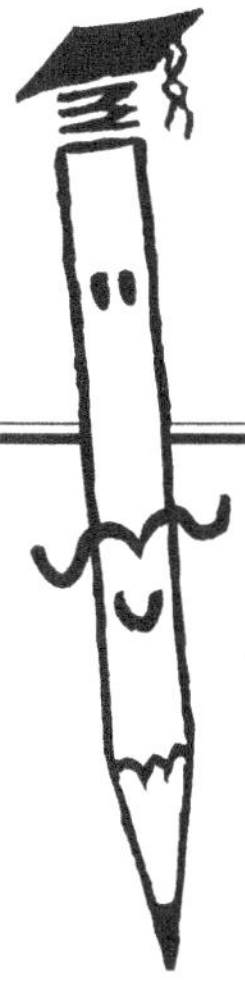

How *did* this happen?
Turn the page to learn the secret.

THE MAGIC IS THE TONES

What are TONES? Essentially, tones are variations from light to dark. They can be in color, or black and white. When black and white combine, they create a practically endless range of grays.

Often called "shades," tones can be separate, or GRADUALLY fade into each other. If this happens, the SUBTLE transition (or merging) is known as CHIAROSCURO. Artists use the principle to help create the impression that something has a solid surface as well as depth, or "girth." An example is shown on the previous page, which prompts another question. HOW were the tones achieved?

Actually, there are many ways to create tones. For instance, if you place your pencil tip gently against the paper and leave some space between strokes the resulting is a SOFT GRAY TONE. Why? Because BOTH the white streaks between marks as well as the marks are VISIBLE AT THE SAME TIME. In turn, a mixture occurs which I like to call VISUAL "ASSIMILATION." Don't let the fancy word throw you. It stands for a simple process. Add strokes, or place them closer together, and/or push harder to apply extra lead and you will see that your LIGHT GRAY soon changes to a darker gray, or MEDIUM tone. Keep going and eventually you produce a DARK GRAY. The more lead you put in a concentrated area, the darker your tone becomes. Eventually, a VERY DARK, nearly black, tone will emerge, as strong as your graphite will allow. But don't just take my word. Test the procedure.

TRY THIS!

HANDLE YOUR PENCIL YET ANOTHER WAY.

As you know, there's more than one method by which to hold, and move your pencil. For instance, in Chapter 10 you learned to grip it further back from the point. As illustration 12-1 indicates (here on the right), you can also direct it UNDER-HANDED, between your thumb, index finger, and middle finger. This mode starts with your thumb facing you. Then, turn your wrist to the left, if you're right handed, or in the other direction if you're a "lefty." Either way, your thumb should end up being sideways to you.

NEXT, on a new sheet of paper, GENTLY place your pencil point at a slight angle, so that the SIDE of the lead can skim the surface. This will enable you to PULL the pencil rather than push it. Before you start, LOCK YOUR WRIST. The action should come from your elbow. Begin by moving your pencil sideways, back and forth to form very narrow convex arcs. That way, your lines can descend. As they do, try keeping your marks fairly uniform in length, while applying a SOFT, EVEN PRESSURE. After you're done, a light gray rectangle will appear, similar to the sample tone shown here on the right (12-2). If yours is darker, it means you were pressing harder and/or your lines were placed closer together. Should patches, or gaps appear, your strokes were probably inconsistent. Practice some more. The worksheet on the following page provides a good opportunity.

12-1 Hold pencil "UNDERHAND," with your thumb facing you. Then, rotate wrist until your thumb turns sideways.

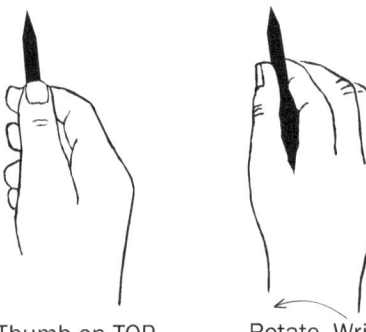

Thumb on TOP   Rotate Wrist

12-2 Glide the pencil side to side in a slight curve while moving downward. Your elbow provides action.

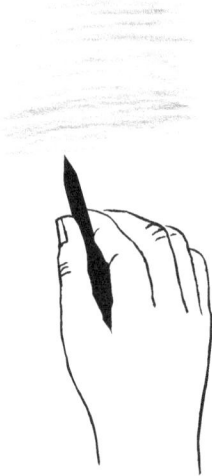

Worksheet F   Duplicate TONES

DIRECTIONS: Match the intensity of each tone example, one at a time, by using the "underhand," side-to-side motion you learned. You can choose the easy route by repeating the SAME tone five times ACROSS. Or, you can elect the more difficult procedure by advancing from light to dark, as you move *DOWN the column,* five times. "Lefties" may invert your page. That way, your hand doesn't block the samples. Erasing is not permitted, and "reworking" is not allowed either. The goal is to help you feel the pressure, gain reasonable control, develop consistency, and improve agility.

Terrific! Now that you've mastered
INDIVIDUAL tones, learn to COMBINE them.

STEP 1   On a fresh sheet of paper, form a very pale gray square section about the size shown, by appyling light, gentle, consistent strokes (12-3).

12-3   Tone a LIGHT gray field.

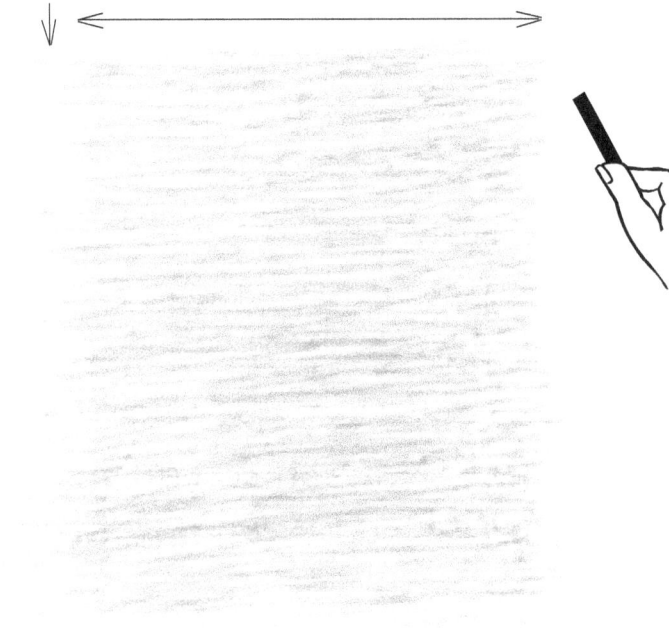

STEP 2   Add another layer of light gray OVER your field. BUT, leave a small margin (or space) from the LEFT. The span should be less than the width of your "pinkie" (little finger). When done, your rectangle should have a **narrow** stripe of **light gray** and a **slightly darker tone** over the remainder (12-4).

12-4   Fill another layer, leaving a slight margin from the left (arrows show area).

STEP 3 Take a look at the arrow on illustration 12-5. It's one more space over and another coat of light gray has been added. You need to do the same. After completion, your rectangle will show a light gray stripe, a slightly darker stripe to the right of it, and a darker field for the rest.

12-5 Arrows point to a 3rd tone of gray. It starts 2 spaces over from the left.

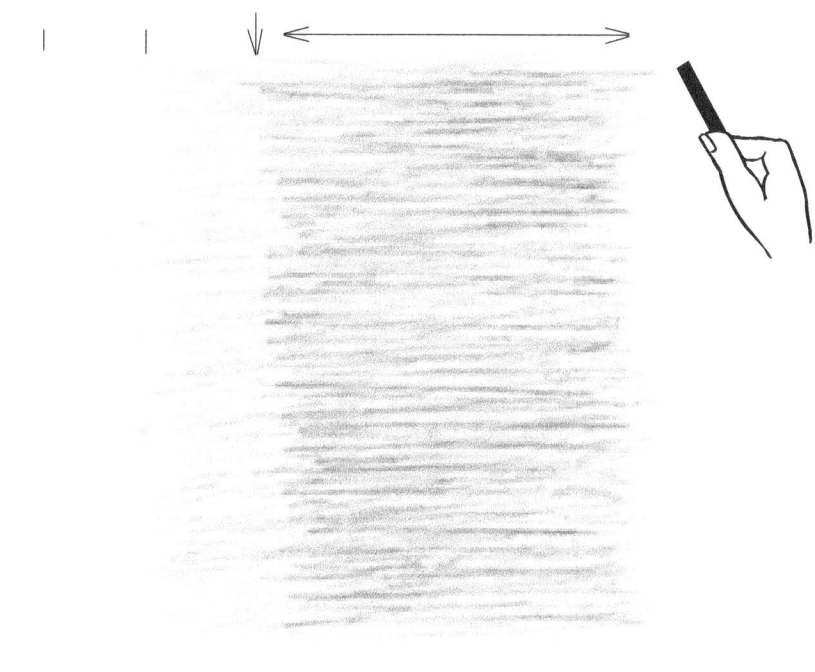

STEP 4 Yes! You guessed it. Repeat the procedure one more interval to the right (as shown by the arrow in illustration 12-6.) Then your field will also have FOUR different grays with the largest area on the right, being the darkest.

12-6 Initiate from your 3rd space and add another layer.

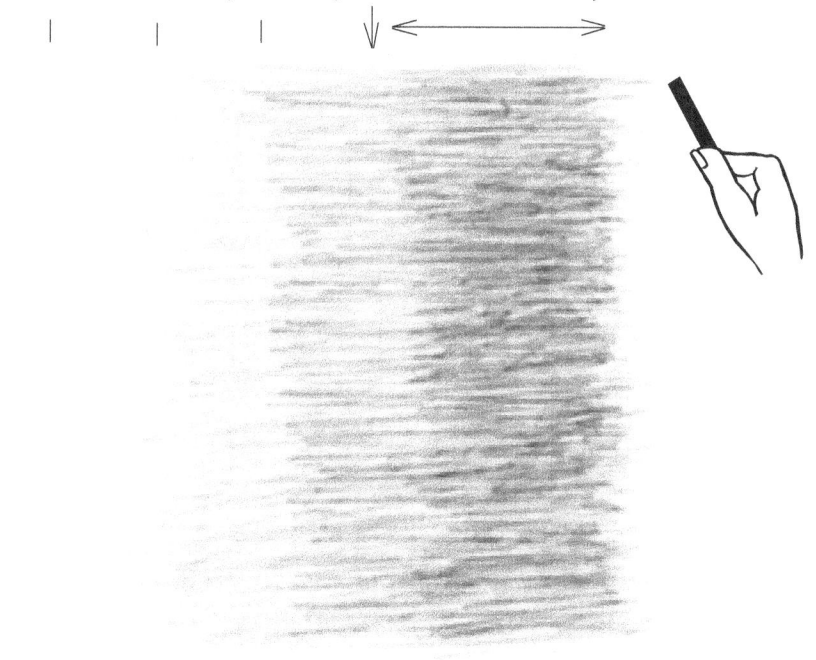

Go for one more pass. Start another interval to the right. The arrow in illustration 12-7 shows the general location. When finished you will have 5 stripes of gray, ranging from fairly light to quite dark.

12-7 Layer your field once more, beginning four columns to the right.

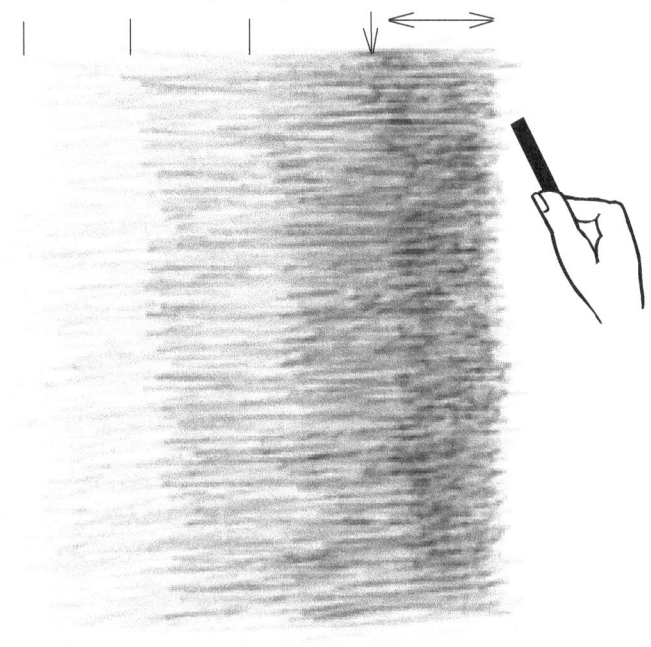

Prop up your drawing consisting of five tones. Then, move your drawing several feet away from you (12-8). When you observe it from a distance, you will find your INDIVIDUAL stripes of gray will seem to flow (or mix) more evenly, and smoothly from one into the next. Because of that, another type of *visual* effect, known as *DISTANCE* "assimilation, occurs and this one tends to give the impression (or illusion) that your tones have a combined length, width, as well as *depth*. How is such magic possible? Simple. Darker tones generally appear as though they are further from the viewer than lighter tones of equal size and distance. As a result, your gradually darkening tones will seem to curve away from you, despite the fact that your paper is flat. This is one reason why you can better appreciate pictures from a few paces. That's when you get the full impact.

12-8 Observe your tones from a few paces.

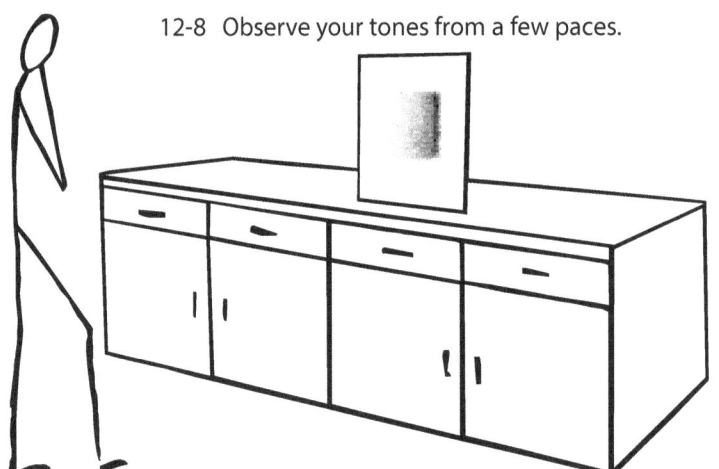

Pretty amazing to see what tones can do, when observed from just a few steps, isn't it? Next, explore another way to merge them.

STEP 1

With a cotton swab, or your finger, GENTLY rub the area between the first and second column (or stripe of gray) on YOUR set of tones. Stroke ONLY in ONE direction (from LIGHT to DARK). Advance with a left to right motion, LIFTING your hand after each sweep, as you descend. Go only half way down. Soon your first SEAM on the left (to mid-point) will appear to vanish, like the one shown in example 12-9. Notice the SUBTLE difference between its upper and lower half.

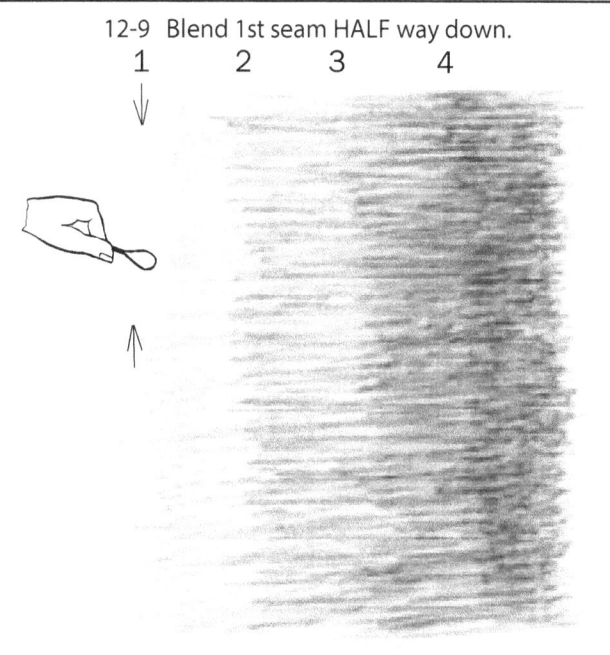

12-9 Blend 1st seam HALF way down.

1   2   3   4

TIP Rubbing tends to darken tones a little. Why? Because the pores of the paper get filled-in. To avoid the darkening effect, as much as possible, press LIGHTLY. Don't use a BACK and FORTH motion. If you do, your TWO DIFFERENT grays will join as ONE larger mixture. The idea however, is to keep the tones separate, but indistinct at the seam. In other words, it should be difficult to see where they join. This kind of toning method is often called "modeling."

STEP 2

Repeat the "modeling" technique by lightly blending the remaining bottom half of your first seam. Then fade the next boundary entirely. Complete ALL the seam connections, INDIVIDUALLY until they are "softened." When finished, your blends should appear somewhat like illustration 12-10, shown here on the right. Compare it to illustration 12-9 (above). Pay special attention to the softer, more gradual appearance the tones have taken AFTER blending. They seem to "meld," or "fade" into each other, much the way they appeared VISUALLY from a distance, BEFORE they were blended, don't they?

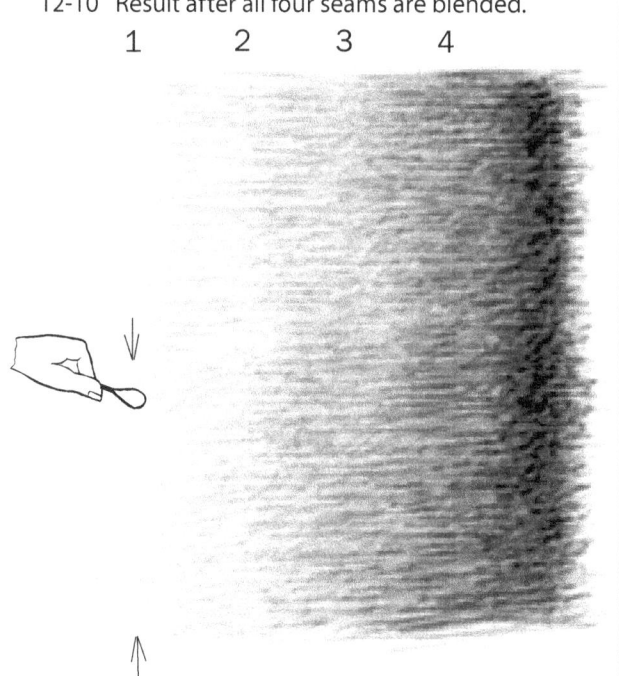

12-10 Result after all four seams are blended.

1   2   3   4

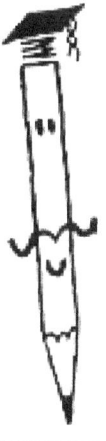

Now that you realize tones optically mix when viewed from a distance, and you know how to apply and blend them by hand, you're ready to put the CHIAROSCURO method to work.

(EXERCISE 12)

OBJECTIVE: Cause a seemingly hollow, flat shape to appear solid and curved.

BEFORE   AFTER

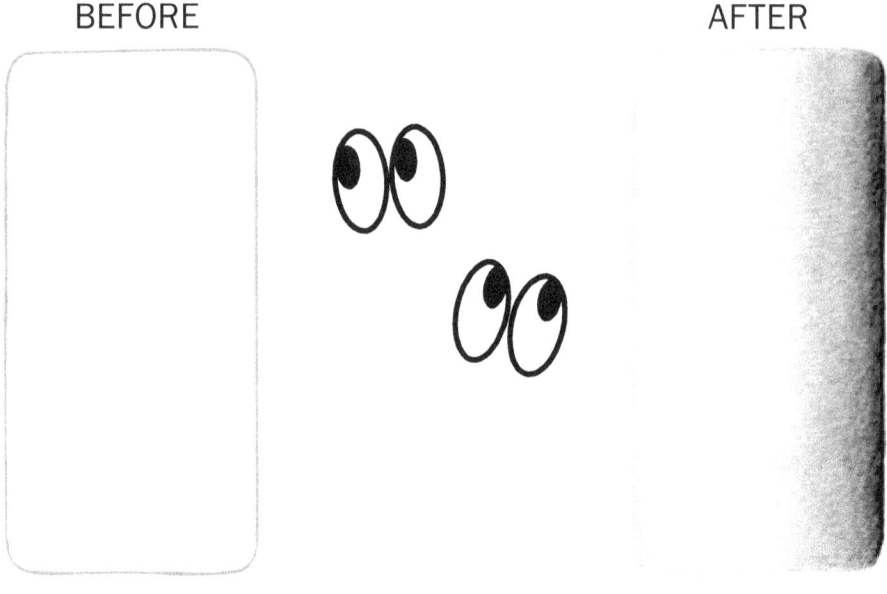

STEP 1   On a new piece of paper, LIGHTLY center a fairly large, vertical rectangle that's twice as tall as it is wide (12-11).   Then round the corners slightly (12-12).

12-11 LIGHTLY draw a fairly large rectangle
        at a 2 to 1 vertical proportion (or ratio).

12-12 Slightly round the corners.

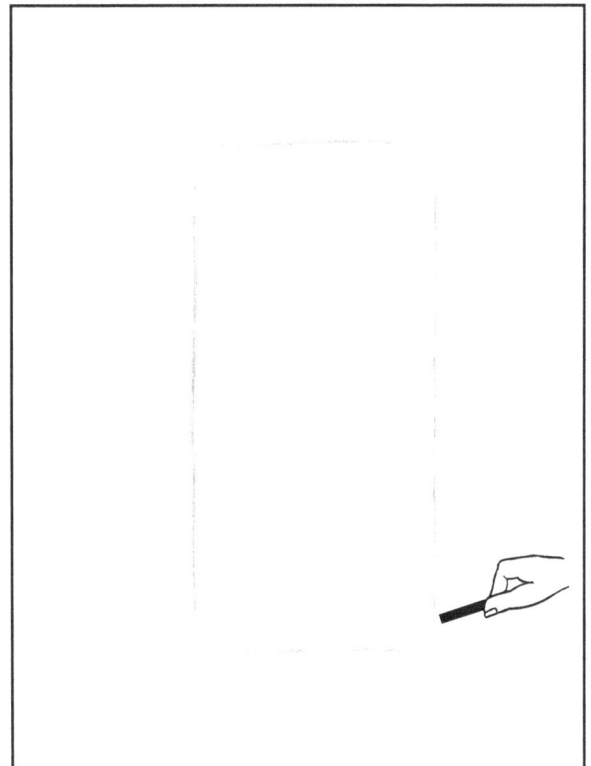

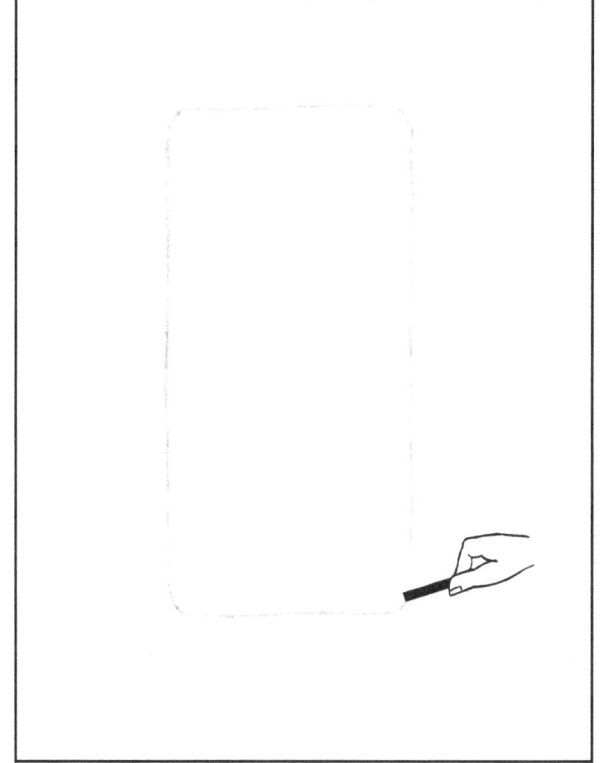

STEP 2 Using the "underhand method" you practiced, cover the right HALF of your rectangle with a faint, even gray tone from top to bottom (12-13). Then, lightly apply another layer, starting about a fourth of the way into the RIGHT of your light gray field (12-14).

12-13 LIGHTLY tone the right half of your rectangle.

12-14 Tone 3/4 of your darkened field.

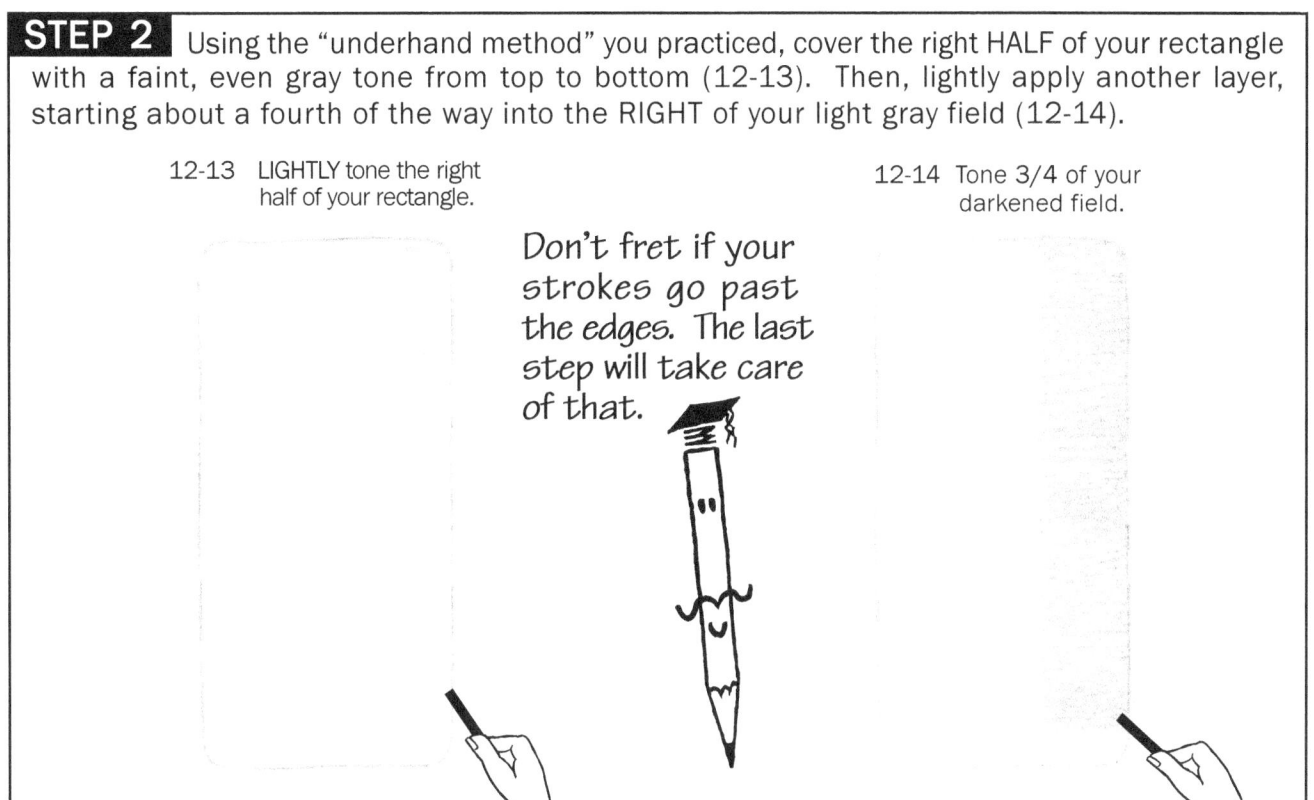

Don't fret if your strokes go past the edges. The last step will take care of that.

TIP Try to stay within your lines as you progress. If you exceed a little, it's OK. Erasing now will only cause smears. The cleanup method will be explained during the final phase.

STEP 3 Include 2 more layers of gray (12-15 and 12-16). The objective is to complete FOUR different TONES, ranging from light to dark in a left to right sequence

12-15 Tone right HALF of your field.

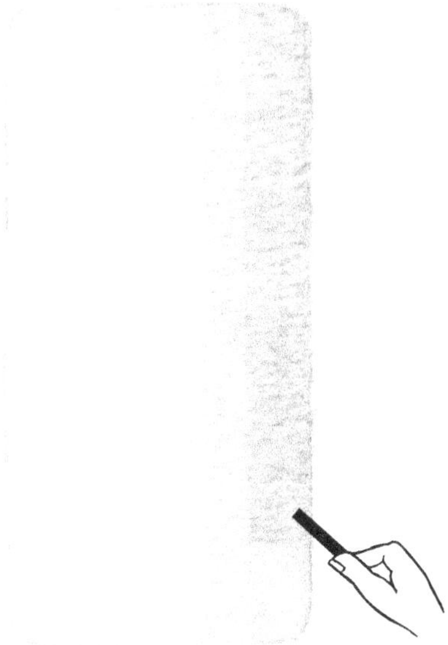

12-16 Tone right QUARTER of your field.

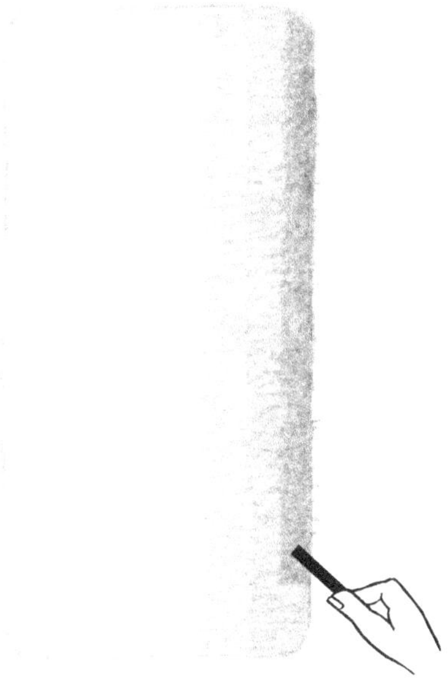

STEP 4 Apply a light **narrow** tone on the **LEFT** side of your rectangle. Make sure to leave a large white gap between it, and your other stripes of gray (12-17).

12-17 Lightly tone the left edge.

TIP Move your pencil side to side, NOT up and down, as you descend.

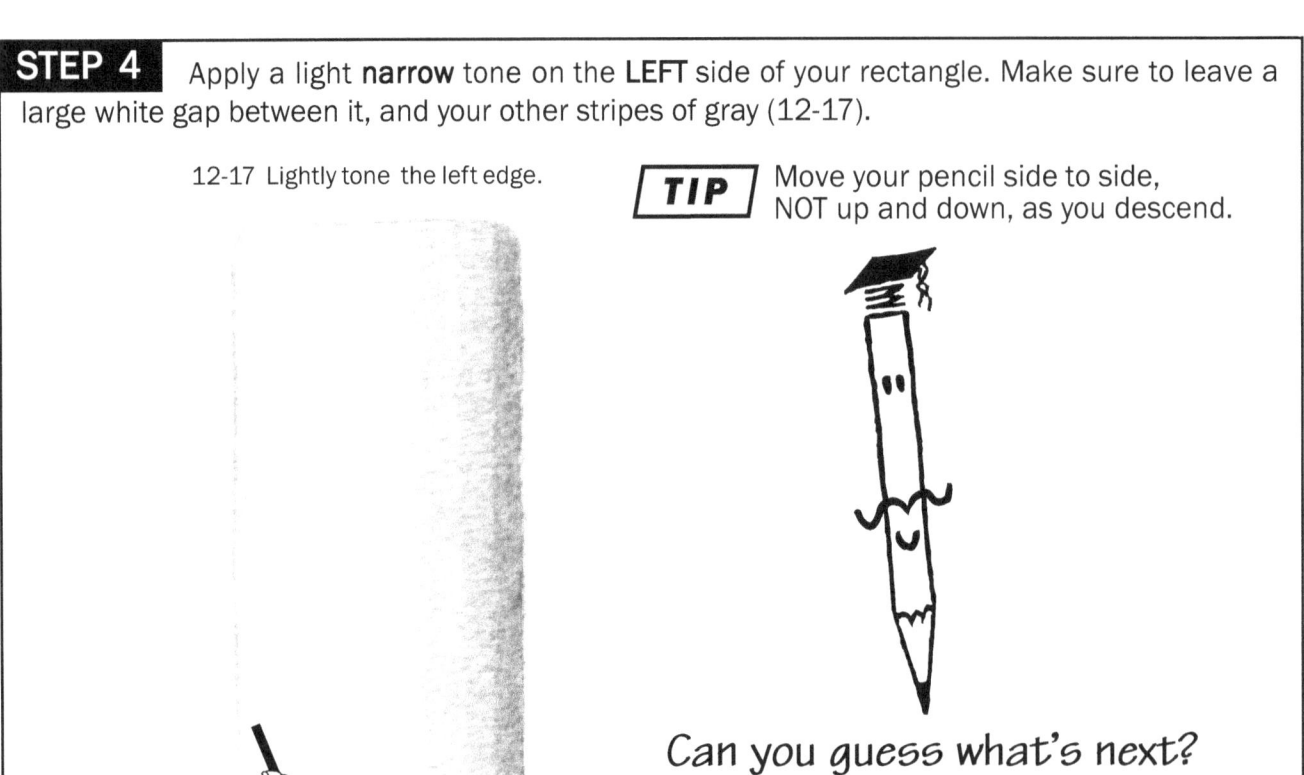

Can you guess what's next?
Yep! "Blending."

STEP 5 Take advantage of the same"modeling" technique you practiced on page 219 in order to blend the seams on YOUR drawing. GENTLY stroke from LEFT to RIGHT to merge the LEFT tone into the WHITE area. Notice the difference between the *blended TOP* half, and the *unblended* BOTTOM half (12-18). The upper half now has what is known as a "SOFT" left edge. Once the entire left side is "softened," blend the light gray tone (near center), into your white space.   In this case, use a RIGHT to LEFT direction to keep most of the WHITE area intact (12-19).

12-18   Blend left side tone
gently into the white.

12-19   Blend 1st seam
at center into white.

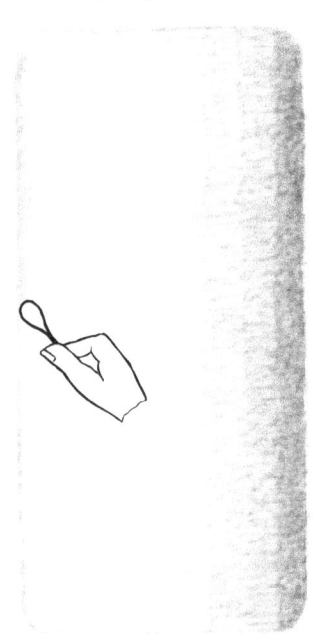

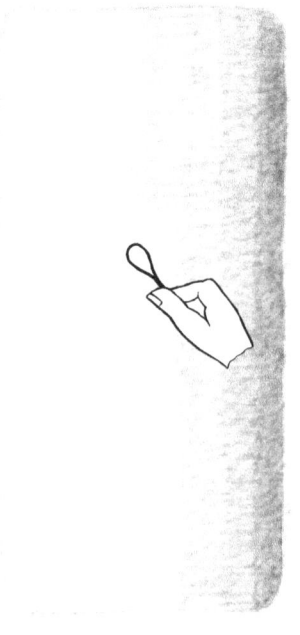

STEP 6   Proceed to the right of center and blend the next seam by switching to a soft *back and forth* motion. This will enable the edge to "diffuse" on boths sides of it (12-20). Press harder near the start and ease up at the end of your sweeps. It's like a concave action.   Yes, I know that earlier I said you should blend only in one direction, but by now you've got more practice. As long as you are gentle and careful, you can handle the dual blending technique.

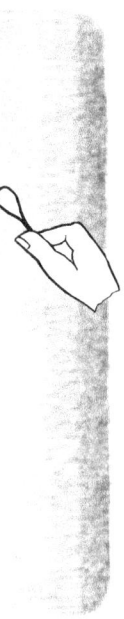

12-20 GENTLY blend your seam
        on BOTH sides of it.

STEP 7   Maintain a GENTLE back and forth motion to soften your remaining 2 tones, ONE AT A TIME.   After blending, your grays should flow gradually from one into another, somewhat like illustration 12-21, here.   Compare it to illustration 12-17 (previous page). It changed quite a bit since then, didn't it ?

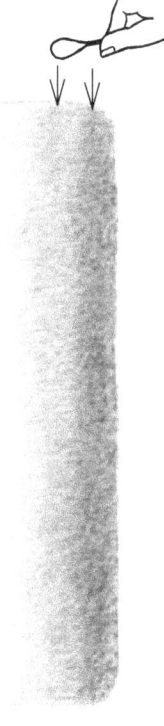

12-21 Result after blending
        3rd & 4th seams.

STEP 8 To give your work a "sharp, polished look," darken the right side of your figure just a little more and fade the tone into the lighter one to the left of it. Then, "clean" around all perimeters (edges) with your eraser (12-22). This will help remove the over-strokes and smudges, thereby improving quality. Compare illustration 12-22 to 12-23 to see an example of what finishing touches can do.

TIP If you accidentally erase too much, carefully replenish (add back) tone to match.

12-22 Softly fade more dark to RIGHT side & erase excess around edges.

12-23 Finished example.

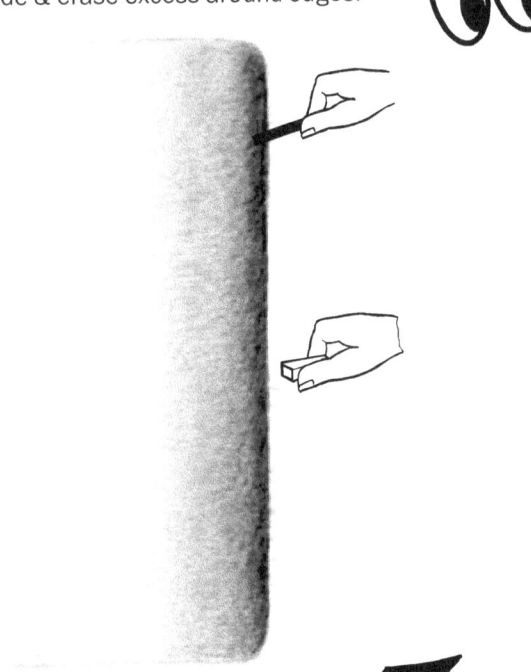

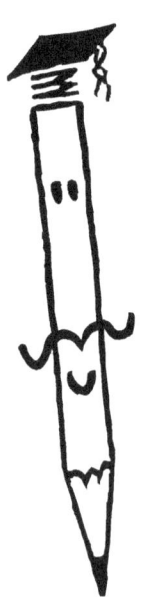

Bravo! At this stage you will have created the "illusion" that your rectangle is solid, and its surface is arched, even though your paper is flat. Next, take a look at how some of your fellow students' work turned out.

Model

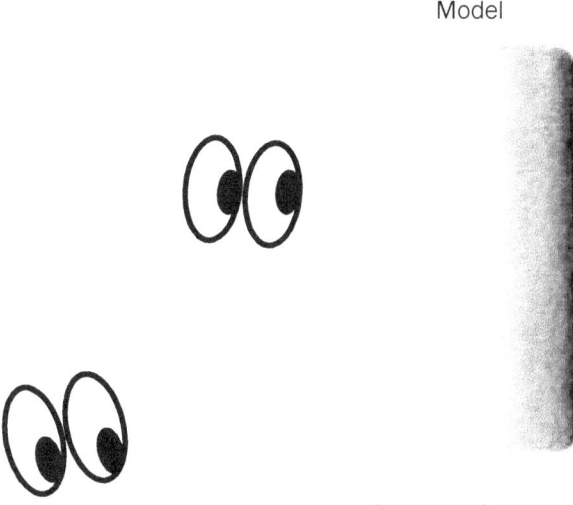

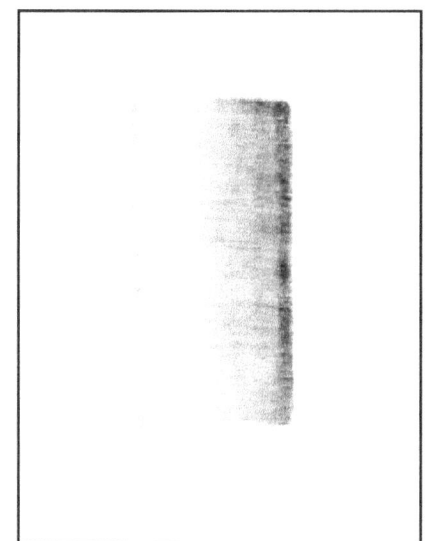

STUDENT SAMPLING

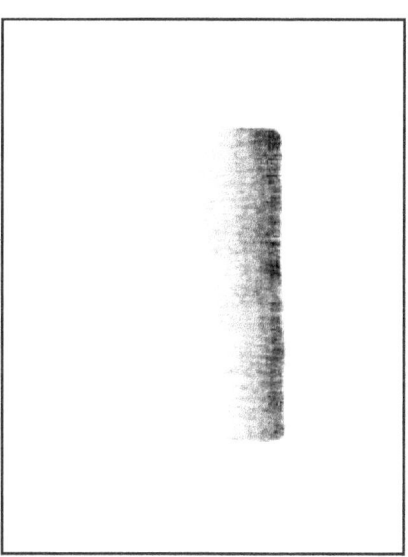

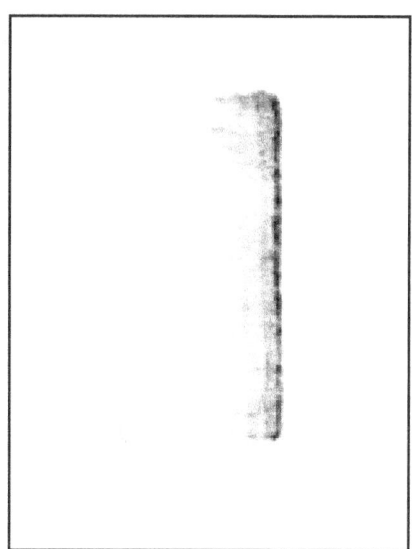

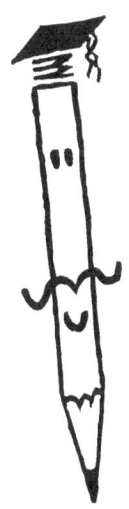

For a first toning exercise, these examples are dandy aren't they? Yours, I'm sure, is good, too. And with practice you will continue to improve. Prepare to apply what you've learned. Please go and get your outline drawing of the vase you created in Chapter 2, then turn the page. The supplemental exercise awaits.

CHAPTER 12
SUPPLEMENTAL EXERCISE

OBJECTIVE: Add TONE to the vase you drew in Chapter 2.

BEFORE

AFTER

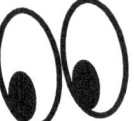

HOT TIP *There's something different going on here.* Unlike the rectangle you modeled in the previous exercise, your vase has *angular and wavy sides, so the TONES must also be angular and wavy.* **Notice how the gray stripes gradually WIDEN near center** (12-24).

12-24   Tones follow the WAVY
          shape of the figure.

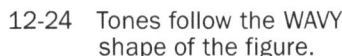

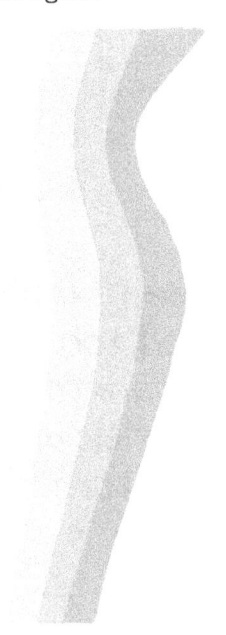

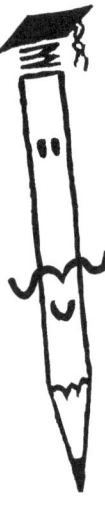

Tally Ho! Grab your pencil
and let's do some toning.

STEP 1   LIGHTLY TONE THE LEFT *EDGE* OF YOUR DRAWING

Your strokes should be fairly short. Illustration 12-25 shows how the tone should appear, more or less.

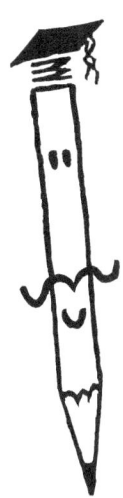

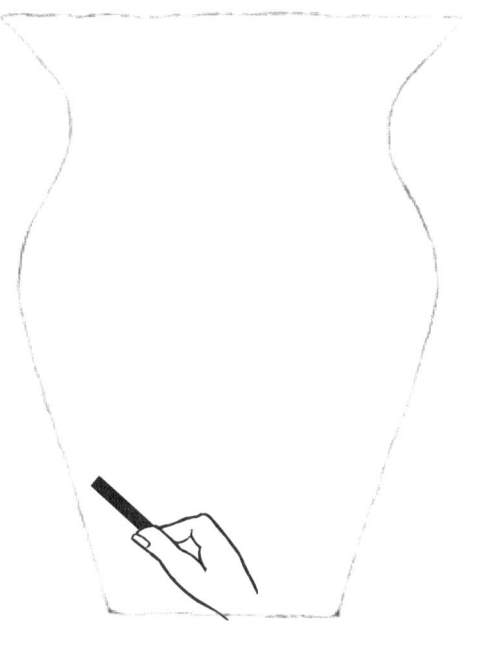

12-25   You should follow a "backward letter "s" shape on LEFT side.

Reminder: You don't need to be concerned if your strokes exceed the boundaries. Don't do any erasing now. Save it for the finishing touches.

STEP 2   LIGHTLY TONE THE ENTIRE RIGHT *HALF OF YOUR DRAWING*

Take a look at illustration 12-24 (previous page). Observe that the LARGE field is made with four WAVY "S"shaped tones. Keep this in mind as you fill your field with side to side strokes (12-26).

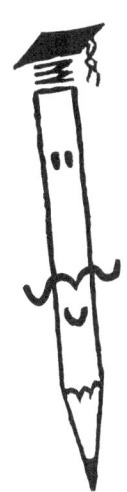

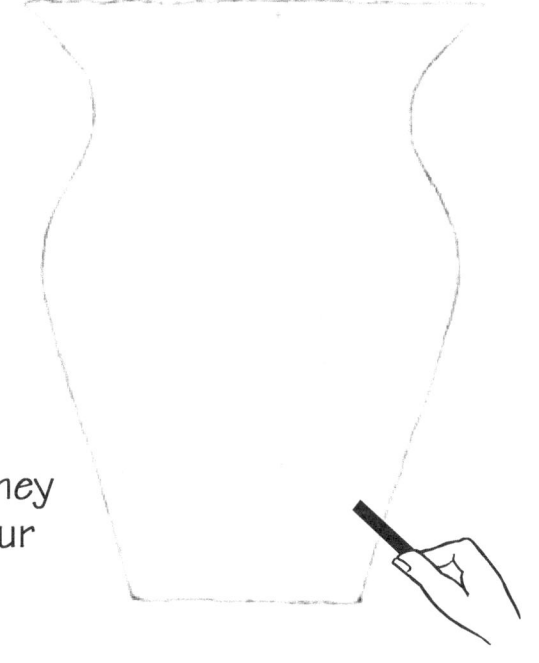

12-26   Form your tone with *sideways* strokes to create a slightly WAVY "S" shape.

Set a course for your WAVY "S" shaped tones with very faint dots. They will help you stay on track. Later, your dots will disappear during blending.

STEP 3 TONE THREE QUARTERS OF THE RIGHT HALF

Leave a quarter space from the right of center, and LIGHTLY add another layer of tone on your drawing. Remember to stroke *sideways* to fill a *slightly wavy shape.* *Again, you can put dots along the way.* Illustration 12-27 shows how your figure should more or less appear, as you progress downward.

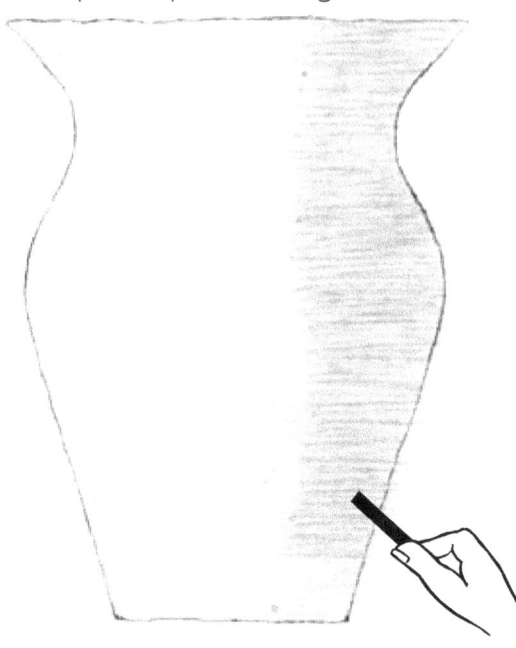

12-27 Apply a coat of tone starting a quarter space to the right of center.

STEP 4 ADD ANOTHER LAYER

Move one quarter space to the right, and fill the right half of your figure with a slightly darker wavy tone (12-28).

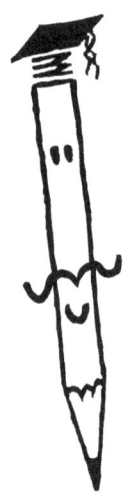

Are you lightly placing dots to help form your wavy stripes of tone?

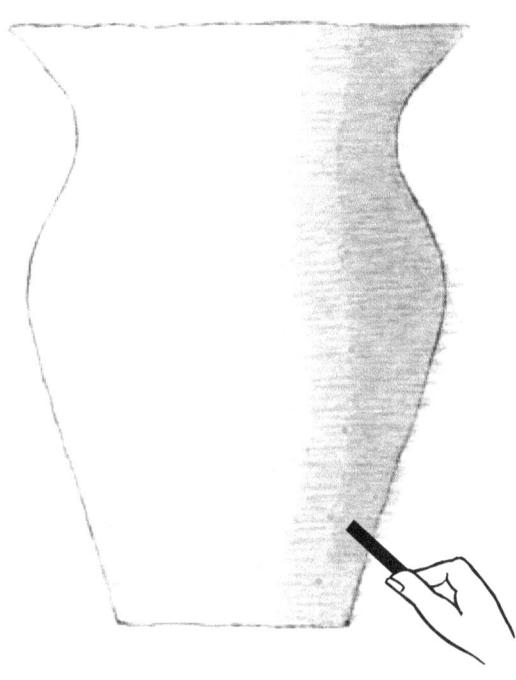

12-28 Lightly tone the right HALF.

STEP 5 — LAYER THE RIGHT QUARTER OF YOUR FIELD

Go for one more pass. *Notice that the last wavy shape is a little more exaggerated* (12-29). When completed, you should have a wavy stripe of *faint* gray on the FAR LEFT edge of your vase, and a *white* section to the right of it. From there, FOUR wavy stripes should range from light gray to dark gray.

12-29 Lightly tone the 4th quarter.

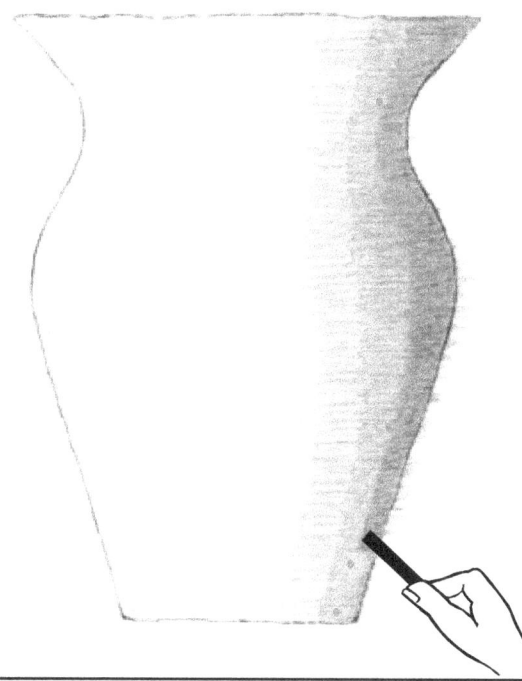

STEP 6 — GENTLY BLEND LEFT & CENTER EDGES INTO THE WHITE PORTION

Starting with your figure's side on your left, gently blend the border line and tone until they both soften and fade at the edges. *If your line is too dark, dab it first with your eraser.* Next, blend the first light gray tone (near the CENTER) *barely* into the white area (12-30). Be sure that most of the white section remains white.

12-30 Fade your LEFT edge from LEFT-to-RIGHT.
Fade your CENTER edge from RIGHT-to-LEFT.

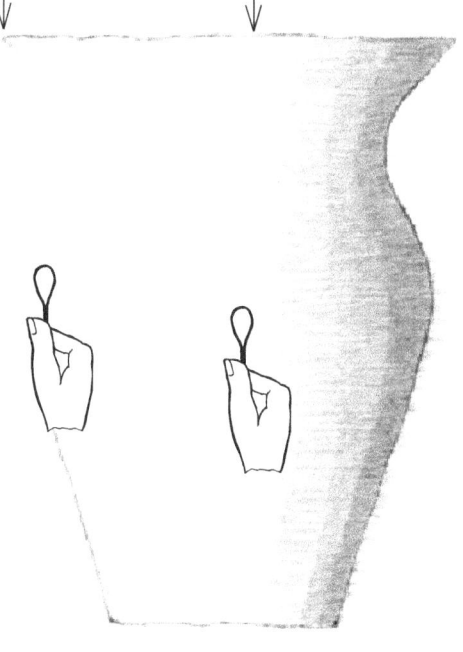

STEP 7 | BLEND TWO MORE SEAMS, ONE AT A TIME

Gently fade the connection between your 1st and 2nd tone from center. Then fade the seam between your 2nd and 3rd tone (12-31).

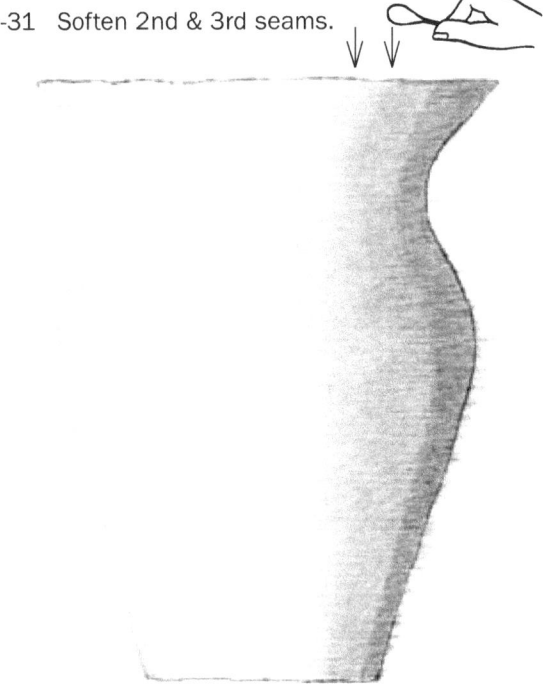

12-31 Soften 2nd & 3rd seams.

STEP 8 | FADE YOUR FOURTH SEAM

Repeat the blending process once more by "softening" the edge between the third and fourth (or last two) tones. When completed, you should have a fading gray on the left edge of your vase drawing, followed by a range of light to dark grays advancing from the center to the right edge (12-32).

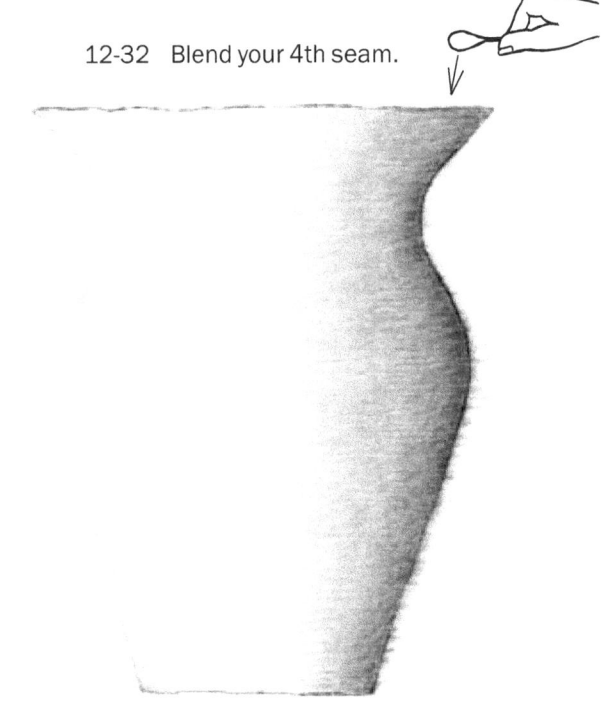

12-32 Blend your 4th seam.

STEP 9 | DO THE FINISHING TOUCHES

"Feather" in a little more dark on the RIGHT edge of your figure. That means press harder when you start, and gradually reduce pressure as you stroke from **right to left.** This will help fade the dark into the slightly lighter tone. Next, carefully erase any smears, or over-strokes. Then, soften some of the top and bottom edges with your eraser (12-33). When completed, your vase will appear "sharper" and seem to lift from the page, similar to the way mine does (12-34).

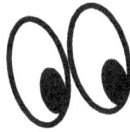

12-33   Slightly darken right side and erase excess.

12-34   Example of finished drawing after right side is feathered and edges are cleaned with an eraser.

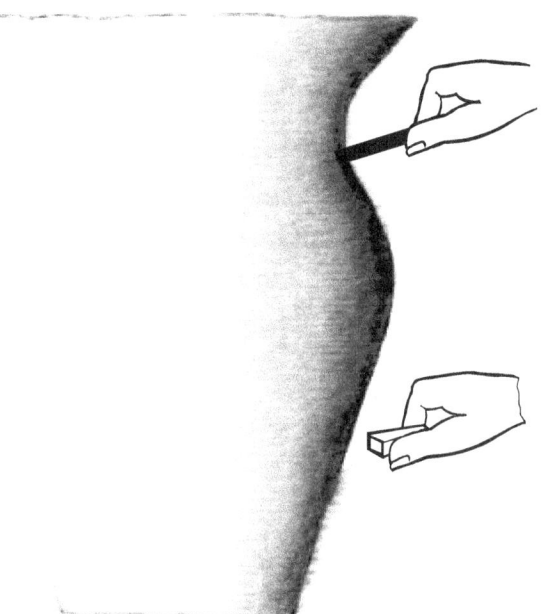

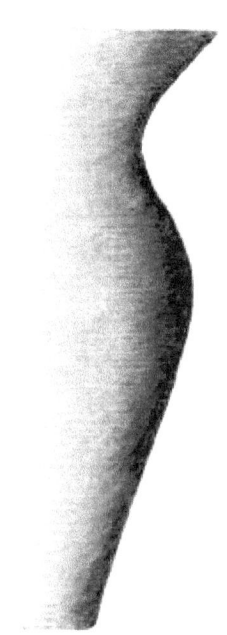

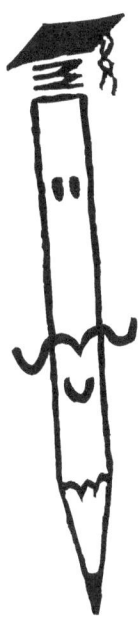

Be proud of your achievement. Toning takes practice. You're learning. Don't expect your version to be as refined as the model. Besides, how "good" your cylinder, and now your vase, turned out is not important. Your focus should be on where they took you. The follow-up explains.

Chapter 12
FOLLOW-UP

Shapes are nifty, although tones seem to be quite impressive too, wouldn't you agree? With variations of gray, your drawings can take on another dimension. Plus, it's fun to include them. You saw how much your cylinder and your vase changed, didn't you? The snag is that because of such lures, students tend to become impatient. They hurry past the *formative* phase so they can start *toning* much sooner, and that usually gets them into trouble!

What am I implying? I'll tell you. Having been introduced to a method commonly referred to as "shading," you moved into a whole new territory. Consequently, from here on, you may be tempted to neglect certain basics. After all, your tones will hide the "flubs," right?

Not necessarily! If you buy into the idea, odds are you will be disappointed. *SHAPING* and *SHADING go hand in hand.* They depend on each other, similar to the way construction works. For instance, a house with sturdy framing develops as other parts are added, yet put them on ineffective supports and things fall apart. *Drawings* aren't much different. For quality, you should strive to master BOTH techniques. And now, having said that, I'm honored to present you with the official announcement...

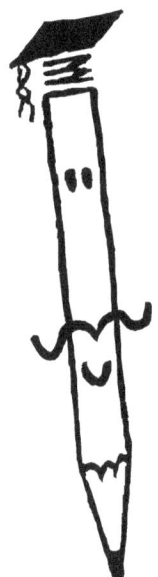

Congratulations!

You've graduated Anyone Can...Arts
DRAWING MAGIC
Guidebook 1

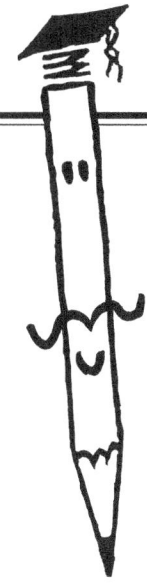

This isn't the end.
It's a beginning.

By now I'm sure you've realized that the exercises you completed were not necessarily meant to be frame-worthy. Rest assured though, what they taught you is the treasure. You now have a better understanding that the process of drawing is not an instantaneous event. It's a series of events, and *each* is a miraculous achievement.

As your lines begin to transform an empty page and fill it with awe and wonder, dozens of procedures you've learned will cross your mind. At those times, you will want to be able to summon all of them. For example, *Streamlining* will come in handy, as will the *Crisscross Method*. Another amazing tool will be the *Inverse Approach* and the wisdom to remember, it's the parts that make the whole.

Despite this powerful awareness, however, occasionally you may still forget you're human, and that it actually takes three of your natural abilities to draw. These are your vision, thoughts and actions. When they compete and things don't go exactly the way you'd like, you could lose patience, make undue changes, become anxious, or rush. In turn, you might cut corners and skip important stages. That's why it's usually smart to study your subject before you begin to draw, check your progress regularly as you draw, and review your work after your picture is completed.

I'll say again, *drawing is a marvelous experience.* The answers are right there in front of you, along with a world of sights to behold, with fresh eyes, when you take the time to observe. Look forward with joyful anticipation to all the exciting ways you will be able to apply your advancing skills with DRAWING MAGIC Guidebook 2, and keep exploring that special artist in you.

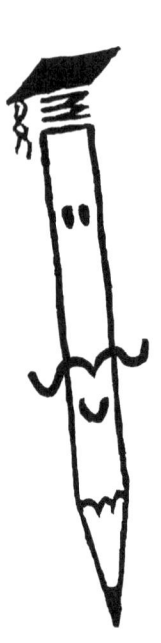

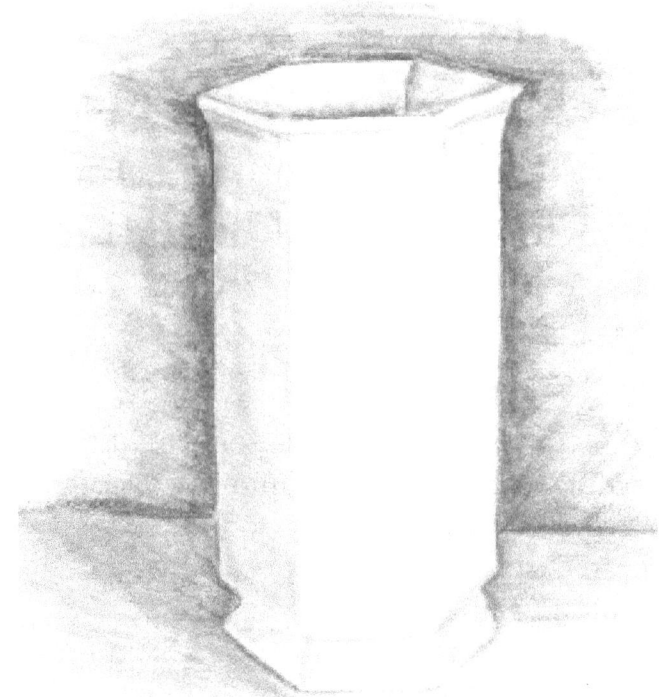

After completing the course, students found delightful things to draw. Here's a hexagonal vase and a polar bear mother with her cub.

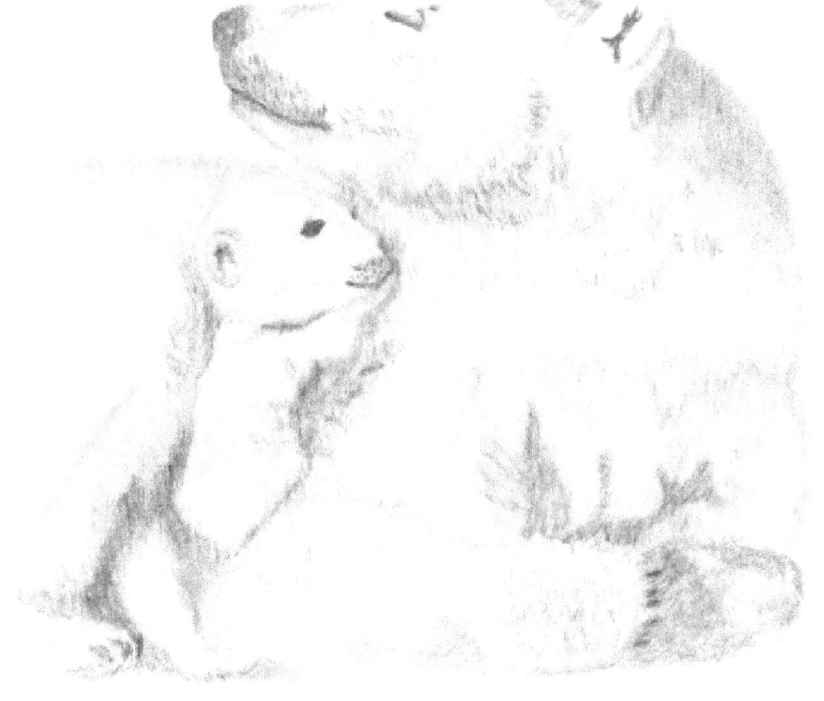

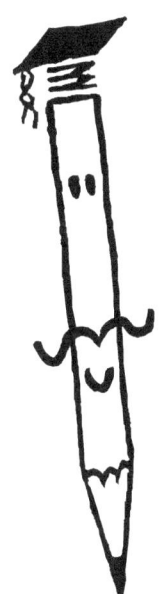

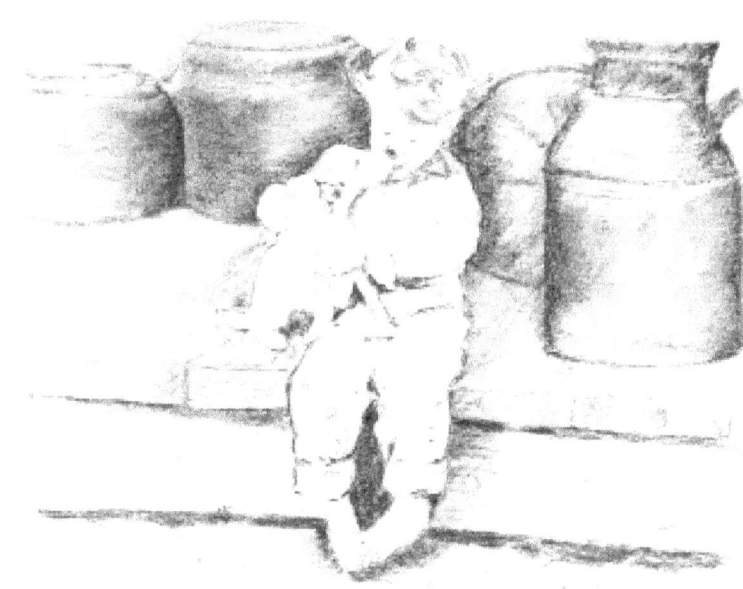

The little boy with his dog and the hands were also terrific sources of inspiration.

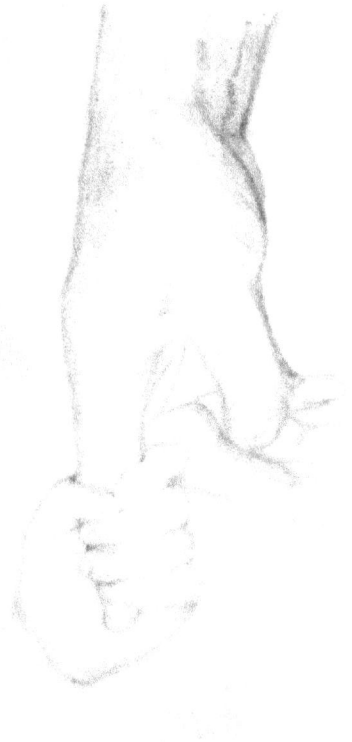

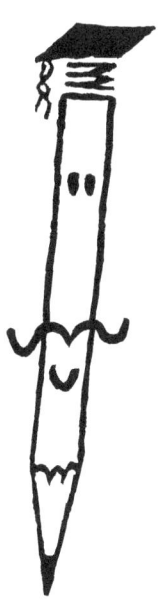

See what wonderful results you can achieve. Pick the subject matter you like, and keep it simple.

ARTIST'S GLOSSARY

Terms and Phrases as defined by Professor Pencil

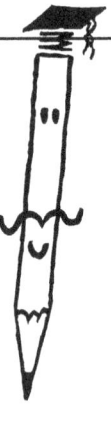

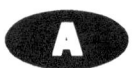

ACCENT - emphasize, increase, heighten, or improve

ACCURATE - reasonable likeness, but not expected to be a perfect or exact match

ADEPT - skillful or capable

ADJACENT - next to or beside something

ADJOINING - next to or beside something

AD-LIB - figure out or find a way to make things work

ADVERSE - not wanted

AGILITY - move easily and effectively

ALIGNMENT - when two or more things, or reference points, locate along a straight line

ALTERNATIVE - replacement, switch or change

AMISS - not in proper order or accurate appearance

ANGLE - any direction other than plumb or level
Other words with similar meanings: SLOPE, INCLINE, DIAGONAL, SLANT, TILT

ANTICIPATE - expect or foresee

APPARENT - visible to the naked eye or obvious

APPROXIMATE - almost or nearly accurate

ARC - a curve; or to bend, as in a curve

ARTIFICIAL - imitation

ASCEND - move upward in a straight direction or at a slant

ASPECT - visible characteristic or appearance

ASSESS - survey, examine, evaluate, study

ASSET - advantage or valuable possession

ASSIMILATION - a process of merging different tones, by blending them, or by viewing them from a distance, to give the impression that they gradually fade into each other

ASTRAY - move away from

ASYMMETRICAL - irregular, uneven, not precise in shape

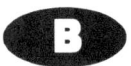

BASE LINE - lowest horizontal span between two points

BISECT - divide in half

BLEND - combine or mix together

BOUNDARY - a limitation showing where something starts, or ends
Other words with similar meanings: BORDER, PERIMETER, EDGE,

BOW - amount of bend, or flex, in a curve

CHARACTERISTIC - appearance

CHIAROSCURO - variation of tones to help give the impression that a subject has light shining on it

COINCIDE - two things in the same place

COMPONENT - part or portion

CONCAVE - curve that bends inward

CONCEPT - thought, idea, principle, approach, procedure or method

CONFIGURATION - arrangement or format

CONFIRM - make sure something is accurate by checking yourself

CONSECUTIVE - follow one after the other without any gaps

CONSIST - made of

CONSISTENT - regular, not varying or changing

CONTINUOUS FREEHAND LINE - a line that starts at one point and moves nonstop until completed at an ending point

CONTRAST - visible difference between 2 or more things (for example-black and white)

CONVERGE - come together

CONVEX - curve that bends outward

COORDINATE - a position, or reference point, where a vertical and horizontal alignment intersect

COORDINATION - two or more things that work together, like hand and eye coordination

CORNER GUIDE LINES - horizontal and vertical lines that help draw curves

COUNTERACT - reduce, reverse, or undo

CREATIVE FREEDOM - ability to change, or modify by choice

CREST - maximum, or furthest extent of bend in a curve

CURVE - bent line

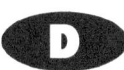

DECLINE - downward direction, at a slant, or angle

DEFORMITY - distortion

DELETE - remove or take away

DEPICT - create a likeness

DESCEND - move downward in a straight direction or at a slant

DESTINED - meant for

DEVIATE - stray, go past or away, or to change

DEVISE - figure out or invent

DISTINCT - stand out or easily visible

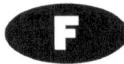

EDGE - where one shape stops and another begins

EFFECTIVE - able to achieve accurate result

ELABORATE - fancy or stylish

ELEVATION LINE - imaginary guide line along a curve crest

ENHANCE - improve or emphasize

ENTAILS - involves or requires

EQUIDISTANT - equal distance

ESTABLISH - bring something into being or cause it to appear

ESTIMATE - a reasonable opinion, or judgment based on observation (best guess)

ETCH - cut

EVALUATE - examine accuracy

EXPANSE - distance, or span between two reference points

EXEMPLIFY - show by example

EXTREMITY - furthest distance

EYEBALL - estimate visually, without the aid of mechanical devices, rulers, etc.

FACSIMILE - reasonable likeness or similarity to something else

FADE - gently or gradually change a tone from dark to light, or from light to dark

FAINT - barely visible

FEASIBLE - likely to work well or be useful

FEATURE - characteristic or special attraction

FEATHERING - sweeping pencil strokes in 1 direction, with gradually reduced pressure for blending tones

FIDGET - unable to stop moving

FIGURE - a shape; also the ability to think through, calculate, or estimate

FLAW - not accurate, defective, undesired

FLEX - to bend a curve; or amount of bend or "bow" in a curve

FLUB - goof, botch, bungle, flaw, inaccurate, undesirable result

FLUSH - two or more things that line up (or are aligned) evenly

FOOLPROOF - always works

FORETHOUGHT - think ahead

FORM - a shape, or the procedure which makes it
Other words with similar meanings: FASHION, DEVISE, DRAW, PRODUCE

FORMAT - shape, template, or foundation, made with guide lines, to serve as a *flexible* boundary from which to develop a drawing

FREEHAND - draw without a straight edge, ruler, or any other artificial or mechanical device

FUNDAMENTAL - basic

FUSS - overwork or overdo

FUSSY - too precise or exact, difficult to satisfy

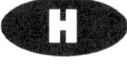

GAUGE - strength, intensity, or amount of something; or to observe, survey, figure out, estimate, judge, assess, analyze.

GIRTH - form seen as both front and side view in order to give the impression of not only 2 dimension (height and width), but also the 3rd dimension known as depth

GLANCE - look quickly

GLIDE - smooth, easy movement

GLIMPSE - quick look or observation

GLITCH - problem or malfunction

GUIDE LINES - temporary lines that help draw a shape

HORIZONTAL - sideways

HITHER - here

IDENTICAL - visibly alike, apparently the same

ILLUSION - a visual effect or amazing prank played on the eyes

IMAGINARY ALIGNMENT - invisible line between two or more reference points

IMPLEMENT - tool or put into action

IMPROVISE - figure out; or to find solutions by applying resourceful thinking

IMPLORE - strongly request

IMPULSE - feeling, urge, or whim

INCLINE - upward direction at a slant

INCONSISTENT - varying, changing, or irregular

INCREMENT - division, or section of distance, equal to the one before it

INDENT - leave a slight gap, space or margin between one location and another

INDISTINCT - not easy to see

INITIAL - first or original

INITIATE - start; or make a choice/decision and act on it

INITIATIVE - willingness to make decisions and choices, plus act on them, or carry them out

INSIGHT - understand

INSTILL - cause or make something happen

INTACT - remain whole, or as is

INTENSITY - strength, stress, pressure, force, rate, measure, or amount of something

INTERLUDE - in between amount of time (meantime)

INTERMEDIATE - between

INTERPRET - translate, change, convert, depict, or replicate

INTERVAL - a span, space, or distance

INTRICATE - delicate or something having many parts

INTRIGUE - interest or curiosity

INTUITION - an impulse, or hunch, based on feeling rather than thought

INVERT (INVERSE) - position upside down, reverse, backward, or in the opposite direction

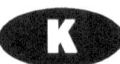

JUT - extend past or stand out

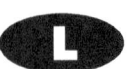

KILTER - something that appears to be in proper position, size, or condition (see "out of kilter")

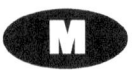

LATERAL - sideways position or direction

LAX - not careful

LATTER - second, recent, or closest to the end

LAYOUT - a written or illustrated plan

LEEWAY - extra space or amount of freedom

LEVEL - HORIZONTAL (sideways) position without apparent angle

LIMBER - not rigid; flexible, able to move easily

LOPSIDED - larger, higher on one side, or tilted

MALFUNCTION - not working properly (inaccurate)

MANUALLY - by hand

MARGIN - a distance, or interval, inset from the edge; or a space between two locations

MARVEL - appreciate or admire

MAXIMIZE - get the full benefit or to increase as much as possible

MAXIMUM - most amount, distance, or intensity

MEDIAN - center or middle location between two reference points

MELD - combine, mix, diffuse, blend, fade, or merge

MESH - fit together

MINIMIZE - reduce to the least strength or amount

MODEL - subject or picture of a subject you intend to replicate

MODELING - blend variations of gray, or tone

MULL - think about, ponder

MULTITUDE - many

NEGATIVE SPACE - area that borders a shape

NIMBLE - flexible, quick, agile and skillful, such as with the hands

NOTCH - a gap or interval of space

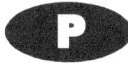

OBSERVE - look carefully

OBVIOUS - easy to see, stands out

ODYSSEY - an adventure in learning and experiencing new things

OMIT - take away

OPT - choose

OUTLINE - the surrounding shape of something revealed by a line

OUT OF KILTER - not in accurate condition
Other words with similar meanings: AWRY, ASTRAY, ASKEW

OUTSET - beginning or the start

OVERALL PROPORTION - comparison of maximum horizontal to maximum vertical distance

PACE - speed

PARALLEL - two or more things that are the same distance from each other at both ends

PEEPERS - eyes

PERCEPTION - understanding based on observing and thinking

PERIMETER - boundary of a shape

PERIPHERY - edge or outer margin, like the perimeter or maximum boundary of a shape

PINPOINT - locate or place accurately

PLEASANT SURPRISE - unexpected result that turns out well

PLOT - devise or plan a course of action, such as to locate reference points

PLUMB - VERTICAL (upright) position/alignment without apparent angle

POLYGON - a shape made with three or more STRAIGHT lines that connect

PONDER - think carefully

PORE - small hole, or examine carefully

POST - after

PRECAUTION - action to prevent unwanted result

PRELIMINARY - first or starting point

PREMISE - an assumption that something makes sense

PREVIOUS - before

PRINCIPLE - method or a way to do things

PRIORITIZE - select steps in *order of importance or effectiveness* - these can be a choice to proceed from large to small, or from basic to more elaborate refined stages

PROCESS - a method, or an ability to figure out and understand

PROFICIENT - skillful

PROPER - reasonably accurate

PROPORTION - a comparison of length to width, or a size comparison of one thing to another

PUN - funny use of a word with two meanings

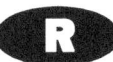

QUADRANT - quarter section

RANDOM - action by choice or preference rather than logical sequence

RATIO - proportion or scale estimation by comparing how big something is to something else

REFERENCE POINT - a location or position

REFINE - improve

REFLECT - think back or relate to, represent

RELATIVE PROPORTION - size comparison of one shape, or one part of one shape, to another

RENDITION - a drawing that resembles something but is not an exact match

REPLICATE - create a reasonably accurate likeness

RESOURCEFUL - ability to use skills effectively, so they work well
        Other words with similar meanings: AD-LIB, IMPROVISE, INVENT

REVERSE SPACE - The adjacent area at the edge of a shape
        Also called: NEGATIVE SPACE, OPPOSITE SPACE, INDIRECT SPACE

ROTATE - turn, pivot, twirl

ROTUND - big

RUNG - bar on a ladder

S

SECTION - part or portion of the whole

SECTOR - specific part or location

SEE - observe and understand

SEISMOGRAPH - machine that measures earthquakes and movements on, or in, the earth

SEQUENCE - a particular order or procedure arranged one after the other

SHADING - toning by creating variations of gray

SHAPE - visible boundary of something

SILHOUETTE - a shape, filled in with one tone

SIGNIFY - indicate or show

SIMPLIFY - streamline, or make the drawing process easier by reducing forms to very basic
        shapes with straight lines

SIMULTANEOUS - at the same time

SKETCH LINE - a freehand line made with overlapping strokes

SKIM - glance through quickly

SPACE - shape or area that borders a figure

SPAN - distance (or expanse) between two reference points

SPONTANEOUS - unplanned, or to act without much forethought

SQUIGGLE - draw impulsively by following your whims, feelings, or mood

SQUINT - observe with your eyes partly closed

STATUS - current situation

STREAMLINE - simplify a shape to a minimum of straight lines

STRICT - too precise, fussy

STRIDE - pace, rate of advancing speed

STRUCTURE - a shape or a combination of several shapes which total one entire shape

SUBDIVIDE - divide into smaller parts

SUBJECT - item/model to be replicated, or a topic

SUBORDINATE - secondary, or something not as important as something else

SUB-PROPORTION - a size subdivided into smaller units in scale

SUB-SHAPE - part, portion, or section of a larger shape

SUBTLE - slight, barely noticeable difference between one thing and another

SUCCESSION - organize in a particular order or sequence (one after another)

SUPPLEMENTAL - additional

SURFACE - exterior, or top layer of something

SURPASS - improve, outdo

SURVEY - examine, study, observe

SYMMETRICAL - even, balanced, uniform, consistent, regular,

SYNCHRONIZE - work well together

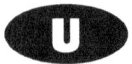

TALLY - examine, evaluate, total

TANGIBLE - something real or touchable

TAPER - gradually narrowing, or two lines that come together at a point

TECHNIQUE - method or procedure

TEMPLATE - temporary shape (or format) made by guidelines which serve as a flexible boundary in order to plot (or locate) reference points

TEMPO - speed

TONE - range of light to dark color or gray

TRAIT - visible characteristic or feature

TRANSFORM - change from one appearance to another

TRANSITION - the in-between stages during which something changes from one appearance to another; or a switch from one procedure to another

TRIO - group of three

TRUSTY SEVEN - basic structural components used to help draw shapes (reference points, alignments, proportions, straight lines, curves, angles, reverse space)

ULTIMATE - last or final

UTILIZE - use

UNCONVENTIONAL - unexpected or unusual

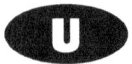

VARIATION - slightly different, not an exact match

VARY - differ or change

VERIFY - check to be sure

VERSATILE - ability to apply skills in many ways

VERSION - appearance, opinion, or point of view

VERTICAL - upright

VICE VERSA - other way round, reverse sequence

VIRTUALLY - mostly accepted or believed, seemingly real

VIA - with or by way of

VIABLE - likely to work

VISION - eyesight or understanding based on observation and thinking

VISUAL - relating to eyesight, such as estimating sizes or proportions by eye

VISUALIZE - picture in your mind, imagine, pretend, or make believe

VISIBLE - able to be seen

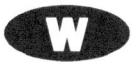

WHIM - act with little or no forethought

WITHIN RANGE - apparently near the desired size or area

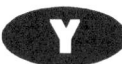

YON - there

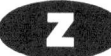

ZEAL - enthusiasm, interest

INDEX

ACCURACY 35, 58, 125, 197

AD-LIB 118, 136

ALIGNMENT
Explained 3
Diagonal 8
Horizontal 3
Imaginary 3, 8, 100, 195
Level 17
Parallel 17
Plumb 16
Vertical 3, 14

ANGLES
Explained 8, 9
Angle Extension 9
Angle Guide Lines 8, 9, 10
Worksheet 10

ASSIMILATION 214, 218

BLENDING TONES
Manually 219
Visually 214, 218

CHECKING STATUS
Alignments 19, 125
Angles 19
Arm Length 14, 36, 61
Before, During & After 36, 38, 61
   125, 146, 147, 150, 190, 191, 193, 208
Curves 36, 38, 113, 170, 179, 193
Distance 146, 168, 170, 201, 218
Double Check 19, 61, 122, 123, 150
Final Check 22, 44, 150
Inverted/Rotated 208
Proportion 14, 53, 146, 191
Reference Points 19
Reverse Space 86, 108
Side by Side 146, 168, 190, 201, 208
Squiggle (base) 179

CLOSURE PRINCIPLE 79

CONTINUOUS STRAIGHT LINE
Explained 4
Worksheet 5

COORDINATES
Plot Reference Points 18, 100, 106, 201

CRISSCROSS
Explained 92

CURVES
Explained 31
Check Accuracy 36, 38, 113, 170, 179
Trace in air 149, 169, 203
Worksheet 34

DIAGONAL ALIGNMENT 8

DOODLES
Explained 174
Examples 173, 180, 211
Experiments 175, 176, 178
Purpose 175, 177, 179

ELEVATION
Curve guide line 32

ESTIMATING 58
(See "plan ahead" and "pencil readings")

EXTENSION
Angle Guide Line 9

FINISHING TOUCHES 22, 38, 61, 147, 150, 231

FORMAT/TEMPLATE 12

GUIDE LINES
Angles 8
Curves 32, 33
Formats 12

I

IMAGINARY ALIGNMENT 3, 8, 32, 101, 195

IMPROVISE 117, 118, 136

INDIRECT SPACE 82, 108

L

LEVEL ALIGNMENT 8, 17

N

NEGATIVE SPACE *See "reverse space"*

O

OBSERVE 27, 36, 56, 70, 146, 152, 208, 218
    See "checking status"& "streamline-squint"
    See "plan ahead" & "pencil readings"

OPPOSITE SPACE *See "reverse space"*

OVERDOING 22, 35, 60, 61, 131, 135, 147, 150

P

PATIENCE 37, 59, 62, 123, 144, 150, 200, 232,

PARALLEL ALIGNMENT 8, 17

PENCIL READINGS 29, 58, 121, 122, 132, 133

PENCIL TECHNIQUES
    Squiggle 175, 176
    Tone 214
    See "straight lines," "angles," "curves"

PLAN AHEAD 51, 65, 119, 131, 135, 187

PLUMB ALIGNMENT 8, 16

PROPORTION/SCALE
    Explained 3
    Estimating 27
    Distance Pencil Checks 130, 132
    Distance Proportion Conversion 131
    Overall Proportion 3, 50
    Relative Proportion 50

R

REFERENCE POINTS
    Explained 3
    Coordinates 100

REVERSE SPACE 82, 86, 89, 108, 109

RULER (vs.Freehand Drawing) 4, 7, 20

S

SCALE - *See "proportion/scale"*

SHAPING (STRUCTURE) PRINCIPLES
    Alignments 3, 16, 17
    Angles 8 , 9, 19
    Curves 31
    Proportion 3, 9, 17, 50
    Straight lines 4
    Reference Points 3
    Reverse Space 86, 89,108,109
    Trusty Seven 90
    See "checking status"

SIDE-BY-SIDE COMPARISON
    146,147,168,170,208,218

SIDEWAYS COMPARISON/REVIEW 208

SKETCH LINES
    Drawing Examples 154,211
    Straight 4

SQUIGGLES *See "doodles"*

STARTING 12, 179 (*See "plan ahead"*)

STRAIGHT LINES - *freehand*
    Explained 4, 7
    Continuous 4
    Sketch 4

STREAMLINE
    Explained 84
    Examples 83, 93, 129
    Squint 129

STYLE 7, 154, 176

T

TONES
    Explained 214, 219
    Experiments 214, 216, 219
    Worksheet 215

TRUSTY SEVEN 90, 108, 125, 147, 179

V

VERIFY RESULT 125, 168, 170, 179, 193, 201
    See "checking status"

VERTICAL ALIGNMENT 3

VISUALIZE 18, 19, 33, 51, 118, 119, 131. 135,
    186, 187, 193, 195, 199

WHY DRAW 3

"Drawing isn't just for some, it's for everyone."

"Just as there are methods by which to learn how to read and write, there are methods by which to learn how to draw."

Peter Kraus

ABOUT THE AUTHOR

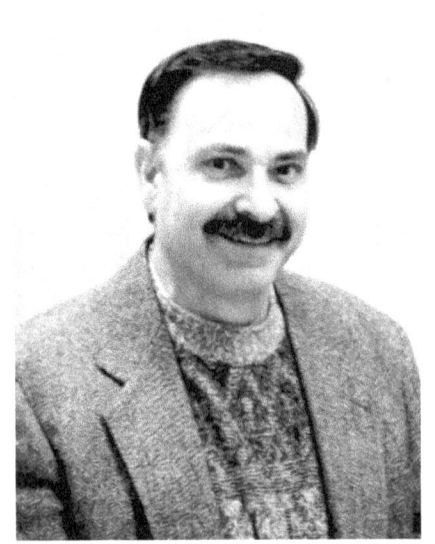

Accomplished fine artist, speaker, graphic designer, and instructor with over thirty-five years of excellent teaching experience, Peter Kraus is the founder of ANYONE CAN...ARTS and the author of the *Drawing Magic* series of books. Born in Hungary, Peter emigrated to the United States as a child in 1956. Following graduation from high school, he opened his studio and gallery where he created commissioned pieces and fine custom frames. Studying psychology and art education, he earned his degree from California State University, Northridge. In addition to his dedication to *Anyone Can...Arts*, Peter Kraus is also an eminent instructor in a Los Angeles Community College. Highly proficient with multi medias and styles, Peter's aim is to bring out the expressive quality of each student. His unique approach to teaching is remarkably successful with not only the artistically inclined, but also with the artistically challenged, special needs children and adults, senior citizens and at-risk-youth. Proven correct time and again, his conviction that drawing skill CAN be learned is the heart of his ANYONE CAN...ARTS philosophy. "When we are growing up, we are taught that a very small percentage of people have the ability to draw well, but I'm convinced the opposite is true," confides Peter. While he was busy studying psychology, he questioned why some people have the talent to draw well and others don't. Was it in their DNA, did they have an extra gene? Something inside told him it was more than talent and his investigations led him to conclude that people were not only not getting the right encouragement, but that they were also getting instruction based on faulty premises. Schools teach that art comes from "intuition" and it simply flows from us. If a child isn't showing any artistic instincts from the get go, he never will. Peter doesn't deny the existence of artistically gifted individuals, but he believes drawing should be taught analytically as a skill. Instead of using the historically great artists as absolute models, our learning should start from the basics and evolve step-by-step at one's individual pace. This method gives the student a fair chance to discover he or she can actually draw well and do something with the skill. In fact, Peter prefers to look at drawing as "functional and we can use it any way we want."